THE MANAGEMENT AND REGULATION OF BANKS

The last ten years have seen a dramatic increase in the interest taken by national authorities in the activities of banks. In this first serious work to spotlight this development, John Cooper explains how official interest has grown from separate but parallel pressures to elaborate prudential controls for the protection of depositors and the preservation of the existing banking mechanisms, national and international, and to elaborate monetary controls as a key instrument in the conduct of macroeconomic policy, particularly in controlling inflation.

On prudential controls, he traces the pressures for their elaboration back to the secondary banking crisis in Britain in 1973–5, the uncertainties in the foreign exchange markets following the abandonment of fixed exchange rates in 1973, the problems caused for banking systems by the need to recycle oil money internationally following the oil price rises in 1973 and 1979–80 and the traumatic consequences for borrowers of all types and their bankers of the world recession accompanied by widespread tight money policies since 1979. He explains how these prudential controls have been developed both nationally and internationally and sets out clearly the principles which lie behind them.

On monetary controls, the author traces the pressures for their elaboration in the political debate on how economic policy should best be conducted, before but particularly after the accession to power of the Thatcher Government in 1979. Whilst the gradual enthronement of monetary control as an essential element in economic policy generally is described primarily in the context of the British experience, the principles and arguments which lay behind that enthronement are set out in a way to give them a much wider application.

As a background to the discussions on both prudential and monetary controls, the author describes the main types of banking institutions, the financial markets in which they operate and the principal risks which are, in fact, involved in the business of banking. In doing so, he adds a practical perspective to the continuing debate on the techniques and desirable extent of both prudential and monetary controls and contributes some incisive and forthright comments on the relationship between national authorities and bankers, the controllers and the controlled.

John Cooper is a Managing Director of Singer & Friedlander Ltd. Having graduated at Oxford with a first-class degree in philosophy, politics and economics, he entered merchant banking in 1959 and has remained a merchant banker ever since, specialising in foreign exchange, eurocurrency operations and commercial lending.

Since leaving Oxford he has retained an interest in academic economics and particularly in its relevance to the practical world of finance. In 1968 he published a Penguin Special on British economic policy, particularly relating to the balance of payments; and he has contributed articles to the national press on international finance and foreign exchange.

As a member of the Executive Committee of the British Bankers' Association 1975–81 and its Chairman 1980–1, he was deeply involved in the discussions which led to the Banking Act 1979 and to the subsequent arrangements for banking supervision in the United Kingdom. He has also been involved in discussions on the co-ordination of banking regulations within the European Community.

THE MANAGEMENT AND REGULATION OF BANKS

John Cooper

M
MACMILLAN

First published 1984
Reprinted 1985

Published by
MACMILLAN PUBLISHERS LTD
(Journals Division)
and distributed by
Globe Book Services Ltd
Brunel Road, Houndmills
Basingstoke, Hampshire RG21 2XS

Printed in Great Britain by
Antony Rowe Ltd
Chippenham

ISBN 0-333-34234-8

Contents

To

The Rt Hon. Lord Richardson of Duntisbourne, K.G., P.C., M.B.E., T.O.
Governor of the Bank of England 1973–83

under whose governorship the regulatory arrangements described in this book were developed and put in place

Preface

The last five or six years have seen an unprecedented debate in Britain, prompted by a series of events described in Chapter 1, on the prudential control of banks. Participants in the debate include officials of HM Treasury and the Bank of England and members of the banking community representing their own individual banks, their immediate trade associations, such as the Committee of London Clearing Banks or the Accepting Houses Committee, and their main British trade association, the British Bankers' Association. The immediate conclusions of the debate were enshrined in the Banking Act 1979 and the papers subsequently published by the Bank of England on *The Measurement of Capital*, *The Measurement of Liquidity* and *Foreign Currency Exposure*. Simultaneously, but starting from a slightly earlier date, a similar debate took place between bankers from the different Member States of the European Community in the forum of the Banking Federation of the European Community (European Banking Federation), between these bankers and officials of the European Commission in Brussels and between those officials and the national supervisory authorities of the Member States. The immediate conclusions of this debate were enshrined in the First Banking Co-ordination Directive of the European Community, which was finally adopted in December 1977 and in other directives and proposals subsequently emanating from the European Commission in Brussels.

Having been privileged to participate in these debates, through both the British Bankers' Association and the European Banking Federation, I thought it worthwhile to set down between one set of covers the main conclusions of the debate so far: that is, to describe the conceptual framework in which the arrangements for the prudential control of banks have been developed and put in place in Britain and, as important, the particular participative techniques which the Bank of England has developed for effecting this prudential control. This is the first purpose of this book. Inevitably, the key documents describing the conceptual framework and the Bank of England's approach to prudential control emanate largely from the Bank itself; and I am grateful to the Bank for permission to quote extensively from them. On the side of the bankers in the debate, I am grateful to the officials of both the British Bankers' Association (BBA) and the European Banking Federation for the tireless briefing they provided, and provide, for me, my colleagues and successors on the Executive Committee of the BBA and on the working parties of both the BBA and the European Banking Federation.

Alongside, but distinct from, this debate on prudential controls, another debate has developed in Britain, on monetary controls. Again, the events leading up to this debate are described in Chapter 1. Whilst the debate on monetary control embraces a wider group of participants, including economists, journalists, politicians and others concerned with the country's macroeconomic policy, as well as bankers and officials from HM Treasury and the Bank, the banking system inevitably provides the practical setting and background against which this debate takes place; and there seems room for a description of the institutional infrastructure of this setting, in terms of banking institutions and the financial markets, and for some observations of the practical effects on this infrastructure of some of the proposals put forward. This is the second purpose of this book. In describing the institutional background I have been fortunate to have been preceded by the Wilson Committee (to Review the Functioning of Financial Institutions), which provided a mine of information on the institutions of British banking, not only in its own Report and its Appendices, published in 1980, but also in the massive volumes of evidence submitted to it. I have quoted extensively from the Report and the Appendices and also from the written evidence submitted by the Bank of

England, the Committee of London Clearing Bankers (CLCB) and the Accepting Houses Committee: these extracts are reproduced with the permission of the Controller of Her Majesty's Stationery Office and, where appropriate, the CLCB. A major contribution to the debate on monetary control was provided by a consultation paper by HM Treasury and the Bank of England published in March 1980 and entitled *Monetary Control*. I have quoted extensively from this paper: again, these quotations are reproduced with the permission of the Controller of Her Majesty's Stationery Office. In describing the debate, I have received valuable advice from Mr Tim Congdon, who not only allowed me to quote extensively from his recent book on *Monetary Control in Britain*, but also read the drafts of the relevant passages in Chapters 1 and 6 and made some very valuable suggestions.

Again, alongside the debates on prudential and monetary control, and related to but distinct from them, two further developments have taken place in the relationship between the British banking community and 'the authorities', particularly the Bank of England: the development of Lifeboats for domestic industrial borrowers and of international Lifeboats for sovereign borrowers. The third purpose of this book is to describe these developments as they affect practising bankers; and this is done in Chapter 6.

Mr Lionel Price and Mr John Beverly of the Bank of England have both read the draft of the entire book, as has Mr Ian Morison of Midland Bank, formerly of the Inter-Bank Research Organisation. I am grateful to all three for the valuable advice they have given me on aspects of both prudential and monetary control and also on Lifeboats for both domestic industrial borrowers and sovereign borrowers. Any remaining errors of fact are, of course, my own, as are all the opinions expressed, except for those specifically attributed.

Finally, I should like to thank my secretary, Mrs Joyce Reid, and Mrs Daphne Jarvis for their patience in typing and retyping the text.

London JOHN COOPER

1 Official Preoccupation with the Banking System

INTRODUCTION

In the 1970s and early 1980s, control of the banking system has become a major preoccupation of governments and control authorities in the United Kingdom, the other members of the European Community and generally throughout the world. This preoccupation has focused on two quite separate types of control, prompted by two distinct groups of factors: prudential control, designed to ensure that banks are prudently run, with the aim of protecting depositors and avoiding major upheavals in confidence and the movements of funds; and monetary control, designed to use the banking mechanism as a positive tool in the conduct of macroeconomic policy generally or, at the very least, to prevent the banking mechanism from pulling in the opposite direction from, and thwarting, other measures of economic policy.

This preoccupation with prudential control and monetary control has produced a series of measures in the United Kingdom to formalise and codify existing control arrangements and, in some areas, to extend them. The Banking Act 1979 is the keystone to such measure of prudential control. The arrangements for monetary control have proved to be less easy to encapsulate in a single document, but the series of proposals put forward by the Bank of England which culminated in the paper entitled *Monetary Control – Provisions*, published in August 1981, will probably emerge as the keystone of these arrangements.

The formalisation of prudential and monetary control has been preceded and accompanied by very considerable public debates. Inevitably, these debates have been as much concerned with the institutions of banking and their interrelationships in the financial markets as with the actual controls themselves. And this concern has itself forced the debate back a further stage to analyse not just the functions of specific institutions but why they behave in the way they do and how they can be expected to respond to a change in the conditions in which they operate: in other words, how individual banks are managed. The purpose of this book is in part to describe the present arrangements for prudential and monetary control in the United Kingdom. But it recognises that these arrangements will inevitably be subject to a continuing process of modification and continuing pressures for their extension. In the expectation of a continuing public debate on such modifications and extensions, a second important purpose of this book is to set out, as background for such a debate, a description of the institutions of British banking, the financial markets in which they interrelate and the philosophy and techniques by which they are managed.

A constant thread running through any discussion of either prudential control or monetary control must be the relationship between the regulatory authorities and the banks in the case of the former, and the monetary authorities and the banks in the case of the latter. Any effective system of control of either sort, and any useful discussions about such systems, must by their very nature incorporate some fairly precise allocations of responsibilities between controllers and bankers. Opinions may and probably should differ as to precisely where the lines of demarcation should be drawn; but no workable and effective system of control can be complete unless these lines are drawn and are drawn in such a way as to leave both bankers and controllers in no doubt as to which side of them they stand. For this reason, the relationship between controllers and controlled will feature largely and continuously in the chapters that follow.

Although the discussion in this book centres predominantly on British banking, its control and management, it inevitably spills over into an international dimension, for at least five reasons. First, a large part of the business of British banks is essentially international in character: it consists of taking deposits from sources outside the United Kingdom, often in currencies other than sterling, and lending them on to borrowers also outside the United Kingdom. Secondly, British banks are major operators in markets which are essentially international in character – the foreign exchange markets, eurocurrency markets and eurobond markets, for example – and this has prompted both prudential and monetary controllers in the United Kingdom as well as elsewhere to ask whether these markets can or should be brought specifically under their control. Thirdly, as we shall see in Chapter 2, a significant proportion of the banking community based in the City of London are foreign-owned: that is to say, they are either branches or subsidiaries or associated companies of banks whose head office is located in another financial centre outside Britain, in, for example, the United States, continental Europe or Japan. These 'overseas banks', as they are termed in the statistical tables, participate actively in the domestic British banking scene as well as in the international money markets based in London. Fourthly, and as a consequence of the general spilling of banking activity over national frontiers, there has been an increasing tendency for prudential controllers – if not, as yet, monetary controllers as well – to liaise in the co-ordination of their controls and regulations on an international basis: examples are the activities of the Advisory Committee set up within the European Community under the first EEC directive on the co-ordination of banking regulations which was adopted in 1977 and the activities of the Cooke Committee of bank supervisors set up under the auspices of the Bank for International Settlements in Basle and named after its current Chairman, Mr Peter Cooke of the Bank of England. Fifthly, and in consequence of the first four reasons, the philosophy and techniques of bank management and regulation in other countries, particularly in other member states of the European Community and in the United States, have already become integral factors in the debate between controllers and controlled in the United Kingdom and are beginning to rub off in practical effects. For all these reasons, the descriptions and discussions which follow are not confined parochially to purely British banking; and it is hoped that their relevance will have a wider application as well.

THE PRESSURES FOR PRUDENTIAL CONTROL

The prudential control or regulation of banks has become an increasingly important function and preoccupation of national 'authorities' in the 1970s and 1980s. (The exact identity and constitutional position of these authorities varies from country to country. In the United Kingdom they consist of HM Treasury and the Bank of England.) Whilst this development has probably been as marked in the United Kingdom as in any other country, it has in fact been a world-wide phenomenon spanning both developed and less developed countries in one dimension and both socialist and capitalist, free-enterprise countries in another.

This increasing attention to the prudential regulation of banks has been prompted by two sets of factors, separately identifiable but interacting on each other: first, the factors of philosophy or policy and secondly, the course of recent events which have thrown the requirements of philosophy and politics into a sharper focus.

The principle of protecting depositors

The political factors lying behind the prudential regulation of banks centre on one distinct principle though, as we shall see, many subsidiary political principles have intervened in recent years and will inevitably continue to do so. This principle is the protection of depositors from the danger that a bank which has accepted their deposits will fail and be unable to repay them. Governments rightly see national banking systems as a crucial piece of machinery in the infrastructure of economic activity and, particularly, economic development. A part of the function of this machinery is the collection of savings, both long and short term, in the form of deposits from those individuals and corporations who are receiving more money than they are spending and the channelling of these funds, by way of loans, into the hands of those individuals and corporations who are spending more money than they are receiving, usually on capital items capable of producing future income rather than on current consumption. It is an essential characteristic of any such deposit-taking mechanism that it should at all times retain the confidence of the depositing public in its ability to repay their deposits on their due date; and this is a main political reason for governments to ensure that depositors with the national banking system are not only secure from the possibility of a default by their bankers, but are seen to be secure and protected.

In the United Kingdom and the European Community generally – and also in other countries of the world – this political reason has been reinforced in recent years by a marked emphasis on consumer protection and 'consumerism' generally: a widespread acceptance that it is a function of national governments (and, in the European context, of the European Commission as well) to protect the consumer in all his activities from exploitation by manufacturers of the products he consumes and providers of the services he uses. Within this philosophy, the protection of depositors – and, particularly, small individual depositors – is seen as a proper responsibility of government in its own right, quite apart from the more general responsibility to preserve the confidence of the depositing public in the banking system and thus preserve the stability of that system.

These general philosophical reasons for involving national government in the protection of depositors have been reinforced in the 1970s and early 1980s by four groups of events, each of which caused tremors of anxiety about the solidity of the British and other banking systems collectively and of individual institutions within those systems, and which therefore gave rise to new and more urgent calls for tighter and more effective prudential controls. These events were the secondary banking crisis in the United Kingdom which was sparked off by the collapse of London and County Securities in November 1973; the uncertainties in the eurocurrency and foreign exchange markets which followed the widespread abandonment of fixed exchange rates in 1973 and the collapse of Bankhaus Herstatt in 1974; the dramatic increases in the price of oil in 1973 and 1979–80 and the consequent recycling problem resulting from the international redistribution of cash wealth between oil-producing countries and oil-consuming countries; and the consequences for both banks and their borrowers of widespread tight money policies and recession since 1979.

The secondary banking crisis, 1973–5

The secondary banking crisis in the United Kingdom provided a classical demonstration of the fragility of a developed and sophisticated banking system and its dependence on the continuing confidence of depositors.[1] The crisis was preceded by three particular developments which taken together can be seen in retrospect to have sown the seeds from which it sprang. First, there was the mushrooming growth of fringe banking institutions which was both encouraged by the policy of competition and credit control, inaugurated by a Bank of England discussion paper published in 1971, and left uncontrolled by the untidy state of banking legislation prior to the Banking Act 1979, which split responsibility for supervising deposit-taking institutions between the Bank of England and the Department of Trade in such a way as to leave virtually unsupervised those fringe institutions which most required supervision. Secondly, there was the marked emphasis on property development and its finance, particularly by the new, fringe banking institutions although many of the established banks, including the clearing banks, got caught up in it as well: this particular type of lending carries with it a very particular sort of credit risk which will be discussed in greater detail in Chapter 4 and which, if left unmixed with other sorts of risk in a bank's lending portfolio can prove dangerous, if not lethal. Thirdly, there was the dramatic growth of the wholesale sterling deposit markets in London, both intercompany and interbank, which gave the fringe banks access to almost unlimited supplies of funds, albeit on a pretty short-term basis, from sources which, in retrospect, can be seen to have been much too uncritical and unselective in the placing of their funds. These money markets and their relevance to bank management and regulation are discussed in some detail in Chapter 3; it is sufficient at this point to note that in these as in other financial markets the greater the size and sophistication of the market, the greater the danger it presents to the unwary and imprudent.

The secondary banking crisis was sparked off in November 1973 by the collapse of London and County Securities. London and County was itself a fringe bank, unsupervised by the Bank of England – and effectively unsupervised by any authority – which had tapped the money markets as well as the general public for short-term deposits and employed a large proportion of them in loans to property developers. The collapse was triggered by the inability of London and County to renew short-term deposits from the money markets and general public as they became repayable – or, if you like, by the unwillingness of depositing institutions and individuals to renew such deposits. In the words of the Bank of England's chronicle:

> Its troubles had been well publicised, culminating in the resignation within five months of joining the company of a respected City banker who had been appointed to strengthen the banking division. Meanwhile the uncertainty that had been introduced into the property scene following the imposition of a freeze on business rents in December 1972 had been overlaid with an increasing awareness of the potential effect of the rapid increase in interest rates on property companies (particularly on their asset valuations) and on those lending to them. In such circumstances the resignation was sufficient to trigger a liquidity crisis for London and County, but it very soon became apparent that some more sophisticated depositors in the money markets were taking fright at their potential exposure to any such institution.[2]

As has been clearly shown by evidence which has since come to light, the crisis was sparked off by imprudence and straight bad banking in relatively few institutions, of which London and County was one; but it soon spread – and threatened to spread even wider – to institutions which could claim to be prudently and properly managed but, through no fault of their own, got caught up in a panic withdrawal of confidence. To quote again from the Bank of England's chronicle of the effect of London and County's collapse:

> The Bank thus found themselves confronted with the imminent collapse of several deposit-taking institutions, and with the clear danger of a rapidly escalating crisis of confidence. This threatened other deposit-taking institutions and, if left unchecked, would have quickly passed into parts of the banking system proper. While the U.K. clearing banks still appeared secure from the domestic effects of any run – indeed the money market deposits withdrawn from the fringe were largely re-deposited with them – their international exposure was such that the risk to external confidence was a matter of concern for themselves as well as for the Bank. The problem was to avoid a widening circle of collapse through the contagion of fear.[3]

The incipient crisis of confidence which followed the collapse of London and County prompted three courses of action by the Bank of England, in its capacity as regulator or controller of the banking system: two ongoing and, as it were, permanent improvements to the system of regulation and one more immediate and, hopefully, temporary arrangement. The first permanent change was the establishment of a system of bank supervision designed both to widen the net of supervision to cover all deposit-taking institutions – and not exclude the weakest, as was the case in the system forced on the Bank by the existing legislation – and at the same time to give more precision to the techniques of supervision: this change, if effective, should prevent any similar crisis of confidence developing in the future, by removing the possibility of a weak institution collapsing or threatening to collapse through imprudent management. The second permanent change, prompted as much by the political emphasis on 'consumer protection' as by a need to improve the banking system, was the establishment of a system of deposit protection, effectively insuring small depositors at the expense of the banking community generally against a proportion of any loss sustained as a result of the collapse of a deposit-taking institution. Both these changes were effected by the Banking Act 1979 and are discussed in Chapter 5.

The more immediate and urgent action by the Bank of England prompted by the collapse of London and County and its aftermath was to prevent the collapse of confidence from bringing down the whole banking system by the establishment of the 'Lifeboat'. The reasoning behind this action has been clearly set on record by the Bank:

> It is hardly necessary to dwell here on the damaging consequences that a collapse of confidence extending into the banking system would have had. As a result of their experiences with the Overend Gurney crash of 1866, the Baring crisis of 1890 and the prolonged international crisis of 1929–33, the Bank – and the world at large – had come to regard the taking of prompt and decisive action to prevent a spreading loss of confidence as one of the essential roles of a central bank. In the circumstances of the closing weeks of 1973, therefore, the Bank felt it essential to meet their responsibility for fully-recognised banks by mounting a rescue operation for the benefit of the depositors of a group of institutions which were not fully-recognised banks, but whose otherwise inevitable collapse would have threatened the well-being of some recognised banks. The need for rapid joint response to the developing situation was immediately accepted by the English and Scottish clearing banks when the Bank approached them.[4]

Three points are worth making about the Lifeboat in the present context. First, in appealing to the English and Scottish clearing banks to join them in their task of establishing the Lifeboat, the Bank of England drew a clear distinction between problems of 'liquidity' and problems of 'solvency': liquidity problems could bring a prudently managed institution to its knees through no fault of its own, whilst blame for a solvency problem had to be laid at the door of the management of the institution in question. Put in another and more direct way, an appeal by the Bank of England to members of the Lifeboat for help from an institution with *liquidity* problems need not, and should not, be an appeal for charity or be anything more than appeal to lend funds at a commercial rate of interest which would ultimately be repaid in full; an appeal for help for an institution with *solvency* problems could be seen as a direct appeal for charity – an appeal that the shareholders in the institutional member of the Lifeboat should, in fact, make a gift to the shareholders in the institution in trouble.

In appealing to the English and Scottish clearing banks for help in establishing the Lifeboat, the Bank of England was very specific in limiting its appeal to that help required by those with *liquidity*, not *solvency*, problems. Before agreeing to provide support for a company which sought it, the Control Committee of the Lifeboat had to be satisfied that, among other criteria, the company in question 'was currently trading solvently and, on the basis of best estimates possible at the time, was likely to remain solvent provided it received liquidity support by way of recycled deposits'.[5] Stated thus boldly the principle is clear and simple enough; but, of course, to estimate the future solvency of any company is far from simple and makes up a large part of the process of credit assessment discussed in Chapter 4.

The second point to note regarding the Lifeboat is that the very action by the Bank of England of putting it together and calling on the clearing banks for their support was generally regarded as a perfectly proper thing to do – by the Bank itself, by the clearing bankers, by the rest of the banking community and by the public at large. It can confidently be predicted that had the Bank not intervened with the speed and effect that it did, the result would have been a carnage of financial institutions, the destruction of British banking as we know it, both national and international, and a very severe jolt to the economy as a whole. In other words, the creation of the Lifeboat as a vehicle for recycling funds was undertaken by the Bank of England – and accepted by everybody else – as a proper function of a central bank in its role of banking supervision: this principle will be referred to again in Chapter 4, in the context of the liquidity stance it is appropriate for an individual bank to take in the mismatching of maturities of its incoming deposits and outgoing loans and in the reliance it is reasonable for it to place on the commitment of the central bank to ensure the smooth running of the cycling and recycling of deposits. This will be referred to yet again in Chapter 6, when we come to consider the problems of cycling and recycling funds between banks, countries and currencies through the euromarkets and the role which central banks can and should play, individually or collectively, in ensuring that these mechanisms of recycling never seize up.

The third point to note regarding the Lifeboat follows naturally from the first: it is the extreme arbitrariness of the distinction drawn between liquidity problems and solvency problems. Technical accounting definitions and conventions may make it possible to say categorically as a matter of fact whether a company is solvent today (or, at least, at the latest moment for which detailed accounting information is available); but the decision as to whether a company will be solvent *tomorrow* will always remain a matter of judgement rather than of fact. And a judgement as to the future solvency of a company already with liquidity problems will almost certainly be more complicated and difficult than one as to the future solvency of a company without such problems.

The decisions as to whether an institution should be supported by the Lifeboat were taken by a Control Committee of the Bank of England and the English and Scottish clearing banks, consisting of senior representatives of each under the chairmanship of the Deputy Governor of the Bank. In discussions as to the future solvency of any applicant institution, it can be assumed that there was inevitably some tension and conflict of interest. The clearing banks would clearly be reluctant to provide support in the form of loans for any institution which seemed unlikely to be able to repay those loans, with interest calculated at a commercial rate, at some reasonably predictable time in the future. To do so would be to flout the most basic rules of prudent banking. The clearing bankers would have been right to argue that this would have been an act of grave irresponsibility towards their shareholders; and they might well have added that by indulging in imprudent banking practices they might well threaten the profitability, if not the very solvency, of their own institutions and thus exacerbate the very crisis of confidence which the whole Lifeboat exercise was designed to allay. The Bank of England, on the other hand, would be keen to extend the net of support to as wide a group of institutions in trouble as it reasonably could. Its self-imposed brief, as we have seen, was 'to avoid the contagion of fear'; and the fear would in no way be alleviated by explanations that an institution had been allowed to collapse because the Control Committee had decided after much deliberation that its future solvency was in doubt.

Indeed, in the final stages of the support operations to stem the secondary banking crisis, the Bank of England went it alone, without the rest of the Lifeboat, and supported several institutions whose future solvency could not be described as undoubted but whose collapse might have given further impetus to the crisis of confidence. The Bank has recorded two such cases of particular significance:

> In late 1975 Slater Walker Limited, the authorised banking subsidiary of the financial group, Slater Walker Securities Limited, found itself in difficulties, as in May 1976 did Edward Bates & Sons Limited, which had originally joined the Lifeboat for a strictly limited amount in September 1974. Both were part of sizable groups with sensitive external ramifications. Foreign currency obligations of the non-banking companies of the Slater Walker group, for example, amounted to some £75 million equivalent, a significant part of which was publicly held. Additionally, the Group was responsible to a large number of investors and pensioners through the funds managed in its unit trusts and life assurance business. As regards Edward Bates, a reconstruction had been put in hand in 1975 involving the introduction of new shareholders from the Arab world. During 1976 it became increasingly apparent that further reconstruction would be required of both groups, which in each case would be likely to involve a substantial writing down of assets. The reconstruction schemes entered into for the Bank's own account both held promise that they might in fact reduce the loss that would have been sustained if the Bank had followed routes involving liquidation.[6]

The last paragraph demonstrates very clearly that in pursuit of its own objective, the Bank was prepared to go a great deal further than simply the solution of liquidity problems of individual institutions by establishing a mechanism of recycling, and to shore up ailing institutions by the injection of funds which it almost certainly would not recover in full. That it was right to do so on its own account, there can be little doubt: the support operation itself was a remarkable achievement by any standards, and it is most improbable that it would have succeeded if the Bank had stopped short at supporting only those institutions with liquidity problems and letting the others go. But whether it would have been right for the Bank to persuade the clearing banks – or for the clearing banks to be persuaded by the Bank – to commit their own funds in such a way to a significant extent is another matter.

In the event, and whatever estimates of the future solvency of candidate institutions were made by the Control Committee at the time, it is clear that the clearing bank members of the Lifeboat did, in fact, participate in support of institutions which subsequently became insolvent. The Bank implies as much in its summing up of the whole saga:

> The lifeboat and subsequent support operations were undertaken in the compelling interests of maintaining confidence, domestic and international, in the banking system. In this they were wholly successful. Such operations rarely prove to be costless, even when on a scale much smaller than was required in this case. But the potential losses have been fully provided for in the books of the members of the support group; and whatever the ultimate losses may prove to be, they will be far less than those that would have been sustained by the support group and the economy at large had the support operations not been undertaken.[7]

Whether the clearing bank members of the Lifeboat deliberately and positively acquiesced in the use of their funds in supporting institutions which were, or were likely to become, insolvent, or whether they allowed their funds to be used in support of only those institutions which they genuinely believed were likely to remain solvent and were subsequently proved to be wrong in their credit assessment, only they personally will ever know. The point to be made in the present context is that however tidy the distinction between liquidity problems and solvency problems in theory, in practice they cannot be distinguished with such precision. It follows that any action, such as the recycling of funds through a Lifeboat-type mechanism or any other, to solve the liquidity problems of individual borrowing institutions, taken for the public good, cannot in practice be totally disentangled from the solvency problems and potential solvency problems of such institutions: any such mechanism will thus inevitably involve somebody – Bank of England, clearing banker or other participant – in undertaking credit risks beyond what they would normally regard as prudent limits. The ramifications of this for central banks, the banking institutions which they supervise or control and the relationship between the two will be discussed in some detail in a domestic and an international context in Chapter 6.

One further and related point must be mentioned. The secondary banking crisis prompted the Bank of England to commit its own funds and almost certainly to persuade the clearing banks to commit their funds to the exposure to commercial risks which considerations of normal banking prudence would have rejected. The sole – and sufficient – justification for this was the common good: in the Bank's words, already quoted, 'the lifeboat and subsequent support operations were undertaken in the compelling interests of maintaining confidence, domestic and international, in the banking system'. There have been plenty of other examples in the 1970s and the 1980s where lending banks have felt themselves under pressure – sometimes from the Bank of England, more often from the politicians and the public at large – to go beyond their normal rules of prudent lending to support some borrowers whose survival is thought to be in the 'national interest': the public reaction to the collapse of Laker Airways and Stone Platt Industries early in 1982 were two such. Unlike the pressures to join the Lifeboat or any other support group to recycle funds within the banking mechanism, these pressures have little to do with the requirements of prudential control: they stem from the arguments for intervention by the central authorities not merely to preserve the good health of the banking system, but rather of the economy as a whole. These pressures and the reactions of the Bank, other central authorities and lending bankers will be discussed in Chapter 6.

The same pressures are to be found on lending bankers to stretch their normal rules of prudence in some of their international lending to retain or restore the good health of the international economic community: the political pressures on international bankers to reschedule the debts of Poland, Mexico and other sovereign borrowers in trouble in 1981, 1982 and 1983 are examples. Again, these pressures and the reactions of central authorities and lending bankers are considered in Chapter 6.

Uncertainties in the foreign exchange markets since 1973

The secondary banking crisis highlighted two of the major risks undertaken by banks as a normal and integral part of their lending activities: the credit risk of lending to a borrower who may not be able to repay and the liquidity risk of financing lendings with short-term deposits which may suddenly not be renewed. At about the same time that domestic bankers in the United Kingdom were living through the crisis and learning, both directly and by example, the lessons it had to teach, international banks all over the world were being subjected to another, separate but almost equally shattering change in the conventional environment in which they had become used to operate: the abandonment of fixed exchange rates by the world's major central banks and their replacement by a market of floating rates, with varying and limited degrees of intervention.

The old post-war system of fixed exchange rates – named the 'Bretton Woods' system after the historic international monetary conference at which it was established, held in Bretton Woods, New Hampshire in July 1944 – lasted until 1971. To call this a system of fixed exchange rates is not entirely accurate. A more precise definition has been given by Professor John Williamson:

> The exchange rate regime incorporated in the Bretton Woods system has become generally known as the 'adjustable peg'. The essential characteristics of this system are that at any time a country undertakes to maintain the value of its currency within a narrow margin of a par value, while the par value can be changed under certain circumstances. This arrangement was intended to provide a compromise between the desire to stabilize exchange rates in order to avoid the disorderly markets and competitive depreciations of the 1930s, and the desire to avoid forcing countries to revert to the gold standard 'rules of the game', under which defence of the exchange rate overrides the pursuit of domestic full employment policies.[8]

This system of adjustable pegs was effectively brought to an end by the suspension of the official convertibility of US dollars into gold in August 1971; although this was followed by attempts to shore up some system of fixed but adjustable pegs – notably at the Smithsonian Conference in Washington in December 1971 – all attempts to retain a fixed, if adjustable, pattern of exchange rates between the world's main currencies were abandoned in favour of more freely floating rates in March 1973. An immense literature has grown up – official, academic and other – to analyse the causes of the failure of the system of adjustable pegs, to assess the shortcomings, national and international, of the system of freely floating rates and to recommend reforms to the international financial system which might mitigate these shortcomings.[9] Whilst it is not the purpose of this book to add further to this particular debate, the main characteristics of the systems of fixed but adjustable pegs and of freely floating rates do require a brief description as the replacement of the one by the other represented a major change in the environment in which banks operate, highly relevant to the management – and regulation – of banks operating in the foreign exchange and eurocurrency markets.

Against the background of a regime of fixed but adjustable pegs in national exchange rate policies, the 1950s and 1960s saw a huge growth in the foreign exchange markets and the related eurocurrency markets, both principally based in

London. The actual mechanisms of these markets and their impact on the activities – and profits – of individual banks will be described in Chapters 3 and 4 respectively. At this point it is simply necessary to show how both were affected by the regime of fixed but adjustable pegs up to 1971 and by the move to more freely floating rates thereafter.

The system of exchange rates set up at the Bretton Woods Conference in 1944 and subsequently presided over by the International Monetary Fund (IMF) required all members of the IMF – effectively covering all significant trading nations in the non-Communist world – to fix a par value of its currency in terms of gold (which, itself, was convertible into US dollars at a fixed price until this convertibility was brought to an end in 1971) and to maintain the value of its currency in the foreign exchange markets within a bracket of 1 per cent on either side of its par value. If a par value became demonstrably unrealistic – in terms of, say, its purchasing power parity with other currencies or of a wide imbalance in the balance of payments of the country in question – a mechanism existed for a par value to be changed, after consultation with the IMF.

This situation provided a perfect nursery in which to develop the post-war foreign exchange markets: dealers could take substantial positions in a currency – buying more than they were selling, or vice versa – in the virtually certain knowledge that the possible loss of such a position or mismatch was limited by the 2 per cent bracket in which a currency's par value could move – unless, of course, warning signs were flashing, heralding an imminent change in par values. And it was a crucial characteristic of the system that warning signs always *did* flash before a major change in par values. It is true that they sometimes flashed for a very long time before a national government was persuaded to change the par value in the direction the warning signs and market pressures were predicting; but taking the whole period from 1944 to 1971, many more and bigger changes in par values of currencies were well and widely predicted by dealers than those which took the dealers and the public at large by surprise. The reason for this general predictability of par value changes was simple. National governments had a general reluctance to change par values unless there was an overwhelming case for doing so; and the evidence for such an overwhelming case would usually be as obvious and accessible to dealers in the markets and the general public as it was to the national governments.

This predictability of par value changes put dealers in a wonderful position to 'take a view' or speculate for or against a currency. If a currency had been pushed by market pressures against the limit of the bracket in which the government was obliged to maintain it, and if the evidence strongly suggested that a change in the par value ought to be, and therefore probably would be made, then speculators felt themselves to be on almost a 'heads I win; tails you lose' type of deal: short of a dramatic new change in circumstances, it was most unlikely that the currency would rebound to the other limit of the bracket (thereby losing the speculator 2 per cent of his position) and more than likely that the par value would be changed to his advantage (thereby making him anything from, say, 4 per cent or up to 12 per cent or more, of his position). The position of the speculator was not, of course, as clear cut as that. Timing, for example, was very important: a delay between the opening of such a position and the actual change in the par value would require the speculator to borrow the suspect or weaker currency;[10] and the pressures of other speculators all wanting to do the same thing could push such interest rates up to astronomic levels, which could erode considerably any ultimate profit. Again, central bankers attempting to ward off speculative pressure on a currency grew adept at forcing up the relevant rates of interest to punishing levels. But taking all the par value changes together over the period – the devaluation of sterling in 1967 and the floating of the D-Mark from a fixed peg in 1971 and again in 1973 are amongst the most dramatic examples – the clear lesson to the speculator was that to take a position against a currency which was under pressure to devalue – or in favour of a currency which was under pressure to revalue – was almost certainly to be on to a good thing. (The term 'speculator' is used here to cover any operator in the market who takes a position with a view to making a profit: it is not intended to connote approval or, as in some circles, abuse. The methods of speculation and the motives behind them are discussed in Chapter 3.)

Whilst the era of fixed but adjustable pegs was educating a whole new generation of foreign exchange dealers in getting used to handling substantial and growing transactions at minimal commercial risk in longish periods between changes in par values, and at the same time whetting their appetites for speculative gains when changes in par values actually occurred, another equally important development was taking place: the rapid growth in the movement of short-term capital across national frontiers. Indeed, it was massive movements of short-term capital – 'hot money' – across national frontiers and from one currency to another, reaching a final crescendo in the later 1960s and early 1970s, which ultimately made the system of adjustable pegs unworkable.

This growth in short-term capital movements sprang from several separate causes. In the words of Professor Williamson:

> International trade, with its opportunities for shifting funds between currencies by leading and lagging payments, grew at an unprecedented pace: its value multiplied more than 5-fold between 1950 and 1971, and import penetration rose substantially in most countries. An international capital market re-emerged in the 1950s and expanded dramatically with the emergence of the Euro-Currency Market after 1958; one of the attractions of the offshore currency markets was, indeed, their greater immunity from exchange controls. Multinational corporations, which have ample opportunities for avoiding exchange control through variations in the timing of payments between subsidiaries, became a major economic force. (For example, the earnings in the U.S. direct foreign investment expanded from \$1.8 billion in 1950 to \$10.6 billion in 1971.)[11] As a result, the world of the late 1960s had become one of intense capital mobility.[12]

This increased mobility of capital enormously expanded and deepened the burgeoning post-war foreign exchange and eurocurrency markets. By increasing both the size and number of those keen to participate in both markets, it substantially increased the turnover of the banks who 'made the market' and acted as dealers; it also provided a much greater vehicle for speculation, for those who were minded to use it. As to this scope for speculation, Professor Williamson has remarked that 'by the time that the adjustable peg was abandoned, capital mobility had developed to the point where the Bundesbank could take in well over $1 billion in an hour when the market had come to expect that another parity change was pending'.[13]

By 1973, therefore, when the regime of the adjustable peg was finally replaced by one of floating rates, the banks in London and elsewhere which dealt in the foreign exchange and eurocurrency markets had got their dealing rooms into a high gear, used to dealing in very substantial amounts, learning to live with a degree of mismatching in terms of currency exposure and also maturity exposure in the forward markets. They were also made aware of the possibilities of speculative gain in a market which up to that point could almost be said to have been rigged in the speculator's favour.

The switch to floating exchange rates provided a significant jolt to dealers in the foreign exchange and, to a lesser extent, the eurocurrency markets. The volume of trading remained pretty high: the floating exchange rates and an increase in the volatility of domestic interest rates themselves kept up the impetus of short-term capital movements from one currency into another. But the odds in the speculators' game had changed dramatically. During those periods under the old regime when no change in par values was expected, an unmatched position in one currency against another was most unlikely to represent an exposure to potential loss of more than 1 per cent, with an effective maximum of 2 per cent and a real possibility that an adverse movement would right itself in a day or two in the ebb and flow of a market which, by definition, was fairly static. Under floating rates, on the other hand, the same position could represent an exposure to potential loss of 5 per cent or more, with no absolute maximum at all; and experience quickly taught the folly of assuming that a position which had gone wrong was more likely to 'come right' than go much more wrong through the ebb and flow of a market which had become almost viciously unstable.

This change in market conditions required a complete reassessment by bank managements of the risks represented by open exposure in outright foreign exchange positions, one currency against another; or in mismatched maturity positions in the forward market or, consequentially, in mismatched maturity positions in the eurocurrency deposit markets. Almost certainly, existing limits on all these positions would need to be drastically reduced, for the simple reason that a limit of, say, £1m on an outright foreign exchange position would represent an exposure to potential loss several times greater than that represented by the same position under the old regime.

Besides the need to renew the limits on a bank's own foreign exchange positions, the introduction of floating rates prompted, or should have prompted, banks to undertake two other urgent reviews as well. The first is a review of its internal controls to see that the internal limits fixed by the bank's management are properly observed. If a bank sustains a substantial loss in its foreign exchange operations, it is not usually the consequence of dealing within too large limits set by the bank's management, and getting it wrong; it is much more often the consequence of dealers going well outside those limits – and getting it wrong – or, in a large bank with complex exposures in foreign exchange, a simple inability of the internal accounting systems to be able to tell the bank's senior management exactly what the bank's exposure to the various risks is at any one time. The sudden pressures which followed the floating of exchange rates in 1973 imposed a severe and crucial test on the internal controls of banks in their foreign exchange operations: systems which had proved adequate in the quieter times of adjustable pegs were suddenly found wanting under these new pressures.

It is worth remarking that bank managements should feel no inhibitions in tying their dealers down with tight controls out of feelings for the self-respect of the dealers. Any dealer with experience in the foreign exchange markets – and probably many other markets as well – will confirm the positive comfort they feel at the imposition of tight and effective controls. Most dealers will admit that their close attention to the very short-term movements in the market may often cloud their judgement of the wider picture of the risks to which they are exposed: and most dealers who are actively trading in the market with the profitability of their operations as the primary aim will instinctively be pushing up against the limits imposed on them in order to maximise a position which they regard as potentially profitable. Realising this, many dealers positively welcome the constraints of precise limits and rigid controls to enforce those limits and despise a management whose lack of control throws what they regard as an unfair burden of responsibility on them the dealers. In many cases where losses have been sustained through large positions being taken which have subsequently gone wrong, it has been possible to say that the bank's management could not be faulted on the size of the limits and simply that the fault lay in the transgression of those limits; but in many of those cases, it would also have been proper to argue that the bank's management *was*, in fact, at fault for the exercise of inadequate control.

The third review which the introduction of floating rates should have prompted in bank managements is a review of the limits imposed on the exposure to individual counter-parties. The precise exposure to the risk of the failure of a counter-party – and how to weigh that risk in relation to the risk of, say, making a loan to the same counter-party – is not at all easy to determine but is discussed briefly in Chapter 4. At this point, it is simply worth remarking that the increased risks in foreign exchange operations described above as following the introduction of floating rates apply equally strongly to one's counter-party as they do to oneself. There is therefore a case for assessing very carefully the philosophy and ability of a counter-party and fixing limits based on that assessment before accepting their name in the market. This point has been given added force in the United Kingdom by the abolition of exchange control in 1979, which gave access to the foreign exchange market to individuals and corporations who had not until then had the benefit of experience enjoyed by authorised banks but denied to most other UK residents by the Exchange Control Act 1947.

These lessons from the floating of exchange rates since 1973 were rubbed home to both the banks themselves and the supervisory authorities by the brutally real experience of substantial losses realised by several leading – and other – banks. In June 1974, just over a year after the floating of exchange rates, Bankhaus Herstatt in Cologne closed its doors as a result of massive foreign exchange losses which brought down the whole bank; later the same year both Westdeutsche Landesbank in Germany and the Union Bank of Switzerland announced swingeing foreign exchange losses and in September Lloyds Bank International announced that their Lugano branch had suffered exchange dealing losses of £33m – though in this case the cause was fraud. Commenting on these events in its paper on the Lifeboat the Bank of England remarked that 'the reaction of international bankers was in many ways very similar to that of U.K. institutional depositors in December 1973 – lines to smaller banks were drastically reduced or withdrawn'.[14] No wonder that the Bank of England saw the proper management and internal control of banks' foreign exchange operations as being crucial not only to the good order of the foreign exchange markets but to that of the financial markets, domestic and international, generally. The Bank's role in supervising these operations is discussed in Chapters 4 and 5.

The problems of recycling oil money since 1973

The third group of events which coincided with the UK secondary banking crisis and the turmoils in the foreign exchange markets, and which added to anxieties about the solidity of the international banking system was the train of consequences which followed from the dramatic rises in the price of oil in 1973 and 1979–80. Like the traumas in the foreign exchange markets since the floating of exchange rates in 1973, the effects of these price increases have been felt by the entire international banking community, and by no means exclusively by British banks; though the pre-eminence of London as a centre of international banking is reflected in as great a concern in the matter being displayed by the Bank of England as any other central bank.

As is well known, the price of oil quadrupled in 1973, following the war in the Middle East and the disruption in supplies; it increased abruptly again in 1979 and 1980. The broader effects of these price increases on the world economy, and the domestic national economies which form its integral parts are and will continue to be the subject of intense academic and political debate. In this book, we are concerned only with the effects of the price rises on the international banking mechanism; and these spring from the dramatic reallocation of cash resources from the oil-consuming countries to the oil-producing countries.

The oil price rises in 1973, 1979 and 1980 – but particularly the first – suddenly generated a massive increase in the cash receipts flowing into the oil-producing countries, most of which were members of the Organisation of Petroleum Exporting Countries (OPEC). By the same token, the price rises had the equal and opposite effect of making equally massive reductions in the cash resources of the oil-importing countries. The 1973 price rise was so sudden that neither the recipients of the new cash surpluses nor those who were denuded of them were able quickly to react to their new circumstances; the result was that the oil-producing countries allowed their newly acquired wealth to pile up in the form of cash deposits whilst those who found themselves the providers of this cash were obliged to seek short-term borrowings to settle their immediate debts.

As we have seen, the period from the Second World War to 1973 saw the development of a broadly-based international market for foreign exchange and eurocurrency deposits; and an essential adjunct to these markets, if not an integral part of them, was a growing institutional machinery of international banking, capable of giving and taking deposits, borrowing and lending, across national frontiers and in different currencies. It was this institutional machinery, already in place, which provided the main vehicle for recycling the new-found deposits from the oil-producing countries on a short-term basis back to the oil-consuming countries who had originally provided the cash that made them up, and this eased the jolt to the world economic system inflicted by the rises in the price of oil. Commenting on this role in February

1979, the Governor of the Bank of England remarked that

> perhaps it is helpful to think of the international banking system as performing the function of an intermediary between different domestic economies in much the same way as any financial intermediaries perform specialised functions within a single domestic economy, matching differences in supplies and demands for credit. And just as in an evolving domestic economy those forms of intermediation which are most efficient or most attuned to the needs of the time will expand the fastest, so has it been for international banking.[15]

But if the international banking mechanism can claim some credit for coping with the problem of recycling the oil money and thus relieving central banks and other official financial institutions from undertaking responsibility for the task, the sheer size of that task caused some anxieties in official, political and academic circles as to whether the institutional machinery was, in fact, up to it. Some of these anxieties were voiced by the Governor in the same forum a year later. In 1980, the Governor prefaced his anxieties by remarking that

> the last six years have clearly demonstrated that international financial markets are resilient and constructive. International banking activity has grown fourfold since the end of 1973 and with it has increased the ability of the banking system as a whole to take deposits and to lend on a large scale.
>
> Accompanying and underpinning this growth has been a considerable prudential tightening by the banks themselves and by the authorities in major financial centres. We, and our colleagues in other centres, believe in continuing this process and further improvements are now in train. Reinforcing the soundness of the international banking system in this way will help to provide a secure basis for sustainable growth in its financing capacity.[16]

The resultant tightened and improved techniques of the

prudential supervision of banks, both domestic and international, are discussed in Chapter 5.

In his speech in February 1980, the Governor listed three anxieties which lay behind this tightening of prudential controls and, indeed, behind the Bank's attitude to the international banking mechanism generally. First, he pointed out the rapid increase in the debt burden of the non-oil-producing countries and emphasised the general expectation that these debts would inevitably go on increasing in the future. Having stressed earlier in his talk the need, and the greater recognition of the need, for current account adjustment, especially by countries with a relatively weak external position, the Governor went on to emphasise that

> however vigorous the adjustment effort, payments imbalances cannot be quickly reduced. Many countries will still need finance on a considerable scale. These countries will tend to be the ones that have already accumulated a very heavy burden of outstanding debt. Well before the end of the 1970s the debt service commitments of the non-oil developing countries were growing more rapidly than their exports. Now with maturities closely bunched, world trade slowing down and interest rates high, the debt service ratios for many must be rising – and will go on rising – uncomfortably fast.
>
> The financial needs of these countries cannot be met without further heavy recourse to the international markets. For there may be greater reluctance than in 1974 to draw upon foreign exchange reserves – much of which reflect market borrowing and which in many cases are not large in relation to import needs. Moreover, the finance available from official international and multinational sources, although greater than in 1974, is still modest in relation to current and prospective needs.[17]

The significance of this growing debt burden of borrowing countries for the lending banks – and the central banks in their capacity as prudential supervisors – is the extent to which it weakens the borrowers' ability to repay the principal loan on schedule, or even to pay interest as it falls due and thus increases the credit risk undertaken by the borrower. The plight of Poland and Mexico – and their bankers – in 1981 and 1982 are but two examples of an excessive burden of debt.

But central bankers have other interests as well as the prudential supervision of banks. One is the good health of the international financial system: it is the central bankers who remain largely responsible for ensuring that disruptive events such as the rise in oil prices do not cause chaos in, or even the disintegration of, the international financial system and, as important, that the disruptive effects of such events are not transmitted through the international financial system itself into the real economies of individual nation states. This interest may sometimes tug policy in a different direction from what lending bankers regard as their best interests in the cause of prudence. Just as the Bank of England saw the solution, or at least the alleviation, of the secondary banking crisis lay in its persuasion of the major banks to recycle the funds pouring into their coffers (even if that meant in the later stages encouraging them to extend their lending criteria beyond the point that they would normally regard as prudent), so the central banks saw the alleviation of the short-term balance of payments imbalances, resulting from the oil price increases, as lying in the persuasion of the international banks to recycle the funds pouring into their coffers from the oil-producing countries, even if it meant encouraging them to accept sovereign credit risks which they would otherwise have declined to take. There was a hint of anxiety, rather than approval, in the Governor's comment in the speech already quoted that

> the growing burden of market debt which these countries have already incurred is mirrored in the balance sheet of the banks. The greatly increased international exposure of the banks, recent political developments and the more cautious attitude on the part of monetary authorities across the world towards expansion in the euro-markets may together temper the banks' willingness to lend.[18]

The role of the Bank of England and other central banks in

nudging practising lending bankers to 'be statesmanlike' and go beyond their prudent lending criteria in the interests of the greater international good will be discussed in Chapter 6. In particular, that chapter includes a discussion on the validity of the analogy between the risks involved in the recycling of liquidity in the domestic secondary banking crisis which the Bank of England's Lifeboat was designed to achieve in 1973–5 and those involved in the recycling of funds between sovereign states in the early 1980s.

The second anxiety voiced by the Governor and others about the effects of the oil price rises relates to the balance sheets of the lending banks. These banks may find it more difficult to bear the brunt of recycling, he remarked:

> because of the risk that, as their international business grows, their internal ratios of own funds to deposit liabilities and to total lending may come under strain. Competition has kept lending margins so narrow for the last couple of years at least that the scope for generating internal capital must have been very limited. Given the present state of equity and bond markets, such capital constraints could become increasingly serious.[19]

The importance of the ratio of a bank's capital resources to its external liabilities as a principal tool of bank management will be discussed in Chapter 4, together with the sorts of factors by which bankers judge what numbers that ratio ought ideally to show.

The third anxiety of the Governor and others about the effects of the oil price rises is related to the second: it is the fineness of the profit margins secured by the banks in their recycling of deposits from oil producers, induced very simply by the sheer weight of those deposits. In a sense this is a rather perverse consequence of the very competitiveness of the international deposit markets: banks dared not turn down massive deposits from the oil-producing countries nor to offer rates of interest substantially below the market, lest those depositors should move permanently to competitive banks. Thus the major international deposit-taking banks were awash with deposits which they had to on-lend to somebody simply to clear their books; and such a volume of money seeking profitable employment made the international money markets rather less critical than normal, or possibly prudent, about the risks they should take and certainly gave less prudent, about the risks they should take and certainly gave the borrowers the initiative in driving down profit margins to minimal levels. As the Governor remarked:

> evidently it will be helpful if the returns to the banks are commensurate with the risks they assume. I have for some time been convinced that spreads and margins on international\lending had fallen too low; and more especially that the differentials between the best risks and less good risks had narrowed too much. There are now indications that spreads may be edging up for lending which is considered to be more risky. This is a development to be welcomed, both in itself as a more realistic assessment of risk and because it may encourage a further increase in total lending by drawing on a wider circle of banks.[20]

It may be questioned, with the benefit of hindsight, whether the Governor was not too sanguine in detecting this widening of margins. Certainly there has been a widening of profit margins in terms of interest since he spoke; but equally there has been an even greater downgrading of many of the credit risks involved – that is, the likelihood of default, or at least of 'rescheduling' has become significantly greater in many loans to sovereign borrowers. But the main point that he made still stands: that in 1980 and the years immediately prior to it, the margins of profit were unhealthily low: if they covered the overheads of the banks concerned, they certainly left nothing over to build up an adequate reserve against future losses, or deferred payments, of both capital and interest.

The consequences of tight money and world recession since 1979

An integral part of the complex economic consequences of the oil price rises of 1973, 1979 and 1980 was a rapid acceleration in the rate of price inflation throughout the Western world. That same inflation was an integral part of the process whereby, in part deliberately and in part passively, the Western world came to live with those oil price rises without a major economic upheaval or disaster – at least until the time of writing in early 1983. As we have seen, the immediate palliative of the consequences of the price rises was a massive recycling of money from the oil-producers to the oil-consumers; and the main reason why this palliative was so effective for so long was the accompanying high rate of inflation which steadily eroded the *real* value of the money deposits being recycled.

This point was well made by Mr Anthony Harris in an article in the *Financial Times* on 2 September 1982:

> The world's debt schedule was allowed to reach its present tottery state because inflation made both lenders and borrowers complacent. Lenders got the best return they could, borrowers relied on inflation to erode the real obligations they had signed. Inflation in this context is a solution rather than a problem: it is an adjustment mechanism by which excessive credit expansion becomes manageable. Indeed, the inflation of the 1970s was the adjustment required to make sense of the world-wide refusal to respond to high oil prices by cutting real incomes: the recycled opec surpluses were the source of unsustainable credit expansion, and the fiscal squeeze now being mounted would have been more appropriate in 1974. The inflation has robbed opec of much of the real value it thought it had secured when investing its surpluses.
>
> However, as financial markets and interest rates adjust to past inflation, only accelerating inflation can keep the adjustment going; and in the end governments were faced with a stark choice between indefinite acceleration – hyper inflation – and a determined attempt to reverse the process. It was the stress produced by this reversal which produced the murderously high interest rates we have recently seen.

The stress produced by the attempt to reverse the process of accelerating inflation from 1979 onwards had other even more dramatic consequences for the international banking community and for its customers. We shall see in the next section of this chapter how monetary measures have become the principal weapons for fighting inflation within the UK domestic economy; and this choice of weaponry has been shared by the United States and other major developed economies. We shall see, too, the effect which these monetary measures have had on banking institutions and markets and how they have come to be seen as the source of, and sometimes blamed for, some of the harsher consequences of the measures on their borrowing customers. The point of mentioning these monetary measures and their consequences in this section is simply to point out the general anxiety amongst governments and central banks, not particularly that banks' customers were being driven to the wall by the anti-inflationary policies, but that some of the banks themselves might go the same way. And we have already seen the particular interest which governments have in ensuring orderly banking systems, particularly to protect depositors.

The real causes of the world recession of the early 1980s will no doubt be the subject of academic debate for years to come, as will the apportionment of 'blame' for it between, for example, the OPEC leaders for instigating the oil price rises in the 1970s and the national governments of the United States, the United Kingdom and other developed countries for initiating a major monetary squeeze. What is beyond any dispute is the severity of the squeeze and the depth of recession at the time of writing in early 1983. Commenting on the worldwide consequences of the US monetary squeeze since 1979, the *Financial Times* remarked at the time that

> interest rates have risen well above the rates of inflation, and impose their own forbidding discipline on borrowers. Subsequently the world recession has almost eliminated the opec surpluses . . . and has sharply depressed the prices of all commodities not controlled, like oil, by cartels. The earning power of many developing countries has collapsed just as their financial obligations increased.[21]

Almost by definition the main casualties in a credit squeeze are the major borrowers, be they individuals, corporations or countries. By raising the rate of interest, a credit squeeze reduces the profitability or solvency of these borrowers and pushes them closer to bankruptcy than they would otherwise go, unless, of course, they can recoup the cost of these high borrowing costs by, for example, charging higher prices for their products. One of the characteristics of the recession of the early 1980s was not only high rates of interest in money terms, but more particularly historically very high rates of interest in *real* terms (that is, adjusted to take account of the rate of inflation). Indeed, the very success of monetary policies in bringing down the rate of inflation increased the severity of the monetary squeeze designed to effect the policies, thereby imposing even greater burdens on borrowers.

The combination of restrictive monetary policies, with their accompanying high real rates of interest, and worldwide recession with its slackening of demand for both raw materials and primary products hit several major groups of borrowers very heavily indeed. First, those countries to which the international banking system had recycled the oil surpluses thrown up by the oil price rises of the 1970s found themselves hard hit by rising interest charges just at the time when their own external balance of payments was being squeezed by the recession in demand for their exports. These countries included some which were not oil-producers at all and which required the recycled oil money to pay the inflated bills for oil imports: examples were Portugal and South Africa; Eastern Europe in general, but particularly Poland and Romania; and Latin America, particularly Brazil and Argentina. The external financial position of Eastern Europe was heavily affected by the USSR; and this in turn was exacerbated by a poor grain harvest, lower gold sales to the West and a decline in the price of gold. The external financial position of Argentina was, of course, much complicated by the Falkland Islands crisis in 1982 and its aftermath.

Another group of countries to whom OPEC oil surpluses had been recycled were those which were themselves producers of oil but whose development plans and consequential external financial requirements had been set at levels greater than forecast – and certainly greater than actual – receipts of oil revenues. These countries could be said to have borrowed from the international banking system to finance current expenditure in anticipation of the receipt of oil revenues: in the event, they were doubly squeezed by the dramatic increase in interest charges mentioned above, accompanied by a significant drop in their oil revenues below earlier forecasts caused by both the fall in world oil consumption and the fall in the US dollar price of oil. Examples of countries in this group were Nigeria and, dramatically, Mexico.

A second group of borrowers hit by the combination of restrictive monetary policies and world-wide recession were oil producing companies who had borrowed heavily from the banking systems, national and international, to develop production facilities for oil and gas, particularly in North America. These companies had based their plans on optimistic forecasts about the continued growth in the world demand for oil and gas and continued rises in its price; in some cases, it is probably true to say that their lending bankers were carried away by the euphoria caused in the oil industry by the price rises of the 1970s. Again, this group of borrowers received a double blow by the sharp increase in their interest charges, caused by higher interest rates, accompanied by an equally sharp decrease in their earnings, caused by the fall in oil consumption and in the price of oil. Examples of such borrowers are the ill-fated Dome Petroleum in Canada and some of the oil-producing borrowers from Penn Square Bank in Oklahoma City. The inability of the latter borrowers to pay the interest and repay the principal when due on some of their loans caused the collapse of Penn Square in July 1982 and severely dented the profits of other US banks including Seafirst Corporation of Seattle and Continental Illinois in Chicago, which had participated in some of Penn Square's loans; indeed, so great was the damage sustained by Seafirst Corporation as a result of these bad debts to oil-producing borrowers that it was obliged in April 1983 to agree to be taken over by Bank of America.

A third group of borrowers hit by the combination of restrictive monetary policies and world-wide recession included all those companies, not specifically related to the oil industry at all, who had borrowings outstanding to their bankers at the end of the 1970s and therefore suffered increased interest charges as a result of the high real and money rates of interest and also suffered a squeeze on their earnings as a result of the recessionary decline in the demand for their products. This group probably included most manufacturing companies in the United Kingdom – and in the developed countries as a whole – though the smaller their borrowings at the onset of the recession, the lighter the pressure from increased interest rates. Not all such companies will, of course, go to the wall before the tide turns, real rates of interest recede and demand picks up for their products; but a great many, large and small, were pushed into bankruptcy by these influences. Each bankruptcy resulted in some loss of capital to one or more banks as well as a period, in many cases, over which the loans were 'non-performing' in the sense that interest was not paid to the banks on loans outstanding; and it is worth remarking that a 'non-performing' loan is much more painful to a bank in periods of high interest rates than in periods of low interest rates, for the simple reason that the bank has to borrow the funds it provided in making the loan, and the cost of such borrowings obviously reflects the going rate of interest.

Whether the banks collectively were sensible in making all these loans will be discussed briefly in Chapter 4, as will the criteria used in making the loans and subsequently deciding to extend them. The point to be made in the present context is that banks all over the Western world probably had more potential bad debts on their books in the early 1980s than at any other time in the living memory of then practising bankers, and the potential threat of this overhang of bad debts to the very solvency of individual banks and to the national and international banking systems as a whole became a major preoccupation of bank supervisors, and national governments, at that time.

These preoccupations were shared, in differing ways, by those responsible for both prudential controls over banks and monetary controls over national economies. To some extent, the losses sustained by individual banks – and the potential exposure to further losses in the future – were the consequence of downright incompetence on the part of lending bankers, failing to observe the elementary criteria for lending discussed in Chapter 4; the huge exposure, in terms of its own size, of Penn Square Bank to dubious credit risks and the consequent grotesque size of its losses are probably an example of this incompetence. And it is the business of the prudential supervisors of banks – as well as of the management of the banks themselves – to prevent such incompetence. But to some extent, and perhaps a larger extent, the losses and potential losses of individual banks in the early 1980s were the result of restrictive national monetary policies throughout the developed world in terms of abnormally high real rates of interest and a significant recession in demand. In these circumstances, it may well be that the prudential supervisors and others interested in the continued health of the institutional machinery of banking, national and international, should look to the monetary controllers and economic managers of the developed countries, as much to the management of banks, to ensure this continued good health. Action to this end could, of course, involve a change in the monetary policies. It could also include specific government intervention to prevent the default of a major borrower and the consequent pressures on its bankers: such intervention was proposed, for example, in the case of Poland and, in a different way, Mexico as major sovereign borrowers on the brink of bankruptcy in 1981 and 1982, and of International Harvester and the German electrical giant, AEG in the same condition at the same time. These proposals for official intervention to prevent the default of major borrowers are discussed in Chapter 6.

THE PRESSURES FOR MONETARY CONTROLS

Almost by coincidence, the period of the 1970s and early 1980s which saw the growing preoccupation of national 'authorities' with the prudential control or regulation of banks, saw also a parallel preoccupation of national 'authorities' with monetary control as well. Although developing at the same time, this preoccupation with monetary control was stimulated by quite separate pressures from those described above.

Disillusion with 'demand management'

At the most fundamental level, the greatest pressure for monetary control has sprung from a growing dissatisfaction with the conduct of British economic policy and a growing disillusionment with the chosen strategy on which that policy was based and with the weapons used to effect it. Although this dissatisfaction and disillusionment are discussed here in a domestically British context, it should be noted that they were shared in virtually all countries of the developed world.

Writing in 1967, the present author remarked that

> one of the most remarkable changes that has come about in Britain in the twenty years since the Second World War has been in the public's idea of what it expects the government to achieve in its efforts to control the economy. In 1944, the famous White Paper on Employment Policy stated boldly that 'the Government accepts as one of their primary aims and responsibilities the maintenance of a high and stable level of employment after the war'.[22] So far have we moved in our expectations of economic government since then, that it is difficult today to recall what a novel departure this acceptance of responsibility represented.[23]

He went on to comment that, more recently, in its report published in August 1959, the Radcliffe Committee (on the working of the monetary system) devoted a chapter to a consideration of the 'objectives of monetary policy'. The Committee summarised these as follows

> 1. A high and stable level of employment.
> 2. Reasonable stability of the internal purchasing power of money.
> 3. Steady economic growth and improvement of the standard of living.
> 4. Some contribution, implying a margin in the balance of payments, to the economic development of the outside world.
> 5. A strengthening of London's international reserves, implying further margin in the balance of payments.[24]

The strategy of economic policy to achieve these ends from the end of the Second World War in 1945 right into the 1970s was based on the manipulation of 'demand'. The premise behind this strategy was clearly stated by the late Sir Roy Harrod, one of the most articulate of the high priests of the 'demand management' theory:

> I posit [he wrote in 1958] that the objective of policy is the maintenance of demand at a level that ensures comfortably full employment and the steady growth of output in accordance with the potential of the economy. Any sagging down of demand below this level is to be avoided. This is a general maxim applicable to all countries . . . Over-full demand is to be avoided. Britain, and other countries of Europe, have been plagued with over-full demand for most of the period from 1945 to 1957. This is bad for efficiency, may tend to create external insolvency and tends to cause inflation, involving an upward movement in the cost of living, which, if no checks are imposed, may gather dangerous momentum. It seems that the periods 1952–3 and 1956–7 are the only occasions since 1946 when Britain has been exempt from the evil of over-full demand.[25]

Within this strategy of 'demand management' monetary policy had a definite role to play. But it is important to emphasise that monetary measures were seen as relevant and appropriate *only* in their effect on total demand. The point was made very clearly by the Radcliffe Committee:

> It is for monetary measures in association with other weapons of economic policy to pursue, in the balance decided by the Government, the aims of employment policy, of stability in the value of money at home and abroad, and of growth. The impact of monetary measures – the way they push the economy in the desired direction – is on the total pressure of demand for goods and services. To put the simplest case, when unemployment is rising, prices are dropping and economic development is lagging all round, the weight of monetary measures has to be directed to increasing total demand. In the opposite case (not so

easy to diagnose) when the labour market is tight, prices are rising, the exchanges are weak and the smooth progress of the economy seems threatened by speculative distortions, it is for monetary measures to be thrown into the struggle to decrease the total pressure of demand. Unfortunately the situation is usually more complex than either of those we have just described; but however complex it is, the authorities must make up their minds which way on balance they want the pressure to work, and having made their decision, they may look to monetary measures, along with others, to operate either to increase or decrease the total pressure of demand.[26]

The gradual acceptance of the importance of the money supply

The basic credibility of 'demand management' as the main theoretical framework for British economic policy survived into the early 1970s. It began to be eroded by the evident inability of successive British governments to pursue successfully the five objectives listed by the Radcliffe Committee – and widely accepted as the proper objectives of national economic policy: the stop–go policies of the late 1950s and early 1960s and the ever more frustrating 'stagflation' of the later 1960s and early 1970s were the visible consequences of this inability. It was finally dethroned by the surge of price inflation which hit the British economy in the middle 1970s and also left its mark on many other developed economies in Europe, the United States and elsewhere.

This surge of inflation can be – and has been – attributed to many diverse causes: the dramatic increases in oil prices already mentioned in this chapter; the monopoly power of trade unions, supposedly giving the ability to bid up the price of labour irrespective of the relationship between its supply and demand; the inability or unwillingness of successive governments to control public expenditure and the rate of wage increases in the public sector; the willingness of governments to allow the public sector borrowing requirement to increase steadily as a proportion of the country's gross domestic product – these are all examples.

But one factor above all others has been latched onto by many (though not all) commentators as being crucial: the fact that the surge of inflation was preceded by – and later, accompanied by – an almost total lack of constraint or control over the expansion of credit. We have already seen how the system of 'adjustable pegs' in fixing exchange rates set up at Bretton Woods in 1945 was finally abandoned in 1973 in favour of floating rates, and some of the consequences this had for the environment in which banks operate. A separate and every bit as important consequence was the removal it implied of one of the few monetary restraints on the governments of those countries involved. The United Kingdom allowed the pound to float in June 1972, a year earlier than the final abandonment of the old system by other countries. As Tim Congdon has remarked:

> the move was widely welcomed as an escape from the straitjacket of fixed exchange rates, as a chance to break out from the 'stop-go' policies said to have been caused by the \$2.80 and \$2.40 parities. However, it ended the self-imposed discipline of external factors on British monetary policy. Despite some lip-service from the Bank of England on the need to pay more attention to the monetary aggregates, there was no effective constraint on credit expansion. In both 1972 and 1973 the money supply grew by over 25 per cent. The accompanying upsurge in economic activity became known as the 'Barber boom', after the Chancellor of the Exchequer, Anthony Barber, who presided over it.[27]

Mr Congdon has chronicled the conversion of 'informed opinion' to an appreciation of the importance of controlling the money supply in the following stark terms:

> The period from 1945 to 1972 may, from the viewpoint of British economic management, be regarded as a series of mistakes; the Barber boom was a disaster. In 1974 and 1975 inflation rose sharply, reaching a peak, as measured by the retail price index, of 26 per cent. The similarity with the highest rate of money supply growth was uncanny; it

> required considerable stubbornness not to interpret the money supply and inflation movements as related. The impact on informed, though not lay, opinion was as profound as the Weimar hyperinflation on attitudes in Germany. It became widely accepted that the money supply had to be controlled if inflation was to be reduced and eventually prevented.[28]

This acceptance of control of the money supply as a crucial facet of an effective economic policy – and especially one aimed to reduce or control the pace of price inflation – was an important turning point in policy making and of the highest relevance to the subject of this book: it swung the attention of all those concerned with the formulation and conduct of economic policy, and commenting thereon, towards the knotty questions of a precise definition of the money supply and how it can be controlled; and this in turn has led to a new inspection and analysis of the financial institutions and markets which make up the banking system, how they react to different actions or stimuli by the authorities and, in short, how they can and ought to be controlled.

The public acceptance of control of the money supply as a key facet of economic policy took some time to emerge in any coherent form. Again, Tim Congdon has chronicled the development:

> The Bank of England seems to have started adopting money supply objectives in late 1973 and early 1974. In a speech to the Scottish Institute of Bankers on 17th January 1977, Gordon Richardson, Governor of the Bank of England, hinted as much by saying 'In the past we have naturally had aims as to the rate of monetary expansion we wished to see . . . At the end of 1973, for instance, we raised interest rates and introduced the supplementary special deposits scheme with the object of achieving a reduced rate of growth of M_3. Our aim since then has been to keep the growth of money supply moderate.'[29] But official aims were probably not quantified and they were certainly not announced to the public. As a result, monetary policy was incoherent for the next few years.[30]

The next step towards a more public commitment to control over the money supply came in 1976, prompted at least in part by the heavy pressure on sterling in the early part of the year and forced into the headlines by the Labour government's acceptance in December of a number of conditions for a loan from the International Monetary Fund (IMF). Continuing his chronicle of the events of that year, Tim Congdon reports that

> perhaps as a demonstration to the international financial community of their adherence to sound policies, but perhaps also as a response to the evolving climate of opinion, the government moved step by step towards the announcement of money supply targets. In a speech in Brighton on 18th June, the Governor of the Bank of England recognised that other countries had found an explicit target 'a useful way of conducting monetary policy';[31] in a policy package on 22nd July, the Chancellor of the Exchequer stated that the authorities expected money supply growth in the 1976/77 financial year to be 12 per cent and let it be understood that this was to be a 'guideline'; and at the Lord Mayor's dinner on 21st October, the Governor said he believed it 'right to have a publicly-announced monetary target' and also hardened up the 12 per cent figure from a guideline to a target.[32] Since then the authorities have regularly announced and always been committed to an explicit money supply target.[33]

The chronicle continues:

> In December 1976, the government agreed to a number of conditions for a loan from the I.M.F. Borrowing had become necessary following the dangerous fall in the reserves earlier in the year. These conditions were contained in a Letter of Intent and mostly related to monetary and credit limits. The I.M.F. visit consequently gave a further impetus to financial targets. It is, however, wrong to attribute the introduction of money supply targets to the I.M.F. episode. In fact, some of the targets in the Letter of Intent, notably the £7,700m DCE [Domestic Credit

> Expansion] number, were so lax as not to be a serious policy constraint. The purpose of appealing to the I.M.F. [continues Tim Congdon in an aside which is relevant to a theme of this book] was largely political, in that it enabled the Chancellor and the Prime Minister to invoke a higher, outside authority for putting through necessary measures and guaranteeing Labour Party acquiescence in the money supply discipline.[34]

In his narrative of events, Mr Congdon describes the ambivalence of policy between 1976 and 1978 and the evident uncertainty of the policy-makers as to whether to concentrate on controlling the money supply or controlling the rate of exchange for sterling. To the extent that it is relevant to the discussion of the interaction of the authorities and the banking community and the former's attempts to control the money supply and/or the rate of exchange, this ambivalence and uncertainty will be further described and explored in Chapter 6; in this chapter we are simply concerned to trace the acceptance of control over the money supply as an integral part of national policy. Commenting on policies pursued in 1976–8, Tim Congdon concludes that it would be a mistake

> to suppose that the official endorsement of publicly-announced money supply targets in 1976 marked the true beginning of a monetary target regime. For at least a year afterwards the authorities dithered between decisions governed by money supply considerations and decisions governed by the exchange rate. The vacillation reflected strong doctrinal differences between various camps in Whitehall and the Bank, and among economists.
>
> It is not easy to pinpoint the exact dividing line between this phase of uncertainty and the whole-hearted acceptance of money targets. But perhaps the first definite statement that they were made to be paramount came in the speech by Denis Healey, as Chancellor of the Exchequer, to the Lord Mayor's dinner on 19th October 1978. He recognised two vital elements in a money supply target system and, without being too precise about it, pledged the authorities commitment to both.[35]

The first vital element explicitly recognised by Mr Healey was the fact that exchange rate management is in conflict with money supply control: that is, that one can control the exchange rate or the money supply, but not both. The second was Mr Healey's emphasis that the government would be 'determined to control the growth of public expenditure so that its fiscal policy is consistent with its monetary stance'.[36] As Tim Congdon remarks, this 'pledge to keep the budget deficit in line with the money supply target was important . . . as a withdrawal from the standard Treasury view that budgetary decisions should be regulated to adjust aggregate demand in the economy'.[37] Again, the significance of both these elements will be explored in Chapter 6.

The election of the Conservative Government of Mrs Thatcher in May 1979 further established control of the money supply as a central ingredient of economic policy. In his Budget Speech in March 1980 Sir Geoffrey Howe, the Chancellor of the Exchequer, announced a medium-term financial strategy which envisaged gradual reductions in the budget deficit and the money supply growth rate over a period of years and boldly put numbers on these intentions: the eventual aim was stated as being a sterling M_3 rise in the 1983–4 financial year between 4 and 8 per cent; the ratio of public sector borrowing to gross domestic product was projected to be lowered to 1½ per cent in the same year. The fact that these targets for both the money supply and the budget deficit were greatly exceeded in the first year, 1980–1, is less relevant in the present context than the fact that monetary control and the publication of explicit targets were now an element of economic policy to which the government was totally and openly committed.

The philosophy behind the medium-term financial strategy (MTFS) was clearly spelt out in a Green Paper on monetary control presented to Parliament by the Chancellor of the Exchequer in March 1980. It states plainly that

> The Government considers that a progressive reduction in the rate of growth of the money stock is essential to achieving a permanent reduction in inflation. It is a pre-requisite of a sustained revival of the British economy.

> Other Government policies, such as those to restore incentives, support this objective. But control of inflation, and thus control over monetary growth, is indispensable. The relationship between the rate of growth of the money stock and the growth of prices and incomes is complex. They can diverge in the short run, but there are strong grounds for believing that they will not diverge significantly over a period of years. The Government's policy is therefore to sustain downward pressure on prices by a progressive reduction of the rate of growth of the money supply over a period of years.[38]

Whilst the basic philosophy enunciated in this extract from the Green Paper was retained in Sir Geoffrey Howe's two subsequent Budgets in 1981 and 1982, the numerical precision of the first edition of the MTFS of 1980 has been much blurred. Thus the Budget statement published in March 1981 declared that

> the Government's objectives for the medium-term are to bring down the rate of inflation and to create conditions for a sustainable growth of output and employment. It is committed to a progressive reduction in the growth of the money stock and to pursuing the fiscal policies necessary to achieve this without excessive reliance on interest rates. The past year has seen greater monetary growth and public borrowing than was intended, but the Government is determined to ensure that the essential thrust of its financial strategy for the medium-term is maintained.[39]

In March 1982, the Financial Statement reiterated the belief that 'over a period of years there has been a reasonably stable relationship between the monetary aggregates and Money GDP and prices'; and it confirmed that 'the Government's policy is to maintain monetary conditions that will bring about a further reduction in inflation'.[40]

But in both the 1981 and 1982 Budgets, Sir Geoffrey Howe smudged the precision of the monetary targets he set in 1980 in two ways. First, he increased the percentage increases incorporated in the targets, so that the target for sterling M_3

(£M_3), the broadest official definition of money, was raised in the 1982 Budget for the fiscal year 1982–3 from its previous level of 5–9 per cent to an 8–12 per cent increase.

Secondly, and probably more importantly, the Chancellor eased the spotlight from a single measure of money supply (£M_3) and declared that in future the authorities would instead take into account a range of other measures of the money supply, and also less specific indicators of its movements. He thus recognised the danger, pointed out by many commentators, of basing policy too rigidly on a measure of the money supply which demonstrably had major drawbacks. The thinking behind this change was explained by the Treasury in the following terms:

> No single measure of money can fully describe monetary conditions. They have to be assessed in the light of all the available evidence. Sterling M_3 (£M_3) has risen faster than the target range set for it last March. But it has been affected by such factors as the civil service dispute, structural changes in financial markets, in part reflecting removal of controls, and a greater demand for liquid assets, such as bank deposits, as a medium of saving. The effects of these changes may be felt for some time to come. Slower growth in narrow money aggregates and money gross domestic product (GDP), and indicators such as the exchange rate, asset prices and real interest rates, suggest that, as intended, financial conditions have been moderately restrictive during the past year. To make more explicit the way in which a range of indicators is monitored, the target ranges for monetary growth will now apply both to the two broad measures of money – £M_3 together with PSL_2, and to the narrower measure, M_1.[41]

In the same article the Treasury provided the following definitions of the monetary aggregates mentioned: **M_1** is defined as notes and coin held by the public, plus private sector sterling sight deposits held by UK residents. **PSL_2** is defined as the private sector components of £M_3, plus other money market instruments such as deposits with local authorities, commercial bills and certificates of tax deposit, plus savings deposits and securities (mainly held with building societies). The initials PSL stand for Private Sector Liquidity.

This widening of the indicators on which monetary policy is based was confirmed in the Financial Statement accompanying the Budget in March 1983. The Treasury stated that

> In judging the rate of monetary growth needed to reduce inflation the Government will continue to take account of structural influences on the different monetary aggregates, as well as the behaviour of other financial indicators.

But the Statement also confirmed the central role in government strategy of control of the money supply, in the following words:

> The objective over the medium term is to continue to reduce inflation, and to secure a lasting improvement in the performance of the U.K. economy, so providing the foundations for sustainable growth in output and employment. Firm financial policies are an essential means to this end. The medium-term financial strategy sets out the framework within which policy is operated. Control of the money supply is a central part of this strategy.[42]

The impact of this strategy on the banking system, and the role of the banks in its implementation are discussed in Chapter 6.

NOTES

1. The crisis, its antecedents and the response of the Bank of England and the banking community generally are described in a paper entitled 'The secondary banking crisis and the Bank of England's support operations' prepared by the Bank of England for the Wilson Committee and published in the *Bank of England Quarterly Bulletin*, vol. 18, no. 2 (June 1978). For a more detailed and colourful description see Margaret Reid, *The Secondary Banking Crisis 1973–75* (Macmillan, 1982).

2. *Bank of England Quarterly Bulletin* (June 1978) pp. 232–3, para. 24.
3. Ibid., p. 233, para. 25.
4. Ibid., p. 233, para. 26.
5. Ibid., p. 233, para. 28.
6. Ibid., p. 235, para. 48.
7. Ibid., p. 236, para. 49.
8. John Williamson, *The Failure of World Monetary Reform 1971–74* (Nelson, 1977) p. 3.
9. See, for example, John Williamson, ibid.; Andrew Crockett, *International Money: Issues and Analysis* (Nelson, 1977) and the bibliographies in those two books.
10. In this context, the alternative possibilities of speculating in the forward foreign exchange markets are ignored. These possibilities, which will be touched on in Chapter 3, would, however, have very similar costs.
11. Professor Williamson's source for the earnings on US direct foreign investment is Marina v. N. Whitman, *The Current and Future Role of the Dollar: How Much Symmetry?* (Brookings Papers on Economic Activity, 1974 (3)), p. 555.
12. *The Failure of World Monetary Reform, 1971–74*, p. 47.
13. Ibid., p. 50.
14. *Bank of England Quarterly Bulletin* (June 1978), para. 39, p. 235.
15. Speech by the Governor of the Bank of England given at the annual banquet of the Overseas Bankers Club on 5 February 1979, *Bank of England Quarterly Bulletin*, vol. 19, no. 1 (March 1979) p. 49.
16. Speech by the Governor of the Bank of England given at the annual banquet of the Overseas Bankers Club on 4 February 1980, *Bank of England Quarterly Bulletin*, vol. 20, no. 1 (March 1980) p. 59.
17. Ibid., pp. 59–60.
18. Ibid., p. 60.
19. Ibid.
20. Ibid.
21. Leading article, *Financial Times*, 3 September 1982.
22. Cmnd 6527 (HMSO, 1944) para. 1.
23. John Cooper, *A Suitable Case for Treatment: What to do about the Balance of Payments* (Penguin, 1968) p. 18.

24. *Report of the Committee on the Working of the Monetary System*, Cmnd 827 (HMSO, 1959) p. 22, para. 69.
25. R. F. Harrod, *Policy Against Inflation* (Macmillan, 1958) p. 230.
26. Cmnd 827 (HMSO, 1959) pp. 129–30, para. 382.
27. Tim Congdon, *Monetary Control in Britain* (Macmillan, 1982) p. 3.
28. Ibid., p. 3.
29. Speech by the Governor of the Bank of England, reprinted in *Bank of England Quarterly Bulletin* (March 1977) p. 48.
30. *Monetary Control in Britain*, pp. 3–4.
31. Speech by the Governor of the Bank of England, reprinted in *Bank of England Quarterly Bulletin* (September 1976) p. 325.
32. Speech by the Governor of the Bank of England, reprinted in *Bank of England Quarterly Bulletin* (December 1976) p. 454.
33. *Monetary Control in Britain*, p. 4.
34. Ibid., pp. 4, 5.
35. Ibid., pp. 5–6.
36. Quotations from Mr Healey taken from Treasury Press Release, 19 October 1978.
37. *Monetary Control in Britain*, p. 6.
38. *Monetary Control*, Cmnd 7858 (HMSO, March 1980) p. iii, paras 2, 3.
39. *Financial Statement and Budget Report* (March 1981).
40. *Financial Statement and Budget Report*, Part 2 (March 1982).
41. 'The 1982 Budget: the strategy', *Economic Progress Report*, no. 143 (Treasury, March 1982).
42. *Financial Statement and Budget Report* (March 1983).

2 The Institutions of British Banking

The principal function of those institutions which collectively make up the mechanism of British banking is the collection of deposits from those with cash resources surplus to their immediate requirements and the on-lending of these cash resources, in one form or another, to those with an immediate need for them. This function is common to every institution involved in banking: indeed, one of the banking services which must be provided by an institution in order for it to become a 'recognised bank', and thus entitled, among other things, to use the word 'bank' in its title, is the provision of current or deposit account facilities or the acceptance of funds in the wholesale money markets.[1]

Some banking institutions confine themselves to taking certain types of deposit, defined as to size, length of maturity or currency; others specialise in providing certain types of loans and advances, defined for example as to the industry of the borrower or the characteristics of the assets taken as security; others again specialise in domestic deposit-taking and lending whilst others still specialise in overseas deposit-taking and lending. Further, some institutions provide services separate from their deposit-taking or lending but which greatly influence the extent and particular characteristics of their deposit-taking and lending: money transmission services and investment management services are examples.

Not only do the deposit-taking and lending activities of banking institutions provide them with the distinctive characteristics of banks, they also provide their most important sources of profit and, even more significant to a theme of this book, the reason for attracting the attention and supervisory control of the authorities. We saw in Chapter 1 how the whole argument for, and justification of, prudential controls on banking institutions rests in large measure on the publicly accepted requirement to protect depositors. Equally, it is the lending side of the banks' activities which ultimately attracts the attention of those concerned with the control of credit and its direction; though the volume of, and movements in, the deposits taken by the banking system is of crucial interest to those concerned with controlling the money supply.

The functions undertaken by deposit banks are fairly standard throughout the Western world; but the pattern by which these functions, and specific specialisations within them, are grouped in different institutions varies from one country to another. The purpose of this chapter is to give a brief description of the main types of banking institutions which exist in the United Kingdom and, particularly, to note any special characteristics they possess regarding their deposit-taking and lending activities. Although the particular pattern of institutions described is essentially of fairly parochial interest, the general pattern which emerges of the deposit-taking and lending activities of banks, in general, has a more general, universal relevance.

THE LONDON CLEARING BANKS

In the words of the Wilson Committee:

> the London clearing banks are the dominant force in retail deposit banking in England and Wales. They play a very substantial part in sterling wholesale deposit and lending business, and are also active in international banking. Through their subsidiaries they control most of the retail banking business of Northern Ireland and they have shareholdings in the Scottish clearing banks ranging from 16 per cent to 100 per cent.[2]

The clearing banks may be defined formally as those banks

which are members of the Committee of London Clearing Bankers (CLCB). By this definition, there are six London clearing banks at the time of writing: Barclays Bank, Coutts & Co., Lloyds Bank, Midland Bank, National Westminster Bank and Williams & Glyn's Bank. Of these, Coutts is a wholly-owned subsidiary of National Westminster, and Lloyds has a 16 per cent shareholding in the Royal Bank of Scotland Group, the parent company of Williams & Glyn's. Thus effectively the London clearing banks, as generally known, consist of four main banking groups: Barclays, Lloyds, Midland and National Westminster:

> All of the groups have merchant and wholesale banking subsidiaries which, with the exception of Williams & Glyn's, engage in a significant proportion of their business. Practice regarding the organisation of international activities varies, with Barclays, Lloyds and National Westminster having specialist subsidiaries, while Midland and Williams & Glyn's conduct business through specialist divisions of the parent bank. Several of the clearers also participate in consortium banks. All of the groups are involved through subsidiary or associated companies in instalment credit and leasing business.[3]

It is worth adding that the four major groups have become increasingly international in recent years, as is reflected in each case by the acquisition of major banking subsidiaries in the United States and the significant proportion of their profits arising from activities outside the United Kingdom.

Within the United Kingdom, the characteristics of the London clearing banks are broadly shared by the Scottish Clearing Banks – the Bank of Scotland, the Clydesdale Bank and the Royal Bank of Scotland – and by the Northern Ireland banks. 'The Northern Ireland banking system is dominated by the Northern Ireland branches of the Northern Bank and Ulster Bank, both subsidiaries of London clearing banks, which engage in banking throughout Ireland. It also includes branches of two banks registered in the Republic of Ireland, Allied Irish Banks and Bank of Ireland.'[4]

As the Wilson Committee pointed out:

the London clearing banks carry out the bulk of the nation's cash distribution and money transmission activities. They collect notes from the Bank of England's Head Office and seven branches in England and store them in about 100 cash distribution centres for distribution subsequently to their own branches. Money transmission involving payments between branches or between banks passes through the Bankers' Clearing House or Bankers' Automated Clearing Services, both of which are owned by the clearing banks. In 1978 about 80 per cent of the nation's non-cash payments were processed through these two organisations.[5]

The members of the CLCB have been, and continue to be, responsible for the organisation and conduct of the clearing system in England and Wales. This system has grown organically since approximately 1770. It is centred on the Bankers' Clearing House, which is now a limited company and is owned by the six members of the CLCB. In addition to these six members, three other banks – the Bank of England, the Co-operative Bank and the Central Trustee Savings Bank (CTSB) – all have a seat in the clearing house and participate in the clearing system. The Bank of England has had its seat since 1864: the Co-operative Bank and the CTSB since 1975. As the CLCB has pointed out:

> the functional membership of the Bank of England, the Co-operative and the CTSB in the clearing house does not extend to membership of the CLCB, nor do they share in the ownership of the Bankers' Clearing House. They are, however, represented on a number of CLCB committees, particularly on those where functional details of the clearing system fall for consideration. The Scottish banks and, for that matter, the four branch banks operating in Northern Ireland are also represented where relevant.[6]

Alongside the Bankers' Clearing House, the members of the CLCB established an electronic transfer system of payments between banks in 1968. This system was proudly described by the CLCB to the Wilson Committee in 1977 in the following terms:

Now organised as a separate company called Bankers' Automated Clearing Services Limited (BACS) with its own purpose built computer centre, the organisation has grown into the world's largest automated clearing house, with a total staff of about 200 handling 262 million items in 1976. Non-clearing banks and other financial institutions have agency arrangements with BACS, while customers of the clearing banks and other banks are able to initiate payments by presenting magnetic tapes directly to BACS.[7]

The money transmission system provided by the clearing banks has been clearly described by Professor Revell:

> The money transfer system involves the movement of bank deposits from one account to another at three different levels : (1) within the same branch, (2) between branches of the same bank and (3) between banks. As computers increasingly maintain the accounts for groups of branches, the proportion of movements which could be said to be within the same 'branch' goes up, and as banks merge to form larger units, the proportion of movements that are internal to the bank rises. The mechanism for clearing debit and credit transfer items between banks is the same as that between branches of the same bank: all the items affecting the other bank or the other branch are collected together and exchanged for items affecting the same two banks or branches but in the other direction. For example cheques drawn by customers of Lloyds in favour of customers of National Westminster are exchanged at a clearing for cheques drawn by customers of National Westminster in favour of customers of Lloyds. The essence of a clearing system is that only the net difference between the two sets of items exchanged is settled. For transfer between branches of the same bank settlement is made through the account which each branch maintains with its head office, while between different banks the settlement is made through the working balance which each bank maintains with some bank outside its own system – with the Bank of England in the case of the London clearing banks.[8]

Besides providing this money transmission service, the clearing banks are, of course, substantial takers of deposits and lenders of money. This function was succinctly described by the banks themselves in their evidence to the Wilson Committee:

> The U.K. has a wide range of financial intermediaries with the common functions of providing a repository for funds not required for immediate use and of facilitating their productive employment. Within this range is a number of intermediaries whose particular contribution is to provide a repository which is highly liquid, so that the owners of funds can have them fully available either on demand or at short notice. The clearing banks are among this number, and this determines in a fundamental way their approach to the lending side of their business.[9]

Besides the highly liquid nature of deposits taken by the clearing banks, that is, in effect, the fact that they can be withdrawn at very short notice, another characteristic of many of these deposits is that they are made up of a large number of small amounts, that is, the deposit-taking activities of the clearing banks are very much a *retail* operation. This point was well taken by the Wilson Committee itself. It reported in 1980 that

> There are a large number of commercial banks, and they vary considerably in the range and scope of their operations. Their activities can be divided into retail and wholesale business. Retail banking on the deposit side is mainly concerned with cash withdrawal and money transmission – usually the most important reason why people keep back accounts. This requires a network of branches and is therefore mainly the province of the London and Scottish clearing banks, the Northern Ireland banks and certain other banks like the Co-operative Bank and the Yorkshire Bank who between them have a total of more than 13,000 outlets spread throughout the U.K. Cash withdrawal and money transmission facilities are also provided by the National Girobank, which operates

through some 21,000 Crown and sub-post offices, and by the trustee savings banks. The terms on which retail funds are taken are standard and usually published. The level of current account (non-interest bearing) deposits tends to move with money payments in the economy, but funds may be moved fairly easily between current and deposit accounts in the banks and other intermediaries in response to interest rate differentials, so that the banks are not able to control the level of retail deposits very precisely.[10]

The deposits taken by the clearing banks, then, are predominantly very short-term and predominantly retail, or, individually, small in size. Indeed a substantial proportion of the deposits taken by the clearing banks are 'sight deposits' or, in effect, credit balances on current accounts: of their total sterling deposits of £60029m in December 1982, £22155m[11] or 37 per cent were in the form of sight deposits. These deposits, whilst a crucial prerequisite of the more profitable banking business of the clearing banks are, in a sense, a 'fall-out' or by-product of the clearing banks' functions of providing cash withdrawal and money transmission facilities: as we shall see, other banks requiring deposits to finance their lending activities are obliged to attract such deposits by paying the market rate of interest. It would, of course, be wrong, as any clearing banker will tell you, to assume that since the sight deposits acquired by the clearing banks as a by-product of their cash withdrawal and money transmission services are interest-free in a formal sense, they are, in fact, interest-free and costless in any practical sense. The point is simply that in calculating the charges made to customers for these services, the banks do take into account the interest-free balances that come as a result: in other words, the interest which the banks save as a result of the interest-free deposits they enjoy is used, in part at least, to subsidise the money transmission and cash withdrawal services they provide. What *is* true is that whilst the costs of providing the two services remain fairly constant – increasing with price inflation but, hopefully, restrained as a result of increased efficiency and computerisation – the level of interest rates, and thus the direct benefit of interest-free deposits, fluctuates fairly widely. One need not pin-point the exact break-even rate of interest at which the benefit to the clearing banks of interest-free deposits exactly equals the cost of providing the services which generate those deposits – a recent estimate of the figure was around 9 per cent per annum[12] – to accept the point that very high interest rates give the clearing banks a bonus to their profits (known as the 'endowment effect' of their interest-free deposits) and, equally, that very low interest rates – less than 9 per cent, if the above estimate is correct – give the clearing banks a burden on their profits. The point to note is that both the bonus and the burden are a direct consequence of factors entirely outside the control of the clearing banks themselves.

The lending operations of the clearing banks, and their particular characteristics, have been summarised by the Wilson Committee:

> The lending business of commercial banks tends to be less specialised than that of the other deposit-taking institutions. Bank loans vary in size from an overdraft of a few hundred pounds or less to loans of several hundred million pounds to multinational companies or sovereign governments. When a loan is too large for one bank to take on it can be provided by a number acting as a syndicate. The British clearing banks have traditionally preferred to lend to both their personal and business customers on overdraft within limits reviewed each year and in principle callable on demand. There has, however, been an increasing tendency for lending to industry to take the form of term loans with periods of between two and seven years, and sometimes longer, and with repayments geared to particular circumstances. This has reflected in part recognition of the comparatively permanent nature of some of the lending previously done on overdraft and in part the advantages of term loans for the financing of distinct investment projects. As well as overdraft and loan finance to personal customers the clearing banks have long provided bridging finance for house purchase and loans for home improvements. They have now also begun to enter the mortgage business directly. Other facilities provided by commercial banks

include industrial instalment credit and equipment leasing.[13]

As the Wilson Committee noted, the clearing banks traditionally have preferred to make most of their lending on an overdraft basis, which theoretically gave them the right to call for repayment at very short notice. The rationale behind this policy was quite simply that since a significant proportion of their deposits were withdrawable 'at sight': that is, at no notice at all, and the greater part of their deposits were fixed for very short periods – the Wilson Committee noted that at the time it was reporting 'about three-quarters of the London clearing banks' larger deposits have a maturity of less than three months'[14] – it seemed only prudent to undertake most of their lendings on a similar short-notice basis. But again, as the Wilson Committee noted, the clearing banks have recently abandoned too rigid an adherence to this principle.

The 1970s saw a steady increase in term loans to industry by clearing banks for periods of between two and seven years or even longer; and the early 1980s have seen a dramatic incursion by the clearing banks into the house mortgage market. Apart from the pressures from their borrowing customers, both corporate and personal, for such term loans, this policy seems to have been based on a perception, based on historical fact, that deposits with clearing banks are not very volatile, and on the emergence of the inter-bank deposit market as an immediate source of funds. As the Wilson Committee put it, 'the clearing banks with their large branch networks can be confident that a substantial proportion of their deposits will remain with them and banks generally can expect to be able to obtain deposits from the money markets at the going rate'.[15] The implications of this change of policy, and the whole question of how mismatched a bank should prudently allow itself to be, in terms of the maturities of its deposits and lendings, will be discussed in Chapter 4.

One further point should be made about the clearing banks. The characteristics noted above relate specifically to their operations as domestic clearing banks. Over the years, but particularly in the 1960s and subsequently, the Big Four clearing banks – Barclays, Lloyds, Midland and National

Westminster – have built around themselves groups of institutions which include many other types of bank as well as the 'central' domestic clearing bank. The characteristics of these subsidiaries depend, of course, on the type of institution which they are and will be described here in that context. Barclays Merchant Bank, County Bank (owned by National Westminster) and Samuel Montagu (owned by Midland), for example, share the characteristics of other merchant banks; Mercantile Credit (owned by Barclays), Lombard North Central (owned by National Westminster) and Lloyds and Scottish (partly owned by Lloyds) share the characteristics of other finance houses.

THE MERCHANT BANKS AND ACCEPTANCE CREDITS

The main independent merchant banks are grouped together in a trade association known as the Accepting Houses Committee (AHC), which currently has sixteen members. Whilst the accepting houses, as members of the AHC are known, still account for the greater part of the business conducted by merchant banks, other and newer rivals have grown up in recent years. As we have seen, the big clearing banking groups have now got their own merchant banking capability: the Midland Bank achieved this by buying an existing accepting house, Samuel Montagu, in 1973; Barclays Bank and National Westminster Bank by creating their own merchant banks in Barclays Merchant Bank and County Bank respectively, and Lloyds by developing a merchant banking division within Lloyds Bank International. Again, several American-based and other foreign banks have established their own wholly-owned subsidiaries to undertake merchant banking activities in London: Chase Manhattan Limited, Citibank Limited, Orion Royal Bank (now wholly-owned by the Royal Bank of Canada) are all examples. The Standard and Chartered Bank group has established its own Standard Chartered Merchant Bank and the Hongkong & Shanghai Banking Corporation has acquired Antony Gibbs

& Son Ltd., a former member of the AHC, as a wholly-owned subsidiary.

Whilst the emphasis given to different activities will vary from one merchant bank to another, and the total list of activities undertaken by merchant banks is in a constant state of change as new opportunities are taken and older functions become redundant, the activities of the larger merchant banks can be grouped under three main headings: lending banking, the provision of corporate financial advice, and the provision of investment advice. Although we are primarily concerned in the present context with merchant bankers as takers of deposits and lenders, this role is in itself effected by their other activities. As corporate financial advisers, the merchant banks arrange the procurement of funds from the long-term capital markets as well as assisting in capital reorganisation, mergers and take-overs; and the contacts made in this activity provide a natural 'catchment area' for both deposit-taking and lending activities.

As investment advisers, the merchant banks manage the investment of considerable institutional savings, among which pension funds are now the largest single element, and they also advise wealthy private individuals. Again, this investment activity has a direct effect on the banking operations of merchant banks, in that the banking operation can provide a safe and administratively simple short-term employment for funds awaiting investment in bonds and shares; and at the same time, an investor wishing to borrow funds for investment in the stock market can be a natural borrower from the merchant banks.

One of the characteristics and boasts of the merchant banks is that, although small in size, they have a position and influence in the financial markets proportionately much larger than their own resources. The point was made with characteristic immodesty by the AHC in its evidence to the Wilson Committee. 'In terms of financial resources,' it declared:

> the Accepting Houses represent only a small part of the banking system in the U.K. At the end of 1976, their combined assets represented 4 per cent of the total assets of

all banks in the U.K.[16] Accordingly, in common with other independent merchant banks, their success and the maintenance of their competitive position among financial institutions are dependent more upon their ability to exercise their skill and inventiveness for the benefit of their clients than upon their own resources. In a number of areas they have been pioneers. Unlike some other financial institutions, the Accepting Houses do not concentrate on any single activity. Their business is spread, in varying proportions, over a number of fields. Their influence is, however, disproportionate to their resources, by virtue of their role as financial intermediaries.[17]

In the present context of deposit-taking and lending institutions, the accepting houses and other merchant banks are, then, relatively insignificant. To update the figures given above for 1976, the combined assets of the accepting houses in December 1982 represented 3.7 per cent of the total assets of all UK banks: to put this figure in perspective, it compares with 17.6 per cent for the London clearing banks, 17.9 per cent for the American banks in London and 18.4 per cent for the Japanese banks in London.[18]

But in spite of their relatively small size in the total UK deposit banking scene, there are five points which are worth making at this point about the deposit banking business of the merchant banks, and particularly the accepting houses. First, the banking business of merchant banks is predominantly a wholesale banking business: that is, they take in the bulk of their deposits in substantial lumps – probably little less than £250 000 each – and at the same time lend the money out in similarly-sized lumps. This means that most of their borrowers are corporate entities, rather than individuals; and most of their depositors are either corporate entities or other banks. Some such depositors come to them direct; others are contacted through the money markets, described in Chapter 3. Secondly, and consequentially, virtually all the deposits of merchant banks are interest-bearing. Taking figures as at December 1978, the Wilson Committee noted that nearly 80 per cent of the sterling deposits of accepting houses were time deposits or CDs and that a high proportion of their sight deposits were also interest-bearing.[19] The merchant banks do not, therefore, share the interest-free current account balances – and the fluctuating 'endowment profits' which go with them – which play such a role in the balance sheets of the clearing banks, and which are, in fact, a direct spin-off from their cash withdrawal and money transmission services.

The third point to be made about the merchant banks is that a substantial proportion of their lending and deposit-taking business is conducted in currencies other than sterling. In December 1982 only 39 per cent of the total deposits taken by members of the AHC were in sterling and 61 per cent in other currencies; this compared with a proportion of 72 per cent of the deposits taken by the London clearing banks at the same date in sterling and only 28 per cent in other currencies.[20] The deposit-taking and lending business of the merchant banks thus straddles the domestic sterling banking scene and the international eurocurrency banking scene; but the split between the two is not a neat one. For example, some of the borrowers of eurocurrency loans and depositors of eurocurrency funds are, in fact, domestic UK-resident corporations; and some of the borrowers and deposits in sterling are, in fact, resident outside the United Kingdom. Since the abolition of UK exchange control in 1979, London merchant banks – and, indeed, other London-based banks with an international business – have increasingly regarded their banking activities as genuinely international and not divisible between the United Kingdom and the rest of the world; the only exception to this attitude is the ratios and reserves they are obliged to observe for purposes of UK monetary control, which do not affect their international business and which will be discussed in Chapter 6. As in their domestic banking business, the eurocurrency lending and deposit-taking by merchant banks is a wholesale rather than a retail operation. The sources of the deposits are mainly international corporations, foreign central banks and monetary authorities, and other commercial banks.

The fourth point to be made about the lending operations of the merchant banks is a direct consequence of the relatively small size of their own resources, on which we have already remarked. This smallness of resources means that to satisfy the borrowing requirements of their larger customers they must develop techniques for mobilising the funds of others to supplement their own: as the AHC has stated, 'the Accepting Houses should probably be regarded more as procurers of finance (with their own funds leading the way in most cases) than as providers'.[21] One such technique is to put together syndicates of banks which together can provide loan facilities far in excess of the sums which could be offered by a merchant bank on its own. This technique was described by the AHC in its evidence to the Wilson Committee in the following terms, using figures taken in early 1977:

> In their position as managers, the Accepting Houses demonstrate the ability, notwithstanding their own small size, to mobilise and provide substantial funds to meet the needs of industry. In this connection they manage syndicate facilities of £7½ billion of which £1 billion is their own funds with the remainder contributed by other banks, predominantly not British owned. In addition the Accepting Houses manage a further £2½ billion of sterling Buyer Credit facilities. This means that the Accepting Houses are responsible for providing £10 billion of finance in their role as managers. The funds so mobilised are by way of loans, overdrafts and acceptance credits. A substantial portion is for periods in excess of 5 years.[22]

Another method of mobilising the resources of others in order to supplement their own – and the fifth point to be made about the lending operations of the merchant banks – is the technique of providing 'acceptances'. Although this technique for providing funds is by no means exclusive to the merchant banks – it is widely used, for example, by the clearing banks and many overseas banks with London offices – historically, it owes its origins to the merchant banks and is, in any case, the distinctive characteristic of the older merchant banks as emphasised in the name of their trade association, the Accepting Houses Committee.

If a merchant bank wishes to make funds available to a customer it can either make a straight loan to the customer or it can provide an 'acceptance credit'. The AHC has provided a succinct definition of this technique:

> An acceptance credit involves the 'borrower' drawing a bill of exchange, which is virtually the same as writing a post-dated cheque, on an Accepting House. In return for an acceptance commission the Accepting House then 'accepts' the bill of exchange which means that the Accepting House promises unconditionally to pay, on maturity of the 'post-dated cheque', its face value to its then holder. After acceptance the bill of exchange becomes a high-class negotiable document which is sold to the Discount Market (at a discount rate usually only marginally above the going rate on U.K. Treasury Bills) and the proceeds handed to the 'borrower'. On maturity the Accepting House pays the holder of the bill of exchange and is itself repaid by the 'borrower'.
>
> In effect, the Accepting House, by providing its acceptance, has enabled the 'borrower' to gain access to the pool of very short-term funds (mainly overnight funds) within the banking system which are placed in the Discount Market. The effect on the 'borrower' is similar to a short-term loan (the usual term is 3 months). The effect on the banking system is that daily balances can be applied to working capital finance – the use of acceptance credit facilities is normally tied to the purchase of raw materials, the financing of stocks and work in progress or the financing of sales, with special emphasis on exports.

The AHC added that

> bill financing was the basis of merchanting finance provided by the Accepting Houses at the beginning of this century (although initially mainly for raw materials purchased from abroad or finished goods sold abroad) and the Accepting Houses still provide nearly half of all such facilities afforded by the UK banking system.[23]

Whilst the historic part of this statement remains true, the AHC's proportion of all acceptance credits provided by the

UK banking system had fallen to 22 per cent by December 1982. It is worth remarking that the AHC's proportion fell in this way notwithstanding a significant increase in the total acceptance credits provided by the accepting houses from £1084m in February 1977 to £2978m in December 1982 and that the fall in the proportion reflected an even more dramatic increase in the use of acceptance credits in the UK banking system from £2533m in February 1977 to £13 459m in December 1982. The reasons for this revival of the acceptance credit are discussed in the section on the Discount Market in Chapter 3.

One final point should be made about acceptance credits. We have seen that the provision of acceptance credits is a technique by which the merchant banks – and other banks – mobilise the funds available in the pool of very short-term funds placed in the Discount Market, for the use of their borrowing customers. In this way, the merchant banks are able to provide funds for their customers without themselves having to go out and borrow those funds on their own account – as they would have to do, if they were to make the loans direct to the customers themselves. But it is crucial to note that, while not borrowing the funds themselves, the accepting houses do undertake that the funds will be repaid: when a bill matures, it is to the house which has accepted it that the holder will look for repayment, rather than to the original drawer or 'borrower'; and if the original borrower goes bust, and is unable to repay, it is the accepting house which suffers the loss, rather than the holder of the bill. The acceptance credit is thus to be contrasted with that other technique mentioned above by which merchant banks mobilise the funds of others for the benefit of their customers, the management of syndicates of banks. As the acceptor of a bill, a merchant bank is unequivocally taking on the credit risk that that bill will be redeemed; as the manager of a syndicate of banks, the merchant bank, while implicitly recommending that the risk is a fair one, is simply inviting the other members of the syndicate to undertake that risk for themselves.

THE OVERSEAS BANKS AND THE CONSORTIUM BANKS

One of the principal and, in terms of scale, unique characteristics of the institutions of British banking is the mixture of their deposit-taking and lending business between domestic depositors and borrowers and international depositors and borrowers. This mixture opens up many opportunities for profitable activities to the institutions involved, which would not be open to the same extent to institutions operating purely domestically or purely internationally; and it almost certainly thereby increases significantly the contribution to the British balance of payments made by the 'invisible earnings' of the banking community. But the mixture is inherently untidy from the point of view of the student of banking trying to attribute different types of banking, and different areas of geographical specialisation, to different types of banks; it is even more untidy from the point of view of the British regulatory and monetary authorities in their attempts to maintain some sort of prudential and monetary control, respectively, over British banking institutions.

We have seen that in December 1982, the deposit banking operations of the Accepting Houses were split as to 39 per cent in sterling and as to 61 per cent in other currencies and that at the same date the operations of the London clearing banks, whilst predominantly conducted in sterling, were still based in other currencies as to 28 per cent. Again, the operations of both the Accepting Houses and the clearing banks involved dealing with counterparties – depositors and borrowers – split between the domestic sector and the international sector; and, untidily for analysts and controllers alike, this split was not directly related, statistically or in any other way, to the split between sterling and other currencies. Thus, for example, in December 1982 the London clearing banks were lending £45 255m by way of sterling advances: as one would expect, the greater part of this amount was lent to domestic borrowers, but £3251m or 7.2 per cent were in fact lent to overseas borrowers as well. At the same date, the London clearing banks were making market loans and advances in foreign currencies of £22 796m: of this total, about half was going to overseas borrowers, but £9590m went to UK banks and £1419m to domestic borrowers in the United Kingdom. The figures for the Accepting Houses showed a comparable lack of any discernible relationship between the split of their banking business between sterling and other currencies and that between domestic and overseas counterparties.

Students of the institutions of British banking must take account of a third dimension when analysing the division between domestic and international business. Besides the split between sterling and other currencies and that between domestic and overseas counterparties, there is the further split between British-owned banks and foreign-owned banks, including the UK branches or subsidiaries of foreign-owned banks, or, in the names given them in the statistical tables, between 'British banks' and 'overseas banks'.

As the Wilson Committee noted:

> there were 201 overseas banks and their subsidiaries in London at the end of 1978. The American and Japanese banks, which numbered 63 and 22 respectively, formed the largest national contingents. A primary reason for their presence is their desire to participate in the eurocurrency and eurobond markets, but some are long-established and play an important part in the financing of trade, and in domestic banking business. Frequently the latter is based on existing banking connections with the parents of foreign-controlled UK companies, but some banks, especially the American banks, have become actively involved in U.K. domestic banking.[24]

By December 1982, the number of 'overseas banks' reporting statistics to the Bank of England had grown to 225, of which 58 were American and 24 Japanese. It should be noted that these figures simply cover those 'overseas banks' which carry on a significant business of taking deposits and granting loans; it does not cover those other foreign-owned banks which, for example, maintain a representative office in London. *The Banker*, the monthly magazine, publishes an annual survey of all foreign banks in London: its latest tally, published in November 1982, gave a figure of 449 foreign banks represented in London, of which 379 were directly represented through a representative office, branch or subsidiary and 70 were indirectly represented through a stake in a joint venture or consortium bank.[25]

In December 1982, the overseas banks accounted for sterling deposits of £25 791m, or 19.2 per cent of the total sterling deposits in the UK banking system, and currency deposits of £284 424m, or 75.6 per cent of the total currency deposits in the UK banking system. Overall the overseas banks made up 58 per cent of the total balance sheet of the UK banking system, compared with 17.6 per cent for the London clearing banks and a mere 3.7 per cent for the accepting houses. Within this total of 58 per cent for the overseas banks as a whole, 18 per cent was accounted for by the American banks, 18 per cent by the Japanese banks and 22.0 per cent by the other overseas banks. In terms of sheer volume, of domestic and international business taken together, the overseas banks thus dominate the British banking scene.

The Wilson Committee noted that in December 1978 nearly 90 per cent of the liabilities of the overseas banks consisted of foreign currency deposits and that 'their capital resources in the U.K. were only just over 1 per cent of their deposits; this reflects their dependence on the support of their parent banks'.[26] By December 1982, this ratio of 90 per cent had increased to 92 per cent; and capital resources in the UK remained at something under 1.2 per cent of total deposits, though this average for all overseas banks hid a variation of less than 0.3 per cent for the Japanese banks, less than 0.9 per cent for the American banks and 2.1 per cent for the other overseas banks. This heavy dependence of most 'overseas banks' on the capital of their overseas parents raises important questions for prudential regulation. In particular, it emphasises the importance for the health of the UK banking system that overseas parents will stand behind their branches, subsidiaries and, to some extent, associated companies too, in times of trouble: a principle which is being developed by national bank supervisors acting collectively as a general rule of parent company responsibility for overseas operations, supervisory responsibility for such operations being taken by the authorities in the parent company's country. It also raises questions of an even-handed treatment by the supervisory authorities of overseas banks in matters of capital adequacy and limits in foreign exchange exposure, so as to ensure that they do not enjoy an unfair advantage in comparison with the indigenous British banks. These questions will be discussed in more detail in Chapter 5.

On the lending side, the Wilson Committee noted that in December 1978, the overseas banks

> were responsible for 15 per cent of sterling advances and 60 per cent of foreign currency advances to U.K. residents, with quite a strong emphasis on the manufacturing and financial sectors amongst the sterling advances. In their foreign currency U.K. lending they have played a prominent role in supporting loans for North Sea Oil development. Most of the advances are term loans – in early 1977 almost 30 per cent of the American banks' sterling loans and nearly 70 per cent of their loans in other currencies had an initial maturity exceeding one year. The bulk of domestic lending is to medium-sized or large corporate borrowers, institutions and the public sector.[27]

This picture remained broadly unchanged in December 1982.

In December 1978, the Wilson Committee noted that the overseas banks 'match the accepting houses as providers of finance through acceptance credit'. By December 1982, the overseas banks had pulled well away from the accepting houses, and were providing £6429m of acceptance credits out of a total provided by the whole British banking system of £13 459m; the accepting houses were providing £2978m, which while well up on their figure of just over £1500m in December 1978 still represented a significantly lower proportion of the total. These figures reflect two important developments in the acceptance credit market which took place in 1981 and 1982: the dramatic increase in the overall use of sterling acceptance credits prompted by the activities of the Bank of England as a major buyer of bills in the market and the equally dramatic widening of the list of banks whose acceptances are eligible for discount at the finest rate by the Bank of England. Both these developments will be discussed in the section on the bill market in Chapter 3.

One further group of banks must be mentioned in this section, sharing some of the characteristics of the overseas banks but reporting separately from them: the consortium banks. In the Wilson Committee's words:

> there were 29 consortium banks at the end of 1978, created by international consortia of banks to carry out specialist activities which are international in character. While consortium banks account for only one per cent of the sterling deposits of the banking system, they have 6 per cent of the foreign currency deposits, giving them over 4 per cent of the system's total liabilities.[28]

By December 1982 the number of consortium banks operating in London had fallen from 29 to 24 and whilst they had held their share of 1 per cent of total sterling deposits in the UK banking system, they had slipped to 3.7 per cent of total foreign currency deposits and 3.1 per cent of the system's total liabilities. This decline reflects a disillusionment on the part of some of the shareholders in some of the consortium banks about the original concept and the consequent sale of their shares either to one of the existing shareholders or to a new shareholder altogether. In this way, those banks which used to report as 'consortium banks' and no longer do so have not just simply disappeared; in most cases they now appear as 'overseas banks' being wholly-owned subsidiaries of an overseas parent. One of the biggest and most recent examples of this change of status was the £45m takeover of Orion Bank in April 1981 by the Royal Bank of Canada which bought out the other four shareholders – National Westminster, Chase Manhattan, Westdeusche Landesbank, Credito Haliano and Mitsubishi Bank.

The reasons for this change in ownership in Orion (now called Orion Royal Bank) were summarised in an article in *The Banker*'s annual review of foreign banks in London in November 1981. They are worth repeating here in that they underline a definite change in fashion and direction in the approach of several of the world's major banks to 'international business', and particularly international business based in London. Most of the consortium banks grew up in the 1970s as the reaction of several major banks in their own countries to the feeling that they should provide an international service to their larger customers with significant and growing international businesses: by entering the international arena in partnership with other major banks, they were spreading the cost of a new venture whose future expansion and success was unproven and at the same time creating a liaison with other like-minded banks with whom they could share their customers, rather than have those customers seduced away by those major international banks who offered a total world-wide service. Mr William Hall wrote in *The Banker* of the takeover in April 1981:

> Although only ten years old, Orion Bank had outlived its usefulness to its major shareholders . . . Like some other London consortium banks, Orion began to feel in the last few years of its life that it was in a 'Catch 22' situation. If it was too successful, it began stepping on the toes of its shareholders; and if its financial performance flagged, as it did in the last couple of years, its shareholders found that they could deploy their money more effectively elsewhere. The rationale behind the bank's establishment had disappeared by the mid 1970s. By then its big shareholders had moved into international areas which had once been regarded as Orion's special preserve. However, the lessons that emerge from the rebirth of Orion Bank are not universally applicable to all the consortium banks, many of which continue to prosper. . . .
>
> Some stay in business either because they are making decent profits or because they are now so big that it would cause too much bother to close them down. Some have found a life of their own, even if their original rationale has disappeared. One or two more names in the consortium banking community may disappear over the years, but the majority of those that were going, have gone, and the rest have found niches for themselves.[29]

Some eighteen months after the disappearance of Orion from the ranks of consortium banks, the oldest consortium bank of them all went the same way. Early in 1983 Midland and International Banks (or MAIBL as it was generally known in the City) was bought out by Standard Chartered Merchant Bank, a subsidiary of Standard Chartered Bank which was one of the original shareholders with a stake of 19 per cent; the other original shareholders were Midland Bank with 46 per cent, Toronto-Dominion Bank with 26 per cent and Westpac Banking Corporation (of Australia) with 10 per cent. MAIBL, which was founded in 1964, thus succumbed to similar pressures as those which caused the original shareholders in Orion Bank to sell out to the Royal Bank of Canada.

The business of the consortium banks remains basically the same as in 1978, when the Wilson Committee reported that

> the consortium banks' predominant activity is in the provision of term loans in foreign currencies to corporate and public borrowers, mostly overseas. They are active in loan syndications, and some banks manage or underwrite international bond issues. Trade finance through acceptance credit is also provided. Within their U.K. sterling lending there has been some emphasis on lending to the financial sector.[30]

THE BUILDING SOCIETIES

As was stated at the beginning of this chapter, the principal function of those institutions which collectively make up the mechanism of British banking is the collection of deposits from those with cash resources surplus to their requirements and the on-lending of these cash resources, in one form or another, to those with an immediate need for them. It is remarkable that the group of institutions fulfilling this function in greater volume than any other group are not formally regarded or classified as 'banks' at all: the building societies. In September 1982, the deposits taken by the building societies from the public amounted to £64 073m compared with total deposits taken by the London clearing banks of £80 474m, of which £58 249m were in sterling.

Building Societies are mutual organisations which borrow personal savings and lend most of them to individuals buying their own houses. The Wilson Committee described their activities as follows:

> Personal savings can be invested in building societies by means of a share account or a deposit account. The investor in a share account is essentially buying shares in the society and in practice almost all (97 per cent) of the money invested in building societies is in this form. Share capital is not negotiable. Ordinary shareholders are entitled to repayment of their capital with interest and, although the rates of a society may require one to three months notice of withdrawal, in practice, small sums are repaid on demand and larger sums in a matter of days. Most societies also offer regular savings accounts and fixed term share accounts at slightly higher rates of interest.
>
> Building societies make mortgage advances for house purchase at a variable rate of interest and usually repayable over a period of 20–25 years. Repayment is normally made in the form of a regular monthly sum in respect of both interest and repayment of principal . . . Alternatively, societies are prepared to combine a mortgage with an endowment assurance policy; only interest payments are made to the building society during the life of the mortgage, the outstanding debt being repaid when the endowment policy matures.
>
> Mortgages can be repaid in full or in part at any time, although some societies make a charge if the whole mortgage is redeemed in the early years of its life. The actual length of a mortgage averages about seven years, many mortgages being redeemed early when a borrower sells his house and uses the proceeds to pay off his debt. The borrower then usually takes out a new mortgage on his next house.
>
> An important characteristic of building societies' operations is that they borrow short to lend long . . . shares and deposits form the major part (93 per cent at the end of

1978) of building societies' liabilities and reserves and, except for just over 10 per cent of shares which are for a fixed term of a year or more, they can be withdrawn at relatively short notice. Other liabilities include interest accrued, but not yet credited to accounts, tax and other payments due and provisions, and, from time to time, loans made to building societies by the government for special purposes.

Societies' reserves are built up from the small surpluses usually made each year from their operations. Reserves represent the excess of assets (at book values) over liabilities and provide a solvency margin for societies to cover the risk of loss on mortgages or on investments. A minimum reserve ratio (general reserves as a percentage of total assets) is required for trustee status and for membership of the Building Societies Association (B.S.A.). At the end of 1978 accounting years the average reserve ratio for all societies stood at 3.73 per cent.

About 80 per cent of societies' assets are held as mortgage advances. Although these are long-term loans, they are secured against what has in recent years been an appreciating asset, and the risk of loss is low. A proportion of building societies' assets is held in liquid investments to provide working capital and to cover any short-term excess of withdrawals and lending over deposits. These investments are made in cash and short-term bank deposits, short-term public sector debt, and in British government and local authority securities mostly with a residual maturity of less than five years. The financial assets in which building societies are allowed to invest their liquid funds are laid down by the Chief Registrar of Friendly Societies.

The percentage of total assets represented by cash and investments is known as the liquidity ratio. Trustee status and membership of the B.S.A. require a minimum liquidity ratio of $7\frac{1}{2}$ per cent. In practice, however, societies work on much higher ratios, and at the end of 1978 accounting years the average liquidity ratio for all societies stood at 18.8 per cent.

Building societies aim to set their interest rates to investors at a level which will, in the light of the general

> trend of interest rates, retain existing deposits and attract sufficient new deposits to meet their lending programmes once the flow of repayments of principal has been taken into account. The mortgage rate is based on the rate paid to investors with allowance being made for management expenses, a surplus for addition to reserves, and income and corporation tax commitments. Societies like to keep their rates reasonably stable and do not follow every change in competing short-term rates. When other interest rates are high for short periods societies may keep their rates at a level below that required to attract sufficient new deposits and run down liquidity to maintain lending. Liquidity is later restored by maintaining rates when the general level of interest rates falls.[31]

The dominant position of the building societies is a fairly recent phenomenon and is the consequence of dramatic growth in their business throughout the 1960s and 1970s. Deposits taken by the building societies from the public grew from £2273m in 1957 to £53 286m at the end of 1981, a record which represented a very considerable victory in the competition for personal savings over their main rivals – the clearing banks, the Trustee Savings Banks and National Savings.

Some of this success has been the result of taking on the competition in the market place and winning on straight commercial grounds; some, at least in the eyes of the clearing banks, has been the result of 'artificial competitive advantages', arising out of fiscal, prudential and monetary regulation.

As to the commercial grounds for success, two of the main factors must be the rate of interest on deposits which is attractive by comparison with that paid by the competition and the ease of access to the societies' offices. This latter is helped by the rapid expansion in the number of branches of building societies up and down the country – from 1500 in 1967 to 4600 in 1978, as the Wilson Committee noted – and, more importantly, by the opening of these branches on Saturdays, in marked contrast to the clearing banks. In noting this expansion in the branch network of building societies, the

CLCB, in its evidence to the Wilson Committee, commented that their (the building societies')

> savings facilities are increasingly regarded as alternatives to a bank account rather than as outlets for longer-term saving, as the secular increase in withdrawals as a percentage of the societies' gross receipts suggests. Indeed the amount of a societies' shares and deposits, which 20 years ago was of the same order as the clearing banks' 7 day deposit accounts, is now three times as big.[32]

As we saw in the case of the clearing banks, an important magnet for retail deposits is the provision of cash withdrawal and money transmission services. It is no wonder that as the competition for retail deposits hots up, the banks, led by Barclays in mid-1982, should be thinking in terms of re-opening on Saturdays or that the building societies should be experimenting with cash withdrawal facilities, both over-the-counter and through cash dispensers, and with money transmission services by the issue of cheque books. It seems probable that the competition that has broken out between the banks and the buildings societies will cause further encroachment by both into each other's traditional areas of activity, such as the provision of long-term mortgage finance by the clearing banks, to the probable ultimate benefit of their retail customers.

The 'artificial competitive advantages' of the building societies are rather more controversial to describe but are also more relevant to the regulation of banks, the subject of this book. The CLCB drew the attention of the Wilson Committee, in remarkable forthright terms, to the fact that

> many of the mutual and public sector institutions with which the banks are in competition are endowed with artificial competitive advantages . . . The clearing banks strongly believe that these competitive advantages should be terminated. They lead to a mis-allocation of resources in financial markets and distort the market shares of different types of institution. Any subsidies which the government

> wishes to provide should relate to particular financial functions, not to particular financial institutions.[33]

The targets in the CLCB's sights when making these remarks, besides the building societies, were the Trustee Savings Banks (TSBs), the National Savings Bank and the National Giro: the 'artificial' advantages allegedly enjoyed by them will be inspected in the next section.

For the building societies, the CLCB identified four such artificial advantages. First, the fiscal advantage in the arrangements whereby the societies are allowed to pay income tax on behalf of their depositors at the agreed 'composite rate'. This acts as an inducement to those paying income tax to place their funds with building societies rather than with banks; the societies benefit from the fact that tax-paying investors are evidently more sensitive to interest differentials than non-taxpayers. Building societies also have the advantage of a special low rate of corporation tax (40 per cent); moreover neither building societies nor savings banks are liable to corporation tax on gains arising on the sale of government securities, provided they have held them for more than twelve months. This complaint, while apparently perfectly valid, lies outside the subject and therefore the comment of this book.

Secondly, the CLCB commented that

> the building societies, savings banks and Giro are all exempt from the monetary controls imposed on banks, though it is intended in due course to bring the TSBs and Giro within the system. Building societies do have portfolio constraints of their own; but these are in force for prudential purposes rather than to limit the growth of the societies' liquid liabilities. Thus the building societies are not obliged to hold 12½ per cent of their liabilities in the form of reserve assets. Much more important, however, has been the building societies' exemption from credit ceilings in the period up to 1971, and more recently from the 'corset' controls on interest-bearing deposits . . . In addition the clearing banks were subjected between September 1973 and February 1975 to a restriction on their deposit

> rates in order to limit their ability to compete with building societies.[34]

Whilst these specific examples of 'unfair' advantages bestowed on building societies by measures of monetary control are now of historical rather than immediately practical relevance, the point still stands that there is a strong case for even-handedness as between different types of competing deposit-taking institutions when it comes to monetary policy.

The third artificial advantage which the CLCB identified as being enjoyed by the building societies and other 'mutual and public sector institutions' mentioned above is that 'the prudential constraints which these institutions are expected to observe in order to ensure their capital adequacy are also less onerous than those observed by commercial banks.[35] Again, there is as strong a case in prudential regulation as there is in monetary policy for even-handedness as between different types of competing deposit-taking institutions; and this point will be pursued further in Chapter 5.

The fourth artificial advantage identified by the CLCB as being enjoyed by building societies is rather less straightforward:

> The nature of the competition between the banks and the building societies and T.S.B.s is also affected by these institutions' mutual form of organisation. Not only does this mean that they are able to add to their capital resources sums which a commercial bank would have distributed in dividends, but it may also affect their attitude to new investment in their businesses and to the rates of interest they charge and pay.[36]

Whilst this characteristic may well bestow some degree of commercial advantage on the building societies, it is not an advantage which arises from the exercise of either prudential or monetary control: it therefore lies beyond the scope of this book.

The CLCB wound up its comments on the building societies with an eloquent expansion of its point that any subsidies which the government wishes to provide should relate to particular financial functions, not to particular financial institutions. The point is so relevant to the subject of the banking system and domestic economic policy discussed in Chapter 6, that it is worth repeating here:

> In the case of the building societies the clearing banks recognise that the advantages bestowed on them reflect an official commitment to support the ideal of home ownership. The banks do not disagree with the importance of this ideal but they consider that there is a need for some rationalisation of the authorities' sometimes inconsistent attempts to encourage the flow of resources to a multitude of sectors (such as industry, housing, exports and the government itself). The building societies are now of such size and importance that fuller consideration than hitherto should be given to the effects of their activities on other financial institutions and markets so as to avoid undesired distortions in the allocation of savings and credit. In particular, the banks consider that there is a strong case for providing any subsidy to home ownership which the authorities deem appropriate directly to home buyers and letting the building societies compete with other institutions on equal terms.
>
> In the first place this would reduce the present distortion in the distribution of intermediation between the building societies and other institutions and might encourage other institutions to compete with the building societies in the home mortgage market . . . Secondly, the present privileged financial circuit would cease to exist and the way would be open for the building societies to become more integrated with the rest of the financial system . . . Thirdly, the cost of the subsidy would be known and subject to public scrutiny and it would be met by the Exchequer rather than distributed arbitrarily among a range of participants in the financial markets.[37]

THE FINANCE HOUSES

The finance houses are primarily involved in the provision of medium-term instalment credit facilities for both industrial corporations and individual consumers. These facilities are provided for the most part in the form of hire purchase facilities, particularly for motor cars and household goods acquired by individuals, and leasing facilities, particularly for motor car fleets, computers and heavy industrial equipment for industrial and commercial corporations, local authorities and government departments.

The largest finance houses are now either wholly-owned by one of the London clearing banks (such as Lombard North Central which is wholly-owned by National Westminster) or, in the case of Lloyds & Scottish, majority-owned by a clearing bank (Lloyds Bank) with the largest minority held by Royal Bank of Scotland. Whilst these major finance houses look to their parent companies to provide them with a proportion of their finances, they do also look to deposits from the money markets, advances and acceptance credit facilities from other banks and deposits from the public to finance their operations. The smaller finance houses look to the last three of these sources as well. Most finance houses are thus 'deposit-taking institutions', in the terms of the Banking Act 1979 and are therefore required to qualify for authorisation under the Act and to submit to the supervision of the Bank of England, as described in Chapter 5.

Four other characteristics of finance houses are relevant to this book. First, a significant proportion of their business is concerned with financing the purchase of new and second-hand motor cars by individual members of the public. Any technique which the authorities can devise for effecting the supply of funds available from the finance houses for this purpose can have a significant effect on the demand for motor cars – a highly sensitive variable in terms of economic and political management. For this reason, specific controls on hire purchase – usually setting minimum limits for the down-payment and maximum limits for the period over which a hire purchase contract can stretch – have been a familiar tool of British economic management since the Second World War. These controls were finally abolished by the Thatcher Government in July 1982, ostensibly on the grounds that they were too specific a type of monetary control and were thereby likely to distort the financial markets; and this move was generally welcomed by bankers. In their comments on the fiscal privileges enjoyed by the building societies, quoted in the last section, the London clearing banks set out their reasons why any subsidies which the government may wish to provide for specific expenditure should relate to particular financial functions and not to particular financial institutions. Exactly the same case can be made against specific limitations and controls on the provision of finance under hire purchase arrangements: if such controls are sought on, say, the purchase of motor vehicles by the public, they should relate to the markets for motor vehicles and not arbitrarily to one particular technique of financing such purchases and the institutions which provide it.

Secondly, nearly all hire purchase contracts and a proportion of leasing contracts assume a fixed rate of interest throughout the life of the contract, which may extend for two and a half years or more, whereas most of the incoming deposits taken by the finance houses to finance these contracts are for periods of up to three months. Thus, the very nature of their business pushes finance houses into taking involuntarily a risk on movements in interest rates: if rates go up during the life of the contract, the finance house stands to make a reduced profit or even a loss; if rates go down, it stands to increase its profits significantly. This factor means that the profits of finance houses can fluctuate fairly widely from one accounting period to another simply as a consequence of movements in interest rates and not necessarily as a reflection of the quality of the credit risks they take or of their management decisions generally. There is, of course, a limit beyond which a competent management should not allow the interest paid on deposits to be too mismatched against the interest received under hire purchase and leasing contracts and on other lendings: the fixing and observance of such a limit is a discipline which is shared by the management of finance houses with all other deposit-taking institutions and is discussed in Chapter 4.

The third characteristic of finance houses which should be mentioned arises out of their leasing business. If a commercial customer wants finance for a piece of equipment it can either borrow the necessary funds from its bankers, arrange to pay for it by instalment credit under a hire purchase agreement or lease it from a finance house or other leasing company. In the last case, the piece of equipment remains the property of the leasing company, the commercial customer pays a rent to the leasing company calculated to pay for the principal cost of the equipment over its useful life plus a rate of interest in the amounts of the principal outstanding. Leasing companies thus become very substantial buyers of new industrial equipment and, as such, they qualify for the considerable tax allowances available under current UK legislation to buyers of such new equipment. In crude terms, the buyer can offset the capital cost of the equipment against profits in the accounting period in question before arriving at its taxable profits. From the point of view of the leasing company, it must then pay tax in future periods not only on its interest profit (after deducting, of course, the interest cost of the required finance) but also on the proportion of the rental effectively representing the repayment of the principal cost of the equipment. In other words, for the leasing company, the very operation of leasing represents a useful technique of deferring the payment of tax; and as every taxpayer knows, there is a very real sense – the more real, the higher the current rate of interest – in which tax deferred is, in effect, tax saved. Further, under current UK legislation, a leasing company which is part of a larger group, such as a clearing bank group, can reduce the overall tax payments of the group by utilising profits made in other parts of the group – the clearing bank itself, for example – to buy capital equipment for leasing.

As a consequence of this technique of leasing, the tax paid by leasing companies and by banks generally, through their ownership of leasing companies, represents a very much smaller proportion of their profits than is the case for many other companies; and this fact has been the subject of considerable political comment. What is not always recognised by such commentators is that whilst the banks do, indeed, use the technique of leasing to reduce their tax payments, they do not in practice simply pocket the tax saved. Such is the competition between banks and leasing companies for the leasing business available that the greater part, if not all, of the tax saved is passed on to the industrial customers who are leasing the equipment. And this, of course, is precisely the purpose of the tax regulations permitting the capital cost of equipment to be offset against profits: effectively to subsidise capital investment. In other words, by interposing themselves as financial intermediaries between the purchasers of equipment and the ultimate sources of funds used to make those purchases, the leasing companies and the banks which own them, far from making unreasonable or 'unfair' profits at the taxpayers' expense, in fact provide a convenient mechanism by which the government's declared policy of subsidising capital investment can be effected.

Finally, it should be noted that in the retail, hire purchase, end of their business the finance houses have developed very effective techniques of lending money for specific purposes to a large number of relatively small retail customers. In the words of the Wilson Committee:

> finance houses usually operate through branch networks, but their facilities are often offered at the point of sale, with the retailer or dealer having a standing relationship with one or more finance houses for the provision of finance to his customers. Normally the dealer is able to arrange loan, hire purchase or conditional sale finance to suit the customer's requirements. Occasionally the retailer will finance the transaction himself and obtain funds by selling 'blocks' of existing instalment credit agreements to a finance house at a discount. The retailer often continues to collect the instalments on behalf of the finance house. In addition to providing finance for a dealer's customers a finance house will often provide the motor dealer with stocking finance.[38]

The point to be noticed is that hire purchase finance arranged in this way provides a neat mechanism for banking institutions to lend to small retail borrowers, effectively secured by the merchandise bought with the finance, with at least a part of the administrative chore – and credit policing – involved in collecting the instalments being undertaken by the retailer providing the goods. Hire purchase and mortgage lending against private houses are the two principal forms of secured lending in retail amounts to private borrowers in the United Kingdom.

OFFICIAL AND SEMI-OFFICIAL DEPOSIT-TAKING INSTITUTIONS

The Trustee Savings Banks

The Trustee Savings Banks (TSBs) are unincorporated societies providing banking services to the personal sector. They warrant a mention in this chapter as a significant taker of deposits from the public. Having started off literally as depositories for small savings of private individuals, the TSBs now provide a full range of money transmission and personal borrowing facilities. The big change in their activities came with the Trustee Savings Bank Act of 1976. Prior to that, the TSBs' activities were much circumscribed by government restrictions. They were obliged, for example, to invest their depositors' money in Government stock: a restraint which limited their ability to compete effectively for deposits with the clearing banks, the building societies and the finance companies, though looked at from another angle it did, of course, provide the government with a captive source of relatively cheap finance.

In the words of the Wilson Committee:

> the Trustee Savings Bank Act 1976 relaxed government control over the T.S.B.s and removed the most restrictive statutory limitations on their activities. Since then they have been going through a process of transition from being institutions closely aligned with the National Savings movement and heavily circumscribed by government controls to become an independent force in retail banking specialising in serving the personal sector . . . The 1976 Act permitted the T.S.B.s to lend to their customers for the first time, and all the banks now offer a range of credit facilities

> including personal loans, overdrafts and card facilities. Some banks have entered the house-mortgage business and all T.S.B.s are expected to offer mortgages in 1980. The T.S.B.s are also making a phased entry into the market for commercial accounts and loans, particularly for small businesses.[39]

The progress of the TSBs in transforming their business since the 1976 Act has been impressive. In 1977 they made their first loan. In 1978 they brought out their first credit card; and by 1982 they had become the third biggest credit card issuer in the UK with a cardholder base of two million – already larger than that of Lloyds or Midland Bank. As William Hall of the *Financial Times* put it in August 1982:

> T.S.B. Trust Company has been a major success story and an education for some of the sleepier clearing banks. It is the seventh biggest in unit trusts and is rapidly diversifying into life assurance. Meanwhile, the T.S.B.s' bold acquisition of United Dominions Trust, the UK's sixth biggest finance company, has given them an important foothold in another important sector of the market . . . The T.S.B.s have over eight million customers and 13.5 million accounts – more than any other bank – and a much bigger penetration of the section of the market catering for the lower paid members of the community, the area where retail bankers see the greatest growth potential over the next few years.[40]

It should be added that by the end of 1981, the TSBs had assets of £6000m and 1650 branches throughout the United Kingdom.

A major reorganisation of the TSBs was announced in 1982, when it was expected that the necessary legislation would be passed by 1984. The purpose was to rearrange the present federal structure of sixteen unincorporated societies into something more appropriate to their new more commercial stance and ambitions and, particularly, to meet the requirements of the Banking Act 1979 from which they have a specific exemption until 1985. The proposal is that the TSB

Group should have a Companies Act structure and will act as the holding company for all the group's activities. The ownership and accountability of the TSBs will be resolved by the issue of shares in the TSB Group PLC, preferably to depositors. In Mr Hall's words, 'it still has to be decided how to achieve this, consistent with the preservation of depositors' rights, but it could coincide with a capital-raising exercise and a share quote for the T.S.B. shares'.[41]

The National Savings Bank

In the words of the Wilson Committee:

> the National Savings Bank has two objectives – to help finance the public sector borrowing requirement and to provide facilities particularly suited to the needs of modest personal savers. It offers simple deposit-taking and withdrawal services operating through two types of account – the ordinary account and the investment account. The ordinary account offers a comparatively low, stable rate of interest, which is tax free up to a limit of £70 a year. The investment account offers a higher rate of interest which moves broadly in line with market rates and which is taxable.[42]

Both facilities are marketed to depositors through post offices and most sub-offices: at the time of the Wilson Report, this provided some 21 000 outlets in all, spread more or less uniformly over the country in a pattern closely linked to population densities.[43]

The National Savings Bank is effectively a vehicle by which the central government borrows money for its own use from small depositors: as such, it does not really qualify as a 'bank' in the normal sense nor share those characteristics of other banks which are the subject of this book. Its only relevance to our present discussion is as a direct competitor for deposits with private sector banks, particularly the clearing banks, and with the building societies. The exemption from income tax of the first £70 of interest earned by a depositor on ordinary accounts offers a direct fiscal advantage to the National

Savings Bank over its private sector competitors; and this is in direct conflict with the principle enunciated above that any subsidies which the government wishes to provide should relate to particular financial functions and not to particular financial institutions. In their evidence to the Wilson Committee the CLCB commented that the fiscal advantages enjoyed by the National Savings Bank and other national savings instruments

> inevitably lead to distortions in the savings market and the clearing banks believe that they should be abolished or else extended in some common form to all retail savings instruments. Their removal would presumably lead to the payment of higher rates of interest on national savings but the resulting situation would have the advantage of making the true cost of government borrowing more apparent.[44]

The National Girobank

To quote the Wilson Committee again:

> The National Girobank was originally established as a bank within the Post Office in October 1968 after a long period of discussion following a recommendation by the Radcliffe Committee. Its original objectives were to provide a simple money transmission service and to extend the use of current account banking in the personal sector, and it was aimed principally at lower income groups who had traditionally been reluctant to use commercial banks. But providing these services at a time when the clearing banks, partly in response to the threat posed to them by the creation of the National Girobank, were also vigorously marketing their current account services proved to be unprofitable. The original forecasts of the number of account holders and the average level of balances which could be expected were wildly optimistic. After a review in 1970–71 the original concept of extending personal banking was deferred, charges were substantially raised and new financial targets were set. These changes, coupled with an almost complete concentration on business customers and

on the provision of specialised services such as rent collection for public authorities, enabled the Girobank to achieve profitability in 1975, ahead of the revised target.

In the same year it was authorised to begin a phased and cautious expansion of the services it offered, and in 1976 its capital was reconstructed. About half past losses, amounting to about £17 million, were written off and half of the remaining loan capital of £13 million was converted into public dividend capital.

Since then the Girobank has made steady progress. It has progressively increased its profits and met the financial targets set for it. It has broadened its range of services to include deposit accounts, personal loans and limited overdraft facilities and cheque guarantee cards. The money transmission service is, however, still its main activity . . . The National Girobank depends for a large part of its deposit base on a few large customers (in particular the Department of Health and Social Security, Post Office Telecommunications and a number of large business customers) whose deposits tend to be volatile. It has therefore been obliged to maintain a high level of liquidity and advances to customers as yet form only a small part of the balance sheet. The bulk of its long-term assets are high-yielding non-marketable local authority mortgages and bonds.[45]

Since the establishment of the National Girobank in 1968 a great deal of significance has been attached to its role as a major competitor of the clearing banks, both by its protagonists and by the clearing banks themselves. The Wilson Committee, for example, was quite clear that 'the competition it (The National Girobank) provides to the clearing banks, alongside the trustee savings banks and the Co-operative Bank, has undoubtedly contributed to reducing charges and improving services to bank customers generally'.[46] The same point has been made by Professor Jack Revell, an academic commentator, writing some years after the establishment of the National Girobank:

Perhaps the greatest service which Giro has rendered so far

> is to act as a prod to the deposit banks for the modernisation of their money transmission services. The deposit banks certainly opened their credit transfer services to non-customers and introduced their direct debit system earlier than they would have done had there been no prospect of a cheap and competitive Giro system.[47]

For their part, the clearing banks, in their evidence to the Wilson Committee, 'welcomed the increased competition in financial markets because it fosters efficiency and benefits customers'. But they emphasised strongly that

> in order for competition to be effective, however, it is of paramount importance that all institutions compete on fair terms. This principle underlay the reform of the credit control arrangements in 1971 . . . as a result of which all commercial banks were placed on more or less the same footing. But it remains the case that many of the mutual and public sector institutions with which the banks are in competition are endowed with artificial competitive advantages.[48]

We have already noted some of the 'artificial competitive advantages' ascribed by the clearing banks to other institutions; the principle advantage they identified as being enjoyed by National Girobank was the 'totally inadequate capital base on which the Giro is being allowed to expand its range of banking services'.

All dispassionate commentators would probably agree with the verdict of the Wilson Committee set out in the following paragraph:

> The intention of the last government was to allow the National Girobank to continue to diversify its services subject to the constraints of monetary policy and normal banking prudence, and on the understanding that as far as possible it should not be given any competitive advantage, nor disadvantage, over the commercial banks by virtue of its special status. We endorse this approach. We believe that it has a useful function in the banking system both as an

> alternative to the commercial banks and because of its social role.[49]

In the context of this book, it remains to note how the National Girobank is treated in respect of both monetary and prudential controls. The situation regarding monetary control is simple, and remains as reported by the Wilson Committee: 'it was granted listed bank status in 1978 and is consequently subject to the same monetary controls as those imposed on commercial banks'.[50]

The situation regarding prudential control is more complicated and is discussed in Chapter 5.

THE DISCOUNT HOUSES

There are currently eleven discount houses, defined as members of the London Discount Market Association (LDMA). In the words of a famous textbook:

> The discount houses make their money by absorbing surplus funds from the banking system and investing it, mainly short-term, in a range of securities including Treasury and local authority bills, government stocks, bank and trade bills, bonds and stock and sterling certificates of deposit. They are also engaged in currency transactions, buying and selling London-issued certificates of deposit, bank and trade acceptances expressed in U.S. dollars, bills and notes drawn in foreign currencies, and Euro-currency commercial paper of many kinds.[51]

The scale of their operations can be judged from the figure for their total sterling borrowings of £5124m in December 1982, of which £4701m was at call or overnight and of £162m for their total borrowings in other currencies at the same date.[52]

By undertaking this activity, the discount houses provide two valuable services for the banking community as a whole: they provide a secured, profitable employment for surplus funds on an overnight basis or at short notice and they make a market, as principals, in the main instruments mentioned above – particularly Treasury Bills and bank bills.

The discount houses have an important place in this chapter, as a significant group of deposit-taking institutions on the British banking scene; and they have an important, if sometimes controversial, place in the two main discussions with which this book is concerned: monetary control and prudential control. They are important in discussions on monetary control, in that they collectively provide the chosen mechanism by which the Bank of England pumps money into the banking system when it takes the view that credit is getting too tight, and withdraws money from the banking system when it takes the view that credit is getting too easy; this mechanism is described in some detail in Chapter 3.

The discount houses are relevant to a discussion on prudential control for several reasons. First, they differ from the other deposit-taking institutions described in this chapter in that they do not take deposits from the general public in retail amounts: all their deposits are taken in largish, wholesale amounts and most of them, as we shall see, come from other banks. The public interest in ensuring that they are properly regulated from a prudential point of view rests not so much in the consumerist case for the protection of depositors, which was one of the main pressures giving rise to the Banking Act 1979 and, particularly, to the Deposit Protection Fund; it lies rather in the integral part they play in the overall banking mechanism.

Secondly, very few of the assets of a discount house represent a credit risk which is not, effectively, the credit worthiness of another bank or of the central government. In view of this, they are allowed to 'gear up' their balance sheets to much higher ratios than is thought appropriate for other sorts of banks, that is, they are allowed to borrow a much higher multiple of their capital and reserves than are other banks. Thirdly, and as a result of this second characteristic, they can, and occasionally do, take substantially greater risks on their interest rate mismatching or liquidity than other banks. These last two characteristics will be discussed in more detail in Chapter 4.

NOTES

1. Banking Act 1979. The criteria for granting the status of 'recognised banks' are set out in Part I of Schedule 2 of the Act; the limitation on those who may 'use any name or in any other way so describe himself or hold himself out as to indicate, or reasonably be understood to indicate, that he is a bank or banker or is carrying on a banking business' is in Section 36 of the Act.
2. Committee to Review the Functioning of Financial Institutions, *Report*, Cmnd 7937 (HMSO, June 1980) appendices, p. 407, para. 3.36.
3. Ibid., p. 407, para. 3.37.
4. Ibid., p. 411, para. 3.49.
5. Ibid., p. 408, para. 3.42.
6. *Evidence by the Committee of London Clearing Bankers* to the Committee to Review the Functioning of Financial Institutions (CLCB, 1978) pp. 176–7, paras 16.5, 16.6.
7. Ibid., p. 40, para. 3.15.
8. Jack Revell, *The British Financial System* (Macmillan, 1973) pp. 171–2.
9. Committee to Review the Functioning of Financial Institutions, *Evidence on the Financing of Industry and Trade*, vol. 5, Evidence of the Committee of London Clearing Bankers, p. 115, para. 7.
10. Cmnd 7937 (HMSO, June 1980) p. 40, para. 144.
11. Figures taken from *Bank of England Quarterly Bulletin* (March 1983) statistical annex, table 3.2.
12. The Wilson Committee noted an earlier estimate: 'Branch and other associated costs contributed by current accounts are estimated to have cost the equivalent of 7 per cent interest per annum in 1976.' Cmnd 7937 (HMSO, June 1980) appendices, p. 408, para. 3.41.
13. Cmnd 7937 (HMSO, June 1980) p. 42, para. 147. The Committee used the term 'commercial banks' to cover all banks other than the savings banks and the Bank of England.
14. Ibid., p. 43, para. 151.
15. Ibid., p. 43, para. 151.
16. The AHC added, in a footnote, that this figure of 4 per cent 'should be seen in perspective. The combined assets of the

London Clearing Banks represent only 20 per cent, while those of the American banks established in the U.K. represent 27 per cent of the total assets of all banks in the U.K. (*Bank of England Quarterly Bulletin* (March 1977) tables 2/1 and 2/5.)'

17. Committee to Review the Functioning of Financial Institutions (the Wilson Committee), *Evidence on the Financing of Industry and Trade*, vol. 5 Written Evidence of the Accepting Houses Committee, p. 6, para. 3.
18. *Bank of England Quarterly Bulletin* (March 1983) statistical annex, table 3.
19. Cmnd 7937 (HMSO, June 1980) p. 413, para. 3.53.
20. *Bank of England Quarterly Bulletin* (March 1983) statistical annex, table 3.
21. Evidence to Wilson Committee, vol. 5 Written Evidence of the Accepting Houses Committee, p. 8, para. 7.
22. Ibid., p. 10, para. 21.
23. Ibid., pp. 8–9, paras 12–14.
24. Cmnd 7937 (HMSO, June 1980) appendices, p. 416, para. 3.69.
25. 'Foreign Banks in London', *The Banker* (November 1982) p. 79.
26. Cmnd 7937 (HMSO, June 1980) appendices, p. 417, para. 3.70.
27. Cmnd 7937 (HMSO, June 1980) appendices, p. 417, para. 3.71. The proportions of 15 per cent for sterling advances and 60 per cent for foreign currency advances to UK residents had moved slightly to 13 per cent and 70 per cent respectively in December 1982.
28. Ibid., pp. 417–18, para. 3.72.
29. William Hall, 'Consortium banks adapt to a new environment', *The Banker* (November 1981) p. 135.
30. Cmnd 7937 (HMSO, June 1980) appendices, p. 418, para. 3.73.
31. Cmnd 7937 (HMSO, June 1980) appendices, pp. 435–6, paras 3.128, 3.130–3.136.
32. Committee of London Clearing Bankers, *Written Evidence to the Committee to Review the Functioning of Financial Institutions*, November 1977, p. 188, para. 18.9.
33. Ibid., p. 189, paras 8.11, 8.13
34. Ibid., pp. 189–90, para. 18.14.

35. Ibid., p. 190, para. 18.15.
36. Ibid., p. 190, para. 18.16.
37. Ibid., pp. 190–1, paras 18.17, 18.18.
38. Cmnd 7937 (HMSO, June 1980) appendices, p. 430, para. 3.114.
39. Cmnd 7937 (HMSO, June 1980) appendices, p. 422, paras 3.89, 3.90.
40. *Financial Times*, 5 August 1982.
41. Ibid.
42. Cmnd 7937 (HMSO, June 1980) p. 364, para. 13.75.
43. Ibid., appendices p. 427, para. 3.102.
44. Committee of London Clearing Bankers, *Written Evidence to the Committee to Review the Functioning of Financial Institutions*, p. 189, para. 18.12.
45. Cmnd 7937 (HMSO, June 1980) pp. 362–3, paras 1369–73.
46. Ibid., p. 365, para. 1379.
47. Jack Revell, *The British Financial System* (Macmillan, 1973) p. 166.
48. Committee of London Clearing Bankers, *Written Evidence to the Committee to Review the Functioning of Financial Institutions*, p. 189, para. 18.11.
49. Cmnd 7937, p. 365, para. 1380.
50. Ibid., p. 363, para. 1373.
51. F. E. Perry, *The Elements of Banking* (Methuen & The Institute of Bankers, 1981) 3rd edn, pp. 115–16
52. *Bank of England Quarterly Bulletin* (March 1983) statistical annex, table 4.

3 The Financial Markets of London

We saw in the last chapter that the principal function of those institutions which collectively make up the mechanism of British banking is the collection of deposits from those with cash resources surplus to their immediate requirements and the re-lending of these cash resources, in one form or another, to those with an immediate need for them. We saw, too, the wide diversity and large number of institutions which make up the total banking mechanism and also the way that the borrowing and lending activities of many of them cut across any neat divisions of those activities in terms of the geographical location of the depositor or borrower or, indeed, the currency in which the deposit or lending is denominated.

An obvious point to be made about any banking mechanism is that where there is more than one institution taking the deposits and making the loans, it is most unlikely that the incoming deposits and outgoing loans of each individual institution will exactly match and therefore there is a definite need for some mechanism by which the institution with deposits surplus to its immediate requirements can lend them, short-term, to the institution in the reverse situation, with immediate requirements in excess of its incoming deposits. And if it is an acceptable function of the national authorities, as it is in Britain and most other developed economies, to intervene in the banking mechanism in such a way as to increase or decrease the amount of money or credit available, then the mechanism must be such as to give access to the national authorities, through which they can achieve this aim.

The larger the number of institutions making up the banking mechanism and the more diverse the type of deposits taken and lendings made, in terms of currency and maturity, the more sophisticated must be this mechanism as a necessary infrastructure for the banking community. This mechanism through which individual banks can match their borrowings and lendings is, of course, to be distinguished from the *clearing* system provided by the clearing banks, through which are cleared debits and credits arising out of the money transmission services provided by those banks.

As one of the oldest and one of the largest centres of international finance, the City of London has one of the largest and most sophisticated mechanisms in the world through which banks can match up their borrowings and lendings. The core of it is provided by the discount market, the sterling interbank deposit market, the interbank market in foreign currencies and the foreign exchange market; and these are the subject of this chapter.

THE DISCOUNT MARKET

Principal functions

Traditionally, the mechanism for evening out surpluses and shortfalls in short-term funds between different banking institutions has been provided by the discount market. This consists mainly of the eleven members of the LDMA, briefly described at the end of the last chapter. As we have seen, the discount houses borrow sterling, either overnight, at call or for a fixed period, mainly from banks but also from other financial institutions and commercial companies. Their borrowings are normally secured on collateral comprising the short-term instruments (for example, Treasury bills, Local Authority bills, Bank bills, Sterling Certificates of Deposit (CDs)) and short-dated British Government Securities, which they acquire with the money they have borrowed. As the Bank of England has remarked, 'This activity enables them to play a large or predominant part in the secondary market in most of the assets in which they deal.'[1]

A main function of the discount market, then, is to provide a cushion for other banking institutions, which will absorb funds, overnight or for short periods, surplus to their immediate requirements and which at the same time will provide funds at short notice, or for short periods to fill a temporary shortfall in a bank's cash position. The provision of funds in this way is effected either by a bank withdrawing funds from a discount house which it had deposited at short notice, or, alternatively, selling short-term assets – such as Treasury bills, commercial bills or CDs – to a discount house for immediate settlement in cash.

A second main function of the discount market follows from this first; that is, the provision of a credible secondary market in these short-term assets. Not only does such a market provide banking institutions with an immediate source of short-term funds in the manner described above; it also endows the relevant short-term assets held by a bank with much higher degree of liquidity than it would otherwise have. And this provides a very real service to those responsible for the liquidity management of banks. This subject will be discussed in some detail in Chapter 4. At this point it is sufficient to note that, say, a three-month Treasury bill, commercial bill or CD has quite a different quality and attraction to a bank which holds it if it is immediately sellable for cash than if it has to be held by that bank to the date of its maturity.

The third main function of the discount market is to provide the Bank of England with access to the banking mechanism. Each member of the LDMA holds a discount account at the Bank of England: they alone have the right of access to the Bank's lender of last resort facility and it is through them that the Bank conducts the bulk of its open market operations.

To appreciate fully the significance of this function, it is important to understand the precise aims of the Bank in the provision of its last resort facility and in its open market operations.

The discount market and the Bank of England

Traditionally, one of the crucial, if unspectacular, functions of the Bank of England has been the maintenance of an orderly money market: that is, to ensure to the best of its ability that the myriad of transactions which flow through the banking system and the money markets each day, do so without any hiccups or sudden shortages which might otherwise cause wild and disruptive swings in rates of interest or, more disastrously, leave one or more institutions fatally, if only temporarily, short of liquid cash. This function is, of course, quite distinct from that other function, allocated to the Bank of England only fairly recently, and highlighted in the recent debate on 'monetarism', of controlling the money supply. Indeed, it is worth remarking at this point that some of the cruder recommendations of monetarist commentators for rigid control of the money supply would, if accepted, have forced the Bank to fail in its responsibilities in the maintenance of an orderly money market. The jeers of some of the commentators who noticed in 1979 and 1980 that the Bank was on occasion pumping money into the banking system to avert a chronic shortage at a time when the stance of government policy was tight control of the money supply were not – as some of them thought – exposing the muddle-headedness of the Bank and its officials but rather the very real dilemma set by the simultaneous pursuit of orderly markets and of uncompromising and inflexible control of the money supply. The point was well made by Tim Congdon in the preface to his recent book on monetary control in Britain: that 'there may be a trade off between the exactitude of money supply control and the microeconomic efficiency of the financial system. This helps to explain the Bank of England's perception of its traditional role as the "accommodation" of financial institutions'.[2] It is with this 'accommodation' as a major determinant of the Bank's activities in the money markets with which we are concerned in this section.

Related to, and interwoven with, the Bank's function in the maintenance of an orderly money market is its role as main banker to the Government, maintaining a major group of official accounts. Indeed, the Government does not hold balances, other than working amounts, with other banks. As the Bank itself has remarked, 'this centralised system provides the Bank with an up-to-date picture of much of the Government's financial position, and enables it to minimise government balances by employing any surplus cash to reduce the amount of official debt outstanding, thus avoiding unnecessary interest payments by the Government'.[3]

In the present context, the important point is that as banker to the Government, the Bank of England is banker to a substantial proportion of the economy: as such, it is a substantial giver and receiver of funds from and to the accounts of its official customers to and from the accounts of the customers of other banks. The Bank of England is thus a key member of the banking community for whom the discount market provides the ultimate mechanism for matching borrowings and lendings.

As we have seen, this mechanism deals primarily with evening out imbalances between the borrowing and lending activities of individual banks; but there is also a need for a similar mechanism for evening out imbalances in the clearing activities of banks in their provision of the principal money transmission service to the economy as a whole. As we saw in the last chapter, this function is provided by the clearing banks, all other banking institutions holding clearing accounts with one or more of the clearing banks, who effectively provide a money transmission service for these other institutions. In a similar way, each of the clearing banks holds accounts at the Bank of England, and it is through these accounts that the final settlements take place between the clearing banks themselves and between them and the Bank of England. But it should be emphasised that this settlement of balances between the clearing banks and the Bank of England through their accounts at the Bank is very much a final settlement of the day; the vast bulk of the settlements are made during the day through the mechanism of the discount market.

The Bank itself has described its function at the apex of the clearing system in the following terms:

> The final daily cash settlements within the banking system and between the banking system and the Bank (embracing

the Government), take place principally across a small number of accounts – those of the London clearing banks – at the Bank. These banks therefore need to hold sufficient balances at the Bank to cover such settlements. The Bank maintains accounts for other customers too – including, for instance, other domestic banks and overseas central banks – but these normally play only a minor part in determining the daily flow of funds between the Bank and the banking system. The clearers' accounts bear the final daily adjustment of the system.[4]

It is with Bank's role in the mechanism for matching imbalances arising out of the borrowing and lending activities of individual banks with which we are primarily concerned in this section; and we have seen already that traditionally this mechanism is centred on the discount market. As a background to this role, it is worth noting at the outset that the Government, the Bank's principal customer, is a permanent borrower from the rest of the community: this borrowing is managed by the Bank, acting as agent for the Government, and is largely effected by the weekly issue of 3-month Treasury bills and by Government bonds or 'gilt-edged' securities. These latter are issued with varying lives to maturity by the Bank, one of the aims being to achieve a reasonably orderly pattern of maturity over the years, so as to spread fairly evenly into the future the refunding requirements resultant from the maturity of these bonds.

Some of this borrowing is effected directly from the public outside the banking system – by, for example, the sale of government bonds to the pension funds and life assurance companies; but a significant proportion is effected with the banking community itself. In the Bank's words, 'normally, that part of the Government's borrowing requirement which is not financed by the sale of debt outside the banking system is met by the sale of debt – in particular Treasury bills – to the banking system which thus acts as the residual source of borrowing for the Government'.[5] To the extent that the borrowing is effected by the sale of Treasury bills to the banking system, these sales are usually made in the first instance to the discount houses who then, in their capacity as the principal market-makers in bills, act as a vehicle through which the bills are disseminated around the whole banking system.

Taking the current account transactions which take place daily between the Government on the one hand and the rest of the community on the other together with the capital account transactions – particularly the issue and final repayment of an endless series of Treasury bills and Government bonds – it can be seen that the flows of funds passing each day between the Bank of England (acting as banker to the Government) and the rest of the banking system (acting as bankers to the rest of the community) is very substantial, highly diverse and extremely variable in volume and direction from one day to another.

This last point, the extreme variation in the volume and direction of flows between the Government and the rest of the community, can best be illustrated by listing a few examples of the irregular payments which take place. First there is the bunching of corporation tax payments by companies to the Government. Secondly, the very substantial payments of petroleum revenue tax made by the oil industry to the Government on just two days in the year. Thirdly, there are the payments flowing into the Government from the rest of the community resulting from the successful issue of a Government bond, payments made all the greater, if only temporarily, if the issue is a great success and thus heavily oversubscribed. Conversely, there is the flow of payments from the Government to the rest of the community in repayment of these bonds on their final maturity, together with half-yearly payments of smaller amounts representing the interest payments on the bonds. Fourthly, there are the flows of funds to and from the Government, from and to the rest of the community resulting from any heavy intervention by the Bank of England, acting as agent for the Government, on the foreign exchange markets: any very heavy selling of sterling will result in borrowings of the same amount from non-Government sources by the Exchange Equalisation Account, as the particular account at the Bank of England is called; and conversely, any heavy buying of sterling by the Bank of England in the foreign exchange markets will be reflected in a reduction in borrowing by the Government from the rest of the community. Fifthly, of course, there is the flow of funds to the Government from the rest of the community resulting from the issue of Treasury bills by the Bank on behalf of the Government and, equally, the flow of funds in the opposite direction representing the maturity of these bills.

As we have seen, the smoothing out of these flows of funds between the Government and the rest of the community is one of the principal and traditional functions of the Bank of England. And its traditional, but consciously chosen, vehicle for gaining access to the money markets to achieve this smoothing is the discount market. That it is the traditional vehicle is common knowledge to every student of banking. That it is still the consciously chosen vehicle was emphasised in 1980 when, after a considerable public debate on the techniques of monetary control, initiated by the publication in March of that year of the green paper on the subject[6] the Bank announced changes which would be developed in its methods of intervention in the money market. In outlining these proposed changes, the Bank remarked that

> it is envisaged that the Bank's intervention will place a greater emphasis on open market operations and less on discount window (lender of last resort) lending. It has been decided that these operations should continue to be conducted in the bill markets rather than through the inter-bank market, and in large part through the existing intermediaries, members of the London Discount Market Association, to whom discount window facilities would remain confined.[7]

This decision by the Bank to continue its traditional technique of conducting its open market operations through the discount market rather than, say, the interbank deposit market raised some controversy when it was announced; the clearing banks, in particular, stated a preference for Bank of England intervention in the interbank market. The Bank itself has given two reasons for preferring the traditional technique. The first, which was founded on historical experience and has a particular relevance to those involved in the development of similar mechanisms in other financial centres, was the desire to be even-handed in its treatment of different financial institutions and different groups of such institutions. Delving back into history, Mr Tony Coleby, an Assistant Director of the Bank, has made the point in the following terms:

> Given the importance of bill operations to it, the Bank not surprisingly came to have close relations during the nineteenth century with the bill specialists – first, as bill brokers and later as discount houses. Relations with the commercial banks were less close. At least for the first part of the century, the Bank and the joint stock banks regarded each other as commercial rivals, while the latter considered that borrowing from the Bank of England could be construed as a sign of weakness. The Bank for its part came to understand that access to its lending facilities was a valuable privilege. Consequently, it had the problem of how to retain these facilities (and thus underpin confidence in the financial system) without giving the privileged institutions the ability to on-lend more easily or cheaply than those without access to them. The Bank's conclusion was to concentrate its lending facilities on the discount houses because they did not compete with the banks for overdraft or other lending business, or initiate new lending outside the banking sector. There is now, of course, a much wider range of assets potentially available to the Bank for managing the cash position of the banking system, but the reasons which led us to the present position remain valid.[8]

The second reason for the Bank's preference for continuing to conduct its market operations through the discount market was, in Mr Coleby's words, 'the presence, among the objectives underlying last year's monetary control arrangements, of the desire to find a market mechanism which would allow much greater scope than before for market influences to play a part in determining short-term interest rates'. In a sense, this desire to give greater scope to market influences in determining short-term interest rates may seem odd at a time of increased emphasis on control of the money supply as an important objective of economic policy and the rate of interest as an important weapon achieving that objective. But, as we shall see in Chapter 6, monetary policy is based on the proposition, among others, that 'the level of short-term interest rates at any time is determined by the interaction between the markets and the authorities'.[9] As Mr Coleby has pointed out, in building in 1981 the new arrangements for official intervention in the money markets

> the monetary authorities did not intend to abandon taking a view of the level of short-term interest rates likely to be consistent with their wider monetary objectives, expressed as targets for various monetary aggregates. But that view, and the market operations associated with it, were intended to provide no more than a sort of dragging anchor at the very short end of the market. The term structure of rates, out to the three-month point and beyond, was to be fully responsive to market influences; and the outcome of that response was itself to be an important ingredient in the continuous reassessment of the aptness of the official view on the level of very short-term interest rates.

One of the necessary conditions for this process to work satisfactorily was seen to be that 'operations should be conducted at arms' length from the principal counterparties'; and this in itself was an important factor in the decision to continue doing those operations in the bill market. Mr Coleby explained the reasoning in the following terms:

> If the Bank operated directly in the inter-bank market, it would inevitably find its operations concentrated on the clearing banks, upon which any cash imbalance is thrown by virtue of their central function in the settlement of daily cash flows. The resolution of the cash imbalance would consequently be likely to involve a small number of, effectively, bilateral deals. It would not be an exercise that allowed any real scope for market influences to bear on the interest rates arrived at for official operations. In the bill market, by contrast, those influences are more widely

diffused. It is an asset market, rather than a liability market, in which there are many participants each with potentially different circumstances and expectations.

To be effective in smoothing out the diverse and huge payments, already described, between the Government and the rest of the community, the Bank requires an elaborate and quick intelligence system to give it both a forecast of the major anticipated movement of funds and also, as it were, a thermometer to measure the state of the market several times a day as trading proceeds. The details of how the Bank operates in this way are set out with great clarity in the Bank's paper 'The Role of the Bank in the Money Market', already quoted several times in this section. A relevant point in the present context is the extremely close liaison which is required and maintained between the Bank and the discount market in achieving, day in day out, an orderly flow of funds between the Government and the rest of the community at the apex of the whole banking mechanism of both money transmission and borrowing and lending. In a sense, the Bank and the discount houses should still be seen as competitive participants in a market for money, the price for which results from the play of market forces between the participants; but this is not the whole picture. The discount market should also be seen as a highly sophisticated piece of machinery, integral and crucial to the whole banking mechanism, in which the technicians on both sides, but particularly in the Bank, are engaged in a continuing daily, indeed minute-by-minute, effort to ensure the smooth functioning of the market and thus of the banking system as a whole. Seen in this light, it is not surprising that

> the Bank's regular contacts with the LDMA and its members are extremely close, [as the Bank pointed out to the Wilson Committee] The Chairman and Deputy Chairman of the Association attend weekly on the Governor to discuss matters affecting the market, and there is daily contact at various levels which may relate to any aspect of the operations of the market. In such an environment any development in market practice or proposals for new

> instruments to be traded in the market are always fully discussed with the Bank.[10]

Notwithstanding this close market relationship between the Bank and the discount houses, and in part as a result of it, the Bank exercises prudential supervision over the activities of discount houses on a more frequent and detailed basis than that exercised over the activities of other banking institutions.

It remains to describe the actual techniques employed by the Bank in its interventions in the discount market. As has been mentioned, these techniques were reviewed and revised in 1980 and 1981. Under the new arrangements the Bank continues to conduct its operations with the market chiefly through transactions in bills with the discount houses. In simplest terms, if the Bank foresees a shortage of cash, caused by a large flow of funds to the Government from the rest of the community, it will buy bills from the discount houses; conversely, if it foresees a surplus of cash at any time, it will offer to sell bills to the market at rates to make them attractive. Much the greater part of the Bank's intervention is conducted through these purchases and sales of bills; but for the sake of completeness, five further techniques should be mentioned. These have all been succinctly described by the Bank.[11]

First, 'in addition to, or separately from, any bill operations, the Bank may let the houses know that it is willing to lend, at an interest rate of its own choosing. Such occasions are exceptional, and are in contrast with the earlier arrangements under which the houses could at times borrow continuously': such lending is available only to the discount houses and is always on a secured basis. The Bank has given two examples of circumstances in which it may prefer to lend rather than to purchase bills: first,

> when there is an isolated or unexpected shortage – perhaps on a large scale – arising for technical reasons, such as an oversubscription to the new issue of stock by the Government or a half yearly payment of petroleum revenue tax. In such circumstances the Bank may not wish to relieve the shortage entirely by bill operations for fear of causing

unnecessary distortions to interest rates, and may therefore choose to lend – in which case the rate charged may be close to market rates.

The second example is

when the Bank wishes to see very short-term interest rates higher but believes that the discount houses will not offer – or discovers, having invited business, that they have not offered – sufficient paper at high enough rates for the upward adjustment to be effected quickly through bill operations. The Bank may then decline to deal in the bill markets, or may limit its dealings, and thus force those houses that are short of cash to borrow; the Bank then sets a lending rate consistent with the higher level which it is seeking to establish in the market.

A second technique for withdrawing funds from the money market is the calling of special deposits from all banking institutions. As the Bank has described:

the special deposits scheme remains available, with some adjustment of coverage. This scheme enables the Bank to call non-operational deposits, which earn interest at a rate close to the Treasury Bill rate, from most institutions above a certain size in the monetary sector, as a means of withdrawing cash from the money market. Administratively, a call for or repayment of special deposits requires a period of notice, so that the scheme is best suited to occasions when there is the prospect of a protracted period of surplus cash which the Bank wishes to offset. Once special deposits have been called, their release can be timed to suit the expected pattern of market flows – in particular, to match an expected shortage. Special deposits were last called in December 1979.

Special deposits of this sort are, of course, distinct from the Supplementary Special Deposits, or 'corset', a technique aimed at limiting the amount of credit granted by the banking system.

A third technique, 'which the Bank used on three occasions

during 1981 to remove cash from the market for release at a specific future date, is a special tender for Treasury bills of less than three months' term, set to mature on the desired date'. This technique is, if you like, simply a variant on the more usual intervention of buying and selling bills in the market.

Fourthly, the Bank noted in March 1982 that in the previous few months it had 'also revived an earlier practice of placing some funds directly into the local authority short-term deposit market. This has been carried out in order to help relieve the extreme pressure on bill resources caused by the very large money market shortages'.

Fifthly, the Bank has invented the device, first used in 1980, of offering to purchase specified Government bonds from all banks and licensed deposit-taking institutions, the contract including a firm undertaking from the sellers to buy back the bonds at a given price on a specified date in the future: this was tantamount to lending the same amount to the relevant institutions for the period up to the date of repurchase at a rate of interest which was reflected by the difference between the price of the bonds when sold and repurchased (adjusted to take account of the interest coupon payable on the bonds). The amount of bonds which each institution can sell to the Bank under these arrangements is fixed as a proportion of its 'eligible liabilities' – a statistic which effectively reflects the size of a bank's lendings outside the banking system. This device was first used in February 1980, when the offer to purchase and resell was extended only to the clearing banks, it was used again later in the same year, when the offer was extended to all listed banks and finance houses. The technique was revived in January 1983 when the offer to buy government bonds and resell them after one month was extended to all recognised banks and licensed deposit-taking institutions and was designed to inject £1000m into the money markets: this offer was extended for further periods when it matured.

But it is the purchase and sale of bills, from and to the discount houses, which remains the Bank's principal technique of intervention in the money markets. Prior to the new arrangements introduced in 1980 and 1981, the Bank

> aimed to keep the market at least slightly short of cash from day to day, so as to provide the means to bring about a change in the interest rate structure, if that should be judged necessary. The Bank fixed the quantity of Treasury bills on offer at the weekly tenders so as to assist this aim. All bills on offer were sure to be taken up, because of the discount houses' long-standing agreement (still operative today) to underwrite the tender.[12]

The Bank's stated aim of keeping the money market slightly short of cash from day to day kept, as it were, the reins of control taut so that more often than not the discount houses would be obliged to sell Treasury bills to the Bank, which gave the Bank the opportunity to adjust the rates at which it dealt on a daily basis. And by keeping the market short of cash by its tactics at Treasury bill tenders – the weekly issue of new Treasury bills by the Bank – the Bank was effectively ensuring that the market was long of Treasury bills, thus providing the ultimate means for the Bank's intervention in the money market. For the technique to work properly, it is, of course, necessary for both the Bank and the discount market to have an ample supply of bills to trade between themselves; and, in one sense at least, as the agent through which the Government conducts its borrowing, the Bank has the ability to create an almost inexhaustible supply of Treasury bills on which it can draw to soak up funds from the money market. This last point simply reflects the facts that the Government is a continuing and substantial borrower, that the borrowings are made principally in the form of issuing Government bonds or Treasury bills and that, in theory at least, any increase in the supply of Treasury bills that was needed for the Bank's intervention manoeuvres in the money market could be engineered by a reduction in the issue of Government bonds – or indeed, the repurchase of existing Government bonds in the secondary market.

This was, generally speaking, the system which prevailed until 1980, with the Bank making certain that it created enough Treasury bills to effect its market intervention – that it supplied, if you like, sufficient chips to make the game playable between it and the discount market. In 1980 it became increasingly difficult to ensure that the market held sufficient Treasury bills to permit the Bank's established technique of intervention to operate properly. Again, the reasons have been succinctly described by the Bank itself:

> The circumstances which had provided the banking system with sufficient holdings of Treasury bills to sell to the Bank on most occasions when cash was short did not persist. Increased attention was given to the control of the stock of money, but a buoyant trend developed in bank lending to the private sector. At least in the short run, unduly rapid monetary growth could most easily be moderated by selling government debt to the non-bank private sector on a larger scale than hitherto in relation to the Government's borrowing requirement. This combination of circumstances created persistent underlying shortages in the market. The Bank responded in the first instance by reducing the quantity of Treasury bills on offer at the weekly tender. Even so, the Bank still found it necessary to buy Treasury bills – often more than were being issued. Inevitably the proportion of these in the banking system's portfolio declined.[13]

In stark statistical terms, the ratio of Treasury bills held by the banking system (excluding the Banking Department of the Bank) to its total sterling assets fell from an average of about 6 per cent in 1975–7 to 1 per cent in 1981. In short, the perfectly proper new policies for controlling the stock of money had deprived the discount market of sufficient Treasury bills to feed the Bank's technique of intervention in the money market: the game was becoming unplayable under the old rules.

The Bank got round this constraint in three ways. First, it introduced the device, already described, of buying gilt-edged securities from the banking system, with a firm contract to re-sell, thus pumping more cash into the money market or, as a mirror image of this action, enabling it to issue more Treasury bills than it otherwise would. Secondly, it increased the amounts it was prepared to lend to the discount houses for short periods and on a secured basis in the manner already mentioned. Thirdly, and most importantly, it began to buy eligible bank bills from the discount market in increasing quantities – either outright or for future repurchase by the market. After a period of relative decline in their importance as part of the British financial scene, these bills have thus assumed a renewed significance through their use by the Bank in its money market intervention, and this has led to a dramatic increase in their volume, with implications for both prudential regulation and monetary control.

Eligible bank bills

The use of acceptance credits by merchant banks as a method of providing funds for their customers was described in Chapter 2. It is worth requoting in the present context the definition of an accepting credit given by the Accepting Houses Committee:

> An acceptance credit involves the 'borrower' drawing a bill of exchange, which is virtually the same as writing a post-dated cheque, on an Accepting House. In return for an acceptance commission the Accepting House then 'accepts' the bill of exchange which means that the Accepting House promises unconditionally to pay, on maturity of the 'post-dated cheque', its face value to its then holder. After acceptance the bill of exchange becomes a high-class negotiable document which is sold to the Discount Market (at a discount rate usually only marginally above the going rate on U.K. Treasury Bills) and the proceeds handed over to the 'borrower'. On maturity the Accepting House pays the holder of the bill of exchange and is itself repaid by the 'borrower'.[14]

From the point of view of the discount houses a bill of exchange is a very similar sort of animal to a Treasury bill. There are two crucial and interrelated distinctions. First, the ultimate credit risk of the Treasury bill is the British Government – the risk of the bill not being paid is the risk that the British Government will not fulfil its obligations – whereas the credit risk of a bill of exchange is the risk of the bank which accepts it – or, if the acceptor fails to meet its obligations – the original drawer of the bill. Secondly, the bill of exchange will be of similar quality to a Treasury bill in the eyes of a discount house only if it is as rediscountable, that is, sellable to the Bank of England. It can readily be seen that a bill of exchange which is 'eligible for discount at the Bank of England' is a more valuable instrument than a bill of exchange which is not so eligible and that the 'eligibility' of a bank's name as the acceptor of a bill is a prized and jealously guarded privilege. Traditionally, until 1981, the privilege of being an eligible name at the Bank of England was confined to the clearing banks, the accepting houses and certain other British banks. Reporting in 1959, the Radcliffe Committee noted that

> a bill of exchange accepted by a British bank or by one of the eighteen accepting houses is, if it has one other British name on it, 'eligible' paper at the Bank of England, and has therefore the highest degree of liquidity, shared only by Treasury bills and short-dated Government bonds. Having this maximum liquidity and the complete assurance of payment (on which of course the liquidity depends), it commands the lowest rate of discount available for any non-Government paper. An accepting house thus, when accepting a bill, confers on the drawer of the bill (and on anyone who discounts it for him) the certainty of being able to get sterling in exchange for it from a bank or discount house in London, at the least possible sacrifice in discount.[15]

The Radcliffe Committee went on to comment that, in order to retain the power described in the quotation above, 'an accepting house has continually to satisfy the Bank of England that it has adequate capital and adequate liquidity and that it is maintaining its reputation generally'. Since the passing of the Banking Act 1979, all 'recognised banks' must submit to the same sort of scrutiny of their affairs by the Banking Supervision Division of the Bank of England, and it must be assumed that the Bank applies similar criteria of prudential competence to all recognised banks, although probably expecting to find the highest degree of such competence amongst the accepting houses that it can find in other recognised banks.

Prompted by the need to provide more bills in the hands of the discount market eligible for discount at the Bank of England, the Bank introduced, as part of its new arrangements for operating in the discount market, a substantial increase in the list of eligible banks, that is, banks whose bills are eligible for discount at the Bank. The reasoning behind this extension of the list was set out in the Bank's paper on 'Monetary control – the next steps', dated March 1981:

> Increased reliance on open-market operations in eligible bills will require an adequate supply of these bills. In this connection the Bank has felt for some time that the present list of eligible names needs to be extended. The present list consists broadly of the London and Scottish clearing banks, the members of the Accepting Houses Committee and the major British Overseas and Commonwealth banks. It dates from a time when the Bank's supervisory arrangements were primarily concerned with British banks. Apart from being a British bank of the requisite standing, the main criterion for inclusion on the list was that the acceptor should have a broadly based and substantial acceptance business which commanded the finest rates in the market. In recent years there have been major changes in the Bank's supervisory arrangements and the number of foreign banks in London has increased. The Bank has concluded that these developments should be recognised in extending the criteria for eligibility.[16]

In publishing the new list of eligible names in August 1981, the Bank stated that it had

> judged applications, by recognised banks wishing their acceptances to become eligible for discount at the Bank, according to the following criteria:
>
> (i) whether the applicant has and maintains a broadly based and substantial acceptance business in the United Kingdom;

(ii) whether its acceptances command the finest rates in the market for ineligible bills;
(iii) whether, in the case of foreign-owned banks, British banks enjoy reciprocal opportunities in the foreign owners' domestic market.

The Bank then commented drily that

> a bank may apply for eligibility at any time. An eligible bank which wishes to renounce its eligibility is free to do so on giving notice to the Bank.[17]

Under the new arrangements, the close supervision of eligible names by the Bank noted by the Radcliffe Committee will continue, in that all banks on the new, expanded list are 'recognised banks' under the Bank of England Act 1979 and are thus the subject of regular reporting to, and supervision by, the Bank. What this supervision entails will be discussed in Chapter 5; but it may be relevant to note at this stage that, in supervising the British branches of overseas banks, whether or not they are eligible names, the Bank depends heavily on the supervision exercised over the parent bank by the national supervisory authority of that parent bank's country of residence.

Under the new rules, eligible banks undoubtedly enjoy some sort of privileged status, at least so far as their bills are concerned. But they must pay for this in a tangible way, as well as satisfying the Bank as to their prudential excellence. In its March 1981 paper, heralding the extension of criteria for eligibility, the Bank remarked that it considered

> that it would be right to link the criteria for eligibility with arrangements for ensuring an adequate availability of funds to the bill markets. Eligible acceptors have an interest in ensuring that the bill markets function efficiently, which complements the Bank's interest in ensuring that its open-market operations can be conducted effectively. The Bank would therefore like to discuss arrangements which would incorporate a link between eligibility and an undertaking to make available, at least initially,

> secured funds to the discount houses in such a way as to help them fulfil their role as market-makers in those and other bills.[18]

When the new arrangements were finally unveiled in August 1981, the membership subscription for the club of eligible names was set out in the following terms

> From 25th August 1981, each eligible bank undertakes to maintain secured money with members of the L.D.M.A. and/or secured call money with money brokers and gilt-edged jobbers – all at market rates appropriate to the nature of the lending – such that:
>
> (i) The total funds so held normally average 6% of that bank's eligible liabilities;
> (ii) The amount held in the form of secured money with members of the L.D.M.A. does not normally fall below 4% of eligible liabilities on any day.
>
> In relation to the above undertaking, such eligible bank will
>
> (i) aim to meet the daily average ratio over either six or twelve month periods (having first notified the Bank of its choice of period), the ratio on any particular day in a banking month being calculated as a proportion of eligible liabilities at the last but one make-up day,
>
> and
>
> (ii) provide monthly returns of its daily figures, which the Bank will use to assess the bank's performance relative to its long-term commitment.
>
> A bank will go below the minimum only in exceptional circumstances and will be ready to explain such action to the Bank when the relevant monthly return is made.[19]

The impact of these new arrangements on the actual pattern of the Bank's intervention in the money market is dramatically illustrated in Table 3.1, showing figures, published by the Bank, giving the total value each year of the Bank's operations to offset shortages in the money market by bill purchases and by lending. (Operations to offset surpluses, for example by the sale of Treasury bills, are not shown).[20]

TABLE 3.1

	Purchases of			
Year beginning 1 March	*Treasury bills (£m)*	*Local authority bills (£m)*	*Commercial bills (£m)*	*Lending (£m)*
1977	14740	1392	47	21663
1978	16049	1509	2503	9737
1979	16337	2529	3846	18217
1980	11876	2874	15873	21173
1981	3810	4349	39771	4640

Source: *Bank of England Quarterly Bulletin* (March 1982).

In his paper delivered in November 1982, quoted above, Mr Coleby disclosed that 'the Bank's purchases of bank bills (outright and for resale) over the twelve months to end-October [1982] were over £87 billion. To illustrate just how dramatic a turnaround this represents from the not so distant past, the corresponding figure for the year to end-February 1978 was £50 *million*. Meanwhile, operations in Treasury and local authority bills, then at a level of £16 billion, had fallen to £7 billion in the latest twelve months'. He made the same point in a different way by disclosing that the peak of the Bank's holdings of eligible bank bills 'in the main 1981 revenue season (March) was £3½ billion, a year or so later £8 billion and, recently, the figure has been around £9½ billion'.[21]

THE STERLING INTERBANK MARKET

Since the early 1960s a second market has grown up in sterling deposits, totally independent of the discount market and differing in many respects from it. In origin, it sprang from the rigid structure of interest rates observed by the major deposit banks, the clearing banks. At that time, the clearing banks paid 2 per cent below Bank Rate for deposits, that is, 4 per cent if Bank Rate was 6 per cent. On the other hand, they charged ½–2 per cent over Bank Rate on overdrafts, depending on the quality of the borrower, that is, 6½–8 per cent, if Bank Rate was 6 per cent. With this wide spread between lending and borrowing rates imposed on the clearing banks by the conventions they observed, there was a strong incentive for enterprising financial institutions such as the merchant banks, unfettered by such conventions, to attract lenders by paying more than, say, 4 per cent and to attract borrowers by charging less than, say, 6 per cent, making a small return on the money employed. This sort of operation is profitable only if the overhead costs are lower than those borne by the clearing banks and this means that the sums involved in each deal must be relatively large. This activity could be undertaken only if the merchant bank – or other 'wholesale' banker – had access to the funds required. Sometimes, and particularly in the early stages, they looked to their traditional customers and contacts for the necessary deposits, such as major industrial companies or overseas central banks; but very soon they were augmenting these funds by borrowing from other banks, including the clearing banks, funds surplus to their own immediate requirements and offering the considerable inducement to those banks to on-lend such funds by offering rates of interest substantially in excess of those obtainable in the discount market. Once this interbank market had become established, the big clearing banks did not stand idly by and watch the merchant banks and other competitors take this profitable business away from them: most of them established subsidiary companies to participate in the market and thus channel funds to and from the market, from and to the parent clearing bank. At the same time, as the volume increased, a new breed of entrepreneur emerged to provide a needed service in the form of money brokers, putting together borrowers and lenders, as agents, and taking a commission for their services.

The market is conducted entirely by telephone or telex; some dealing is conducted directly between principals, but the greater proportion of deals are effected through the money brokers. Most of the participants, as both borrowers and lenders, are banks; but other participants include local authorities (who are primarily borrowers), building societies, pension funds, finance houses and other financial institutions, and many other commercial and industrial companies. Deposits dealt in vary from overnight, two or seven days' notice and fixed periods from seven days up to one year and occasionally beyond. All deposits in this market are unsecured; and the amounts of individual deposits vary from a minimum of £100 000 up to £5m and even £10m in the very short-dated deposits. Funds come into the market from any institution that has deposits temporarily surplus to its requirements – overseas and foreign banks, through their London branches, the merchant banks and the clearing banks and their subsidiaries, for example.

As a general rule, the Bank of England does not participate in this market; all its operations in the money market being channelled through the Discount Market, as described above. The interbank market can thus be seen as an unofficial clearing system for borrowings and lendings which has grown up spontaneously in the private sector to fill the need for such a system on an unsecured basis. It now deals in very substantial sums and for many smaller and overseas-owned banks it probably provides their principal source of deposits. Rates of interest are entirely dictated by supply and demand for deposits with a particular maturity – say, three or six months; though changes in interest rates initiated in the Discount Market by the Bank of England are, of course, quickly reflected in the interbank market, since many of the participants operate in both markets.

Alongside the sterling interbank deposit market has grown up a market in sterling negotiable certificates of deposit. This market was founded in 1968 and developed markedly in the early 1970s. The sterling certificates of deposit (CDs) are fully negotiable bearer documents, evidencing a sterling deposit with the issuing bank, which are transferable on delivery. They are issued for a minimum period of three months and a maximum period of five years; the minimum denomination of a CD is £50 000 and the maximum is £500 000.

The attraction to a depositor of buying a negotiable CD rather than putting his funds on deposit with a bank for a similar period lies in the negotiability of the CD. Assuming the buyer can find a seller when he wants to sell, the CD represents a much more liquid asset than the fixed deposit, the significance of which will be discussed in Chapter 4. But the saleability of the CDs is dependent on an efficient secondary market; and it is worth noting that the principal dealers in the secondary market are the Discount Houses. Where a CD is readily saleable – and the extent to which it is will depend in part on the standing of the issuer and in part on its remaining life to maturity – the CD will probably command a slightly lower rate of interest – say, by $^1/_8$ per cent per annum – than a deposit placed with a similar bank for a similar period.

Whilst the Bank of England does not generally participate in the sterling deposit market nor the sterling CD market as a principal, it nevertheless feels, and exercises, a responsibility for the good order of the markets, more from a prudential point of view than a monetary one. A close prudential control over the main principal operators in the markets – the banks – is, of course, exercised by the Bank in its regular supervisory activities, which are described in Chapter 5; but the Bank has also sought to exercise some control over the brokers and, as importantly, the relationship between the brokers and the banks by the issue of a Code of Conduct for transactions in the sterling money markets and also the establishment of a Joint Standing Committee representing brokers and principals under the Bank's chairmanship to monitor observance of the Code of Conduct and give advice on any amendments or additions which may become necessary.

The Code of Conduct was first issued by the Bank in July 1979. In the press notice issued at the same time, the Bank was at pains to point out that the Code of Conduct was 'based on extensive discussions between the Bank, brokers and banks and other principals in this market. The Bank consider that observations of this code will be to the advantage of all participants'. The Code of Conduct itself is in no way controversial and simply sets out standard rules as to the maintenance of confidentiality, the preservation of the anonymity of the market and the prohibition of the exchange of confidential information in respect of third parties; it sets out standard rules of conduct for such matters as the prompt passing of details of transactions by brokers to principals, the prompt checking of confirmation by principals, and the procedures to be followed in the event of disputes; it sets out the rule that 'brokers shall be free to pass commercial names, but they shall be fully equipped to give information to customers upon the latest published financial statements of such principals'; it sets out rules as to the extent of entertainment in the course of business and the giving of gifts or favours by brokers to dealers in banks and it states firmly that 'the making or arranging of bets between Brokers and Principals is unacceptable'. At a more technical level, it sets out a standard calculation for the proceeds of sale of sterling CDs and, in two fairly complicated pages, it sets out a standard of calculation of interest in a leap year.

The issue of the Code of Conduct was accompanied by an announcement by the founder members of arrangements to form, with the obvious encouragement of the Bank, a Sterling Brokers' Association, which any firm offering a brokering service on a significant scale could – and can – apply to join. As the Bank pointed out at the time, 'an undertaking to observe the Code of Conduct issued by the Bank will be a condition of membership of this Association', but it added that 'principals, however, remain free to deal at their absolute discretion with any broker, whether or not he is an Association member'. As already noted, the Bank subsequently established a Joint Standing Committee to monitor observance of the Code of Conduct and give advice on any amendments or additions: this Committee is chaired by a Bank of England official and otherwise consists of representatives of the brokers, appointed by the Sterling Brokers' Association, and representatives of the Banks, appointed by the British Bankers' Association (but with the understanding that one banking representative will always be drawn from the LDMA).

It may be worth noting that this machinery for the prudential supervision of the sterling deposit and CD markets was based in its conception very much on the longer-established machinery for the prudential supervision of the foreign currency deposit and foreign exchange markets, with its brokers' association, bankers' association and Joint Standing Committee with representatives from each and a chairman from the Bank of England. This older precedent is described in the next section.

THE EUROCURRENCY DEPOSIT MARKETS

The markets and their participants

Alongside and, since the abolition of British exchange control in 1979, increasingly integrated with the sterling interbank deposit market has grown up a substantial market in interbank deposits denominated in currencies other than sterling. The deposits dealt in on this market are distinguished by the name 'euro'; thus deposits denominated in US dollars, German marks or Swiss francs become known, when traded in this market, as eurodollars, euroD-Marks and euroSwiss francs.

The textbook definition of a eurocurrency is a deposit made with a bank outside the territory in which the currency in which it is denominated is the national currency: the distinguishing characteristic is thus the country of the bank in which it is deposited rather than the country of the holder of the deposit. Thus, for example, a eurodollar deposit is a deposit held in a bank in London – including the London branches of US banks – Frankfurt, Zurich or any other country outside the United States: it can be owned by an individual or corporation resident in the United States as well as those resident elsewhere in the world. Similarly, a euro-Swiss franc deposit is a deposit in Swiss francs, deposited with a bank outside Switzerland: a Swiss franc deposit with a bank in Switzerland is termed a 'domestic' Swiss franc deposit, a US dollar deposit with a bank in the United States, a domestic dollar deposit, and so on. And it should be noted that sterling deposits with banks outside the United Kingdom – in France or Switzerland, for example, are traded as eurosterling.

The nature of the eurodollar is probably best understood by a brief reference to its historical origins. As in the case of the interbank market in sterling deposits, the market in eurodollar deposits grew up in the first instance as a result of the rigid structure of interest rates – in this case, in the United States. Indeed, until 1970, by which time the London market in eurodollar deposits was already established, US banks were strictly limited by law as to the amount of interest they were allowed to pay on deposits and the reserves to be held against them. This led banks outside the United States to offer higher rates of deposit interest to holders of dollars wherever resident, than were obtainable in New York and other US financial centres, and at the same time to offer these dollars as loans at a lower rate of interest than would have been obtainable by the borrower from banks in the United States. It also led American banks to open branches in London, who could take eurodollar deposits in the London market and send them back to their head offices in the United States, who could relend them profitably to domestic borrowers. (This particular technique, which still continues, is obviously more profitable at times of domestic credit squeeze in the United States. And this is a good example of the way the existence and operations of the eurocurrency markets can frustrate attempts by national governments, including the British Government, to control the domestic supply of credit.)

The eurodollar market was originally, and still is, based in London, where it was given an early boost by the relaxations in exchange control in December 1958. More recently it has expanded to embrace deposits in the principal European currencies – primarily, Swiss francs and German marks – and Japanese yen as well as dollars. The markets in these different currency deposits are closely intertwined with the operations of the foreign exchange market, as we shall see below.

The main participants in the eurocurrency deposit markets of London are the banks. In the early days of the market, some of the bigger depositors were central banks with substantial holdings of US dollars in their external reserves, and these included central banks of the Communist countries who, whilst keen to hold a proportion of their external reserves in US dollars for the sake of convenience, had a political prejudice against holding such dollars in the United States. Major international commercial and industrial corporations, such as the great international oil companies, have been direct participants in the markets for a number of years as both borrowers and lenders: for example the market provided a useful employment of short-term funds being put aside by the oil companies in readiness for regular payments of royalties and taxes.

In its operations, the London interbank eurocurrency deposit market is very similar to the interbank sterling deposit market. As in the sterling deposit market, all deals are transacted by telephone or telex. Some deals are transacted directly between banks, but most are effected through the intermediation of brokers. Deposits dealt in vary from overnight, two or seven days' notice and fixed periods from seven days up to one year. From time to time depositors for longer periods – up to, say, five years – appear in the market, but deposits with maturities of more than one year are the exception rather than the rule and it would be thoroughly imprudent of a bank to assume that it could count on the market to provide such deposits at any time. As in the sterling deposit market, all deposits are unsecured, and the amounts of individual deposits vary from $250 000 up to $10m or more.

In addition to the market in interbank dollar deposits, a market has grown up in London in eurodollar Certificates of Deposit (CDs). Domestic dollar CDs were first issued in the New York market in 1961, where they were so successful that they were introduced in the London market by the London branches of several New York banks in 1966. Partly in the light of its general supervisory responsibilities for all the financial markets in London, but particularly because these responsibilities for markets dealing in foreign exchange and instruments denominated in foreign exchange were reinforced by its powers and responsibilities under the Exchange Control regulations, the Bank of England took a close interest in the introduction of eurodollar CDs. It has made clear that the first issues were made in 1966 only 'when the Bank had been satisfied that the banks generally felt that such instruments would constitute a useful addition to their range of liabilities and that a viable secondary market would develop'. It went on to point out that

> because the C.D. (whether dollar or sterling) is a bearer instrument, exchange control consent is required by anyone proposing to make an issue. Such consent has, in practice, only been granted to authorised banks and is subject to the condition that the term to maturity of the C.D.s should not exceed five years. The Bank have also imposed certain non-statutory requirements on the market to reinforce the quality of the instrument traded in London, including that the secondary market in $ C.D.s shall be confined to C.D.s issued by London banks, and that C.D.s may not be denominated in currencies the responsible monetary authorities for which are known to be anxious to discourage the use of their currency in this way (e.g. deutschemarks and Swiss francs).[22]

The attraction to a depositor of buying a negotiable eurodollar CD rather than putting his money on deposit with a bank for a similar period is the same as the attraction of buying a negotiable sterling CD: that is, its negotiability. And again, the negotiability of the eurodollar CD depends on the existence of an efficient secondary market. There is an additional attraction of eurodollar CDs, in that they provide the profitable employment of relatively small amounts of dollars – held, for example, by an individual investor who is holding dollars prior to investing in dollar securities, or simply taking a view on exchange rates – which would be too small to deposit at market rates in the interbank market.

As we have seen, the main participants in the London eurocurrency markets are banks, but that does not mean that they are the ultimate source of the deposits, nor yet the ultimate users. The banks are, in fact, simple intermediaries providing a vehicle through which the dollars flow from those with surplus cash to those with an immediate cash requirement. Many of these ultimate lenders and borrowers are commercial entities, particularly the major US international corporations. A major source of funds into the market in recent years has been the surpluses of cash built up by the oil-producing states since the price rises of 1973 and subsequent years, and a major group of ultimate borrowers has been sovereign states for whom those same oil price rises have caused major deficits in their overall balance of payments. To these should be added those oil-producing states, such as Nigeria and Mexico, who in the euphoria of the oil price rises entered into elaborate development plans and other spending sprees which more than exhausted their immediate oil revenue and brought them to the market to borrow further funds. We saw in Chapter 1 the dimensions and the consequences of this transfer of wealth between sovereign states as a result of the rises in the price of oil; and we saw, too, how it fell to the world banking system to be the main agent for recycling this flow of wealth, in the form of deposits from the new rich to the new poor – or rather to those sovereign states newly short of immediate cash to balance their international payments – and thus to avert the major, and wildly deflationary, financial snarl-up which would otherwise have ensued. A great many of the funds flowing through this recycling mechanism have passed – and repassed – through the interbank market, and in the passing and repassing the participating banks have between them transformed the cash from the short-term deposits with major banks which were what the oil-rich countries wanted into short and medium-term loans, up to nine or ten years, which were what the borrowing nations required. By and large, this involved the participating banks in undertaking two separate risks – the ultimate credit risk of the borrower and the risk of the mismatch in the maturities of the incoming deposits on the one hand and the outgoing loans on the other.

The London interbank market in eurocurrency deposits has thus provided a crucial mechanism by which the considerable risk of mismatching maturities has been disseminated throughout the international banking community. To take a practical example, it would not be unusual, particularly in the early days of its new wealth, for an oil producer to decide to place a proportion of its liquid funds at, say, seven days' notice with a major international bank (Bank A). Bank A might have a use for a proportion of these funds in its own lending activities; but it would probably put a substantial proportion into the interbank market – and, as we shall see in Chapter 4, all banks would expect to have employed a certain proportion of their deposits in deposits with other banks as a matter of prudence. Because the market was probably awash with funds at seven days' notice – since many oil producers had the same preference to hold a significant proportion of their liquid assets in deposits at such short notice – and because the main demand for funds from the ultimate users was more likely to be for three or six months, or for longer periods with interest-rate adjustments every three months – the rate of interest on three- or six-month deposits would almost certainly be significantly higher than that payable in seven days' notice deposits. In being so, it would probably drag up the rate of interest payable on deposits with intermediate maturities, say one month. Thus many banks participating in the market – and let us take Bank B as an example – would be tempted to take some deposits from Bank A at the seven days' notice rate and put them back in the market for one, three and six months – and so on. The deposits would thus flow and reflow through the interbank market until the banks which had contracted to lend to the ultimate lenders on a six monthly basis – and let us take Bank Z for example – were able to find enough banks like Banks A and B, to provide the funds they required at six months' notice. Thus, whilst the ultimate credit risk was taken by Bank Z, the maturity risk was disseminated between Banks A and B and all other banks in the chain. The risks run by the participating banks in undertaking this 'maturity transformation', as it has come to be called are discussed in Chapter 4.

One further characteristic of the eurocurrency markets should be mentioned. There is a very real sense in which these markets are 'offshore' from the point of view of the British and all other national governments. This means that the market represents a great pool of funds which are outside the control, monetary or exchange, of all national governments. Sometimes the existence of this pool can be turned to great advantage by a national government. For example, prior to the abolition of British Exchange Control in 1979, the regulations included the sensible requirement that, with certain exceptions, any British corporation wishing to make a direct investment outside Britain must finance the investment out of funds borrowed outside Britain: this had the double advantage that, initially at any rate, the investment would involve no pre-emption of Britain's external reserves at all, and secondly that it focused the attention of the investing corporation on the fact that no benefit would accrue to it or the country at large until the return on the investment exceeded the cost of borrowing the external funds. Such a policy, if it was not to be unduly restrictive on outward direct investment, required a stable and significant pool of funds outside Britain from which the investor could borrow, and it should be noted that many countries – including Britain, so long as exchange control lasted – were reluctant to allow direct investors from abroad to borrow in their domestic market more than a limited proportion of the funds required for the investment.

A real, historical example will make this point clear. In the late 1960s, a US corporation wanted to build a major plant in Britain. The British Government was enthusiastic that the plant should be built and was therefore willing to permit a proportion, but only a proportion, of the necessary funds to be borrowed in the domestic sterling market. The US government was at the time taking measures to limit the capital outflow out of the country, in order to protect the US balance of payments, and was willing to permit only a proportion of the necessary capital to be remitted out of the United States. The existence of the offshore eurodollar market made possible a solution acceptable to all parties: one third of the cost was exported out of the United States, one third was raised by borrowing in the domestic sterling market and one third was borrowed offshore to both countries, in the eurodollar market.

Further examples of the beneficial effects of the eurocurrency markets for national governments are the access it gives such governments to borrowable 'external' funds with which to boost their external reserves, when such a boost is necessary. Some of the obvious beneficiaries of this who are now in trouble, such as Mexico, Argentina and Brazil may find the euromarkets less forthcoming for the foreseeable future, until they have put their houses in order. But there are many other countries, Britain and France, for example, who have tapped the euromarkets with great ease and for considerable amounts in recent years to tide them over a shortage of external reserves.

But equally, there are important ways in which the pool of offshore funds provided by the eurocurrency markets can be a thorn in the flesh of national governments, and not only those whose domestic economic policies are isolationist and eccentrically parochial. Two ways that this can happen should be mentioned. First, we have already noted how a restrictive domestic credit policy in the United States can be frustrated by the ability of US banks to fund their domestic lending by borrowing eurodollars through their London branches. Until the abolition of exchange control in 1979, a domestic credit squeeze in Britain was reasonably immune from such a leak, in that British banks were strictly limited by the Bank of England in the amount of eurocurrency borrowings they could convert into sterling and relend to their customers, and their customers themselves were simply not allowed to borrow eurocurrencies, including eurosterling. But since the abolition of exchange control in 1979, it is much less easy to prevent funds from leaking into the economy from the eurocurrency markets in times of credit squeeze and thus, to some extent, thwarting the policy of squeeze itself. Indeed, there was a significant leak of funds into the domestic British economy from the eurocurrency markets in the months immediately following the abolition of exchange control, prompted by the quantitative restrictions on bank lending imposed at the time by the 'corset'; and it was the effect on domestic bank lending of the unwinding of these leaks when the 'corset' was finally removed in June 1980 which was one of the principal reasons for the marked growth at the time in the figures by which the money supply is measured, and the consequent tension between the Government and the Bank.

A second way in which the pool of funds mobilised by the eurocurrency markets can embarrass domestic policy is to be found in the ammunition it provides to speculators in times of exchange rate uncertainty to those who want to take a position long or short of a particular currency; and, as we shall see later in this chapter, there are often good commercial reasons for taking such positions. One of the ways of taking such a position for or against a currency is to borrow a currency one thinks will go down in value and convert the borrowing outright into the currency one thinks will go up: such an operation requires a source from which to borrow the first currency, a safe home in which to deposit the second currency and a market in which the outright conversion can easily be made and the profit (or loss) easily taken once the speculation has been closed. The eurocurrency markets provide the first two of these requirements in respect of many currencies and the London foreign exchange market provides the third.

The markets and the Bank of England

As in the case of the sterling inter-bank deposit market, the eurocurrency deposit market is virtually free from any formal controls from the Bank of England or any other authority, and it is not the subject of any formal intervention by any such authority. Nevertheless the Bank does feel some responsibility to see that the market is an orderly one, and to that end does impose – or, at least, strongly encourage – some prudential rules. Some of its prudential supervision is, of course, effected through the Bank's prudential supervision of the banks themselves, who form much the greater proportion of participants as principals in the market; but it has been at pains to exercise some control over the market itself: that is, over the brokers who participate in the market, particularly over which brokers are permitted to enter the market, and over the relationship between the brokers and their principals, the banks. Initially, the Bank had powers to exercise this control derived from the exchange control regulations, but its authority in this respect has survived the abolition of exchange control in 1979, based largely on its traditional position in the City of London and its markets and the respect which that position attracts.

As we shall see in the next section, the eurocurrency deposit market is inextricably intertwined with the foreign exchange market: to a large extent the same brokers and the same banks operate in both markets, and many deals actually involve participating in both markets simultaneously. It is, therefore, natural that the Bank should exercise its prudential control over both markets by a common mechanism. Writing in 1978, before the exchange control regulations were abolished, the Bank described this mechanism and the historical factors which lay behind it, in the following terms:

> Only banks which are authorised under the Exchange Control Act 1947 to deal in foreign exchange are permitted to participate as principals in the London foreign exchange market. These banks mostly employ the services of broking intermediaries, both to identify willing counterparties to transactions and to obtain up-to-the-minute information on the rates being quoted, both spot and forward, for all major and most minor currencies. The brokers have combined to form an association called the Foreign Exchange and Currency Deposit Brokers Association. Those banks that wish to employ the services of a broker are required as far as their dealings with other banks in London are concerned, to operate exclusively through members of the F.E.C.D.B.A. (with an exception for *de minimis* amounts in which they may deal directly between each other).
>
> These arrangements stem from events which occurred prior to the Second World War, when there were a large number of small broking firms in the market, and some unsatisfactory commercial practices developed. With the Bank's encouragement a Foreign Exchange Brokers Association was then formed with membership criteria which included sponsorship from the banks themselves, and an agreed code of conduct. In their turn banks employing a broker were required to pass their London inter-bank foreign exchange business through members of the Association. After an interval covering the war years and those immediately succeeding it, these arrangements were re-activated in 1951 when the exchange market was re-opened. They have been reviewed and revised under the supervision of the Bank on a number of subsequent occasions, notably in 1967 when negotiations were begun to enlarge the Brokers Association to encompass the growing market in currency deposits and, most recently, in 1975 when the trading arrangements and the code of

> practice required by the Bank were restated in a letter sent to all members of the B.B.A. [the British Bankers' Association] by its president, Lord O'Brien. The working of these arrangements is kept under regular review by a Joint Standing Committee, chaired by a Bank of England official, on which banks and brokers are equally represented. The Committee reports back to the Council of the F.E.C.D.B.A. and the Foreign Exchange Sub-Committee of the B.B.A. (which is also the body consulted by the Exchange Control Department of the Bank on exchange control matters affecting banks). The Joint Standing Committee also acts as arbitrator in the event of disputes arising out of foreign exchange and currency deposit transactions completed in the London market.[23]

The broad framework of the arrangements here described, involving the FECDBA, the BBA and the Bank remains essentially the same in 1983 as it was in 1978. Exchange Control has, of course, been abolished, leaving the Bank to fall back on less formal powers for its supervisory actions. The terms of the contract between the three parties have, however, been slightly – though, in the eyes of many participants, significantly – modified by a second and third 'O'Brien letter', dated December 1978 and December 1979 respectively. The second of these letters permits banks using either the currency deposit or the foreign exchange market to deal direct with each other or to use the services of a member of the FECDBA, though they may still not use the services of the UK office of a broker which is not so recognised. Further – and, if you like, as a *quid pro quo*, for this concession to the banks – brokers are permitted by the same December 1979 letter to 'pass commercial names', that is, to put banks in touch with UK non-bank, commercial borrowers or depositors.

This broad institutional mechanism for supervising the currency deposit and foreign exchange markets is, in fact, a curious and not altogether tidy hybrid between the principle of prudential supervision by the Bank and the principle of self-regulation by the participants in the market, represented by the FECDBA and the BBA. It was, however, made a little tidier by the O'Brien letter of December 1978 (which came into effect in January 1979), which in one important respect overtly stated for the first time the *de facto* power of the Bank. Under the previous arrangements, banks which dealt in either market through UK brokers were required to deal only through brokers who were members of the club, the FECDBA (though they were allowed to deal through non-members, provided they were outside the United Kingdom); and formally such members must be sponsored by a specified number of members of the BBA and elected to membership by the FECDBA. In practice, the system was, and is, presided over by a Committee consisting of representatives of the FECDBA and the BBA, but chaired by an official of the Bank of England, which also provides the secretariat: it was thus unthinkable that a broker could be elected – and thus, in effect, empowered to deal in the market – without the implied approval of the Bank. This point was brought out into the open in the second O'Brien letter, of December 1978 which, in the paragraph setting out the 'closed shop' arrangement described above, formally replaced the term 'member broker', by the term 'recognised broker' and added that

> the Bank will maintain a list of Recognised Brokers which will be available on request at all times during normal business hours. Banks are requested to assist the Bank in supervising the conduct of the foreign exchange and currency deposit markets in the United Kingdom and their attention is therefore drawn to the procedure which will be applied by the Bank in according, suspending or withdrawing recognition.

The letter then went on to set these procedures out in detail, listing in particular the criteria to be applied by the Bank in considering applications. Thus, in 1980, an almost imperceptible but, in the present context, significant change took place in the regulation of the two markets. In practice nothing visibly changed at all. But formally, self-regulation with formal advice from the Bank was replaced by Bank regulation with formal advice from the participants in the market.

One final principle relating to its prudential supervision of the foreign exchange and foreign currency deposit markets which is rigorously observed by the Bank and, again, has its roots in the experiences of the inter-war years, should be mentioned. In both markets, the Bank draws a very sharp distinction between brokers and principals: no broker is allowed to act as a principal in the market in which it operates. Among other things, this means that the Bank need not enquire into the activities of brokers with the same prudential questions in mind as it does into the activities of the banks. By and large, as we shall see in Chapters 4 and 5, these questions are related to the *positions* maintained by banks, rather than in the individual transactions which they undertake; and brokers, quite simply, are prohibited from taking positions.

THE FOREIGN EXCHANGE MARKET

Functions and participants

The mechanism of the London foreign exchange market is virtually identical to that of the foreign currency deposit market described above. The market has no physical presence, but is conducted entirely by telephone and telex. Most of the participants as principals are banks, though some larger international industrial and commercial corporations, such as the international oil companies, participate in the market as well.

To some extent, this distinction between banks and non-banks is misleading. *Any* corporation or individual wishing to buy or sell one currency against another will transact the business through a bank; and whether he approaches that bank as a customer or a fellow-participant in the foreign exchange market is not a matter of great moment or interest: suffice it to say that a really substantial customer would almost certainly obtain as fine rates from his bankers as he could if he was another participant in the market. On the other hand a major non-bank with large deals to transact is no longer obliged by the Exchange Control regulations – as it was prior to 1979 – to transact all its business through an 'authorised bank' which had power itself to authorise a transaction in certain circumstances for exchange control purposes; nor, as we have seen in the last section, is it inhibited – as it was prior to 1980 – by the rules of the game in the London market from employing a foreign exchange broker to effect the transaction. Again, major corporations – and, indeed, anybody else who is willing to pay for it – can obtain up-to-date information on exchange rates, and be as well informed on them as the banks themselves, by subscribing to the Reuters information service described below: they thus need not be inhibited from entering the market, as it were, as a professional player by any feeling that other professionals might be better informed. For all these reasons, non-bank corporations may from time to time use a broker to identify a counterparty rather than go to the market via a bank, and in these circumstances that corporation could clearly be said to be itself a participant in the market.

Of more direct interest to the customer, is not whether he is actually participating in the market, 'playing the professionals at their own game', but rather the rates he obtains for his deals. As we have seen, a really substantial customer would almost certainly obtain the finest rates on large transactions, whether he dealt through a bank or participated directly in the market, but most non-banks and even small banks dealing in odd amounts must expect to deal at something less advantageous than the finest terms. As the Bank has pointed out:

> usually, a customer will want to deal for an uneven amount, quite possibly below the minimum for which the best rates are available in the market, thus leaving the bank with an amount to cover on less favourable terms, unless it has other customer business to offset it. The bank may have to aggregate several such small deals and cover them together, in the meantime remaining vulnerable to an adverse change in exchange rates. Moreover, the bank must reckon with the risk that the counterparty might fail to fulfil his side of the contract – a failure which would leave the bank with an unbalanced position and therefore, if rates moved unfavourably, a potential loss. The difference between the finest rates at which business is done – for

large, round amounts between banks of the highest standing – and the rates at which banks normally deal with customers reflects the higher cost and possible risk of doing such customer business.[24]

Some banks which appear in the market do so purely to transact the business of their customers. Many others deal to a greater or lesser extent for their own account; and it is the presence of so many banks in London who are prepared to take positions of their own which makes the London market one of the largest in the world and which reduces what would otherwise be wild fluctuations in rates. As the Bank of England has remarked, 'customer business is uneven in timing and amount, and exchange rates would be more volatile if many banks did not also deal on their own account. Their operations give the market depth and continuity, and facilitate the transaction of customer business.'[25]

The more active banks maintain working balances in the currencies in which they trade: these usually take the form of balances on current account with their principal correspondent banks in the appropriate centres – New York or another US centre for banks holding US dollars, Frankfurt for D-Marks, Zurich or another Swiss centre for Swiss francs, Tokyo for Japanese yen. On top of these working balances, banks may well take modest positions, 'long' (with an excess of assets over liabilities) in those currencies where they think the rate is likely to go up or 'short' (with an excess of liabilities over assets) in those currencies where they think the rate is likely to go down. (And it need scarcely be remarked that a 'long' position in one currency automatically involves taking a 'short' position in another.) These long or short positions can be taken in two main ways. First, as was mentioned in the last section, a bank or other trader wishing to be long of US dollars and short of Japanese yen can borrow yen in the eurocurrency market (if it can find a lender), sell the yen outright for dollars in the spot foreign exchange market (in the manner described below) and put the dollars on deposit on the eurodollar deposit market. Alternatively, the bank or trader can take his long and short position by buying dollars for yen in the forward foreign exchange market (again in the manner described below). In both cases the bank will end up with its dollar assets exceeding its dollar liabilities and its yen liabilities exceeding its yen assets.

Besides keeping working balances in foreign currencies and taking occasional 'positions' in the manner described above, some banks are 'market-makers' in one or more currencies – playing a role comparable to that of a 'jobber' on the London Stock Exchange. Like the jobber, these banks consistently quote rates at which they are ready to buy or sell: in the words of the Bank, 'this provides a considerable service to other participants in the market because it enables business to be executed quickly and in substantial amounts'.[26] Like jobbers – or, indeed, like book-makers on a racecourse – these market-makers react entirely to the pressures of supply and demand upon them. If there are more buyers than sellers at the prices they quote they will raise their prices, and vice versa; and it is these traders who effectively set the prices which the rest of the market quickly adopts. Similarly, a market-maker will react to violent fluctuations in the currency in which it deals by widening the spread between buying and selling prices.

A substantial amount of foreign exchange business is transacted directly between banks. Indeed, it is an important part of a foreign exchange dealer's expertise to know which banks are the market-makers in which particular currency. And before trading with another bank, a foreign exchange dealer is nowadays very well equipped to know exactly what rates of exchange other banks are quoting for the currency concerned. In part, this is the consequence of a highly developed criss-cross of direct bilateral telephone lines linking the dealing-rooms of dozens of London banks at the push of a button at either end. An experienced dealer can obtain quotations from several other banks in a matter of seconds, by these direct lines. And in part, dealing-rooms today enjoy what is effectively a multilateral information service provided by Reuters, the information transmission company. Each bank who subscribes to the Reuters system has a video screen on which are displayed the rates quoted by certain banks for certain currencies. Those banks who are willing to do so, and there are many of them, take a 'page' in the Reuters service to display their rates, and in a form that can be continually and instantly updated. Thus, by pressing the appropriate buttons on his control unit, a dealer in one bank can instantly throw up on his screen a full table of exchange rates in several currencies at which another bank is in principle prepared to deal, and by deft button-pressing, he can work through the tables displayed by several banks in a single minute. Conversely, the bank who subscribes to display his rates, as well as to receive on his screen the rates quoted by other banks, may well have his rates being inspected visually by forty or fifty or more banks at any one moment. Once a bank dealer identifies by this method the bank at whose rates he is prepared to deal, it is a quick step to phone or telex that bank's dealing room, by either direct or public line, to propose and clinch a specific deal.

And this telephone, telex and Reuters infrastructure not only links up individual London banks dealing with each other: it also links them up with other banks in other financial centres – New York, Frankfurt, Zurich, Paris, Tokyo, Hong Kong, Singapore, and so on. Many London branches of overseas banks which are active in foreign exchange trading are linked to their head offices by direct telephone and telex lines, which greatly increases the speed and efficiency with which London dealing rates and other market information can be disseminated throughout the world, so that a significant proportion of the foreign exchange business of London banks active in foreign exchange is conducted directly with banks in other financial centres overseas as well as with other banks in London.

But besides this interbank dealing, with both London and overseas banks, a great deal of business in the London market is conducted through foreign exchange brokers. Brokers provide two main services for the banks who are their customers: first, they provide up-to-the-minute information of the rates in any particular currency. Again, a competent dealer in a bank will know which dealer in which broking firm or firms specialises in any particular currency and, if the bank deals a lot in that currency, he will probably have a direct line installed to that particular dealer. Secondly, it is the business of the broker to find counterparties for his customer, that is, to bring together buyers and sellers. As the Bank has pointed out, 'once a broker has quoted a rate to a bank, and the bank has chosen to deal, the broker is committed to providing a counterparty'.[27] Once a deal has been done through a broker, that broker charges a fee or commission, payable by the principals, at rates which are fixed at irregular intervals by the Joint Standing Committee, chaired by the Bank and described in the previous section. This is the only source of profit to the brokers: unlike the banks, they do not – indeed, are not permitted to – take positions in currencies, but act purely as intermediaries.

The spot market, forward market and currency swaps

Exchange rates are quoted in the foreign exchange market for three different types of transactions: spot transactions, forward transactions and 'swap' transactions which, as we shall see, are a mixture of the first two.

Spot transactions are simply the purchase or sale of one currency against another for immediate settlement: in practice, spot transactions are conventionally settled the second working day after the deal has been clinched, thus giving time for the paperwork to be completed and the other necessary arrangements made. A market-making bank will quote a two-way rate for one currency against another, the lower rate being the rate at which it will buy the first currency and the higher rate the one at which it will sell. With several different currencies being quoted at any one time, there is obviously a large number of potential cross-rates in which any currency can be dealt in against any other currency; but for the sake of simplicity, each currency is in practice normally quoted against the US dollar. A bank wishing to buy, say D-Marks against French francs can easily calculate the market rate by ascertaining the rate at which he can buy D-Marks for dollars and that at which he can sell French francs for dollars. If any dealer is rash enough to quote a cross-rate – at which he will buy, say, D-Marks against French francs – which is out of line with the main market rates, in this case for D-Marks/dollars and French francs/dollars, other dealers in the market will quickly take advantage of the situation by taking him up on his rates and then undoing the transaction by buying D-Marks against dollars and selling French francs against dollars at market rates with other banks, and taking a consequent profit. Indeed, a high proportion of the deals undertaken by an active bank will be of this purely professional nature: jumping into the market to take a small profit if disparities appear between cross-rates, or, for that matter, between any quoted rates. The greater the number of banks acting as pure professionals in this way, the greater the 'depth' of the market, the closer all rates quoted by all participants will keep to each other and the more attractive and efficient the market becomes to its ultimate customers and to other banks overseas.

The rates normally quoted in the market are good for large, round amounts. To quote again from the Bank:

> for very large amounts, or for smaller or odd amounts, a bank would normally quote a wider spread, and the range of amounts for which a quotation is good will vary to some extent with the currency concerned and market conditions. Generally, however, a quotation in sterling/dollar would be good for round amounts of £½ million, between £½ million and £5 million, and a quotation in dollar/deutschemark would be good for round amounts of $½ million between $½ million and $5 million.[28]

As well as quoting 'spot' rates for one currency against another, the foreign exchange market quotes 'forward' rates as well. A forward deal is one in which both parties to the deal formally agree the rate at which they will exchange an agreed amount of agreed currencies at an agreed date in the future. In fact, a forward deal is exactly the same as a spot deal except that whereas the spot deal is always for settlement two working days ahead, a forward deal can be settled a week, a month, a year or even longer ahead. The spot market ultimately exists because there are always a number of people who want to exchange one currency for another – to pay for imports, convert the proceeds of exports, make capital investments overseas, and so on: it is not simply a playground in which professionals deal with each other, despite the fact that a great many of the deals concluded are, in fact, between professionals. Similarly, the forward market ultimately exists to satisfy a very real demand for forward foreign exchange cover.

For example, traders and other companies importing goods or raw materials from abroad will know with some precision how much they will need to pay the suppliers at some fixed date in the future. If they have been invoiced in sterling by the overseas supplier, there is no foreign exchange problem for the importer (though there is a foreign exchange problem for the overseas exporter, who will know with some precision exactly how much sterling he will receive in the future and on what date; and he will then have to decide what arrangements to make to exchange that sterling into his own currency at that future date). If, on the other hand, some British importer is invoiced by the overseas supplier in a currency other than sterling – US dollars, for example – then he will have a known commitment to pay away a known amount of US dollars on a known date in the future. Under the system of fixed exchange rates which prevailed from 1945 to 1972–3, the British importer could reasonably expect to buy his dollars at a known rate on the appropriate date in the future – often three months ahead, since this is a common period of credit given by suppliers in international trade; he would, therefore, probably wait until the appropriate date and buy the necessary amount of dollars on the spot market two days before he was required to pay them to the supplier. Since the breakdown of the system of fixed exchange rates in 1972–3, the British importer has had no certainty as to the rate at which he might be able to buy dollars three months, or any other period, ahead; and therefore there is a strong incentive for him to enter into a firm commitment to buy the dollars forward at an agreed rate, for settlement on the appropriate date in the future. The floating of exchange rates since 1972–3 has thus given a considerable boost to demand in the forward market.

There are, of course, many other types of 'end-user' of the forward market. Exporters, for example, who have invoiced their overseas buyers in currencies other than sterling are in a position which is a mirror-image of the British importer, described above: they will be expecting to receive a known mount of foreign currency on a known date in the future and hey have a strong incentive to fix the rate of exchange at vhich these foreign currencies, when received, are converted nto sterling just as soon as the amounts and dates of receipt re known, rather than to wait until the foreign currencies are ctually received. And it is worth emphasising that this ncentive is not to take a 'super-profit' out of their international trading, still less to make a speculative gain on the xchange markets. The incentive is simply to fix in sterling erms the precise amounts of future payments to, and receipts rom, counterparties overseas and thus at the same time to emove one uncertainty from their forward planning and, nore important, to close off the real possibility of large inintended losses (or profits) resulting from movements in xchange rates. The point is even more important to importers and exporters of capital goods which may be a long time n their construction and for which there may be a delay of everal months or even years between the dates when the ontracts to buy and sell the goods in question are signed and he dates on which payment has to be made.

There are many other ways in which commercial and ndustrial organisations, as well as individuals, can find hemselves with firm forward commitments to pay or receive oreign currencies in the future and whom common prudence will lead to the forward exchangc market to cover their otherwise open exposure to the risk of movements in the rate of exchange. These include the payments of royalties and dividends to parent companies, the payment of salaries and pensions to individuals and firm commitments to make capital payments in either direction, from one currency into another.

But the biggest users of all of the forward foreign exchange markets are the banks themselves, using the forward market as an integral part of their eurocurrency deposit operations, described in the previous section. As we saw then, banks engaged in the eurocurrency deposit markets stand ready to take deposits in several different currencies, but principally US dollars, Deutschemarks, and Swiss francs; and they stand ready to make deposits with other banks and to make loans to commercial and industrial customers in a similar range of currencies. It is frequently the case that a bank which needs to lend, say, Deutschemarks for three months, is short of the required number of three-month D-Mark deposits but long of, say, three-month dollar deposits: in this situation the Bank will turn to the market in spot and forward D-Marks against dollars and use the three-month dollars to 'manufacture' three-month D-Marks by means of a 'swap' transaction.

A 'swap' transaction is one in which a bank buys one currency spot against another and in the same transaction sells it back 'forward' to the same bank. The difference between the spot rate and the forward rate in a swap transaction is known as the 'swap margin', and it is these margins which are quoted in the market as, as it were, the cost – or premium – that a bank will charge – or pay – for undertaking the two-part transaction of spot purchase and forward sale, or vice versa. Going back to our example in the previous paragraph, a dealer with a commitment to provide a three-month D-Mark deposit may well 'manufacture' this deposit by borrowing three-month dollars and simultaneously undertaking a three-month D-Mark/dollar swap: that is, he will sell the dollars spot for D-Marks and buy them back against D-Marks for settlement in three months time. He will thus have D-Marks available to lend for three months but will at the same time have ensured that he has the dollars back in his hands in three months time, with which to repay the dollar deposit which matures on that date. Indeed, a competent dealer faced with the need for three-month D-Marks will not just ask the market for a quotation for three-month D-Mark deposits: he will also ask for rates for, say, three-month US dollar deposits and three-month dollar/D-Mark swaps. And he will deal in whichever market will give him the D-Mark deposits at the lowest effective rate of interest. The effective rate of interest on the D-Marks 'manufactured' out of dollars will be the underlying interest cost of the three-month dollars plus or minus the forward discount or premium for three-month D-Marks against dollars: this discount or premium is simply the difference between the spot and forward rates of exchange incorporated in the 'swap'.

An important point should be made at this stage about the technique described above of manufacturing deposits in one currency out of deposits in another and a swap. In the example given above, it should be noted that the dealer sold and repurchased the same amount of dollars in the swap transaction: he was thus taking no open exposure to the risk of movements in the exchange rates. Equally, the incoming dollar deposit, the outgoing D-Mark loan and the swap which converted them were all for the same maturity, three months: the dealer was thus taking no risk in terms of maturity or interest-rate mismatching. All these potential risks – foreign exchange, maturity mismatch and interest-rate mismatch – will be discussed in Chapter 4.

So much is the forward foreign exchange market dominated by the swap transactions that the market itself does not deal in outright forward transactions between participating banks at all. A bank which has been asked by an industrial or commercial customer to quote a rate for a forward transaction for one of the reasons outlined above will have to calculate the rate and effect the forward transaction in the market in one of two ways. Taking the example that his customer wants to buy yen three months forward against US dollars, a dealer can undertake a three-month swap in the market selling spot yen and buying them back three months forward; he can then enter the spot market and buy back the spot yen against dollars, leaving him long of three-month forward yen to sell to his customer. Alternatively, he can borrow three-month dollars in the market, sell them spot for yen and place the three-month yen on deposit in the market: at the end of the three months, the yen deposit will have matured, giving him the yen to pay to his customer and the customer will in turn pay him the dollars with which to repay the three-month deposit.

In the above example, it should again be noted that the dealer has not exposed his bank by either method to the risk of movements in foreign exchange rates, nor to the risks of mismatching as to either maturity or interest rates. On the other hand, the second method of manufacturing an outright forward, by giving and taking deposits in the respective currencies, does increase the 'gearing' of the bank's balance sheet and the risks associated with such an increase. These risks are discussed in Chapter 4.

From this description of the spot, forward and swap markets in foreign exchange, it should be clear how closely intertwined are these markets with those for eurocurrency deposits. And from this, three more lessons may be drawn. First, the opportunities for arbitrage between the various markets by an astute dealer or team of dealers are almost infinite. We have already seen how an astute dealer can arbitrage between the spot markets for different currencies, taking a quick turn when the cross-rates get out of line. The markets for foreign currency swaps and eurocurrency deposits provide, as it were, multidimensional opportunities for arbitraging between the various markets; and it is by no means surprising that a major proportion of the deals undertaken by active banks in all the markets taken together should be deals between professionals – taking advantage of tiny discrepancies in rates to take equally tiny turns, but on substantial volume. And the point to be made about these deals is that they need not – and usually do not – involve the bank concerned in open foreign exchange risks or the risks of mismatch in maturities or interest rates. The only risks that are involved in such deals are the credit risk of the counterparties and the 'gearing' risk mentioned above: these will be discussed in the next chapter.

The second lesson to be drawn is that the very scale of these 'professional' operations undertaken by the dealing rooms of active banks does in itself provide almost unlimited opportunities for a bank to take horrendous risks either through mismanagement – such as sloppy book-keeping – or through dishonesty by dealers. Happily, the second of these risks has proved unusual in the London market; but banks active in the foreign exchange markets ignore them both at their peril. And the Bank of England is quite right to have perceived the checking of management controls of foreign exchange positions – and the internal limits within which dealing rooms operate – as a proper part of their responsibilities for prudential supervision.

The third lesson is the almost frightening efficiency with which the markets, backed by formidable batteries of information-disseminating technical equipment, can and do react to changing interest rates, changing exchange rates and the changing monetary, economic and political conditions which influence them both. Unless deliberate exchange or other monetary controls are erected to prevent or limit it, the foreign exchange and eurocurrency markets provide a kind of highly sensitive conductor which transmits, via exchange rates, the monetary and other pressures on interest rates in national financial systems – on occasion to the evident satisfaction or discomfort of national governments. Precisely how these pressures build up, and the factors which initiate them, are discussed in the next section.

The pressures of supply and demand in the market

In conditions of freely floating exchange rates, the rate of exchange between two different currencies is entirely set by the pressures of supply and demand in the market. The efficient system of arbitrage between the spot markets for individual currencies, mentioned above, ensures that the *total* supply of a currency, against all other currencies, is equated very quickly and on a continuing basis with the *total* demand for that currency, against all other currencies. Thus the pressures on a currency, up or down, from world-wide supply and demand are reflected very accurately in exchange rate movements, which thus become a key barometer for the measurement of such pressures.

In the days of fixed exchange rates, prior to 1972, the pressures of supply and demand on the foreign exchange market were similar in strength to what they are today, but were manifested by different results. For example, if the supply of sterling exceeded the demand for sterling the exchange rate was not permitted to move by more than a very limited amount: it was, in effect, held at the agreed rate by the Bank of England entering the market and buying sufficient sterling – usually against US dollars but also against other currencies as well – to mop up the surplus supply. Conversely, if demand for sterling against all other currencies exceeded the supply in the market to such an extent as to push the rate of exchange beyond the agreed limit, then the Bank of England would satisfy the excess demand by selling sufficient sterling, that is, buying sufficient dollars and other currencies, to bring the supply and demand for sterling back into equilibrium. In these circumstances, the pressures of supply and demand were brought into equilibrium, not by a movement in exchange rates, but rather by a movement in the external reserves of the United Kingdom, or whichever country was buying or selling its own currency in the market. And in this case, the barometer of the excess pressures of supply over demand, or vice versa, was the size of the external reserves of gold and foreign currencies of the country concerned. If and when these external reserves were in danger of being exhausted – or if the country concerned came to believe that, for whatever reason, the exchange rate it was defending had become unrealistic and therefore ultimately indefensible – then it would alter the rate at which it stood ready to intervene in the market to siphon off a surplus of supply or a surplus of demand for its own currency.

British readers who lived through the 1950s and 1960s will recall the almost continual preoccupation with monthly fluctuations in the level of the external reserves and with the ability of the country to maintain a fixed rate of exchange for sterling which provided a continuing backcloth for, and a major influence in the conduct of, Britain's economic policy. Other readers have only to study a simple economic history of the times to realise how central to policy-making this preoccupation had become.

One of the reasons for the abandonment of fixed exchange rates in 1972 was almost certainly a desire by some national governments to be rid of this apparent major constraint on domestic economic policy; but if this was the case, the desire has scarcely been fulfilled. The heavy pressure on sterling in the early part of 1976 was noted in Chapter 1 as being a major factor forcing the Labour government of the time to turn away from some of its cherished policy aims and ambitions and submit to a number of politically unwelcome conditions for a loan from the IMF at the end of that year. Again, the anxious, sidelong glances cast by the Thatcher Government at the rate of exchange for sterling, particularly in 1981 and early 1983 when fears for sterling prompted increases in interest rates in direct conflict with the political aim of economic recovery, are testimony to the fact that a regime of floating exchange rates is insufficient in itself to eliminate the exchange rate as a major preoccupation of economic policy-makers. For these reasons, the pressures of supply and demand in the exchange markets are of considerable importance to the conduct of economic policy and thus, by implication, to monetary control by the national authorities – a principal theme of this book.

Before inspecting these pressures, it is worth recalling another reason for the abandonment of fixed exchange rates in 1972, already noted in Chapter 1. It was there remarked that it was the massive movements of short-term capital – or 'hot money' – across national frontiers and from one country to another, reaching a final crescendo in the later 1960s and early 1970s, which ultimately made the system of adjustable pegs unworkable and forced the world into a system of floating rates. The main causes for this growth of short-term capital movements were set out in Chapter 1; at this point it is sufficient to repeat that this growth in itself enormously expanded and deepened the foreign exchange and eurocurrency markets and that they in turn become a major vehicle for 'speculation' both for and against currencies.

In a simple world of fixed exchange rates the buying and selling pressures on a particular currency would derive from underlying transactions, conducted on an evenly-timed basis. These would include, for example, demand for foreign currencies from British importers of goods from overseas, timed for settlement at the usual time for such contracts (frequently, three months after the contract was signed); they would equally include a supply of foreign currency from British exporters, converting the foreign currency proceeds of these exports into sterling – again timed for settlement at the usual time for such contracts (frequently, again, three months after the contract was signed). In the more complicated world, in which there is a credible possibility that exchange rates may change – as, for example, in the present world of floating rates or, indeed, in the world which preceded it, of fixed *but adjustable* pegs, the whole pattern of supply and demand for foreign currencies is greatly distorted as to both the size and timing of the pressures on either side.

In other words, the expectations of the international

trading and business community of changes in exchange rates have become a dominant factor influencing the pressures of supply and demand in the foreign exchange market. Thus, for example, in a stable world of no such expectations, an importer contracting to pay for goods in a foreign currency three months after the contract will wait until that three months is up before buying the appropriate currency: in a less stable world where there is an expectation that, say, his own currency is likely to fall against that in which the imports are invoiced (the currency of the overseas supplier, for example), the importer will have a strong incentive to protect his position in one of two ways. He can either borrow sterling (if he is British), convert the sterling outright into the overseas currency at the current spot rate of exchange and then put that overseas currency on deposit for three months, maturing on the day on which the payment to his overseas supplier is due. Alternatively, he can buy the appropriate foreign currency three months forward against sterling from a bank, in the manner described above.

Equally, in a world of unstable exchange rates, an exporter who expected his own currency to fall against that of his overseas customer would have a strong incentive to delay as long as possible the date on which he converted the foreign currency proceeds of his export sales into his own currency. He could do this by borrowing his own currency from the date on which he would normally have made the conversion – to fill the hole in his finances which would otherwise be caused by the delay in receiving the export proceeds – and putting the foreign currency proceeds of his export sales on deposit for the same period. If his forecast was correct, he would be able to convert his foreign currency proceeds into his own currency at a more favourable rate than if he had made the conversion on the date he received payment.

These techniques of advancing and retarding the conversion of payments and receipts in foreign exchange arising out of normal commercial transactions are known as 'leads' and 'lags'. And they can, of course, be applied to the conversion of any payments or receipts which are known to fall due on a specific date in the future, whatever the underlying transaction giving rise to the payment or receipt: besides payments arising from normal trading transactions, they can also be applied, for example to payments of dividends, royalties and other commitments on capital or current account.

Several points should be made about these leads and lags. The first is the sheer scale of their potential. In 1982, for example, the total imports into the United Kingdom has a value of £53 158m.[29] Assuming the normal terms and conditions of these imports allowed for payment three months after the contracts were signed, this implies that, under normal conditions, payments relating to a quarter of these imports, or £13 289m would be outstanding at any one time. In this situation a sudden and unanimous change in the expectation of United Kingdom importers, to the effect that they suddenly believed that the pound was going to weaken in the foreign exchange market could thus cause increases in the supply of sterling in the foreign exchange market, spot and forward taken together, of £13 289m.

The second point about leads and lags is that the scope for effecting them has been vastly increased by the growth of the foreign exchange markets, described above. But it is worth remarking that the very size and efficiency of these markets can confront the potential leader and lagger with some fine questions of judgement. Thus, for example, if many other traders, in his own and other countries, take the same view as our importer that his currency is likely to weaken, then the demand for deposits denominated in his own currency in the eurocurrency markets will rise, thus increasing the rate of interest on such deposits and the rate of exchange for his currency in the forward market will fall: there may well come a point when the effective forward rate quoted by the market fully discounts the fall in the currency anticipated by the trader, and at this point he must decide whether his leading or lagging is a worthwhile exercise at all. (It should be noted that the market will adjust quickly in this way only if there is some sort of dam, such as exchange control, between the eurocurrency deposit markets and the domestic deposit market for the currency in question, or if the domestic monetary authorities are content to see the pressures in the foreign exchange markets push up – or down – interest rates in the domestic market. This susceptibility of domestic deposit markets to influences generated in the foreign exchange markets – and, indeed, generated in other domestic markets, but transmitted by the foreign exchange markets – is discussed in Chapter 6.)

The third, and perhaps the most important point about leads and lags is that most, though not all, of such transactions are prompted by common commercial prudence and not, as is sometimes supposed, by the greed for speculative gain. In the example above of an importer wishing to clinch the rate of exchange at which he must buy the foreign currency to pay for his imported goods, and to do so ahead of the date on which the payment in foreign currency is due, the importer is attempting to do two things. He is ensuring the sterling cost of his imports will not escalate as a consequence of a fall in the value of currency, and he is eliminating the uncertainty about that sterling cost inherent in a situation in which he had not bought the necessary foreign currency forward. And so even if, as suggested in an example above, the importer reckoned that the forward rate at which he could buy the foreign currency fully discounted the fall he expected in his own currency, he would still have an incentive to make the purchase and eliminate the foreign currency risk. It is a widespread and prudent principle of traders and others involved in international payments to minimise the exchange risks they run; and it is certainly an important part of the advice given to their customers by responsible bankers to reiterate this principle.

There are other major pressures on the foreign exchange markets resulting from expectations about future changes in exchange rates, which are based on solid commercial prudence and not simply the taking of a speculative position. One such is the hedging of direct capital investments overseas. An example will make this point clear. In the 1950s and thereafter, substantial direct investment was made in Britain by US corporations which, for example, involved the building of factories and the acquisition of plant and equipment. These factories and the plant and equipment appeared, and appears, in the balance sheets of the US parent in US/dollar terms, though their value in the balance sheet of the UK subsidiary is obviously stated in sterling. If a major devaluation of sterling takes place against the US dollar, as in November 1967, this can throw up a substantial book loss in the accounts of the US parent – in other words, the dollar value of the UK assets as revalued at the new, lower, exchange rate for sterling will be substantially lower than its dollar value before the devaluation – and probably lower than the original book value in dollars in the parent company's books. The same point applies, of course, in the case of a downward float of the pound against the US dollar, as occurred in the latter part of 1982, rather than of a once-for-all devaluation. The US corporation can protect itself against this risk to some extent by hedging its sterling investment in the forward foreign exchange market: that is, it can sell sterling forward against dollars as far ahead as it can in the future to cover the period during which it expects the exchange rate for sterling to fall. When the date comes round for it to settle the forward sale of sterling, it can buy the required amount of sterling in the spot market against dollars: if its expectation was right, and the rate for sterling has duly fallen, it will realise a profit in dollars which it can use to offset, in part at least, the book loss on its sterling investment. Another technique which is often used to help achieve the same result is for the UK subsidiary to borrow as much sterling as it can in the domestic deposit market (or by adjusting its terms of credit with its suppliers and customers) and convert that sterling (together with any sterling cash at its disposal surplus to its normal day-to-day requirements) outright into US dollars and either lend these dollars back to its US parent or, alternatively, deposit them in the eurodollar market. Both these techniques for hedging the sterling investment of the US parent have the direct result of increasing the supply of sterling, spot or forward, on the foreign exchange market.

Yet another group of pressures on the foreign exchange markets resulting from expectations about future changes in exchange rates arise from those individuals and institutions who, for whatever reason, hold substantial wealth in the form of monetary assets which, with the exception of bullion, are inevitably dominated by one currency or another. One of the main preoccupations of these people and institutions is to preserve – and hopefully enhance – the real value of these monetary assets and in pursuit of this aim they will probably be active in the foreign exchange markets, guided by their expectations of future changes in exchange rates. Such operators include the managers of individual private fortunes, often based in Switzerland, who are sometimes seen as the *bêtes-noires* of the commentators, who attribute much of the instability of the foreign exchange markets to the operations of irresponsible 'speculators'. Much more important are such institutions as the managers of the pension funds of international organisations – such as the United Nations and its various subsidiary institutions – whose function it is to preserve the value of the assets under their management and to achieve a reasonable return on them, in terms of interest, dividends and capital gain.

Most important of all such institutions in recent years have become the managers of the external reserves of sovereign states, particularly those in the Middle East and elsewhere whose reserves have mushroomed since 1973 as the result of the dramatic income in the foreign currency proceeds of their oil sales, following the rises in the price of oil. Indeed, so substantial a business has the management of these funds become – and such management to be effective must inevitably invole *some* switching between monetary assets denominated in one currency and those denominated in another – that a considerable industry has been brought into being by London merchant banks and US investment banks, among others, providing advice, for a fee, on such management and such switching.

Pressures from all these sources focus on the foreign exchange and eurocurrency markets and have a direct effect on the spot rates, the forward rates and the rates of interest quoted for eurodeposits in each currency. And, as we have seen, these spot markets, forward markets and eurodeposit markets are all inextricably intertwined by a complex and continuous series of deals involving each of them and arbitrating between them. Given the size, complexity and implications of these markets for monetary and economic policy, not just in Britain but in all those countries whose currencies are traded on the markets, it is not surprising that the good order, mechanism and activities of the markets should be a prime preoccupation of the Bank of England.

The market and the Bank of England

The interest of the Bank of England in foreign exchange and eurocurrency deposit markets springs from its responsibilities in both prudential and monetary control.

The Bank's prudential control over the markets is exercised in two ways. First, it has established a formal mechanism, involving the British Bankers' Association, the Foreign Exchange Currency Deposit Brokers' Association and itself, for supervising the market as a whole and, particularly, the relationship between the banks and brokers, and as part of this mechanism it has formalised at the beginning of 1980 a system of recognition for brokers wishing to operate in the London market. This mechanism was described in some detail in the section above on the eurocurrency deposit markets. Secondly, as part of the supervisory functions in respect of all banks and licensed deposit-taking institutions, assigned to it by the Banking Act 1979, the Bank has established a system of monitoring each bank's position in individual foreign currencies and it has published guidelines for the assistance of banks in the internal control of their foreign exchange dealing operations. This system is discussed in Chapter 5.

The Bank's activities in the foreign exchange market in connection with monetary control – or, at least, monetary policy – is not dissimilar from its activities in the Discount Market. As in that market, the Bank has a presence in the foreign exchange market as a participant in its own right, in its capacity as banker to the British Government and other official institutions. Again, just as it uses the Discount Market as a mechanism through which to intervene to adjust the supply of money in the banking system and the rates of interest obtaining, so it uses the foreign exchange market as a mechanism through which to intervene to adjust the rate of exchange at which sterling is traded. The Bank itself has described these two roles in the following terms. First,

> the Bank deals actively in foreign exchange on behalf of its customers, chiefly government departments, and central banks and other monetary institutions abroad. The Bank is named as agent in many loan agreements in foreign currency contracted by the Government and by other borrowers in the public sector, and is responsible for seeing that the proceeds of the loans are properly received and that the loans are duly serviced and repaid. The Bank is also responsible for carrying out transactions with the International Monetary Fund and other international organisations. Discharging these various functions may also require transactions in the foreign exchange market.[30]

Secondly

> the Bank also manages, on behalf of the Government, the Exchange Equalisation Account (E.E.A.) in which the official foreign exchange reserves are vested. In this role it may also enter the market from time to time in order to influence the rate at which sterling is trading.

The technical operations of the EEA and particularly the implications of these operations for domestic monetary policy and their effects on the availability of bank credit in the domestic economy, are sufficiently important in the present context to warrant a brief description.

In simple terms, the EEA is the mechanism employed by the Bank of England in which to hold the gold, dollar and other external reserves of the country and through which to intervene in the market for sterling, spot and forward. An outright forward deal by the EEA does not, of course, involve the movement of funds, sterling or other currencies, into or out of the EEA until the deal comes up for settlement. But a spot deal by the EEA automatically involves an inflow of sterling and an outflow of, say, US dollars to and from the EEA in those cases where the transaction is a purchase of sterling against dollars, or it will involve an outflow of sterling and an inflow of US dollars where the transaction is a sale of sterling against US dollars. At its inception in 1932, the EEA was provided with £150m from government funds (specifically, the Consolidated Fund), and these sterling holdings were lent to the central government against Treasury bills. When the EEA purchased foreign currency from the market (or, rather, from the limited number of banks who then made up the foreign exchange market) it ran down its Treasury bills to provide the sterling to pay for such foreign currency; when it sold foreign currency it used the sterling it received to take up more Treasury bills. 'The crucial point was,' as the Bank has subsequently emphasised, 'that, in either case, the central government's need to borrow from other sources was altered, and this had to be allowed for in the authorities' issue of, or market dealings in, Treasury bills.'[31]

When the EEA was set up, and for many years afterwards, the fact that an inflow of sterling into the EEA resulted, not in an inflow of sterling cash into the domestic economy, but rather of Treasury bills, was regarded as a neat device to insulate the ability of the domestic banking system to lend money to the private sector from the inflow and outflow of sterling to and from the EEA. This view was based on the assumption that the ability of domestic banks to lend to the private sector was directly related to their cash holdings; but this assumption, as we shall see in Chapter 4, was quickly overtaken and rendered redundant by subsequent changes in the banking system.

This point was made with great clarity by the Bank in an article already quoted, published in December 1968.

> When the EEA was set up the view was widely held that the Account would help to moderate some of the effects of inflows and outflows of foreign funds. It would do this – in conjunction with official operations on Treasury bills – more or less automatically by transferring the impact of the flows from the cash reserves of the banks to their Treasury bill holdings.
>
> The mechanism through which external flows impinge on the economy is now recognised to be very complex. Also, since the 1930s markets in London have become much more varied and sophisticated: whereas foreign funds seeking a haven in London in 1932 might have naturally turned to British Government securities, there

> are now many other possibilities open to the foreign investor . . .
>
> Given the way in which the authorities respond to an inflow or outflow, the effect on bank liquidity depends to a large extent on the assets into which, or out of which, funds are moving and on who holds those assets . . . An inflow of exchange resulting from, say, a trade surplus will cause the authorities to issue or sell more Treasury bills (or other government debt) to pay for the foreign currency that they are offered – for the Government's own cash is minimal. The overall effect on the banks' cash reserves is likely to be small, but the effect on their liquid assets (and their deposits) will depend on who takes up the additional government debt and what form it takes. To the extent that there is no additional demand from outside the banks, the Government will have to borrow more from the banking system. If the additional government debt taken up by the banks is in the form of Treasury bills, the total of the banks' liquid assets and their liquidity ratio will be larger than before the inflow. Subject to official credit restraints, the banks could then expand their lending to the private sector or to local authorities. On the other hand, the Government may cover their need for additional finance in whole or in part from outside the banking system. If the whole requirement is met in this way, the rise in both deposits and the banks' liquid assets which the inflow would initially have caused will be offset, and accordingly no scope for the expansion of credit will be provided.
>
> In the case of an outflow of funds, the sequence of events outlined above is reversed; the Government's need for finance is reduced, and to the extent that their repayment of domestic borrowing leaves the banks with a lowered liquidity ratio, the ability of the latter to provide domestic credit will be reduced.[32]

The Bank sums up the article just quoted by concluding that

> the functioning of the E.E.A. mechanism and consequent changes in the Government's borrowing requirement help to moderate the impact of an inflow or outflow of foreign

> exchange on the banks' capacity to lend. The extent to which they do so, however, depends on how far the change in the borrowing requirement is met, directly or indirectly, from outside the banking system.[33]

As we saw in Chapter 1, control of the domestic money supply has in recent years become a central plank of the British Government's domestic economic policy. As we shall see in Chapter 6, key pieces in the mechanism by which control of the money supply is claimed to influence the real economy and, as important, by which the central authorities can themselves influence the money supply, are the rate of interest and the rate of exchange. The direct and indirect consequences of Government intervention in the financial markets to influence either of these variables are thus crucial to an understanding of the working of monetary policy and its effects on the banking system through which it operates. These consequences are discussed in Chapter 6, the long and rather technical descriptions in this chapter of the mechanisms by which the Bank of England intervenes in the foreign exchange market as well as the Discount Market, and particularly the connection between the two represented by the EEA, are provided as an essential background for this discussion.

Let us return now to the Bank's own description of how, as manager of the EEA, the Bank intervenes in the foreign exchange market in order to influence the exchange rate at which sterling is trading:

> In the past, [it wrote in 1980] such intervention has sometimes been very heavy, notably before June 1972 when for most of the time sterling was permitted to move within only a narrow range against the U.S. dollar, but more recently, especially in 1976, when sterling fell heavily, and again in 1977 when an attempt was made to hold down the rise in the rate. (That attempt was abandoned because official sales of sterling eventually added too much to the money supply.) Recently, intervention has been largely confined to smoothing out fluctuations in the rate – for example, selling sterling when it is in strong

> demand, with the aim of buying it back at a profit quite soon, perhaps even the same day. Such operations help to lessen short-term fluctuations without affecting the overall trend.[34]

It is particularly worth noting the reference above by the Bank to its experience in 1977, when its attempt to hold down the rise in the exchange rate for sterling by heavy sales of sterling in the spot foreign exchange market was abandoned 'because official sales of sterling eventually added too much to the money supply'. This is a practical example of the point made above in the paragraph explaining the working of the EEA: any sales of sterling – that is, purchases of other currencies – by the EEA will automatically increase the Government's borrowing requirement; and to the extent that the Government has to turn to the banking system to provide these borrowings an increase in the domestic money supply will be created.

As to the Bank's actual method of entering the market, it

> usually intervenes covertly through the agency of commercial banks (and may continue to deal in other markets outside normal trading hours in London). These banks will handle the Bank's business with the discretion and confidentiality which they would give any other customer. Occasionally, however, the Bank wants its presence to be more widely known, and in these circumstances it gives the broking system exchange rates at which it will deal in stated amounts in the same way as would any price-making bank. It would be a breach of market practice for the broker to publicize the Bank's presence, but he must divulge it to the counterparties with whom the Bank deals, and they may be numerous. In these circumstances, it will become widely known that the Bank is in the market.

We have seen already how closely the spot and forward markets for any major currency are intertwined in the foreign exchange market; and in view of this, there appears to be a case to be made for intervening in the forward, rather than the spot, market for a currency, in order to influence the rate at which it is traded in the spot market. Since forward deals do not have to be settled until they become spot deals, such a manoeuvre might be thought to be a neat way of avoiding the side effects on the domestic money supply of spot dealing by the EEA – described above.

As the Bank has pointed out, its 'operations are not, in fact, confined to the spot market. In the years before the 1967 devaluation, official purchases of forward sterling were very large'. For example, 'following the decision in 1964 not to devalue sterling, the Bank bought sterling forward': this was an attempt to ease the pressures on the spot rate – by letting the effect of the intervention percolate through from the forward market to the spot market, by way of the swap market, during what was hoped would be a temporary period until economic policies designed to ease the underlying pressures took effect. Unlike the situation in 1977, when the authorities were dissuaded from intervening in the spot market in an attempt to stem a *rise* in the rate for sterling because of the effects of such intervention on the domestic money supply, the situation in 1964 was one which the authorities were reluctant to intervene in the spot market in an attempt to stem a *fall* in the rate for sterling; for the stark and compelling reason that the EEA's reserves of foreign exchange against which to buy sterling were small and dwindling rapidly. In the event, however, as the Bank reports on this early experiment in intervention in the forward market:

> sterling was devalued; the E.E.A. incurred losses on its forward transactions, and in retrospect it seems likely that the volume of the Bank's forward purchases far exceeded the spot reserves saved, since the tactic of forward support, whereby others could sell to the Bank sterling which they did not own and did not need to borrow, encouraged heavier sales.

The simple lesson to be drawn from this exercise in forward intervention in the mid-1960s is not that such intervention is ineffective or necessarily exorbitantly expensive. It is rather that forward intervention, just like spot intervention, is a sensible exercise only if successful: that is, if it succeeds in protecting the currency in question from an upward or downward pressure which is set to threaten its existing rate. What the experience of forward intervention in defence of the sterling exchange rate in the mid-1960s does demonstrate is that the cost of failure to maintain the defended rate is probably higher to the extent that the intervention was in the forward market than it would have been if the intervention had been confined to the spot market. But where the intervention is aimed to alleviate a relatively short-term pressure – and the pressure indeed turns out to be short-term – then, for reasons apparent above, forward intervention almost certainly has a valuable and sensible role to play.

Finally, as well as intervening in the spot and forward markets, the Bank can intervene, and has intervened in the past, in the 'swap' market. As the Bank has recorded

> when sterling came under pressure in the 1970s, it became the occasional practice for the Bank to sell sterling forward (rather than buy it), though with an offsetting spot purchase (i.e. to do swaps). The effect of borrowing sterling in the exchange market in this manner was to widen the difference between spot and forward rates, increasing simultaneously the cost of closing out speculative positions by a spot purchase and the cost of continuing them. If others had responded to the greater difference between spot and forward rates by selling sterling spot and buying it back forward, the Bank's work would simply have been undone. However, exchange control prevented U.K. non-bank residents (and, outside rather tight limits, U.K. banks) from responding, and in general did not allow non-residents to borrow sterling in London. Non-residents could take advantage as their sterling deposits matured, and as fast as they could arrange to sell marketable sterling assets, but the tactic proved briefly useful on critical occasions.

The lesson to be learnt from this experience of intervention in the swap market is implicit in the Bank's own words. It is that such intervention can add a very valuable tactical weapon to the armoury of the intervening Bank, *provided* that the market for sterling swaps – or, effectively, eurosterling deposits – is reasonably well insulated from the domestic money markets by exchange control. Without such exchange controls, the technical weapon of intervening in the swap market is so blunted as to be rendered ineffective. Indeed, this is but one facet of a more general truth which has emerged from the descriptions on this section of Bank intervention in the foreign exchange markets: that the abolition of exchange control immeasurably reduces the options open to the Bank – or any national monetary authority – for exercising some influence, except in the shortest term, over the level of the rate of exchange for sterling, or any other national currency. This is not to say that exchange control is a good thing, still less that its abolition was a mistake. It *is* to say that without exchange control, the policy option of maintaining the rate for a currency at a reasonably stable level in the foreign exchange market becomes immeasurably more expensive than it would be in the context of some sort of exchange control (such as was endured in Britain until 1979). It is expensive in terms of unwanted effects on domestic interest rates and money supply and, in the context of maintaining the rate for a currency against severe downward pressures, in terms of the external reserves required (and possibly lost) in supporting the rate.

For the sake of completeness, two further types of official intervention in the foreign exchange markets should be mentioned. First, besides intervention in the swap market to squeeze speculators against sterling and make such speculation more expensive, in the manner described above, such intervention can, and is, used for domestic monetary purposes, in the benign circumstances where such action is beneficial both domestically and in the foreign exchange market. As the Bank has put it:

> it is sometimes profitable for the EEA to lend sterling on the swap, buying dollars spot and selling them back forward, to relieve a shortage of sterling in the money market (or in other circumstances to borrow sterling, to absorb a surplus). Such transactions are occasionally

undertaken where they help the joint objectives of smoothing fluctuations in the exchange rate and domestic money-market management.

Secondly, as a special instance of its willingness to undertake forward commitments, the EEA will, in some circumstances, 'help the banks to absorb long-term forward sales of dollars and deutschemarks arising from export sales guaranteed by the Export Credits Guarantee Department'.

NOTES

1. Bank of England's *Written Evidence* to Wilson Committee in connection with Stage Two of their Enquiry: 'Supervision of Financial Institutions: 3, Supervision of the Markets in Money, Foreign Exchange, Currency Deposits and Gold', para. 8. Reprinted in *Second Stage Evidence*, vol. 4 (HMSO, 1979) p. 104.
2. Tim Congdon, *Monetary Control in Britain* (Macmillan, 1982) p. x.
3. 'The Role of the Bank of England in the Money Market', *Bank of England Quarterly Bulletin* (March 1982) p. 86.
4. Ibid.
5. Ibid., p. 87.
6. *Monetary Control*, Cmnd 7858 (HMSO, March 1980).
7. 'Methods of Monetary Control' (a background note issued by the Bank of England on 24 November 1980), *Bank of England Quarterly Bulletin* (December 1980) p. 428.
8. A. L. Coleby, 'Bills of Exchange: current issues in an historical perspective', a paper presented to a Conference on the Bill of Exchange organised by the Institute of Bankers in London, 17 November 1982. Reprinted in *Bank of England Quarterly Bulletin* (December 1982) p. 515. Unattributed quotations in the next few pages are taken from this paper.
9. *Monetary Control*, Cmnd 7858 (HMSO, March 1980) p. 6, para. 3.1.
10. Bank of England's *Written Evidence* to the Wilson Committee in connection with Stage 2 of their enquiry: 'Supervision of the Markets in Money, Foreign Exchange, Currency Deposits and Gold', para. 9. Reprinted in *Second Stage Evidence*, vol. 4 (HMSO, 1979) p. 104.

11. 'The Role of the Bank of England in the Money Market', p. 90.
12. Ibid., p. 87.
13. Ibid., p. 88.
14. Written evidence by the Accepting Houses Committee to the Wilson Committee, *Evidence on the Financing of Industry and Trade*, vol. 5 (HMSO, March 1978) p. 8, para. 12.
15. *Report of the Committee on the Working of the Monetary System*, Cmnd 827 (HMSO, 1959) p. 66, para. 186.
16. 'Monetary Control: Next Steps', reprinted in *Bank of England Quarterly Bulletin* (March 1981) p. 39, paras 6, 7.
17. 'Monetary Control – Provisions', republished in *Bank of England Quarterly Bulletin* (September 1981) p. 348, paras 9, 10.
18. 'Monetary Control: Next Steps', p. 39, para. 8.
19. 'Monetary Control – Provisions', p. 348, paras 11, 12. Eligible liabilities were broadly defined as the total liabilities of a bank, less funds lent by a bank to other banks and less those funds lent to the LDMA and others under the new arrangements set out above.
20. *Bank of England Quarterly Bulletin* (March 1982) p. 88. The figures for purchases of bills include purchases for later resale to the market. The figures for commercial bills are almost exclusively eligible bank bills. In publishing the figures in this form, the Bank emphasises that 'the figures are gross and merely illustrate turnover in the Bank's operations (Issue and Banking Departments). They are not an accurate guide to the relative importance of different operations to balancing the market, because the maturity terms of the operations are not identified. For example, if £1 million is lent to a discount house overnight on each of two consecutive days, a total of £2 million is recorded in the table, whereas only £1 million is recorded if the initial loan is for two days. Nevertheless, the table illustrates well the increased turnover in commercial bills in the Bank's operations in the last two years, and the relative decline in turnover of Treasury bills.'
21. Coleby, 'Bills of Exchange', p. 517.
22. Bank of England's *Written Evidence* to the Wilson Committee in connection with Stage 2 of their Enquiry: 'Supervision of the Markets in Money, Foreign Exchange and Gold', para. 15. Reprinted in *Second Stage Evidence*, vol. 4 (HMSO, 1979) p. 106.

23. Ibid., pp. 105–6, paras 13–14.
24. 'The Foreign Exchange Market in London', *Bank of England Quarterly Bulletin* (December 1980) p. 439.
25. Ibid., pp. 437–8.
26. Ibid., p. 438.
27. Ibid., p. 438.
28. Ibid., p. 439.
29. *Economic Trends* (Central Statistical Office, February 1983) p. 48.
30. 'The Foreign Exchange Market in London', p. 442.
31. 'The Exchange Equalisation Account: its origins and development', *Bank of England Quarterly Bulletin* (December 1968) p. 379. This article gives a detailed account of the history and technical operations of the EEA; and these operations remain in 1983 broadly as described in the article.
32. Ibid., p. 386.
33. Ibid., p. 387.
34. This quotation, together with other unattributed quotations in the rest of this section, is taken from the Bank's paper, 'The Foreign Exchange Market in London', *Bank of England Quarterly Bulletin* (December 1980).

4 The Risks of Banking

The principal function of banks, as we saw in Chapter 2, is the collection of deposits from those with cash resources surplus to their immediate requirements and the on-lending of these cash resources, in one form or another, to those with an immediate need for them. In fulfilling this function, banks inevitably undertake certain risks; it is the purpose of this chapter to describe and explain these risks. The identification of risks and their measurement are, of course, primarily the responsibility of the managers of banks. But, as we saw in Chapter 1, there have been increasing pressures throughout the 1970s, and early 1980s for national authorities to take a keen interest in the risks undertaken by banks and in their prudential supervision.

CREDIT RISKS

Commercial risks

The first risk confronted by a banker is the credit risk of the borrower: that is, that the borrower will be unable to repay the loan when due, together with the interest due throughout the loan's life. There is, of course, no neat scientific formula for assessing this risk, though some of the more naïve bankers sometimes tend to attribute to their sophisticated, computerised analyses of risk a certainty of prediction which they scarcely warrant, misleading themselves with the false argument that the greater the complexity of the analysis, the greater the chance of its accuracy. On the other hand, some of the modern risks undertaken by bankers *are* extremely complex, reflecting the complexity of the enterprises of some of their customers; and in these circumstances, elaborate techniques of analysis and the ability provided by modern computers to handle and interrelate an enormous number of variables provide invaluable tools with which the banker can gauge the size of the risk he is running. In all the risks he runs, listed in this chapter, the banker must undertake two separate mental processes: the identification of the precise risks he is running, and their measurement. It is probably not too old-fashioned to suggest that the first of these processes depends heavily on experience – either direct, or learnt from others – and common sense; the second, the measurement of risks, can be greatly assisted by technical knowledge and analysis.

One of the simplest forms of lending undertaken by bankers is lending which is fully secured. Some bankers lending on this basis pay little regard to anything other than the basic value of the security taken and its relationship to the amount of the loan given. A homely example of this sort of lender is the pawnbroker; an example on a larger scale is a bank which lends money to finance property development, purely on the value of the property concerned. This sort of banking appears on the surface to require no great expertise. The point was made to the present writer with remarkable naïvety by a young banker in the great property boom of the early 1970s. The role of the banker is easy, he declared: all you need do is get a reputable firm of surveyors (with a prudent level of insurance for professional indemnity) to value the property to be taken as security, agree to lend a proportion of that value to the developer (say, two-thirds – but this proportion was driven up close to 100 per cent in the brisk competition between British banks of all types and sizes to finance the property boom of the early 1970s) and employ a competent firm of lawyers to tie up the deal in a manner which would stand up in a court of law. If the borrower is unable to repay the debt when due, and the security is insufficient to cover it together with the interest accrued, he went on, this can be the result of only three things: either the property is not worth the value put on it by the valuer, in which case you sue the valuer; or the borrower has failed to honour his obligations under the loan agreement, in which case you sue the borrower; or the loan agreement itself is defective, in which case you sue the lawyer who drew up the agreement.

The first part of this young banker's naïvety related to his heavy reliance on the law. It would be plainly incompetent of a banker lending in the manner described not to have a properly drawn-up agreement and not to have a formal valuation with the authority of a competent firm of professional valuers. Indeed to the regret of some of the older generation of British bankers, legal agreements relating to loans have in recent years become much more formal – and lengthy – than they were in the past: a development they see as having originated in the United States, where the banking climate, and the commercial climate generally, is a great deal more litigious than is the case in Britain. But most bankers regard the main purpose of a formal loan agreement as being to set out for easy reference by both parties the terms of the original agreement and to provide, in the context of possible litigation, a safety net to preserve the interests of the lender if the worse came to the worst, rather than a formal legal structure to bear the full weight of the banker's decision to lend and its consequences. Indeed, many old-fashioned bankers would regard the fact that a loan of theirs had led to litigation as a demonstration of their own incompetence or inadequacy: in the example of the property loan above, incompetence either in assessing the honesty of the borrower or in the banker's *own* assessment of value of the property and of future changes in that value, or in the drafting or approving of the documentation. And, of course, our young banker left totally out of account the huge costs of litigation in commercial cases, which can be substantial even in those cases where a court finds in favour of the bank – as the young man's bank did, in fact, learn to its considerable cost.

The point to be made is that even the most secure sort of secured lending *does* require considerable judgement on the part of the banker: judgement as to the character and honesty of the borrower and judgement as to the future value of the assets taken as security. Professional valuers can give an accurate and precise figure for the value of an asset at the time the valuation is made: that, indeed, is their job and their particular expertise. When it comes to future movements in that value, the judgement and expertise is of a totally different order; and it is not obviously or necessarily the case that the professional valuer's judgement is better than the banker's. Certainly, no competent professional valuer would dream of putting himself in a position of being liable if his judgement on future price movements turned out to be wrong.

Another type of fully secured lending which has reached very substantial proportions in recent years is bank lending to oil companies against the security of oil or gas still in the ground. Sometimes these loans take the form of loans made to an oil company with the oil taken as security for the loan: in these cases the lending bank looks in the first instance to the oil company for the payment of interest and repayment of the principal of the loan and may not be particularly interested as to whether the funds to make the payments have been generated from the oil in the ground or from other sources. In other cases, such loans are structured as 'non-recourse' loans: in these circumstances the lending bank looks purely to the sale of the oil it has taken as security for the funds necessary for the payment of interest and the repayment of the principal of the loan; and if the funds from this source are inadequate to satisfy these commitments, the bank has no recourse to the borrowing company itself for the repayment of the loan. These second, non-recourse, loans can be very valuable to the borrowing company in that they do not pre-empt its capability to borrow for other purposes.

The principles involved in making an assessment of the credit risk entailed in making these loans against the security of oil in the ground are essentially the same as making any other loan, fully secured against assets. First, the lender must be satisfied with the honesty and integrity of the borrower; secondly, he must be satisfied with the present valuation of the asset taken as security; and thirdly, he must be satisfied that the present value is not likely to be reduced significantly over the life of the loan.

Valuing oil in the ground is a much more complicated

proposition than valuing a piece of real estate. Besides estimating the selling price of the oil or gas, which is the simplest part of the calculation, it involves assessing how much oil exists in the underground reservoir concerned, how much of that oil can be extracted using existing technology, the costs of that extraction and any unusual technical features which might add unusually to that cost and the rate of that extraction, since 100 tons of oil extracted and sold today is worth a great deal more than 100 tons of oil extracted over a period of, say, ten years and sold as extracted (assuming no change in the price of oil). And an assessment of this last rate of extraction involves an assessment of two totally separate groups of factors: technical and political. The technical factors include such items as the availability of, and access to, pipelines which will carry the oil or gas from the oilfield to the market, and the capacity of extraction facilities which are expected to be applied to the field in question. An example of an important political factor is the environmental question of how much the relevant national authorities will allow the process of extraction to upset the environmental amenities of the surrounding countryside: a classic case of this was the uncertainty surrounding the price to be put on the onshore reserves of oil in the British field of Wytch Farm, when the British Gas Corporation invited, at the Government's insistence, outside bids for its 50 per cent share in the field at the end of 1982: the price was much influenced by the assumptions that were made as to the rate of extraction which would be permitted by the appropriate authorities on purely environmental grounds. Another important political factor is the possibility of a depletion policy being imposed by a national government in an attempt to control the speed at which the national asset represented by the oil reserves is depleted.

Valuing the oil in the ground is only a part of the judgement that must be made in taking such oil as security for a loan. Another is an assessment of the future price of that oil over the period of the loan. We have already noted, in Chapter 1, the dramatic increases in the price of oil in the 1970s; at the time of writing, in early 1983, there is great uncertainty as to whether these high prices will be maintained, at least in real terms, into the later 1980s – in the light of the accelerated production in new producing areas (such as the United Kingdom's North Sea fields), the impressive development of fuel-saving techniques in the main oil-consuming countries (such as the United States, Japan, Britain and continental Europe) as a direct consequence of the hike in prices and the slowdown in consumption as a consequence of the world recession. This uncertainty is a good example of how lending which is fully secured at its inception is by no means risk free.

Enough has been said about these two particular types of secured lending – against the security of real estate and oil in the ground – to highlight the risks involved in such lending. And in each case, a responsible bank attempting to assess these risks requires a considerable specialist and technical expertise on which to base such an assessment. Some of this expertise can sensibly be bought from outside experts: that of the professional valuer of real estate, for example, or of the professional firms which have grown up specialising in evaluating the production potential of oilfields. But ultimately a lending banker who undertakes these risks without fully understanding and assessing the risks he is taking, is by that very action escalating the risks in a quite unnecessary and, some would say, irresponsible way.

Another, and in a sense simpler, type of secured lending is lending by mortgages to individual borrowers the funds they require to buy their residential homes. In Britain and the United States, institutions have grown up to specialise in this type of lending: the building societies and the savings and loans associations, respectively. In most countries, including the United States and, increasingly, Britain, this type of lending is undertaken by the main deposit banks as well: that is, in a British context, the clearing banks. In this case, the lending bank will almost always obtain a professional valuation from a surveyor, both to value the property and to comment on the soundness of its structure and any other relevant features; but it will also have regard to the circumstances of the borrower and the relationship between his income and resources on the one hand and his ability to pay interest and repay capital on the other.

At the other end of the scale, if a bank is entirely satisfied about the ability of a borrower to repay, it may well lend totally unsecured. Thus, for example, no British bank would question the ability or willingness of the British Government to honour its obligations; and hence the wide acceptance of Treasury bills and Government bonds – both representing totally unsecured loans to the Government by banks as prime assets. Again, at least for relatively short-term loans, banks are content to lend to a wide variety of fellow banks, in their own and other countries, on a totally unsecured basis: for example, the sterling and eurocurrency deposits exchanged in the London interbank markets, are all totally unsecured. True, each individual bank will set individual limits up to which it will lend to each other bank in the interbank market; but within those limits, the deposits are always unsecured. In setting these limits, the lending banks will have regard in particular to the size of the borrowing bank, the country of its residence, any special characteristics of its lending business, its reputation in the market place and, to the extent that such an assessment is possible from material available, the extent to which it is 'geared' in the manner described later in this chapter.

But besides national governments and fellow banks, there are many other borrowers to which banks are prepared to lend unsecured, particularly the larger industrial and commercial corporations. In the case of these latter, it is common for the lending bank to write into the loan agreement conditions prohibiting the borrower from giving security to any *other* lending bank and also putting a limit on the total borrowings which the corporation can make – such as fixing a maximum proportion of borrowings to the funds attributable to the shareholders or, with rather more detail, a maximum proportion of current liabilities to current assets. Both the precise definitions of these proportions, or ratios, and the maximum numbers that are written into them vary, depending on the nature, size and financial shape of the borrower's business.

In making these loans to corporations – or any other borrowers – on an unsecured basis, a bank is basically taking the same sort of credit risk as it is in the case of lending on a fully secured basis: at the crudest level, that risk is that the borrower will be unable to repay the loan on the due date or to service it with the specified payments of interest. In the case of secured lending the lending banker may not look much further than the asset he has taken as security to yield sufficient funds to repay the loan and pay the interest on it. But in the case of an unsecured loan, a banker will need to look at the earning capability of the borrower in some detail, because it is basically on those earnings that depends the borrower's ability to repay. But by putting a limit on the ratio which relates a corporation's borrowing to the net value of its own assets (its shareholders' funds), the lending bank is providing some sort of safety net for itself and its fellow lenders, to the extent of increasing the possibility (though by no means ensuring) that in the event of a catastrophe and the liquidation of the corporation, a sale of the assets in its hands would go some way to repaying its debts.

Besides loans on a totally secured or totally unsecured basis, much of the lending undertaken by banks is done on a partly secured basis. A corporation seeking a loan, e.g. for working capital purposes, may have impressed its bankers with the soundness of its business and its future prospects; but for a variety of reasons – such as its size, the experience of its management, its dependence on a single product – the banker may not feel sufficiently confident in the future earning ability of the corporation to rely totally on future earnings as the source from which his loan will be repaid. In these circumstances, the banker may well, as it were, 'top up' the sources available for repaying the loan by taking as security a fixed charge over specific, identifiable assets in the hands of the corporation, such as its factory premises or the land on which it operates. In such cases, the banker will still look primarily to the future earnings of the borrower as the source of his repayment; and he will monitor those future earnings as closely as if they were his *only* source of repayment. But the security he has taken will provide him with that additional comfort, without which he would have felt it imprudent to make the loan in the first place. To put this feeling of comfort in perspective, it should be recorded that many banks which have started off lending to a corporation on a partly secured basis in this way have subsequently felt sufficiently confident after a period of time to release the security and continue the loan on a totally unsecured basis. Such a gesture would demonstrate that circumstances had changed sufficiently to increase the banker's confidence in the ability of the borrower to repay without recourse to the sale of the assets in question; such changes might include, for example, a longer track-record of successful and profitable operations by the corporation or the growth of the shareholders' equity, through retained earnings, to more acceptable levels. Indeed, it is often the case that a banker will lend on a partly secured basis in the first instance, in the clear expectation that the borrower will 'graduate' to the status to justify the release of the security within a foreseeable period of time.

Another situation where a banker may make a loan on a partly secured basis is where the borrower is seeking a loan to finance a particular asset such as, for example, a complex and expensive piece of equipment or a new factory. In such a situation the banker will be looking to the general stream of future earnings of the borrower, augmented by the fruits of the proposed investment, as the main source of his repayment; but he may still take the asset he is financing as specific security to give him additional comfort and, very often, as a discipline to ensure that the new loan is used for the acquisition of the asset in question and not soaked up in other uses. A consequence of this practice is that many large corporations may have given specific parcels of security to different banks in respect of different loans.

Assessing the future earning power of an industrial or commercial corporation is not an exact science. It depends, for example, on the ability of the management in its chosen field, which can be measured in part by its profit record in previous years, though this measure may prove critically misleading in a situation where a corporation is borrowing funds to finance diversification into new fields of activity. It depends on an assessment of the future market for the goods or services produced by the corporation, and experienced bankers will confirm that a corporation's management are not necessarily the best judges of that future market for any but the shortest period ahead. It depends, in the case of corporations with a high level of borrowings where the rate of interest is not fixed, on the future course of interest rates in the country of the borrower. It depends on future movements, many of which may be unpredictable for all but the shortest periods, in the cost of raw materials, local taxes, energy requirements and labour with the particular skills required. And, it should be added, to the extent that the raw materials are imported or the goods or services produced are exported, it depends heavily on the future of the exchange rate for its country's currency.

In spite of all these complications, many bankers feel more comfortable with unsecured, or partly secured, lending to such industrial and commercial organisations than they do with fully secured lending of the type described earlier; this is because they believe that they have some control over the earning power of the borrowers and thus over the fate of their loans. In the case of the secured loan – and particularly where there is no recourse to the borrower, as in the case of some loans secured on oil in the ground, or where the borrower has precious few other assets to which to have recourse, as in the case of some loans secured on property – the banker is relatively powerless, assuming the borrower fulfils all his obligations, to take any action he might feel necessary to preserve his loan. It is rather as if he has entered a casino, taken great trouble and the best advice on placing his chips on the table and then, once the croupier has shouted '*rien ne va plus*', is powerless to intervene until the wheel stops turning. The competent unsecured or partly secured lender, on the other hand, will have required regular management information on the course of the borrower's financial progress – on profits, turnover, profit margins, the return on capital invested, the levels of stocks, cash and other current assets, both as interesting figures in themselves and in relation to current liabilities. These figures, taken together, will give him a very clear picture of where the earning power of the borrower is going; and if he has designed the control clauses in his loan agreement sensibly – setting limits on the ratio of borrowings to shareholders' funds, current assets to current liabilities, the proportion of profits absorbed by interest charges and so on – these will give him the right to discuss the situation with the borrower's management and, if necessary, intervene in its decisions, long before his lending is put at serious risk.

There are five points to be made about these brief comments on lending, not fully secured, to commercial and industrial corporations. First, the lending banker's job is only partly done when he has analysed the future earning power of the borrower – and vetted its cash flow forecast for the next period of time. As important, if not more so, is the establishment of a proper system of monitoring the effectiveness of that earning power and the accuracy of that cash flow forecast as time proceeds. This should include the incorporation in the monitoring system of alarm bells to give early warning of forecasts failing to be met and plans going off the rails. It should also include, as we have seen, trigger arrangements, agreed between borrower and lender such that when forecasts and targets have been missed by a sufficiently wide margin, and when plans have gone sufficiently off the rails, the lender will have the right to intervene and, if necessary, force the borrower to adjust its plans. (The final sanction – the whip placed in the lender's hand by such a trigger – is, of course, that it empowers the lender to call the loan.)

The second point follows from the first: it is that where a lending banker is depending more on the future earning capacity of the borrower than on the security of a physical asset and is thus keeping in relatively close touch with the borrower through reporting and monitoring arrangements made between them, the criteria by which the bank assesses the borrower's ability to repay the loan will quickly become apparent to the borrower. Apart from the general discussions which will inevitably take place between them, the control clauses written into the formal agreement by the banker – limiting, for example, total borrowings in relation to the total shareholders' funds – will give the borrower a clear idea of what statistics the banker is watching and at what point the banker is likely to become unenthusiastic about renewing the loan. And because the market for making loans has been in the recent past, and will probably continue for some time to come to be, a highly competitive one – that is, a 'borrower's market' – the borrowers will soon make themselves aware of what criteria other lending banks are using and what conditions they would be likely to write into the formal agreements. In this way, a fairly standard set of criteria and conditions emerges through the market, to the obvious convenience of both borrowers and lenders. But it is important to note that this standard set of criteria and conditions is infinitely adjustable via innovations or changes of view by one or more bankers in the game; and it is a basic premise of this book that it is in the interests of the bankers, the borrowers and the community at large that this flexibility should continue. It would be a sad day for the banking community and, indeed, for the economic community of a country as a whole, if banks were inhibited from experimenting with new criteria for lending either by their own managements, or by the prudential authorities, or by the monetary authorities and those responsible for economic policy as a whole.

The third point to be made about such lending is one that was touched on in Chapter 1; that is, that in an environment of tight money discipline, such as has been endured from 1980 to the time of writing in 1983, an ever-widening group of corporations has been forced to adjust its future plans, modify its future ambitions, cancel or reduce planned developments and close down existing plant and capacity. In many instances, all this has been the deliberate result of the Government's economic policy; but it appears to many corporate borrowers to be rather the result of the hard-nosed meanness of their bankers. Many of these cut-backs, for example, have been forced on corporations by their bankers as a condition for continuing a loan; and they have been decided by the bankers in their assessment of the continued viability of the corporation concerned. In other words, a change in a bank's conditions is almost always the result of a change in the borrower's ability to meet its forecasts of profits and cash flow, or of a change in those forecasts; and in recent times, a great many of such changes have been the direct consequence of high real interest rates or a high exchange rate for sterling against other currencies, or simply a slackness on demand for the corporation's products. The toughness of the banker's conditions in these circumstances is not a toughening of his attitude to the borrower in the sense that he is not prepared to undertake the same degree of risk in relation to that customer as he was in easier times; it is rather that the economic environment in which the customer operates has deteriorated to the extent that it has materially increased that degree of risk and, in increasing the stringency of his conditions, the banker is simply trying to reduce his risk to its previous, acceptable, proportions. Whilst many bankers must applaud the Government's policies and the salutary financial disciplines they have imposed on British economic – particularly industrial – activity, they must all be saddened, if not a little aggrieved, at the clear case of mistaken identity in the public mind which attributes to them, the bankers, rather than the Government, the main burden of responsibility for the misery and suffering which the disciplines impose.

This last point applies in the British experience of the early 1980s, when the Thatcher Government imposed its monetary discipline through the 'impersonal' market forces of the level of interest rates, the exchange rate for sterling and effective demand within the economy. It applies with equal strength in those situations, such as the period of the 'corset' on domestic lending by British banks in the late 1970s, where the monetary discipline is applied by national authorities in the much cruder form of actual numerical limits, however devised, on the lending of individual banks. In this case, a tightening of the limits on bank lending inevitably means that a more stringent test will be applied by banks to the credit-worthiness of their customers: after the tightening, a bank will be able to satisfy the borrowing requirement of fewer customers than before the tightening and, commercially, the only sensible way of picking out the customers who are to be disappointed is to pick those which represent the biggest credit risk to the lending bank. In this situation the banker may appear to his disappointed customer to be being even more hard-nosed, even unreasonable, than in the situation where the monetary discipline is imposed through more impersonal market forces: in this latter case, the banker can at least demonstrate that the outlook for his customer has deteriorated (admittedly through no fault of his own), whereas in a situation of specific credit restriction he has to explain to his customer that, notwithstanding the fact that his assessment of the customer's credit-worthiness has not changed, he must still call back a loan which he had willingly provided previously. In this case, again, the customer will often attribute the 'blame' for this change of heart to the lending banker, whereas it really resides with the policy of the government.

The fourth point to be made about unsecured lending to commercial and industrial corporations relates to the sources of funds used for repayment. In unsecured, as well as secured, lending the ultimate risk undertaken by the banker is that the borrower will be unable to repay. As we have seen, the ability of an unsecured borrower to repay will depend heavily on its future earning power – unlike the secured borrower where that ability will depend heavily on the future value of the asset taken as security. It can also, of course, depend on the borrower's ability to raise money from alternative sources. A banker which lends to a major industrial or commercial borrower may well do so on a continuing basis, with annual reviews being written into the agreement for the sake of tidiness and good order: the 'overdraft' basis of much of the lending of British clearing banks falls into this category. Alternatively, such lending may be made on the basis of a fixed period – say, five or seven years – after which the agreement clearly states that the loan must be repaid. In relatively few instances will the banker making an unsecured loan for a fixed period of time have based his assessment of the borrower's ability to repay on an elaborate cash flow forecast for the period – which might, for example, relate the capital repayments and interest payments to the earnings generated by the activity financed by the loan. In most instances, the risk assessment of such loans will be based on an estimate of the borrower's capacity to repay *or renew* the borrowing at the end of the period in question. Generally speaking, such an estimate will depend on whether the borrower's financial condition is likely to improve or deteriorate over the life of the loan: assuming that the bankers in general do not change their measures of a borrower's financial condition and thus their assessment of the credit risks involved, during the life of the loan in question, the judgement as to whether a borrower will be able to renew a loan in, say, five years' time, will depend on exactly the same criteria as a judgement as to whether the borrower will be able to repay the loan on the same date.

The fifth point about loans to industrial and commercial corporations which are unsecured or only partly secured is rather a different one. For reasons described above, British corporations find themselves in the situation of having given specific parcels of security to different banks in respect of different loans. Such situations are perfectly sensible in most cases in normal times; but they can become extremely untidy and, indeed, unworkable if the situation of the corporation deteriorates to such an extent as to put its survival at serious risk, at least in the eyes of its bankers. For, at this point, all its separate bankers will start asking for more specific security in support of their loans; and if any one of them feels that it has got less than its fair share of the security available, it may well threaten to call for repayment of its loan. And, almost by definition, the more this situation is likely to arise, the less the borrower is likely to be in a position to repay that particular – or any other – loan. In this situation, the only way out may well be for all the borrower's bankers to get together and put all their lendings on a common basis, specifically in relation to the security the borrower has to offer. It is this type of situation which is most often the background to the creation of industrial Lifeboats, which will be discussed in detail in Chapter 6.

Sovereign risks

One of the fastest-growing types of lending undertaken by banks operating in the international markets in the 1970s and early 1980s has been lending to 'sovereign risks': that is, lending to, or effectively under the guarantee of, the government of an overseas country in such a way that the credit risk of the loan is effectively the risk that that government cannot or will not repay the loan on the due date. As we saw in Chapter 1, the volume of such loans was hugely expanded in the years following the sharp increases in the price of oil in 1973 and again in 1979–80, as an integral part of the process of recycling the increased oil earnings of the major oil-producing states. These loans have been made partly to those countries whose balance of payments have been hit most hard by the oil price increases and for whom the need for external borrowings has been most urgent: obvious examples include Brazil, Argentina and Poland. They have also been made to less developed producers of oil which, dazzled by the sudden accretion to their wealth and in the full expectation that that accretion would be continuing, embarked on elaborate internal development plans the cost of which so exceeded their increased immediate incomes as to require them to borrow externally: obvious examples of these recipients of loans include Nigeria, Venezuela and Mexico.

Not that lending to sovereign risks has been a particularly new phenomenon. In the second half of the nineteenth century and the first half of the twentieth, with pauses caused by the two world wars, the merchant banks of the City of London made a considerable business out of arranging loans for sovereign borrowers, though in these cases the bulk of the funds was provided by finding purchasers of bonds rather than by loans from banks. Borrowers in this market included governments and public bodies in Europe, the United States, Central and South America, the Middle East, Japan and other countries of the Far East, South Africa, Australia and New Zealand.

The new wave of sovereign lending which took off in the 1970s was predominantly unsecured and predominantly in the form of bank loans, though a proportion was, and is, provided by the issue of eurobonds on behalf of the borrowers. One of its characteristics has been that it has involved a very wide group of banks – wider than one might normally expect to become involved in international lending on this scale. The explanation of this is simple. The funds to finance these sovereign loans were provided in the first instance by the new oil-rich states in the Middle East and elsewhere: as we have seen, these lenders kept a high proportion of their new riches in the form of short-term deposits which they deposited with the major commercial banks operating in the international field. These banks, in turn, on-lent some of these deposits to the sovereign borrowers; but for reasons of common prudence, to which we shall return, a considerable proportion was placed on deposit in the London eurocurrency deposit market. And, by the mechanism described in Chapter 3, this immediately disseminated the funds into the hands of a very wide group of banks. Indeed, the 'petro-funds' became available through the London eurocurrency markets to all those many banks in Britain, the United States, Japan, Germany and elsewhere in the world who maintain branches and subsidiaries in London or otherwise enjoy access to these markets.

Alongside this diffusion of the petro-funds from the oil-rich countries into the international banking system, there has grown up an equally effective mechanism, on the other side of the market, for the attraction of these funds to the new sovereign borrowers. Many banks in London and other financial centres have developed an expertise in putting together syndicates of other banks to provide loans to sovereign borrowers: in essence, this involves agreeing the amount, the period and the rate of interest with the borrower and then disseminating – by telephone, telex and letter – these terms to potential lenders, together with some basic financial information on the borrower. It should be added that, for reasons discussed later, the rate of interest is nearly always expressed on the basis of a margin over the cost of eurodollars or other eurocurrency deposits for stated periods – usually three or six months – in the London eurodollar market rather than as a fixed rate for the whole life of the loan: this margin is negotiated separately for each loan and reflects the banking community's general assessment of the credit-worthiness of the borrower, together with the competing pressures of supply and demand in the market for sovereign loans.

In making these loans to sovereign borrowers, just as in making loans to any other borrower, the lending bank must assess the credit risk involved. And, as in the case of all other lending, the ultimate credit risk can be defined in terms of the prospective ability of the borrower to repay the loan on maturity, or alternatively to refinance it with the same or other lenders. Until very recently, many bankers distinguished between sovereign risks and other credit risks with the observation that 'sovereign risks do not go bust'. In the early 1980s this distinction has been blurred from both sides. On the one hand, the possibility of some sovereign borrowers, such as Argentina and Mexico, going bust has seemed much more real than it did even two or three years earlier, if by 'going bust' is meant to default irrecoverably on their loans. On the other hand, such has been the anxiety of national governments to avoid the social and political consequences of major industrial and commercial corporations going bust that they have resorted to a variety of means: from the cajoling of banks to be less prudent in extending their exposure than their commercial judgement would otherwise dictate to the injection of state funds to fill a deficit. Examples of the first are the rescue operations which were mounted for Massey Ferguson and Dome Petroleum in Canada in 1981 and 1982 or of AEG, the major electrical engineering group, in Germany in 1982; examples of the latter are the subsidies and financial aid meted out to steel producers and motor car manufacturers in Britain and many other countries as well. In short, the assumption that sovereign credit risks are different from commercial credit risks in kind, rather than in degree, is now generally recognised to have less basis in fact than it had in the past; and credit analysis of both sorts of risk is now accepted to have much in common.

In 1981 and early 1982, the Basle Committee of Bank Supervisors reviewed the methods by which banks, under the supervision of its members, managed country risk in their international lending business – a review which involved a detailed look at the techniques used by the banks for assessing the credit risk of sovereign borrowers. As a result of this review, the Committee 'considered it might be helpful to banks to set out some general considerations relating to country risk assessment'; and it did this in a paper issued in March 1982 entitled 'Management of banks' international lending: country risk analysis and country exposure measurement and control'. It should be recorded that in issuing this paper, the Committee was at pains to point out that it was not its intention 'to lay down a preferred method of setting about what is generally acknowledged to be a complex exercise. The Committee recognises that some banks have very sophisticated systems and that all banks need to tailor their country risk management systems to meet their individual circumstances and exposure.'[1]

The Basle paper noted the general awareness amongst banks of the existence of country risk and the need for a system of assessing that risk as part of the process of managing their international lending portfolio; and it defined 'country risk' as referring to 'the possibility that sovereign borrowers of a particular country may be unable or unwilling, and other borrowers unable, to fulfil their foreign obligations for reasons beyond the usual risks arising in relation to all lending'. It noted further that

> a wide variety of factors may prevent borrowers of a given country from fulfilling their foreign obligations, which makes the country risk a difficult concept to define with precision. The risks range from the consequences of official actions or important socio-political changes in the borrowing country to largely unpredictable events such as natural disasters or external shocks arising from global phenomena like world depression or the consequences of an oil price rise. A major complication is that the same events will affect borrowers in some countries more than in others and also have varying effects on different borrowers in the same country. Their impact will, moreover, tend to vary over time. Country risk assessment cannot therefore be an exact science, but an art in which a significant degree of unpredictability must be acknowledged . . . For most major banks the starting point is statistical information available from both national and international sources.

This point was subsequently underlined by Mr Peter Cooke, the Chairman of the Basle Committee and Head of Banking Supervision at the Bank of England:

> If the terms of lending are to be got right the analysis and the information on which that analysis is based needs to be as comprehensive and up-to-date as possible . . . Bankers worth their salt are not likely to lend to commercial concerns without looking at the resources, the cash flow and the markets of those businesses. So it must be for lending to countries.[2]

The Basle paper went on:

> For the more industrialised banks may find domestic statistics more useful since they are often the most up-to-date. For developing countries, data produced by international organisations such as the I.M.F./I.B.R.D. the O.E.C.D. and the B.I.S. may be more frequently resorted to. The analyst will of course wish to look at a wide range of macro-economic numbers and at the relationships between them that he believes are significant. Many banks operate sophisticated mechanical scoring systems, with certain risks being weighted numerically to produce country scores or ratings. Such systems can be useful, but should not be relied on too much since economic ratios based on past performance have quite limited predictive ability over the wide range of possible country risks.

Of the statistics required, perhaps the most important, as the paper pointed out, are those on a country's external indebtedness:

> Since the key question is whether there will be impediments to the repayment of external indebtedness, the size, nature and maturity pattern of a country's current external indebtedness are particularly significant. Unfortunately, these data can be most difficult to establish, because of some countries' reluctance to undertake the collection of all necessary data or to reveal the true extent of their indebtedness.[3] The analyst will nonetheless wish to project a path for countries' external debt and to forecast their ability to service and repay, which means looking at the outlook for official reserves and other balance-of-payments items, terms of trade, exchange rates, inflation, the country's record in servicing and repaying external debt and other relevant factors.

Commercial bankers would fully endorse the Basle paper's emphasis on the need to improve statistical information flows, particularly those related to external indebtedness; and they welcomed Mr Cooke's admission that 'the supervisors recognise that they have at least some responsibility for ensuring that official sources make their full contribution to the information flows'.[4] For their part, the bankers took a major initiative in January 1983 with the establishment of an Institute of International Finance, based in Washington, DC, to facilitate the exchange of information between commercial bankers and their sovereign borrowers. The plans were formulated at a meeting in New York in October 1982 of thirty-one major banks from North America, Europe and Japan under the chairmanship of Mr Bill Ogden, vice-chairman of the Chase Manhattan Bank; membership is open to any international lending bank. The proposed functions of the Institute have been described by Mr Ogden in the following words:

> One, it will gather country economic information, not to duplicate what is already being done, but to look for gaps in the information and seek ways to fill them.
> Two, it will discuss with borrower countries on a strictly voluntary basis their economic plans, assumptions, and financing needs.
> Three, when and where appropriate, it will serve as a focal point for dialogue between the international banking community and multinational institutions, central banks, and supervisory authorities in the developed countries.
> Four, it will furnish members with country reports of an informational nature. These will be objective and will avoid making credit judgements, which will be left strictly to each member bank.

In a letter circulating amongst international bankers in March 1983, designed to solicit the interest of potential members, Mr Francis Mason, the Interim Treasurer of the Institute, added further precision to these proposed functions by the following specific exclusions:

> The Institute will not be involved in setting credit criteria nor in establishing ratings for credit-worthiness, nor will it constitute a vehicle for deciding what credits should be provided or the terms of such credits. Neither will it serve as

a vehicle for the exchange of information among its members regarding lending practices. It is not contemplated that members will furnish any particular information to the Institute on their own lending practices.[5]

Once the relevant statistics, however imperfect, have been assembled, how do banks use them to assess country and, particularly, sovereign risks? The ways in which twenty major private sector banks set about assessing the risks attached to sovereign lending in 1980 were the subject of a survey, conducted by Mr F. M. Burton and Mr Hisashi Inoue, whose findings were summarised in an article published in January 1983; the banks concerned were in the United States, Britain, France, Switzerland, Canada, Japan and Germany. Their findings in terms of the factors used by the banks in making their credit assessments are worth recording:

The selection of variables considered to be relevant is similar among the banks, the major ones being as follows: gross national product or G.N.P. a head (or their growth rates); the inflation rate, or its proxy the growth rate of the money supply; the budgetary balance of central government; the domestic savings ratio; foreign exchange related variables (e.g. the change in foreign exchange reserves).

A small number of banks, in considering a country's foreign trade sector, confine themselves to broad aggregates relating to the absolute level of exports and imports. Most banks, however, additionally or alternatively, refer to the geographical and product diversification of exports and the 'import compressibility' ratio (that is, the ratio of food and oil to total imports). Some banks emphasise other components of the balance of payments such as official transfers, the use made of I.M.F. credits, and various elements of the capital account but particularly the trend of foreign direct investment flows.

The majority of banks take a country's external debt situation into account, but the variables they consider to be important range from debt outstanding/exports, debt outstanding/G.N.P. and debt outstanding/foreign exchange reserves. The absence of a clear-cut measure is a conse-

> quence of the ambiguous foundations of debt-related indicators, a practical handicap arising from a two to three-year time-lag before external debt statistics are made available, and the narrow statistical base which usually excludes non-guaranteed private borrowings and short-term debt. Although many banks are critical or the usefulness of the debt-service ratio, ironically, this is one of the commonest variables in use.

Having stressed the similarity of the variables chosen by most banks in their risk assessment, these commentators remark on variables, utilised by two banks:

> the ratio of military expenditure to G.N.P. and exchange rate fluctuations (or the exchange rate parity) in relation to a country's major trading partners. The former variable is regarded as an unproductive expense which contributes to debt service difficulties, but more significantly is considered to correlate with internal or external political instability. The latter variable is used to indicate whether an exchange rate is over-valued and may cause future balance of payments deterioration.

As to political risk analysis, these two writers regard it as

> perhaps, one of the least satisfactory and under developed aspects of country risk evaluation. All banks, more or less, consider the socio-political circumstances facing countries with the main emphasis placed on the quality of the policy makers, evidence of internal stability, relationships with neighbouring countries and, in some cases, the diplomatic relationship of the debtor country with the lending bank's government. General indicators include the ratio of manufactures to G.N.P., the quality of the infrastructure, the quality of human resources measured, for example, by the literacy rate, and the endowment of natural resources (in particular of oil reserves). Most banks construct a country's economic and political profile from that country's experience over the preceding one to five years.[6]

The principal lesson which emerges from this description of the criteria used in risk assessment is its demonstration of the diversity of criteria used rather than the production of a definitive list. To some commentators too much diversity is to be deplored. Dr David Lomax, for example, of the National Westminster Bank, London, in an article in the same journal, draws a very valid distinction between the established and fairly standard criteria used by banks in their assessment of credit risk in their lending to both corporate and personal borrowers in domestic economies and the relative lack of such standard criteria in the international arena of sovereign lending.

Dr Lomax rightly points to three beneficial roles played by such standard credit-worthiness criteria:

> First, lenders and borrowers both know that if they satisfy the conventional credit criteria then they stand little risk of losing their money or of getting into severe financial difficulty. The criteria are guidelines by which prudent operators, both at the corporate and personal level, may handle debt while minimising risks, on the one hand, of loss and, on the other hand, of finance drying up. Second, the criteria tend to endorse reasonably efficient use of resources and a well functioning economy . . . Third, credit criteria play an important role in ensuring the stability of the economic system . . .
>
> The same considerations apply in the international field. As far as companies and financial organisations are concerned creditworthiness criteria are examined in great detail by lenders and borrowers, and are used as strict guidelines for policy. As far as countries are concerned creditworthiness criteria, in the sense in which they apply in domestic markets, are conspicuous by their absence. This should be remedied. Country borrowers, and lenders to countries, need strict criteria of creditworthiness to be applied as one would to companies or in the domestic markets. The market wants and needs criteria. All participants would be easier in their minds if there were such criteria to abide by. [He accepts that] different factors affect the creditworthiness of different countries, some of

> which cannot be captured adequately in any particular statistic. But it is the essence of credit criteria in the corporate sector that one uses relatively standard criteria. These might be modified in certain cases according to one's knowledge of the company, but the criteria are nevertheless relatively strict. The same beneficial impact would be obtained in the country sector if some particular criteria were accepted. Some countries might modify these slightly, but the emphasis would be on slightly rather than on their complete disregard.[7]

It is clear that common, generally accepted criteria for the credit analysis of corporate and personal borrowers has proved immensely beneficial in the context of domestic markets for bank lending; indeed this is one of the conclusions that emerged in the previous section of this chapter. It is equally clear that this common code of credit assessment criteria has emerged as a consensus of the individual views of separate lending banks, independently arrived at, rather than as a rigid regulation imposed from above. As Dr Lomax has put it, 'credit-worthiness criteria are organic developments in society. They have been developed through practical usage and custom, rather than through being imposed from above by government'. It is a premise of this book, spelled out in the previous section, that this is the proper way for the conventions of credit assessment to evolve. And it is also clear that the lack of such common criteria, accepted and applied by borrowers and lenders alike, in the international market for bank lending to sovereign borrowers has been one of the contributory causes of the great disorder in which that market finds itself in the early 1980s.

But is it sensible and realistic – adopting, if you like, the free-enterprise premise of this book in a pure and undiluted form – to wait until a common code of criteria for sovereign risk assessment has emerged through market practice rather than to impose such a code from outside the system or, at least, to use outside influences to prod the system into formulating its own? The practical answer to this question is 'no' – for two reasons. First, time has run out for those who hoped to see the natural emergence of a code, acceptable to both borrowers and lenders. To take but one example, in the situation reached in August 1982, when Mexico sought a moratorium on its public sector debt from its creditors the relationship between that country and its private sector bankers had gone too far to be soluble by the Mexican state and the banking community alone, without the assistance of outside intervention from other national governments and the International Monetary Fund (IMF). Secondly, there are differences between the situation of most corporate and personal borrowers on the one hand and sovereign borrowers on the other – although these are often differences of degree rather than of kind – which make it more difficult for a generally acceptable code to emerge on the international market for sovereign risks.

The first difference between sovereign and other borrowers is that they are susceptible to different disciplines. If a corporate or personal borrower in a domestic market flouts the conventions of credit risk assessment too far, the lending banker will force the borrower into liquidation: in other words, the borrower will go bust. It used to be a widely-held belief that sovereign countries simply do not go bust in the same way, and it is clear that this belief caused many bankers in the 1970s and early 1980s to be a great deal more sanguine – some would say less prudent – in their international lending than they would be today. The problem, as bankers have learnt to their cost in 1982 and 1983, is that countries can go bust in the sense that they can get themselves into that condition of insolvency which, under most national legislations, would put the bankers in a position to call for a liquidation or bankruptcy if it were a corporation or individual involved; but they cannot go bust in the sense that the bankers have an accepted legal right and procedure to clear up the mess and recover as much of their lendings as they can. And since the bankers do not have the legal stick of the threat of bankruptcy or liquidation with which to call a defaulting borrower to order, the balance of power between a sovereign borrower and its banker is vastly different from that between a corporate or personal borrower and his banker. As the Basle paper remarks, 'the special significance of such lending lies in the risk that it might prove impossible to secure redress through legal action, i.e. the borrower might claim immunity from process or might not abide by a judgement'.

In the absence of a legal framework through which he can protect his interests and press his claims, the banker lending to a sovereign state can only rely in the last resort on political pressure. It probably remains true that sovereign borrowers *need not* go bust in any sense, on the simple grounds that they can always live another day, change their internal economic policies and recoup the liquid assets with which to pay their outstanding debts; but such action requires political will on the part of the government of the state in question, its acceptance that that is the policy option it must adopt and its political strength internally to see the policy through. In this situation, where the demands of the banker (to protect his lendings) are effectively translatable into political instructions as to economic policy, the banker simply does not have the political clout to command the same respect from his sovereign borrower as he would with a corporate or individual borrower faced with the threat of liquidation or bankruptcy. For this reason, there is a strong case for concluding that the banking community – and certainly an individual bank, however large and prestigious – simply could not rely on an evolved code of conventions in credit assessment to force a recalcitrant sovereign borrower to accept the disciplines of its policy instructions and that therefore the disciplinary role must be undertaken by some other agent with greater political clout, such as the IMF. There is a further point leading to the same conclusion: the force of a politician's pride. It is bad enough for a national government to be publicly forced to give up, or at least postpone, some of its most cherished political goals at the behest of the IMF; British readers have only to recall the deep chagrin and bitterness felt by many members of Mr Callaghan's Labour Government and their supporters when in June 1976 Britain itself was obliged to submit to the disciplines of the IMF and to forgo, or at least postpone, some of that government's cherished ambitions. It would be even worse – and in practical terms inconceivable – for a national government to have to confess to its electorate that its political priorities were being dictated by a private sector commercial bank, such as

National Westminster Bank or Chase Manhattan Bank. In short, it is easier for a politician to accept a medicine, however distasteful, for his country's economic ills, when that medicine has been prescribed by an official institution such as the IMF rather than by a commercial bank.

A second difference between sovereign and other borrowers is related to the first: that is, that because the policy requirements from a sovereign borrower by its bankers may have wide political implications for the borrower's national government, they may equally and for that very reason have wide political and diplomatic implications for other national governments, including the government of the lending banker's own country of residence. Three examples will make this point clear. First, it must have been abundantly clear to any banker, from the private sector or an official lending institution, that the future credit-worthiness of Mexico required in the closing months of 1982 a policy of domestic economic retrenchment which was bound to cause enormous social, political and economic strains within the country (a point which, incidentally, makes Mexico another good example of the point made in the previous paragraph). The political stability of Mexico is of paramount political importance to other national governments, particularly the United States with whom the country shares a long common border. There are many, for example, who fear that the disintegration of the social fabric of Mexico, brought about by too fierce and sudden a discipline in the internal economy, might well bring to power a Communist regime totally inimical to the United States and many other Western powers. There are others who, brooding on the fiftieth anniversary in 1983 of the rise to power of Adolf Hitler and his Nazi party and policies in Germany, use the benefit of hindsight to see that tragedy for Western Europe as stemming very directly from the harsh economic disciplines imposed on the German economy by the crippling reparation demands by the victors of the First World War through the Treaty of Versailles in 1919. These observers derive from this experience the simple lesson that any demands – made by bankers, governments or anybody else – for such stringent economic disciplines on an internal economy may well provoke a descent into political tyranny and illiberalism which most Western governments would deplore.

A second and rather different example is provided by the case of Poland which, like Mexico, was forced in 1981 and again in 1982 to ask its bankers to rearrange its external debts. Here again, prudent bankers demanded some sort of restraint in Polish domestic economic policy of the sort which, if pushed too far, could cause grave political unrest in that country. And again, the avoidance of such political unrest, with the possible consequence of a tightening grip on the Polish people by the armed forces of the Soviet Union was a matter of extreme political and diplomatic interest to other states. A third, and again different, example is provided by the case of Argentina, which in the last months of 1982 and early months of 1983 was forced to ask its bankers for a rearrangement of its external debts. Again, the bankers demanded some sort of restraint on the domestic spending policies of the government and also on its external expenditure on arms and military equipment. The Argentine invasion of the Falkland Islands in April 1982 and their subsequent retrieval by British forces later in that year generated fears in other countries that the imposition of too great a discipline on the internal economy might provoke the Argentine government into further military escapades overseas (including some further interference with the Falkland Islands); it also generated considerable interest and hostility amongst many political interests elsewhere in the world (particularly in the Conservative Party in Britain) on the matter of commercial banks (particularly British commercial banks) making further loans available to Argentina, with which they might possibly finance further purchases of arms. For all these reasons, the national interests of other countries than the borrower can sometimes be much involved in loans made to sovereign borrowers and in the disciplines on those borrowers which conventional banking criteria might normally require.

A third difference between sovereign and other borrowers is that lending bankers have often seen fit in the past to lend far more to any one sovereign borrower than they would to a commercial customer. This practice reflects the clear belief, widely held amongst many bankers until recently, that sovereign borrowers as a general rule represented a different, and slighter, order of risk than most other commercial and industrial borrowers; it also reflects the sheer size of the requirements of these sovereign borrowers in the later 1970s and early 1980s – as a continuing result of the oil price increase of the 1970s – in relation to the total resources of the lending banks. Thus, for example, by the end of 1982, the total external debt of Mexico was estimated at around US $85 000m, of which around US $65 000m had been provided by foreign private-sector commercial banks:[8] however well distributed amongst the institutions of the international banking community, this figure is substantial in relation to the total lendings made by those institutions and, perhaps more importantly, in relation to their own shareholders' funds (that is, effectively, capital and reserves). One estimate published in November 1982 gave the figures shown in Table 4.1 for the lendings of four major US banks to Mexico as a proportion of their total shareholders' funds.[9]

TABLE 4.1

Bank	*Mexican loans as % of total loans*	*Mexican loans as % of share-holders' equity*
Bank America	3.3	57.0
Citicorp	3.0	50.6
Chase Manhattan	2.9	47.7
Manufacturers Hanover	3.8	78.3

One of the consequences of this is that the lending banks have an interest in their borrowing customers' survival even greater – or, at the very least, more sharply focused – than it would normally be; for a borrower or group of borrowers with loans outstanding from a single bank greater than that bank's capital and reserves to default could effectively cause that bank to go bust itself, in the sense that the writing-off of the full amount of the loans in default on its balance sheet could bring its capital and reserves to a minus figure. And, indeed, there must be many banks around the world whose loans outstanding to the sovereign borrowers of, say, Mexico, Argentina and Brazil taken together exceed those banks' capital and reserves. This means, among other things, that commercial banks wishing to impose disciplines on such sovereign borrowers have definite inhibitions about letting the proposed disciplines push the borrower into serious consideration of a total default as a realistic policy option.

A further difference between sovereign and other borrowers is the number of lending banks which are frequently involved with the former, which greatly exceeds the number of lending banks involved with even the largest industrial and commercial borrowers. To take the example of Mexico again, it has been reported that no less than 1400[10] foreign banks were involved in the rescheduling of that country's existing debts and the provision of $5 bn of new loans which took place in the last months of 1982 and the beginning of 1983. This massive array of lenders has had two consequences. First, it has made it almost impossible for a single bank to exercise any discipline over a sovereign borrower, for the simple reason that the borrower will simply turn for further or replacement funds to a string of other potential lenders. Secondly, and probably more importantly, it has made it unusually difficult for any one lending bank to make an accurate calculation of the total borrowings outstanding at any one time of any sovereign borrower. And as we have seen, the outstanding debt of any borrower, whether or not sovereign, is a key statistic in any serious judgement of the credit risk involved in granting it further loans.

Here, then, are some of the main differences between sovereign and other borrowers; together they provide strong reasons for expecting the conditions imposed by lending bankers on their sovereign borrowing customers (in relation to existing as well as new loans) not to remain the subject of bilateral talks between each lending bank and the borrower. For this reason they provide a strong core for arguing that a common code of criteria for sovereign lending is unlikely to emerge naturally as the by-product of a continuing series of bilateral negotiations, as it has in other lending markets. Such a code seems more likely to emerge partly through initiatives taken by central banks, the IMF or other official authorities, which will be discussed in Chapter 6, and partly through joint initiatives taken by the commercial banking community as a whole.

An example of the latter initiatives was the establishment in January 1983 of an Institute of International Finance, already described. On a more parochial British level, it was revealed in December 1982 that the four leading British clearing banks had set up a secret committee in the Spring of that year to monitor problems in international debt markets and work informally towards a common British bank approach to the payments difficulties of certain sovereign borrowers. The *Financial Times* reported that the committee was set up

> before the Mexican debt crisis revealed publicly the extent of debt problems facing the euro-markets. Its existence was kept confidential at the time for fear of arousing nervousness in the banking community. Since then its practical application has come more to the fore with Argentina's debt problems requiring a joint response from British banks and requests for loans from British banks coming from such countries as Brazil and Yugoslavia. Like many foreign counterparts, British clearing bankers recognise that the debt problems facing many countries in the developing world and Eastern Europe are so serious that the accent has to be on a common approach, rather than competitive solutions to problems which promote the interests of some banks while damaging those of others. It is thought that the sovereign risk committee, which meets regularly on an informal basis, is seen as a potential nucleus for a national negotiating body which could represent the interests of all British banks in debt rescheduling talks.[11]

There is one final pressure for the establishment of a common code of criteria for sovereign risk assessment which should be mentioned; and that is the pressure from the national authorities responsible for prudential supervision. One of the inevitable consequences of the tight money and world recession since 1979, described in Chapter 1, has been the worsening of the financial condition of many bank borrowers, sovereign as well as corporate or individual; and one of the several consequences of this has been some pretty frightening comments on the financial soundness of individual banks and of the international banking system as a whole – politicians, journalists and other commentators vying with each other to predict the demise of the whole system. Such comments must inevitably excite the interest of bank supervisors, whose proper responsibility it is to ensure that banks do not get into trouble and thereby put their depositors' funds at risk. It is, therefore, not surprising that several national authorities for bank supervision should have interested themselves in the techniques employed by banks under their supervision for assessing country risk; the paper issued by the Basle Committee of Bank Supervisors demonstrates that interest.

The US supervisors are a good example. The survey of systems in use by banks for country risk evaluation, quoted earlier in this section, reported that,

> among U.S. banks, systematic country risk evaluation is a semi-official requirement since the sophistication of the evaluation methods they use is an important item checked in regular inspections by the authorities, including the Comptroller of the Currency and the Federal Reserve Board.[12]

Another commentator has disclosed that the US authorities go further than inspecting the methods of evaluation used by the banks they supervise; they also indulge in sovereign risk evaluation themselves. Writing in the same journal, Mr David Lascelles of Carnegie Endowment in New York has reported that systematic monitoring of foreign lending by US banks began only in 1979 when the Federal Reserve Board, the Office of the Controller of the Currency and the Federal Deposit Insurance Corporation formed the Interagency Country Exposure Review Committee (ICERC) to

> set guidelines and bring more consistency to bank regulation. The Committee meets three times a year in Washington to 'rate' country borrowers in six classifications: strong,

> moderately strong, weak, substandard, doubtful and loss. In practice the ratings are made by the Fed. which is the only agency with the staff and expertise to evaluate country risk. Because of its political sensitivity, the ICERC's rating list is highly confidential. But at least four countries are known to belong to the lower categories because of the small likelihood that they will be able to repay their debts in the foreseeable future: Poland, Zaire, Sudan and Costa Rica.[13]

The style and extent of the involvement of bank supervisors in banks' assessment of country and sovereign risks was summarised in the Basle paper in the following terms:

> In the same way that the supervisor would not expect to dictate to banks what specific domestic loans should be granted, he does not set out to dictate to banks decisions about specific international loans. Bank managements are responsible for the risks involved in the credits that they grant, whether to domestic or international customers. At the same time, however, the supervisor has a responsibility to review risks, particularly country risks, and needs, therefore, to ensure that banks have adequate methods of assessing, measuring and controlling their country exposure.
>
> In the first place, the supervisor will wish to see that banks operate at least some form of country risk assessment system, that that system has sufficient resources devoted to it and that it is competently managed. He should be ready to suggest improvements in banks' systems where he believes that his advice would be of benefit.
>
> Secondly, the supervisor will take an interest in banks' country exposure management. Not only will he wish to see that banks have systems that capture the totality of their country exposures in a manner sufficiently detailed to permit adequate control, but he will wish to see adequate diversification of each bank's exposure. He will therefore need to know about individual country exposures and may comment on them in the light of the bank's capacity to sustain losses. One of the main difficulties facing the

supervisor is to judge the true extent of a bank's country exposure, since large differences among banks' measurement systems may make comparisons difficult or impossible. Partly for this reason, standard reporting for at least summary country exposure data has been introduced in several countries. Such reporting allows the supervisor (as well as the banks themselves, when these reports are aggregated and publicised) to compare in a standard way country concentration of lending and lending in relation to capital.

Thirdly, the supervisor will be concerned to see that banks use their country risk assessment to set and maintain continuous controls on their own exposure. He may also wish to ensure that banks have some form of self-imposed limits on their exposure and that those limits function effectively to contain and to diversify their exposure.

Finally, the supervisor will wish to satisfy himself that banks for their guidance have access to the best possible macro-economic statistics. The Committee is well aware of the deficiencies in international debt statistics and is currently pressing for improvements in their consistency, coverage and timeliness. Banks can significantly contribute to the value of international statistics by making their own returns as promptly and as accurately as possible.

Risk concentration

The degree of credit risk undertaken by a bank in its lending policies can be much increased by too great a concentration of that lending into any one area of risk. An immediate recognition of this point is to be found in the fact that all prudent banks fix a maximum limit on their total permitted exposure – in terms of all risks, including loans, guarantees and other contingent liabilities – to any one borrower. Two main factors are taken into consideration in fixing this limit on the maximum exposure to any one borrower: the capital and reserves of the lending bank and the type of credit risk which that bank undertakes. The reliance of the bank's capital and reserves is obvious: at its crudest, when setting any limits on the risks it undertakes, the ultimate question a bank must ask itself is how much it can afford to lose by making a mistake about that type of risk; and whatever the actual number arrived at, any sensible answer to that question must in logic be related to the resources ultimately available. Indeed, in several countries it is a requirement of the regulating authorities that lendings to any one borrower should not exceed a fixed proportion of the lending bank's capital and reserves: examples are the United States, Japan, Italy and Holland. The relevance of the type of risk undertaken by the bank in question is that some specialised banks undertake only certain types of credit risk and that some such types are more risky than others. For example, almost all the credit risks undertaken by a London discount house will be the risk of the British Government or of a bank whose bills are eligible for discount at the Bank of England. Clearly a discount house would be justified in fixing a limit on its exposure to any one eligible name (the British Government being reasonably excepted from its credit limits) substantially greater as a proportion of its capital and reserves than the limits fixed by other banks whose borrowing customers covered a wider variety of riskiness and an inevitably greater degree of risk.

A second reaction of banks to the danger of an over-concentration of risk is to limit that concentration in a geographical sense, that is, to set a limit on their lendings to borrowers resident in any one nation state or wider geographical area. The concept of 'country risk', already discussed, carries with it the clear implication that such risks ought to be the subject of specific limits for each individual bank. The reason for looking at wider geographical areas is that there are such areas in which the dominating factors on which one would base a credit decision are shared by the nation states in that area. For example, many banks put a maximum limit on their exposure to the Comecon group of countries, comprising the Soviet Union and those Eastern European countries whose internal policies and economies are much controlled by it; other banks put a maximum limit on their exposure to certain countries, geographically contiguous, in the Middle East – on the simple but effective grounds of the potential political instability of that particular area.

Many banks do, of course, designate countries as 'unlimited' in respect of country risk. Most banks, for example, would not have a geographical limit on lendings to borrowers resident in their own country, and many British banks would not impose a geographical limit on their lendings to borrowers resident in the United States. But some banks *do* impose a limit on lendings in their domestic economy on the simple logic, not so much that there is a significant geographical 'credit' risk, but rather that a political regime may possibly come to power in its own country less amicable to that bank's type of business – in terms of, say, taxes or regulations – and that prudence therefore suggests maintaining an established banking business and an established group of borrowers outside that country. Many London banks which operate primarily in the eurocurrency markets have a relatively small lending exposure to borrowers within Britain, thus reflecting the 'offshore' international nature of those markets. In most such cases, the limited British exposure is probably the natural consequence of the business undertaken rather than the reflection of a tight geographical limit; but there are probably some such British banks which do have a precise geographical limit for Britain.

One further point should be made about the concept of a tidy set of credit limits, divided by individual nations and groups of nations. The purpose of these limits is to diversify a bank's credit risks by avoiding too much concentration in one geographical area; but this drive to diversify can be taken too far. In the later 1970s several major international banks took on substantial credit risks in relatively small nations, particularly in Africa and Asia, which seemed to some of their fellow bankers to be bold to the point of imprudence. Many anecdotes circulated amongst bankers at the time suggesting that these decisions were based, at least in part, on an inspection of a list of all the nations in the world and the identification of those to which the banks in question did not as yet have a significant exposure. By filling in these gaps the bank would certainly achieve a wider geographical diversification of its portfolio; but as at least one great bank learnt to its cost, it did not automatically enhance the credit risk of that portfolio. In other words, geographical diversification is certainly a proper principle for a bank to observe in shaping its loan portfolio; but it should never cause a bank to overlook the other criteria for judging credit risks, described above. Geographical diversification is a necessary, but in no sense a sufficient, principle to be observed in constructing a loan portfolio.

In fixing geographical limits for credit risk exposure, banks take into account virtually the same set of factors on which they base their sovereign risk limits; though it should perhaps be noted that geographical risks and sovereign risks are not, in theory at least, the same thing. A bank's exposure to a country risk does, of course, include its exposure to the sovereign risk, if any, of that country; but it also includes its lendings to individuals and private sector corporations within that country. Most important of all, it includes deposits with banks resident in that country, whether made through the eurocurrency markets or by any other route together with deposits with overseas branches of those banks.

In the 1960s and 1970s, before the sovereign borrowers became such a dominant part of the scene, there were two main aspects of country risk to which a banker would pay attention, once he had established the credit-worthiness of a non-sovereign borrower. First he would look at the political stability of the country of the borrower's residence, which was relevant to the ability of the borrower to operate and make profits; and secondly, he would look at the 'transfer risk' involved in the lending, meaning the risk that, even assuming the borrower was able to meet its obligations for interest payments and capital repayments from its own resources, it could be prevented from making these payments across the national frontier to the lending bank by government regulation. Since then, this two-pronged analysis of country risk has been overtaken by the more sophisticated sovereign risk analysis described above which, in practical terms, takes, or should take into account all those factors relevant to both the 'political' risk and the 'transfer' risk.

In practical terms the experience of the sovereign debt problems of the early 1980s has provided another reason for regarding the sovereign risks of a country as applying to other borrowers in a country besides its government and official institutions. For example, when the support operations were mounted to reschedule the debts of Mexico at the end of 1982 and of Brazil in early 1983, the pressures were effectively as strong on lenders to private sector banks and other corporations in those countries to hold in, reschedule and not withdraw their loans, as they were on lenders to the two states and their official institutions.

A third reaction of banks to the danger of an over-concentration of risk is to ensure a proper diversification by industrial sector as well as by geography. Again, attention has been focused on the importance of this principle by recent experience in the 1970s and early 1980s. We have already noted in Chapter 1 the problems experienced by many British banks as a result of the collapse of property values in Britain in 1973–5. Several banks had a large proportion of their lending exposure to this property sector; many other banks burnt their fingers to a greater or lesser degree, according to the extent of their exposure; and all banks learnt the lesson of over-exposure to a single sector. A second example of banks over-concentrating their exposure to a single industrial sector can be found in the loans made to ship-owners in the later 1970s. Again, the dramatic decline in the fortunes of the shipping industry, with reduced traffic, a surplus of ships and falling income caught several banks heavily over-exposed. A third example is the heavy concentration of some banks in their lending to the oil industry – to finance production in the United States, Canada, the North Sea and elsewhere. Some fingers have already been burnt at the time of writing early in 1983; the collapse of the Penn Square Bank in Oklahoma in July 1982, and its reverberations in other banks to which it had syndicated loans to oil producers is probably the most dramatic example. But with the future of the oil price, and thus the viability of many recently-developed oilfields, in doubt, there must be many banking managements throughout the world calling for continually updated reports on their bank's exposure to that industry.

The setting of limits to achieve a distribution of risk by industrial classification is a less tidy exercise than by geographical classification. For one thing, there is an overlap, or blurring of the edges, between different sectors. The three mentioned above – property, shipping and oil – are fairly clear cut; but some fairly arbitrary decisions are required to split up the engineering or leisure industries, for example into more precise sectors. A second problem is to decide whether a loan should be classified by the business of the borrower or the nature of the security. As we have seen, many loans to manufacturing corporations are secured, at least in part, on the factory in which the product is manufactured. To the extent that the factory could be used in another industrial sector, its value is less dependent on the prosperity of the industry in question than is the business of the corporation itself: the banker must make an individual decision as to how each particular case should be classified.

One final point should be made about all these techniques of diversification. All three can be implemented effectively only if the bank possesses detailed, accurate and up-to-date records of its loans: even the identification of a bank's exposure to one borrower can be complicated if that borrower is a large group of companies with subsidiaries in many parts of the world. But the keeping of these records is one of the best applications of computer systems to banking management; and a far more sophisticated and useful basis for identifying and classifying the different risks embodied in each loan is now available from computerised records than would ever have been possible before such record-keeping techniques were available.

CAPITAL ADEQUACY AND THE SOLVENCY OF BANKS

The gearing ratio

If a bank lends its own capital to a borrower, it is taking a risk with that capital. If, in addition, it borrows funds in the form of deposits or loans and on-lends these additional funds it is increasing or 'gearing up' the risks to its own solvency. In all discussions about the prudent limits a bank should set for the risk it takes, the ultimate and crude question to be answered is how much that bank can afford to lose in the event of the risk going wrong: we have already seen the relevance of this question to setting a limit on loans to any one borrower; we shall discuss it in the context of liquidity risks and foreign exchange risks later in this chapter; it is equally relevant in the context of the 'gearing' of a bank's credit risk. An over-simplified example will make this point clear: if a bank has £1m in capital and lends it all out to borrowers, it is taking a certain risk on the credit-worthiness of those borrowers: if half the borrowers turn out not to be credit-worthy and default on their loans, the bank loses £500 000, or half its capital. If a bank has £1m and borrows a further £1m and lends the total of £2m, it is said to have a 'gearing ratio' of 1:1, the gearing ratio being the ratio of its external liabilities or borrowings to its own capital. If in this second case one half of the borrowers default, the bank will be able to repay its depositors but its own capital will have been wiped out and, without a further injection of capital, it is bust. If, in a third example, a bank has £1m of capital, borrows a further £2m and lends the total of £3m, it has a gearing ratio of 2:1; if half the borrowers default in this case, the bank loses its capital and goes bust and, as importantly, quarter of the depositors with, or lenders to, the bank lose their money also.

The 'gearing ratio' of a bank is thus of considerable interest to four parties: the management of the bank itself, the shareholders who lose their money if the bank goes bust, the depositors with the bank and the prudential supervisors who are concerned to ensure both that banks do not go bust and that depositors do not lose their money. It is thus a matter of considerable concern to all bank managements to ensure that their gearing ratio is such that, in their own judgement, they are not endangering the bank's solvency; to ensure that it is such as to cause no concern to the prudential supervisors; and to ensure that it appears, from the information available to the depositing public, to be such that it causes no concern with that public – on whose continuing deposits the business of the bank depends.

The 'gearing ratio' is the basic and simplest tool used by both bank managements and bank supervisors for measuring and controlling the solvency of banks or, put another way, the adequacy of their capital resources. In its simplest form, it relates the capital and reserves of the bank to deposits and other external liabilities: the exact definition of 'capital and reserves' and 'external liabilities' varies from country to country and, indeed, in some cases from bank to bank; but as we shall see in Chapter 5 there are concerted moves to achieve some sort of standardisation within each country and, in the context of the European Economic Community, between member states of the Community as well. Another ratio which demonstrates precisely the same degree of gearing is the ratio of total assets to capital and reserves – since the capital and reserves plus external liabilities must, broadly speaking, equal the total assets of the bank by accounting convention, mathematics dictate that this ratio tells the same story as the ratio between capital and reserves and external liabilities.

In Britain, the principal definitions of the variables lying behind the gearing ratio are as follows. The capital and reserves of the bank are taken to be the total of share capital, loan capital, minority interests, reserves and general provisions after deducting the following items: investments in subsidiaries and associates, goodwill, equipment, premises and other fixed assets. External liabilities are taken to be all deposits and other non-capital liabilities excluding contingent liabilities.[14]

The precise numerical ratio which is considered – by the prudential supervisors, the depositors and the bank itself – to be appropriate for any particular bank will vary very much according to the nature of the business and, particularly, of the assets of that bank and also according to its profitability. As we shall see in the next chapter, an appreciation of this need for flexibility and individual assessment is one of the hallmarks of the attitude of the Bank of England in its capacity as prudential supervisor of British banks. In the Bank's own words, it

> considers that to prescribe a precise numerical guideline for the capital needs of all institutions or for groups of institutions would be inappropriately inflexible. Such an approach would endorse overtrading by some companies and be harmfully restrictive to others. Furthermore, it is

> recognised that a sufficient flow of earnings is essential as a first defence against losses and as a source of fresh capital to allow a business to grow or even to maintain the scope of its operations during a period of inflation. Profitability and other prudential considerations have their place within the assessment of capital adequacy so that, within a common framework for the measurement of capital applying to all institutions, the Bank's final assessment of the capital adequacy of a particular institution will involve qualitative judgements depending on the nature of its business. Within the field of supervised institutions there will therefore be a range of capital ratios regarded as adequate.[15]

Some idea of the range of gearing ratios regarded as adequate for British banks can be gleaned from published figures relating to three quite different groups of banks. First, the Committee of London Clearing Bankers (CLCB) in its evidence to the Wilson Committee (dated November 1977) remarked that

> there has been much debate both about the appropriate measure of capital adequacy and about the appropriate levels for the various ratios that can be calculated. A crude approach is simply to relate total capital resources to total deposits. The banks are aware that such a ratio is in practice monitored by many of their depositors (especially overseas banks) and it is important for that reason. The clearing banks' capital ratios on this basis are currently between 6 and 8 per cent, which they believe are comparable with or higher than those of major banks in other countries.

The CLCB went on to point out that

> the limitation of such an approach is that it pays no regard to the nature of the different types of asset that a bank holds. The approach which is now being adopted increasingly is one which seeks to identify the amount of capital required to cover these different types of asset. The amount required will depend on the extent of the risk that the assets may not realise their full value.[16]

The CLCB went on to discuss the degree of riskiness of different assets held by banks, and this is the subject of the next section. But it is worth noting at this stage the point made by the CLCB that

> the public at large is not privy to sufficiently detailed information about the degree of risk of the banks' assets to compute sophisticated capital/asset ratios. But as a compromise between these ratios and the old-fashioned capital/deposit ratio, it is now common practice to compute the ratio of a bank's 'free capital' (total capital less infrastructure assets) to its deposits. ['Infrastructure assets' are defined elsewhere in the CLCB's evidence as essentially the bank's premises, equipment and trade investments.]

This ratio of free capital to deposits is effectively the same as the gearing ratio defined by the Bank of England in the paper quoted above. The CLCB did not put a figure on their member banks' gearing, as measured by this ratio, but they did issue the rather sombre warning that

> during the past few years the clearing banks' ratios of free capital to deposit liabilities have at times fallen to uncomfortable levels, and the banks have duly raised additional capital, both equity and subordinated debt. Even so, their free capital ratios appear less generous when compared with the position in some other countries than their total capital ratios. It is a source of continuing concern that post-tax profits have recently been insufficient to preserve the banks' free capital ratios, after meeting the capital investment needs of the business and after paying modest dividends to shareholders.[17]

A second group of British banks, the limits on whose gearing ratios have been disclosed to the public in very general terms, is the Accepting Houses Committee (AHC). In their written evidence to the Wilson Committee (dated July 1977), they remarked that

> each Accepting House imposes 'gearing' restraints upon itself. It limits the quantity of the deposits that it will take to a multiple of its own resources (its published capital and reserves, plus the inner or hidden reserves allowed by virtue of Schedule 2 of the Companies Act 1967). This multiple will vary from House to House but, typically, liabilities to the public (deposits and acceptances) average about 12 times resources. Each House will limit total loans and advances in the same way.[18]

Writing some two years before this evidence, the Bank of England drew attention to its own preference for a ratio which related the 'free capital' of a bank to its deposits, as mentioned by the CLCB in its evidence to the Wilson Committee:

> Capital adequacy is sometimes assessed by the banks, and often in press comment, in terms of the ratio of capital and resources to total deposits. The Bank of England have preferred in the past and in relation to non-clearing banks to employ a ratio of free resources to public liabilities whereby investment in fixed assets such as premises, in subsidiary and associated companies and in unquoted investments are deducted from capital and resources, and a residual figure is set against deposit liabilities and liabilities on acceptances. A figure of 10% has become known as the basic guideline for accepting houses and similar banks.[19]

This figure of 10, for a ratio relating *free* resources to public liabilities, is, of course, quite consistent with the AHC's figure of 12 for a ratio relating *total* resources to public liabilities.

It should be noted in passing that the 'liabilities' side of the gearing ratio was taken by both the Bank of England and the AHC (in 1975 and 1977 respectively) in the passages quoted above, to include an Accepting House's liabilities on acceptances, whereas such liabilities are now specifically excluded in the Bank of England's definitions for the ratio. The Bank's reasoning behind this change is worth recording. In discussing the non-capital liabilities to which the capital base, as adjusted, of a bank should be related in arriving at the gearing ratio, the Bank comments that

> past practice has been to take account only of deposit liabilities, although to this the Bank has traditionally added liabilities on acceptances. However, these definitions fail to take account of claims by other creditors. Furthermore, acceptances, like other contigent liabilities are more appropriately considered within the risk measure of capital adequacy; and the inclusion of acceptances (which are not always separately identified in published balance sheets) is inconsistent with the objective that the gearing ratio should, so far as possible, be capable of being calculated from published accounts.[20]

The third group of British banks, the limits on whose gearing ratios have been the subject of public discussion, are the discount houses (members of the London Discount Market Association, the LDMA). In the words of the Bank of England

> for many years, the discount houses have observed some simple multipliers relating their trading activities to their capital resources . . . The principle multiplier provided a guideline of 30 times its 'resources' as the maximum size of a house's total book. A subsidiary multiplier of 8 times resources was applied to the house's bond book.[21]

In June 1982 these multipliers or ratios were replaced by a rather more complex measure, which incorporates two multipliers and provides a unified system of measure and control of a house's risks, which for other banks is embodied in three separate ratios: the gearing ratio, the risk assets ratio and the liquidity ratio. In the present context, it is sufficient to note that a house which limits to three months the life of each of the assets it holds – be they eligible bills, ineligible bills, trade bills, certificates of deposit, British Government bonds or anything else – may allow its book of total assets to run up to a maximum of forty times its capital base. (The definition of the capital base for this purpose is similar to that used by other banks, quoted above.)

The wide variation in these multipliers reflects the different degrees of risk which are thought to attach to different types of asset and the proportions in which any bank or group of bank holds these different types of asset. This underlines the limitation of the use of a simple gearing ratio – as emphasised by the view of the CLCB, that it 'pays no regard to the nature of the different types of asset which a bank holds'. It is for this reason that attention has focused increasingly on the concept of a 'risk asset ratio' which takes account of the different types of asset a bank holds, and it is to this more sophisticated concept that we turn in the next section. But before doing so, it is worth considering whether the gearing ratio still has a value as a measure of a bank's risk and a weapon with which to control that risk, or whether it has effectively been replaced by the risk asset ratio.

It would be difficult to argue that the adoption of a risk asset ratio as a sole tool of management and prudential control would eliminate the use of a gearing ratio; but it would be much easier to argue that a risk asset ratio combined with the two liquidity controls discussed in the next section left no real rôle for a gearing ratio in the management and supervision of a bank. But besides the management of a bank and its supervisors, there is one other important group of observers for whom a gearing ratio is extremely useful: the depositing public, including other banks. (For many banks, the shareholders are another interested party for whom the crude gearing ratio is a valuable indicator – to the extent that they do not have access to the detailed information required to make a reasonably accurate assessment of their bank's rating by the other more sophisticated ratios.) We have already seen that the maintenance of depositors' confidence will always remain a paramount concern of any bank's management; and the gearing ratio as disclosed by a bank's published balance sheet is an important factor in determining the extent of that confidence, particularly in the minds of depositing fellow bankers. This point was well taken by the CLCB in its evidence when it remarked that its member banks were aware that the simple ratio of total capital resources to total deposits is, in fact, monitored by many of their depositors (especially overseas banks); and it is also well taken by the Bank of England in its choice of ratios with which to monitor British banks.

Indeed, when choosing the ratios to use in its prudential supervision, the Bank noted that

> the following have been identified as the two most important objectives of capital ratios:
>
> (i) to ensure that the capital position of an institution is regarded as acceptable by its depositors and other creditors;
>
> and
>
> (ii) to test the adequacy of capital in relation to the risk of losses which may be sustained.

The bank went on to comment that

> the first objective makes it desirable that one of the measures of capital to be employed by the Bank should be constructed of elements as far as possible available to the public. Depositors and other creditors have to form judgements about the capital adequacy of an institution using published information, and their reaction to these judgements will have an important bearing on the stability of each institution. The second objective requires information, an important part of which is likely to be available only to the supervisory authority and the institution itself. And the more sophisticated the testing mechanism, the less likely it is that the information will be available to the public in the necessary detail.[22]

For most British banks, the crude gearing ratio has come to be regarded as less useful as a tool of management information and control, the more they develop control techniques based on the risk capital ratio and the liquidity ratios described below; and the same view is taken by the Bank of England. Indeed the switch of emphasis by both the management of banks and their prudential supervisors away from simple ratios of capital to deposits to more specific controls on liquidity requirements and on the capital backing for different types of banking asset is a trend which can be identified in all the main financial centres of the non-Communist world. But notwithstanding this change of emphasis, both the management of banks and their supervisors might still keep an eye on the crude gearing ratio (as calculable from published figures) since it remains a major factor in the fostering and maintenance of the confidence of depositors.

The risk–asset ratio

The risks to its own solvency run by a bank which 'gears up' or supplements its capital resources with deposits and other borrowings were described, in simplest terms, in the previous section. From this description it became clear that the degree of such risk represented by any particular level of gearing, that is, any particular gearing ratio, depends very much on the riskiness of the assets financed by the bank's capital and borrowing. The same point was demonstrated by the fact that the gearing ratio which is generally regarded as appropriate for banks, such as the London discount houses, whose assets carry an unusually low degree of credit risk is appreciably higher than that which is regarded as appropriate for banks whose assets generally carry a higher degree of credit risk.

It follows that a ratio which incorporates a different weighting for different groups of assets, grouped to reflect different degrees of risk, is a much more useful tool for both the managers and supervisors of banks than the simple gearing ratio, in their assessment of the risk to which a bank's solvency is exposed and the adequacy of its capital to support that risk. If a schedule of risk weightings can be generally agreed between bankers and their supervisors, a risk–asset ratio can have additional uses for both. For the bankers, it provides a useful basis for taking decisions about the mix of different assets it should acquire: if, for example, the pressure of competition in the market place has reduced the margin of profit on one group of assets, A, so that it is lower than that available on another group of assets, B, and if the commonly accepted schedule of weightings gives groups A and B the same weighting, an astute banker will at least consider increasing his holdings of B assets and reducing his holdings of A assets by the same amount. For the supervisors, a risk–asset ratio provides a useful yardstick by which to compare the solvency risks, or capital adequacy, of different banks in different categories.

The exact allocation of risk weightings in a risk–asset ratio is not, by its very nature, an exact science, or even a science at all. It must be decided by the individual judgements of individual bankers. But it would be surprising if those individual judgements were to lead to radically different allocations of weightings; so that when a public debate on the matter developed in the 1970s, largely at the instigation of the Bank of England, it was not too difficult for a general consensus to emerge, which could be agreed as the basis for a commonly-observed schedule of riskiness.

A good example of the reasoning behind the construction of a schedule of assets judged by their riskiness, or, put another way, of a schedule allocating capital as cover for the different groups of assets, was provided by the CLCB in its evidence to the Wilson Committee, and is worth quoting in full:

> At one extreme certain types of money market assets, such as Treasury bills, require little or no capital cover; since the risks of a fall in value or of default by the debtor are negligible, it is not unreasonable for them to be financed almost entirely by deposits. The market value of gilt-edged investments, however, can fluctuate and a degree of capital cover is therefore appropriate. Advances to customers do not fluctuate in value in the same way but there is the rather different risk that they may not all be repaid in full. In the case of certain investments, both types of risk apply, while the assets making up the infrastructure of the banks (essentially their premises, equipment and trade investments) require the highest degree of capital cover of all. This reflects not only the fact that they may fall in value, but also their limited marketability. Property values fluctuate at the best of times, and in the event of a crisis a large property portfolio might be extremely difficult to sell at reasonable prices. In the case of the banks' purpose-built

> equipment and some of their trade investments, it would not be safe to assume that their book value could be realised on the open market. It is for these reasons that it is now commonly accepted that infrastructure assets should not normally be financed by deposits (just as the fixed assets of an industrial or commercial undertaking should not normally be financed by short-term funds). For the same reasons, the banks have only a limited role to play in the provision of equity finance to industry and trade.[23]

After a considerable and prolonged debate between British bankers and their supervisors in the Bank of England, and between the different groups of bankers themselves, a generally acceptable classification of assets and risk weightings was published by the Bank of England in 1980 in its paper on the measurement of capital. In introducing the classification, the Bank explained the types of risk of loss which had been taken into account in applying the different weightings, and it should be noted that the risks which are taken into account – as also those mentioned by the CLCB in the passage quoted above – go wider than the simple credit risks described earlier in this chapter. The Bank stated its intention that

> the standard risk asset calculation will take into account three types of risk inherent in the assets themselves but that weightings should be applied to different assets reflecting the extent to which they are susceptible to these risks. The three types of risk are:
>
> (i) *credit risk* – the risk that claims on others may not be redeemable at the due date at their full book value;
> (ii) *investment risk* – the risk that marketable claims on others, or directly held assets may depreciate below their book value;
> (iii) and as a further element within investment risk *forced sale risk* – the risk that actual and additional losses may be sustained because of the need to make untimely sales of assets which, depending on the narrowness of the market, may yield less than their quoted value.[24]

It should be noted in passing that the investment risk and thus, by definition, the forced sale risk as well are also taken into account in the construction of liquidity controls, discussed in the next section.

The Bank further remarked that

> consideration has also been given to whether there would be advantage in going further and attempting to incorporate additional risks such as fraud and other operational risks or concentrations of exposure on special sectoral and geographic risks. The Bank has concluded that to encompass all these elements within a single calculation would involve the construction of an excessively elaborate model whose appearance of accuracy could be dangerously misleading.[25]

Whilst British bankers are probably unanimous in applauding that conclusion in respect of over-formalised models, they should and do pay attention to these further risks in the management of their business.

The classification published by the Bank divides each type of asset which appears in a bank's balance sheet, with three exceptions, into seven categories of riskiness; the three exceptions are plant and equipment, intangible assets and investments in subsidiary and associated companies and these are to be deducted from the 'capital' side of the ratio. A factor representing a risk weight has been applied to each category; the categories range from nil to 2.0. In the Bank's words:

> these weights attempt to reflect the relative risk of loss arising from credit or investment and forced sale risks inherent in a particular class of asset. For this purpose commercial advances are taken as a benchmark to which a weight of unity is therefore ascribed. The risks attaching to other assets may be less or more than those attaching to commercial advances. Thus, for example, the weight ascribed to market loans to listed banks is 0.2 and the weight attached to property is 2.0 . . . The risk asset ratio is calculated by multiplying each balance sheet asset by its weight to produce an adjusted total of risk assets and then

establishing the proportion of this total represented by the capital base as modified by the items requiring a deduction.[26]

LIQUIDITY RISKS

The funding risk

So far, we have considered risks inherent in the *assets* side of a bank's balance sheet. There is another major risk run by banks on the *liabilities* side: the funding risk. As we have seen, it is the principal function of banks to collect deposits from those with cash resources surplus to their immediate requirements and to on-lend these cash resources to those with an immediate need for them. It is crucially important that a bank should always be in a position to repay its depositors when their deposits fall due for repayment: any failure to do so would quickly destroy the confidence of all depositors and potential depositors with the bank in question and thus destroy the business of the bank, causing it to close its doors. The risk that a bank would not be able to repay its depositors when required to do so – known as the 'funding risk' – is thus every bit as important to a bank's health and survival as the other risks considered so far in this chapter.

To some extent, banks can avoid this risk by matching the maturity dates of their incoming deposits with those of their outgoing loans: by taking a three-month deposit, for example, to finance a three-month loan. But even this precaution would not eliminate the funding risk, since there is always the credit risk that a borrower may go bust and thus default on his loan, thereby depriving the bank of the funds with which to repay the deposit; and there is also the much more probable risk that the borrower, while not being insolvent, may itself be less liquid than it planned and therefore not be able to repay the loan until some date later than its due date. (The much publicised 'rescheduling' of debt repayments by sovereign borrowers in the early 1980s is a classic example of this second case.)

In any event, it is most unlikely that all but the smallest

proportion of a bank's deposits and loans will be maturity-matched in this way for two reasons. First, prior to the development in the early 1960s of the interbank markets in deposits denominated in both sterling and other currencies, described in Chapter 3, virtually all deposits with British banks took the form of credit balances on current account which were, and are, withdrawable on demand and without notice, and deposit accounts which are normally withdrawable at seven days' notice. At 31 December 1958, for example, the 'deposits' of the London clearing banks, as reported by the Radcliffe Committee, amounted to £7199m of which £4227m (or 59 per cent) were current account credit balances, £2486m (or 35 per cent) were deposit accounts and only £486m (or 6 per cent) were 'other accounts' (being credits in course of transmission, suspense accounts and internal funds of the banks). The development of the interbank markets in fixed term deposits since that date has, of course, reduced these formally withdrawable deposits as a proportion of a bank's liabilities, but they still remain an important proportion, particularly for the clearing banks.

Another dominant feature of the balance sheets of British banks up to the early 1960s, which is still important today, is the proportion of advances or loans which take the form of overdraft facilities, that is, limits agreed between the banker and the borrower up to which the borrower can draw funds in excess of his current account credit balance, on agreed terms, without notice to the bank. This again increases the uncertainty about the bank's immediate and future requirements for instantly available cash and in this sense increases the funding risk undertaken by the bank. Almost by definition, it is impossible to 'match' an overdraft facility with incoming deposits.

The second reason why it is most unlikely that all but the smallest proportion of a bank's deposits and loans will be maturity-matched is the growing role of the banking mechanism in 'maturity transformation'. We saw in Chapter 3 how the euromarkets have effectively converted the short-term deposits of oil-rich countries and others into medium- to long-term loans to developing and other countries. Precisely the same process has taken place in the domestic British banking system. Current accounts still remain a significant proportion of bank deposits, particularly for the clearing banks – albeit a smaller proportion than before – and other depositors who place their funds with banks are unlikely to do so with most of their funds for more than six months or a year. On the other hand, the average maturity of advances has lengthened considerably since the early 1960s; and where loans are made in the form of overdraft, it is probably the case that both bankers and borrowers now assume that the borrowing will be outstanding for longer than was the case previously. For industrial and commercial borrowers this trend has been encouraged by the drying up of the new issue market for debentures and loan stocks since the early 1970s – the only other major source available to British industry for long-term borrowings. And for individual borrowers, the entry of the clearing banks into the business of lending money for house purchase in the early 1980s marked the acceptance of a much longer commitment to provide funds to such borrowers than those banks had contemplated before.

Against this background of inevitable uncertainty about the continuity of individual deposits and about the timing of the draw-down and repayment of individual loans, coupled with the development of deliberate policies of mismatching prompted by the requirements of both borrowers and depositors, domestically and internationally, the funding risk has become a major preoccupation of banks. The traditional reaction of bankers throughout the ages to this funding risk has been to keep a proportion of its deposits in the form of ready cash (the 'cash ratio'); and since the continued confidence of depositors is a major factor in the actual degree of the funding risk faced by a bank, bankers have been as eager to show a healthy cash ratio in their published accounts as they have to maintain such a ratio for their own and their supervisors' prudential comfort.

The problem about holding immediately available cash is that it does not earn interest; and for cash on deposit, the more immediately available it is, the lower the rate of interest obtainable. This is but one of several examples of the continuing competing pressures in any banker's life between the motives of profit and prudence – or, in the crudest terms, between greed and fear. The actual cash ratio adopted by banks and regarded as a conventional yardstick by depositors and other outside commentators has emerged as a compromise between these competing motives. In the third edition of his classic textbook *Modern Banking*, published in 1951, Professor R. S. Sayers described the evolution of this ratio up to that time as follows:

> The desire for immediate profit encourages the banker to minimize his cash holding, but his desire for liquidity (based on a longer view of profit-earning capacity) encourages him to maximize his cash holding. These conflicting forces, in the course of the evolution of English banks we know today, led to a convention that a 'cash ratio' (ratio of cash to deposits) of ten or eleven per cent. was proper. In the first four decades of the twentieth century this conventional ratio was to an important extent illusory, the published figures of most banks being subject to 'window dressing'; but since 1946 a true cash ratio of eight per cent. has been established and the banks actually work very closely to this figure.[27]

The 8 per cent cash ratio was, in fact, mandatory for the London clearing banks (but not for other British banks) from 1946 to 1971. As we have seen, the ratio represents the proportion of a bank's deposits held in ready cash; and in the context of the London clearing banks, ready cash means cash in the till plus the bank's balance in its account with other banks, of which its account at the Bank of England is by far the most important. While it lasted, the mandatory cash ratio was, in theory at least, a useful weapon in the hands of the Bank of England in terms of both prudential and monetary control. In prudential control, it provided a definite minimum limit on the cash held by the clearing banks. In monetary control, it provided a formal link between the deposits of the clearing banks (and thus the greater part of the credit available in the economy) and their balances at the Bank of England: control of the latter, which the Bank obviously possessed, therefore implied control of the former, should the Bank wish to use it (which it did not).

The mandatory cash ratio was abandoned in 1971 for three

good and important reasons. First, it was imposed on the clearing banks only and since holdings of cash earned no interest, this gave them a clear competitive disadvantage *vis-à-vis* the other British banks which had been making serious inroads in the clearing banks' market share of British deposit banking in the 1960s. But, secondly and thirdly, the ratio had become redundant as an instrument of monetary and prudential control, as a result of the developing trends in the discount market and sterling interbank market, described in Chapter 3.

From a prudential point of view, a substantial cash ratio is clearly appropriate where there are no other assets available which are easily transformable into cash. To the extent that such assets *are* available, the need for a cash ratio of any given size is reduced, and the emphasis of the prudent banker is switched from his total holdings of cash to his total holdings of easily-cashable or liquid assets. The 'liquidity ratio', that is, the ratio of cash, call money, and discountable bills to total deposits, has indeed been an important concept in the management of British banks for many years, going back at least to the 1930s; and there has been a long-standing convention that this liquidity ratio should not fall below 30 per cent. The point is clearly set out in the context of the British clearing banks in the second edition of another famous textbook, by W. Manning Dacey, published in 1958, in the following terms:

> While the assets structure was never completely rigid, the pre-war pattern tended within fairly narrow limits to conform to the following general pattern:

			As % of deposits
Cash			10
Call money, say	6	'Money market assets'	
Bills discountable, say	14		20
		'Liquid assets'	30
Investments	20–25	'Earning assets'	70
Advances	45–50		
			100

> To be sure of meeting the demands of their depositors the banks not only maintained a cash reserve of at least 10 per cent. of deposits producing no income at all; they also buttressed this actual cash holding with money market assets of about double its own size, the return on which throughout the cheap money period was extremely small (for long periods only about ½ per cent.). For the sake of earnings, however, the banks would be unwilling to see the combined total of these three 'liquid assets' rise much above 30 per cent. of deposits, which means that they sought to hold the remaining 70 per cent. of their principal assets in the more remunerative form of investment and advances, the two main 'earning assets'.[28]

We saw in Chapter 3 how call money held by banks with discount houses and bills eligible for rediscount at the Bank of England can both be turned instantly into cash through the mechanism of the discount houses selling bills to the Bank of England: a bank needing cash can either call a call deposit from a discount house which, in turn, will put itself in funds by selling bills out of its own portfolio to the Bank of England, or alternatively it can sell eligible bills to the discount house which can on-sell them to the Bank. We saw, too, how a secondary market for CDs has been developed by the discount houses with sufficient depth to make it reasonable for a bank to regard CDs with a maturity of up to, say, six months as being very nearly cash. For these reasons, the 'liquidity ratio' is clearly more important to a bank's management and its supervisory authorities than a cash ratio from the point of view of the funding risk; and the actual cash ratio which is observed becomes one determined by practical convenience.

But even the liquidity ratio, while not redundant, has become less appropriate as a control on the funding risk than it was before the development of the interbank deposit markets. For one thing, to the extent that a bank *is* able to match the maturity of its outgoing loan with an incoming deposit, its requirement for a holding of cash to limit the funding risk is clearly reduced. For another thing, the very existence of the interbank market, with its present depth and breadth, must also reduce the size of any appropriate cash ratio. Provided a bank's standing in the interbank market and with other depositors is unblemished and the confidence of depositors maintained, and provided that the market continues to exist, a smaller cash ratio is almost certainly appropriate for that bank than would have been the case if the interbank market did not exist. This gives even greater significance – for a bank and the supervisory authorities – to the image of that bank which is given by its published accounts. It also gives, in the eyes of all bankers, even greater significance to the Bank of England's role of lender of last resort, described in Chapter 3, and to the continuation of its policy *always* to accommodate the requirements of the banking system, albeit at penal rates of interest. As one British banker put it when discussing the new principles of supervision with an official of the Bank of England, 'if you look after the liquidity of the market as a whole, we can look after the liquidity of our individual banks'.

The monitoring and control of a bank's exposure to the funding risk, in the circumstances described above, is a subject of some complexity and is certainly not susceptible to neat precision. In order to achieve a conceptual framework in which to discuss each bank's approach to the problem, the Bank of England initiated a rigorous debate within the British banking community with the publication of a paper entitled 'The Liquidity of Banks' in March 1981.[29] Of more importance in the present context is the final version of a paper entitled 'The Measurement of Liquidity'[30] which was published by the Bank in July 1982 and which established 'a framework for measuring liquidity applicable to banks generally, that will serve as a first step towards a qualitative assessment of the adequacy of the liquidity of individual banks taking account of their particular circumstances' (para. 5). This paper distils the best thoughts which emerged in the debate with the bankers and, since it will clearly remain the foundation of British banks' approach to the funding risk for many years to come it is worth quoting at some length.

The Bank's paper set out very clearly the liquidity requirements of all banks, in the following terms:

> Banks must be capable of meeting their obligations when they fall due. Such obligations mainly comprise deposits at sight or short notice, term deposits and commitments to lend, including unutilised overdraft facilities. The mix of these obligations and their incidence in any period of time will vary between different banks but the maintenance of an assured capacity to meet them is an essential principle of banking which is common to all. This capacity may be provided in the following ways:
>
> (i) by holding sufficient immediately available cash or liquefiable assets, subject to the qualification that marketable assets vary in quality in terms of the prices at which they are capable of being sold;
>
> (ii) by securing an appropriately matching future profile of cash flows from maturing assets, subject to the qualification that there may be shortfalls in practice if borrowers are unable to repay;
>
> (iii) by maintaining an adequately diversified deposit base in terms both of maturities and range of counter-parties (bank and non-bank) which depending importantly on the individual bank's standing in the market and on the general liquidity situation at the time, may provide the ability to raise fresh deposits without undue cost (para. 2).

Referring to the traditional measures of liquidity described above, in terms of the 'cash ratio' and the 'liquidity ratio', the Bank comments that

> measures of liquidity which have been employed hitherto have generally involved a comparison of deposit liabilities (in part or in total) with the available stock of certain assets classed as 'liquid'. This approach has the virtue of simplicity but does not take account of the development of liability or asset management techniques for controlling liquidity through cash flows. It also involves an over-sharp distinction between 'liquid' assets and other assets, many of which will be capable of generating cash in particular circumstances. (para. 6)

The bank's chosen measurement of liquidity is a combination of a measure of immediate liquidity together with a forward analysis of calls on that liquidity by commitments to provide funds (net of commitments by borrowers to repay) on various date-bands in the future:

> In this approach, liabilities and assets are inserted in a 'maturity ladder', with the net positions in each time period being accumulated. In the first maturity bands on the ladder this measure, by comparing sight and near sight liabilities with cash and assets capable of generating cash immediately, is similar to a customary liquid assets ratio. Marketable assets are placed at the start of the maturity date, rather than according to their maturity date, but account needs to be taken of limitations on their marketability and their susceptibility to price fluctuations. Commitments are recognised by being included as liabilities or as agreed in specific cases. The measure is thus a series of accumulating net mismatch positions in successive time bands. (para. 8)

As we have seen, marketable assets are placed at the start of the maturity ladder, where they could be said to contribute to the liquidity of the bank, in terms of the old 'liquidity ratio'. The treatment of these assets in the Bank's measurement

> takes account of the extent to which they can be sold for cash quickly (or used as security for borrowing), incurring little or no cost penalty; and of any credit or investment risks which may make their potential value less predictable. It is important that the market for the asset should be sufficiently deep to ensure a stable demand for it. An important factor in this is the willingness of the central bank to use the asset in its normal market operations. These considerations are recognised in the measurement by applying varying discounts normally against the market value of marketable assets, all of which . . . are included at the start of the maturity ladder. (para. 9(b)(iii))

The Bank's proposed discounts for the majority of sterling

assets are set out in Annex 1 to the paper and fall into three groups: a nil discount on, for example, Treasury bills, eligible bank bills and Government bonds with less than twelve months remaining term to maturity; a 5 per cent discount on, for example, other bills and CDs with less than six months remaining term to maturity and Government bonds with less than five years remaining term to maturity; and a 10 per cent discount on, for example, other bills and CDs with less than five years remaining to maturity and Government bonds with more than five years remaining term to maturity.

The lay-out to the maturity ladder, shown in Table 4.2, was illustrated in Annex 2 to the Bank's paper. The key figures to which both bank managements and their supervisors will pay most attention and on which they will put limits are the 'net cumulative position' for each time band. The Bank comments that

> how far into the future it is desirable to measure liquidity profiles depends very much on the circumstances of each bank. The point of maximum excess of liabilities over assets normally occurs within the first six months, although it can be later and it is therefore proposed that the profile should be measured up to 12 months. The Bank recognises, however, that in analysis and discussion it may be appropriate to concentrate more on the earlier maturities. (para. 10)

And it adds that

> as a separate matter, the Bank will also wish to continue to monitor the overall maturity transformation undertaken: for the further ahead a bank's assets mature, the more difficult it is to estimate confidently the credit and other risks which will attach to them until they mature, or to forecast the circumstances in which the bank will then be trading. (para. 11)

One further point should be quoted from the Bank's paper, which is relevant not only in the present context but also in the context of monetary control, discussed in Chapter 6:

In measuring liquidity a distinction has often been made between the position in sterling-denominated business and that in other currencies, although the positions in different foreign currencies have not normally been separately identified. Such distinctions may be appropriate because of the particular circumstances of a bank or its internal management policies. When this is the case, the Bank would expect to take account of these same divisions as a basis for its own monitoring. The Bank, however, also wishes to assess the liquidity of a bank's total business, undifferentiated as to currency denomination, since in principle, through the foreign exchange markets, obligations in one currency may be met by the availability of liquid funds in another. (para. 7)

TABLE 4.2

	Sight– 8 days	*8 days– 1 month*	*1–3 months*	*3–6 months*	*6–12 months*
Liabilities					
Deposits					
Commitments					
Less Assets					
Marketable					
Non-marketable					
Standby facilities					
Available	____	____	____	____	____
= *Net position*					
+/− Carried forward	____	____	____	____	____
= *Net cumulative position*	____	____	____	____	____

The reason why most banks – indeed, presumably all British banks – differentiated until recently between their sterling liquidity positions and their foreign currency liquidity positions was in large part because the two were divided by British exchange control, until it was abolished in 1979. Up to that time, there were very tight limits up to which a British bank was permitted to meet its obligations in foreign currencies by manufacturing such deposits through the swap markets out of available sterling deposits, in the manner described in Chapter 3, and even tighter limits up to which they were permitted to do so by outright purchases of those foreign currencies for sterling. On the other hand, British banks *were* permitted to manufacture sterling deposits out of eurocurrency deposits through the swap market.

The logic of this particular exchange control was simple. The manufacture of eurocurrency deposits of sterling involved a spot sale of sterling and thus a direct reduction in the external reserves of Britain (or, alternatively, a direct increase in the selling pressure on the exchange rate for sterling). The manufacture of sterling deposits, out of eurocurrency deposits through the swap market, on the other hand, involved a purchase of sterling in the spot market and thus a direct increase in the external reserves of Britain (or, alternatively, a direct increase in the buying pressure on the exchange rate for sterling). For most of the time that the exchange controls were in operation, of course, a decrease in the reserves was considered a bad thing from the point of view of economic policy generally, whereas an increase was considered a good thing; and where the authorities wished to restrain an inward movement of funds into the sterling deposit market through the swap, they were able to control it reasonably well by a combination of credit restraint on British banks and exchange controls preventing British resident corporations and individuals from borrowing sterling from non-British banks, or from borrowing eurocurrency deposits and swapping them into sterling themselves. The short period between the abolition of exchange control in October 1979 and the abolition of the 'corset' control on domestic sterling lending by British banks in June 1980 saw the dramatic efficiency with which the unsatisfied demand for domestic sterling credit, pent up by the corset, could, in fact, be satisfied through the eurocurrency and foreign exchange markets, once the exchange controls were taken off; and it was the unwinding of these inward flows which was one of the principal reasons behind the explosive growth of domestic lending by British banks and thus of the money supply figures which followed the abolition of the 'corset' in June 1980.

In the absence of exchange controls, the ever-increasing depth and sophistication of the eurocurrency deposit and foreign exchange markets described in Chapter 3 make it probable that an increasing number of British banks will differentiate less and less between their funding risks and liquidity positions in sterling on the one hand and foreign currencies on the other. The implications of this for both monetary control policy and exchange rate policy will be discussed in Chapter 6.

To conclude this section it is worth repeating that dramatic changes have taken place since the early 1960s in the very nature of the funding risks undertaken by British banks, partly as a result of the operations of the banks themselves but more particularly as a result of developments in the markets in which they operate, described in Chapter 3. These changes have necessitated an entirely fresh approach by both bankers and the supervising authorities to the identification, measurement and control of the risks being run. After a considerable debate involving both the bankers and their supervisors in the Bank of England, a new conceptual framework for such identification, measurement and control has been agreed and established, to replace the simpler but out-dated concepts of cash ratios and liquidity ratios; and this new framework has been defined and explained in the Bank of England's paper, 'The Measurement of Liquidity', published in July 1982 and summarised in this section. At the time of writing, it is much too early to say whether any common conventions will emerge as to what is a prudent level of liquidity for banks in general, as measured by this new yardstick, comparable to, say, the 8 per cent cash ratio and the 30 per cent liquidity ratio of former times; and, indeed, given the wide variety of banks operating in Britain it is doubtful if it will. But at least the bankers and the supervisors now have a framework and a measuring tool to judge the prudence of the banks they manage and supervise respectively, in the context of the funding risk.

The interest-rate mismatch risk

By lending for fixed periods and borrowing for different, usually shorter, periods a bank takes two quite distinct risks. One, the funding risk, was discussed in the last section; the second is the risk of an interest-rate mismatch. If a bank lends for, say, six months at a fixed rate of interest and takes a deposit of the same amount for the same period also at a fixed rate, it has eliminated its mismatch risk. If it lends for six months at a fixed rate and finances this lending with a three-month deposit it has exposed itself to a considerable mismatch risk, in that in three months' time, the rate of interest payable on a three-month deposit, to finance the second half of the period of the loan, may be substantially higher than the cost of three or six months' deposit when the loan was first made. By covering for a shorter period than three months, the bank is taking an even bigger mismatch risk.

Like all the other risks in banking described so far, there is nothing inherently wrong with taking a mismatch risk; indeed a deliberately mismatched position is a major function of the banking system, through maturity transformation, as well as a source of substantial profit – and loss. As in the case of the other risks, prudence does not necessarily, or frequently, require the elimination of the risk. It *does* require its precise measurement and the fixing of limits on its mismatch position by each individual bank.

To some extent, the measurement and control of the mismatch risk can be effected by the same tools as the measurement and control of the funding risk, described above. The concept of a 'maturity ladder' is entirely appropriate for both; and most banks will produce such a ladder on a regular basis for the benefit of their management and supervisors. As in the funding risk, the key figures to which managers and supervisors will pay most attention and on which they will impose limits are the 'net cumulative position' for each time band. But the mismatch risk is rather more complicated to measure, in that it is two dimensional: not only is a high 'net cumulative position' for any one time band indicative of a high exposure to risk, but also the period of time and the number of time bands over which that high net cumulative position extends. The advent of computerised accounting has made it possible for an instantly updatable ladder to be produced showing a bank's mismatched position on each day into the future and thus a net cumulative position for every day until the last maturity date of outgoing loans. Many banks will probably put a limit on the net cumulative position on any one future date, for funding as much as mismatch reasons; but the most important mismatch limit should be expressed as a limit on the average net cumulative position for a specified period of time. What that specified period should be will depend very much on the type of bank in question and thus the type of assets it holds.

But there are two important differences between the funding position and the mismatch position. The first relates to 'variable rate loans'. As we have seen, one of the functions of banking systems, domestic and international, is to transform the maturity of the funds available by taking in short-term deposits – up to, say, three or six months – and lending some of them out in the form of medium-term loans for five to seven years or longer. To lend for, say, seven years at a fixed rate of interest and finance the loan by a series of three- or six-month deposits would clearly be wildly imprudent, as some banks, particularly in Germany, found to their cost in the upward surge of nominal interest rates in nearly all financial centres in the 1970s. The technique has therefore grown up of lending on a variable interest rate basis. On this basis, a borrower agrees at the outset of the loan to pay not a fixed rate of interest throughout its life, but a rate of interest adjusted every three or six months to be an agreed margin over the cost of three or six month deposits in the appropriate currency in the interbank markets. It is worth adding that whilst the variable rate technique neatly eliminates the mismatch risk from the position of the lending bank, in so doing it throws that risk directly on to the borrower and the depositor. Much of the anguish amongst borrowers, personal, corporate and sovereign, which has accompanied the tight money policies in Britain, the United States and most of the non-Communist world of the late 1970s and early 1980s has been the direct result of the high nominal rates of interest obtaining. And a proportion of the loans bearing these high rates were variable rate loans arranged before the dramatic increase in interest rates generally. It should, of course, be added that whilst escalating rates of interest can greatly hurt borrowers on the basis of variable rates, those same escalating rates can greatly benefit depositors with banks. And to the extent that the high real rates of interest obtaining in the early 1980s have hurt many borrowers they have to the same extent benefited depositors.

Variable rate loans should clearly be treated differently in a mismatch risk maturity ladder than in a funding risk maturity ladder. For the former the date of the next refixing of the rate of interest is the relevant 'maturity' date to be entered into the ladder; for the latter, the final maturity date of the loan is the relevant date.

The second main difference between the funding position and the mismatch position relates to marketable securities. We have seen how such assets are placed at the start of the maturity ladder in measuring the funding position, thereby recognising that high degree of liquidity, and that varying discounts are applied against the market value of these marketable assets to take account of any credit or investment risk which may make their potential value less predictable. In measuring the mismatch position, the situation is quite different. A three-month Treasury bill, for example, may be a very liquid asset; but it still has a rate of interest which is fixed for three months. To finance the holding of a three-month Treasury bill with, say, deposits fixed for one week at a time is every bit as mismatched in terms of interest rates as a three-month loan financed by one-week deposits; and the potential loss or profit to the bank holding it is virtually the same. True, the Treasury bill could be sold off at the end of the first week if rates have gone against the bank holding it; but the price at which it can be sold will reflect very precisely the cost of money in the markets for the remaining life of the bill. For this reason, there is a strong case for placing marketable assets in the mismatch maturity ladder on the date of their final maturity.

There is a further point to be made about the treatment of marketable assets, and that is the widely respected accounting convention that marketable assets should appear in the published balance sheet of banks and other corporations at the lower of cost value or market value on the date the balance sheet is drawn up. If this convention is strictly observed, there is a danger that it can distort the commercial judgement of the bank in question. A bank may, for example, wish to obtain a fixed rate of interest for three years on a certain sum of money to fit in with its other dispositions – to match off an incoming three-year deposit, for instance. It has a choice of doing so by lending the money out for three years at a fixed rate of interest or of buying a three-year marketable asset. In both cases, assuming the credit risk to be undoubted in each of them, the bank has no mismatch position; and in acquiring a marketable asset it would be improving its overall funding position, whereas by making the fixed-rate loan it would be leaving that position unaltered. But by buying a marketable asset it has opened up the additional risk that interest rates may be such on the date its balance sheet is drawn up as to cause it to make a substantial provision: that is, that the market price will be substantially below the cost price and the difference will be provided for by a deduction from its profits for the period. No such provision or deduction would be called for in the case of a fixed-rate, non-marketable loan. Various devices have been invented to reduce or eliminate this distortion, the simplest being to treat marketable assets of specified quality and up to a specified maximum maturity as if they were loans: that is, valuing them in the balance sheet at cost and spreading over the period to maturity any difference – premium or discount – between the original cost and the total proceeds to be received on maturity.

This is not the place to discuss the merits of these varying 'smoothing' devices in the balance sheet valuation of the marketable assets. It is sufficient to say that they are sometimes assailed on the grounds that the basic convention of valuing marketable assets as the lower of cost or market value is itself a salutory discipline on a bank's management and that any device designed to mitigate its effect on the bank's profit and loss account would itself weaken that discipline. The purpose of the measurement of the mismatch position proposed in this section is to provide the tools for just that discipline, without the distorting side-effects of the convention of 'lower of cost or market' valuations. A theoretical calculation of the difference between cost and worst possible market is, of course, a crucial factor in answering the basic question involved in setting a limit on the mismatch position: how much can a bank afford to lose by getting its position wrong?

We have seen that there is a strong case for measuring and controlling a bank's funding risk on an overall basis, taking all currencies together. The same does not, of course, apply to the mismatch risk. Indeed, the swap market in foreign exchange, described in Chapter 3, opens up the opportunity to take a whole series of mismatch positions, in addition to those in each individual currency deposit. To take the simple example of a bank which borrows and lends in sterling and dollars but no other currencies: in this case it will have two mismatch positions: one in sterling and one in dollars. It may well arbitrage between the two markets: for example taking one-month dollars, swapping them into one-month sterling and lending the one-month sterling. In this case it has not changed its mismatch position in either currency: the swap will be recorded in its maturity ladder as if it was an incoming deposit in sterling and an outgoing deposit in dollars, both for one month.

But besides this simple arbitrage, the swap market provides the opportunity to take a third mismatch position: a mismatch in the sterling/dollar swap. Thus, in the example above, the bank could borrow the three-month dollars and lend the three-month sterling, but cover the swap not for the full three months but for one month only, with a view to covering off the swap for the remaining two months at a more advantageous rate in a month's time. In this case, the bank would be taking a view not on movements in sterling interests simply or in dollar interest rates simply but in the differential between the two. Put another way, a one against three month position in sterling deposits – lending money for three months and covering with an incoming deposit for one month – is taking a deliberate view that the cost of covering for three months from the start would be higher than the cost of covering one month from the start and the next two months at the end of, say, the first month. A one against three month position on the sterling/dollar swap is taking a deliberate view that the swap cost of swapping for three months from the outset would be greater than the swap cost of covering the first month from the outset and months two and three at the end of, say, the first month. And as we saw in Chapter 3, the efficiency of the foreign exchange market sees to it that the swap cost for one month is effectively the differential between one-month interest rates in sterling and one-month interest rates in dollars, that the swap cost for three months is effectively the differential between three-month interest rates in sterling and three-month interest rates in dollars, and so on.

Bearing in mind that the dealing room of a London bank active in foreign exchange will probably be running active positions on sterling/dollar swaps, dollar/Deutschemark swaps, dollar/Swiss franc swaps – and possibly one or two other currencies, depending on the specialisation and nationality of the ultimate parent of the bank in question – it can be seen that the opportunities provided by the eurocurrency and foreign exchange markets for 'taking a view' on movements in interest rates in individual currencies and on movements in the differential between interest rates in different currencies for different maturities are very wide-ranging indeed. The point to be made in the present context is not that these views should not be taken; indeed, it is exactly because many banks are prepared to take such a view for a limited amount that the London market has the breadth and depth that it has. The point is rather that any bank taking such a view should have to hand a tight and precise mechanism to measure and control the size of the view being taken, that is, of the mismatch risk. The maturity ladder described above to measure and control the simpler mismatch positions in individual currencies is easily adaptable to measure the mismatch in the swap positions in each currency, or between each pair of currencies. And computer programmes are now available to give the managements of banks and their supervisors very precise information on the positions and risks being run.

One final point should be made about interest rate mismatching. In September 1982, a new market appeared in London which provides an opportunity, additional to the deposit and swap markets, for bank managements and others wishing to reduce the risk in an interest-rate mismatch position to do so by 'hedging' the position by contracting to buy or sell financial futures: the London International Financial Futures Exchange (or LIFFE, as it has come to be called). In the words of LIFFE's own introductory booklet, 'a financial futures contract is an agreement to buy or sell a standard quantity of a specific financial instrument at a future date and at a price agreed between the parties through open outcry on the floor of an organised exchange'. The technical terms used in this definition were themselves explained as follows: 'standard quantity' means that each contract for a given type of financial instrument is for the same standard quantity (e.g. $1m); 'specific financial instrument' means that the contract specification lays down not only the type of financial instrument – for example, a three-month time deposit, twenty-year gilt edged stock or a foreign currency – but also its quality in terms of such items as coupon rate and maturity; 'future date' means that the delivery of the amounts specified in the contract must take place during a specified month in the future; and 'open outcry' means that all transactions must be executed on the floor of the exchange and that prices are instantly available to all participants. At the time of writing, three types of contract relevant to hedging interest-rate mismatched positions are traded on LIFFE: a sterling three-month time deposit, a sterling long-dated gilt edged stock (based on a twenty-year Government stock) and a eurodollar three-month time deposit. After only a few months' trading, it is already clear that LIFFE does provide opportunities to limit, if not completely eliminate the risks of a mismatched position; and the experience of the now well-established markets in financial futures in Chicago suggests that as more participants enter the market, thereby increasing its depth, LIFFE may well become an important source of opportunities to reduce the risks in mismatched positions and to do so for longer periods into the future than any opportunities provided by the markets in deposits and swaps.

FOREIGN CURRENCY RISKS

We saw in Chapter 3 that many banks play an active role in the foreign exchange markets, spot and forward and, indeed, how the breadth, depth and efficiency of the London markets in foreign exchange and foreign currency deposits depend on the willingness of a large number of banks to take positions in one currency against another. And we saw in Chapter 1 how dramatically the risks involved in taking such positions have increased since the floating of exchange rates – to the extent that they brought down one relatively small German bank and caused embarrassingly large losses to be taken by three major, well-known European banks. In these circumstances, the foreign exchange risk – the risk that a bank is exposed to if the rate of exchange for one currency against another moves in either direction – is a matter of great concern to both bank managements and their prudential supervisors.

As in the other risks described in the second and third sections of this chapter, the first priority of a bank's management must be to set up a mechanism to identify and measure the risks being run, which can also be used to control them by the imposition of limits. A prerequisite of such a mechanism is a conceptual framework within which the nature of the risks themselves can be discussed and understood within a bank's own management and also between that management and the prudential supervisors.

As in the case of capital adequacy – the risks a bank runs in its gearing ratio and its risk assets ratio – and liquidity risks, the Bank of England initiated a debate with and amongst British bankers, following the enactment of the Banking Act 1979, to establish a common conceptual framework within which it could discuss with each bank its own limits on its foreign currency exposure and also the extent and effectiveness of that bank's internal controls to see that the limits are observed. The Bank concluded this debate with the issue of a paper in April 1981 entitled 'Foreign Currency Exposure' which set out the basis on which the Bank will 'measure, monitor and discuss with banks and licensed deposit-taking institutions . . . their exposure to movements in exchange rates.[31] Since this paper represents a distillation of the views of the British banking community as well as of the Bank itself – in the words of the Bank, it 'reflects the outcome of consultations with the banking community on the discussion paper on the same subject issued in December 1979' (footnote to para. 1) – and since it is the Bank's stated intention that arrangements described in the paper 'will form part of the regular process of supervision' (para. 1), it will be quoted in some detail in this section.

The foreign currency exposure of a bank falls into two quite distinct parts: its dealing position and its structural position. Its dealing position is the result of its normal dealing operations in the spot and forward markets in foreign exchange, already described, and is, or should be, very precisely calculable on a regular basis. Its structural position is more akin to the foreign currency exposure of many industrial and commercial corporations, particularly with fixed assets or long-term borrowings outside their own country, which were mentioned in Chapter 3. The structural position of a bank, like that of any other institution, is not liable to change at short notice; the bank's management may or may not feel it appropriate to hedge a structural position at any particular time by taking an equal and opposite position in its dealing position which is, of course, very easily adjustable at very short notice.

The point is set out in the Bank's paper:

> Banks often find it convenient to identify and distinguish foreign currency exposures which arise from their daily or 'normal' banking operations (henceforth referred to as 'dealing' positions) from those exposures which are intended to be of a longer-term nature (henceforth referred to as 'structural' positions). The Bank believes this is a valid distinction and that structural positions may conveniently be considered separately from dealing positions. It will, therefore be prepared to exclude structural positions from the guidelines agreed with each bank. This distinction does not mean that the Bank considers structural exposures are without risk, and the aggregate foreign currency position included in the risk assets ratio set out in the Bank's paper

> *The Measurement of Capital* encompass dealing and structural positions. (para. 10)

As to the precise dividing line between dealing and structural positions, the Bank accepts that

> each bank will have its own views on the categorisation of exposures as dealing or structural. The dividing line will not always be clear cut and will depend on the particular circumstances of that bank . . . The Bank would normally accept, as structural, exposures arising from banks' fixed and long-term assets and liabilities, including such items as loan capital, premises, and investments in subsidiaries and associates. It might also be appropriate to treat, as structural, positions which banks are obliged to maintain as a result of laws or market conditions to which their overseas affiliates are subject, and positions which arise as a result of reserves or provisions being maintained in currencies appropriate to the banking risks against which they are being held. (para. 11)

The precise limits imposed on the dealing operations of a bank must ultimately remain the responsibility of that bank's management; but these are set in the context of guidelines agreed bilaterally with the Bank of England. As the paper states, 'the Bank will not set any formal limits on the size of a bank's foreign currency positions, but will agree dealing position guidelines with each institution individually. These will take account of the institution's particular circumstances and expertise' (para. 12). Banks' positions are monitored by the Bank through the mechanism of monthly returns:

> The returns will give, in contracted currency amounts, the net spot long or short position and the net forward long or short position in each currency at the close of business on the reporting day. The sum of these positions will give the overall net position in each currency, in currency terms. Where it has been agreed that part of a bank's position in a particular currency should be regarded as structural, this part will be deducted from the overall net position in that currency to give the dealing position. (paras 18, 19)

Perhaps the most significant paragraph of the Bank's paper in the context of the allocation of responsibility is this: 'The return made at the end of each period should also contain a report of each occasion on which the net open dealing position in each currency or the aggregate net short open position has exceeded the guidelines agreed between the Bank and the reporting institutions' (para. 23). In other words, a bank's management may exceed the 'guidelines' agreed with the Bank with impunity but must report the excess retrospectively: the clear implication is that if the bank's management can justify the excess, the Bank will not complain.

As to the guidelines themselves, these

> will be expressed in terms of a relationship between the dealing position and the bank's capital, because it is ultimately from this source that any loss arising from the position has to be made good. As a general rule, for banks which are experienced in foreign exchange the Bank will expect to agree the following guidelines:
>
> (i) Net open dealing position in any one currency: not more than 10% of the adjusted capital base, as defined in the Bank's paper *The Measurement of Capital* for the risk measure.
> (ii) Net short open dealing positions of all currencies taken together: not more than 15% of the adjusted capital base.
>
> The Bank would expect banks inexperienced in foreign exchange to operate within more conservative guidelines. Since exposure to a movement in any exchange rate is represented by both a long position in one currency and an equal but opposite short position in another currency (or several currencies combined), a bank's aggregate exposure can be measured as the sum of either its long or short positions. For purposes of calculating (ii) above, each bank's overall exposure will be measured as the sum of its net short open positions, spot and forward taken together (para. 13).

Setting guidelines with the Bank of England as the supervisory authority and translating them into internal limits for dealers is only part of the business of limiting a bank's risk in its foreign currency exposure. The other, equally important, part is to establish internal control procedures to ensure that the limits are observed – and that the bank's management is properly informed as to the exposure being undertaken. This is not the place to discuss such procedures: the Bank of England circulated a paper on the subject in 1974, following the 'reports of the losses suffered [that year] by banks in a number of countries, as a result of operations in the foreign exchange markets'; and an extract from this circular was attached to the Bank's paper quoted above.

One final point should be made about a bank's exposure to risk as a result of foreign exchange operations. Besides the risks resulting from movements in exchange rates, there is also the risk that a counterparty will not perform under its contract. This risk is particularly acute in the forward exchange market. A classic example was the plight of banks with outstanding foreign exchange contracts with Bankhaus Herstatt when it closed its doors in June 1974. And this particular example underlined the fact that two separate risks may be involved, one a great deal more horrendous than the other. The first risk is that the counterparty will go bust between the date on which the forward contract is agreed and the value date of the contract: in this case the bank taking the risk is left with an uncovered forward foreign exchange commitment, the re-covering of which in the market may or may not involve a loss depending on the movement in forward rates between the date of the original deal and the date on which the re-covering takes place. The second, more horrendous, risk is that the counterparty will go bust on the actual day on which the forward deal is due to be settled; and this risk is, of course, run by entering a spot deal in the foreign exchange market as well as a forward deal. In this case, as several banks found who had deals due for settlement with Bankhaus Herstatt on the day it closed its doors, there is the risk that the bank concerned will honour its side of the deal by paying the appropriate sum in one currency to the failed bank but will not receive the appropriate sum from the failed bank in return. Since foreign exchange deals in the major currencies, spot and forward, can run into the equivalent of millions of US dollars per deal the potential loss resulting from such a situation can be enormous.

Different banks take different attitudes as to the size of the net outstanding forward commitments they should have with any one counterparty; some argue strongly that no such name-by-name limit is appropriate. A fairly common approach is to fix a limit for each bank in the market as a multiple – often, four – of the deposit limit for that bank in interbank dealings, on the logical basis that if the counterparty failed to honour a contract, it could probably be 'undone' in the market at a maximum potential loss of about that proportion.

NOTES

1. These quotations are taken from a covering note issued by the Committee in Basle in March 1982. The paper is available to banks through their own supervisory authorities. The activities of the Basle Committee are described in Chapter 5.
2. W. P. Cooke, 'The international banking scene: a supervisory perspective', speech to the Financial Times World Banking Conference in London, 9 December 1982, reprinted in *Bank of England Quarterly Bulletin* (March 1983) p. 64.
3. The Basle paper carried the footnote that, 'in this connection the analyst may find helpful the Manual on Statistics compiled by International Organisations on Countries' External Indebtedness (BIS Basle, March 1979).
4. 'The international banking scene: a supervisory perspective', p. 64.
5. Letter dated 4 March 1983 to the British Bankers' Association and other national bankers' associations, for onward transmission to their member banks. The function of the Institute, as set out by Mr Ogden, are quoted in this letter.
6. F. M. Burton and Hisashi Inoue, 'Country risk evaluation methods: a survey of systems in use', *The Banker* (January 1983) p. 43.

7. Dr David Lomax, 'Sovereign Risk Analysis Now', *The Banker* (January 1983) pp. 37–8.
8. Estimates quoted in an article by Paul Ellman, 'U.S. banking crisis feared over Mexico'. *The Times*, 20 December 1982.
9. Figures prepared by Goldman Sachs, *Financial Weekly*, 26 November 1982.
10. Figure quoted in *The Economist*, 29 January 1983.
11. 'Banks to monitor foreign lending', *Financial Times*, 2 December 1982, p. 6.
12. 'Country risk evaluation methods: a survey of systems in use', p. 42.
13. David Lascelles, 'U.S. bank regulation after the debt "crisis" ', *The Banker* (January 1983) p. 21.
14. These definitions are now laid down by the Bank of England as the standard basis of calculation for all banks. For more detailed definitions, see 'The Measurement of Capital', *Bank of England Quarterly Bulletin* (September 1980) p. 324.
15. Ibid., p. 324, para. 4.
16. Evidence by the Committee of London Clearing Bankers to the Committee to Review the Functioning of Financial Institutions (CLCB, 1978) p. 63, para. 5.13.
17. Ibid., p. 63, paras 5.14, 5.15.
18. Wilson Committee: Evidence on the Financing of Industry and Trade, Vol. 5: Written Evidence by the Accepting Houses Committee, p. 11, para. 26.
19. 'The Capital and Liquidity Adequacy of Banks', *Bank of England Quarterly Bulletin* (September 1975) p. 241. This paper was the forerunner of the final papers, 'The Measurement of Capital' and 'The Measurement of Liquidity' published in 1980 and 1982, respectively.
20. 'The Measurement of Capital', p. 327, para. 28.
21. 'Prudential arrangements for the discount market', *Bank of England Quarterly Bulletin* (June 1982) p. 209.
22. 'The Measurement of Capital', p. 324, paras 6, 7.
23. Committee of London Clearing Bankers, Evidence to the Wilson Committee, p. 63, para. 5.14.
24. 'The Measurement of Capital', p. 328, para. 31.
25. Ibid., p. 328, para. 30.
26. Ibid., p. 328, para. 33.

27. R. S. Sayers, *Modern Banking*, 3rd edn (Oxford University Press, 1951) p. 33.
28. W. Manning Dacey, *The British Banking Mechanism*, 2nd rev. edn (Hutchinson, 1958), p. 80.
29. Reprinted in *Bank of England Quarterly Bulletin* (March 1981) p. 40.
30. Reprinted in *Bank of England Quarterly Bulletin* (September 1982) pp. 399–402. Where quotations over the next few pages are followed by reference to a paragraph number, they are taken from this paper.
31. 'Foreign Currency Exposure', reprinted in *Bank of England Quarterly Bulletin* (June 1981) pp. 235–7. Where a quotation is followed by reference to a paragraph number in this section, it is taken from this paper.

5 The Prudential Supervision of Banks

THE REGULATORY FRAMEWORK IN BRITAIN

The present arrangements for the prudential supervision and regulation of British banks stem directly from the Banking Act 1979. This, in turn, was a response to growing pressures throughout the late 1970s for a more formal system of prudential regulation than had existed up to that time. As we saw in Chapter 1, these pressures sprang from two sets of factors: first, factors of philosophy or policy and secondly, the course of practical events which threw the requirements of philosophy and politics into sharper focus. The events included the secondary banking crisis of 1973–5, the uncertainties, and losses incurred, in the foreign exchange markets following the free floating of exchange rates in 1973 and the problems of recycling oil money internationally following the major increase in the price of oil in 1973.

The factors of philosophy and politics were part of the growing acceptance of 'consumerism' in Britain, the rest of Europe and the United States: that is, the widespread acceptance of the proposition that it is a proper and necessary function of national governments to protect the consumer in all his activities from exploitation by manufacturers of the products he consumes and providers of the services he uses. Within this general philosophy, the protection of depositors – and, particularly, the small individual depositors – was and is seen as a proper responsibility of government in its own right, quite apart from the more general responsibility to preserve the confidence of the depositing public in the banking system and thus preserve the stability of that system.

These pressures would probably have resulted in new regulations in banking supervision in any case; but the formulation of these regulations, and the enactment of legislation giving them legal backing was given an added impetus by the adoption in Brussels in December 1977 of the First Directive of the European Economic Community (EEC) on the co-ordination of laws, regulations and administrative provisions relating to the taking up and pursuit of the business of credit institutions (document 77/780/EEC). This 'First Banking Co-ordination Directive', as it has come to be called, made it a legal requirement that all Member States of the EEC 'shall require credit institutions subject to this Directive to obtain authorisation before commencing their activities';[1] and it obliged all Member States to lay down the requirements for such authorisations, subject to the detailed provisions of the Directive. These detailed provisions of the Directive will be discussed later in this chapter. At this point it is sufficient to note that at the time of the adoption of the Directive at the end of 1977, Britain and the Netherlands were the only two Member States which had no legal requirements for the prior authorisation of credit institutions. (It should be noticed that the 'First Banking Co-ordination Directive' is concerned with the authorisation of *credit institutions* rather than *deposit-taking institutions*: that is, institutions which *both* take deposits *and* extend loans. As has been pointed out elsewhere, 'by providing for the prior authorisations of all deposit-taking institutions, including those which do not extend loans but which nevertheless finance their own business to any material extent out of deposits, the Act goes further than is strictly necessary under our EEC obligations.'[2])

Against this background, the Banking Act did three main things. It required any institution in the business of taking deposits from the public to be authorised by the Bank of England in one of two separate categories, recognised banks and licenced deposit-taking institutions; it laid down the criteria to be applied by the Bank of England in granting such recognitions and licences and in the supervision of the institutions concerned; and it established a deposit protection fund to which all recognised and licenced institutions have to contribute.

Arrangements for recognition and licensing

The Act lays down that no person or corporation may 'accept a deposit in the course of carrying on a business which is a deposit-taking business' unless it is either the Bank of England, a 'recognised bank', a 'licensed institution' or specifically exempt from the Act; and it defines a 'deposit-taking business' as one where

(a) in the course of the business money received by way of deposit is lent to others, or
(b) any other activity of the business is financed, wholly or to any material extent, out of the capital of or the interest on money received by way of deposit. [Article 1]

The list of exemptions (contained in Schedule 1 of the Act) caused considerable controversy when the Act was being drafted and the bill debated in Parliament. The basic principle enunciated by the British Bankers' Association (BBA) on behalf of the British banking community was that all institutions providing the same services and competing in the same market places should, as far as possible, be subject to the same prudential controls, and that no institution or group of institutions should enjoy privileges not enjoyed by others. This principle is based on two simple premises. First, that simple systems of controls are, on the whole, the more efficient systems of controls and a multiplicity of systems provides scope for individual institutions to escape the full rigours of any of them: the secondary banking crisis in Britain of 1973–5 provided a clear demonstration of this point. Secondly, that the fairer a system of control or supervision, in terms of even-handedness of treatment between competing institutions, the healthier the competition is likely to be between the institutions to the benefit of their customers. Any exemptions from the Act seemed potentially to confer two unfair advantages on the exempt institutions: that they would be subjected to less rigorous supervision than recognised banks or licensed deposit-taking institutions and that they would be exempt from contributing to the deposit protection fund. The most controversial exemptions were the Post Office, and thus the National Girobank, the Trustee Savings Banks and the building societies.

As far as the National Girobank is concerned, the second potential advantage was nullified by a formal undertaking from the Treasury, at the time the bill was being drafted and debated, that the National Girobank would be obliged to make payments to the Treasury exactly equal to the contributions it would have been obliged to make to the Deposit Protection Fund, had it been a member of the scheme. The first potential advantage was countered by an undertaking from the Treasury that the National Girobank would be subjected to prudential controls which would not give it an advantage over the banks and deposit-taking institutions who were the subject of prudential controls by the Bank of England under the Act. But this situation is not clear-cut. As we saw in Chapter 4, virtually all the limits imposed on a bank's operations for prudential reasons relate back, directly or indirectly, to that bank's capital resources; and one of the major principles put forward in that chapter was the principle of flexibility under which the supervisory authority will take into account the particular characteristics of a bank and its business before coming to a view as to the appropriate levels for its capital adequacy. A particular characteristic of the National Girobank, shared with many other banking institutions in other countries, particularly Member States of the EEC, is the fact that it is directly owned by the State. The particular case of the National Girobank and its capital adequacy was highlighted by the CLCB, in its evidence to the Wilson Committee quoted in Chapter 2; and the British banking community can be expected to remain vigilant to ensure that its state-owned competitor is not allowed any competitive advantage.

The exemption of the Trustee Savings Banks (TSBs) from the Act was always seen as a temporary measure and runs out, unless reviewed, in 1985. One of the purposes of the major reorganisation of the TSBs, announced in 1982 and mentioned in Chapter 2, is to give them a legal structure which will meet the requirements of the Banking Act; and it is intended that once this structure is in place, the exemption will be lifted.

The exemption of the building societies was perhaps the most controversial of all. We have seen in Chapter 2 that, in the opinion of the CLCB, the building societies enjoy four 'artificial competitive advantages' over other deposit-taking institutions; and one of these, which they share with other mutual and public sector institutions, is that 'the prudential constraints which these institutions are expected to observe in order to ensure their capital adequacy are . . . less onerous than those observed by commercial banks'. This supposed advantage comes about in two ways: first, the fact that the building societies are regulated by a different authority than commercial banks and, secondly, as we saw in Chapter 2, the very financial structure of the building societies – their mutual form of organisation – does appear to shield them from the very salutory discipline of having to make profits and be answerable for those profits to shareholders.

At the time of the debate which preceded the passing of the Banking Act, these anxieties of commercial bankers were soothed by the assurance that building societies were 'already satisfactorily regulated and supervised under statute' – a reference to the responsibility held by the Chief Registrar of Friendly Societies, under the Building Societies Act 1962, for keeping a register of building societies and for their prudential supervision by means of annual returns. On the matter of building societies' exemption from the requirement to contribute to the deposit protection fund, the bankers were assured that in practice informal arrangements existed under which the larger societies effectively insured the depositors with all members of the Building Societies' Association (BSA) against loss resulting from the failure of any society; and reference was made to Section 43 of the Building Societies Act 1962, which enables the societies to form a deposit protection scheme of their own.

This faith in the existing arrangements was somewhat shattered by the dramatic failure, through fraud, of the Grays Building Society in March 1978. The Building Societies'

Association quickly gave a public undertaking that the Grays' shareholders and depositors would not lose money; and the five largest societies formed a sort of Lifeboat to bail out these shareholders and depositors. But the important point about the Grays episode, from the banks' point of view, was that it demonstrated beyond reasonable doubt that this substantial group of competitors was the subject of a system of supervision which was not only much less onerous than that imposed on the banks but was also totally inadequate. On the question of deposit insurance, some bankers pulled back from the demand that building societies should be required to join the same scheme as the banks, on the simple grounds that the demands on a common Fund from another Grays-style débâcle would probably exceed the contributions of all the other societies put together; but all bankers were united in their demand that, if banks were required to contribute to a Deposit Protection Fund, building societies should be required to contribute to some such scheme as well.

In the event, both the Thatcher Government which came to office in 1979 and the building societies themselves were in general agreement that a new legislative framework had become necessary for the prudential supervision of building societies and, indeed, for their constitution generally. The Thatcher Government indicated that such a framework could be enacted in a new parliament, assuming the Conservative Party was returned to power for a second period of office; the BSA themselves hoped for legislation before the end of 1985 and made their first contribution to the preceding debate by publishing in January 1983 a report of a Committee set up by the BSA in June 1981 to look into the building societies' constitution, under the chairmanship of Mr John Spalding of the Halifax Building Society. The Spalding Report, which was regarded very much as a 'Green Paper' or preliminary discussion document, proposed a fairly massive extension of the powers of building societies to include conveyancing, surveying, hire purchase, consumer lending, banking and insurance. This is not the place to offer any contribution to this debate, except to re-emphasise the principle rehearsed by the bankers in the run up to the Banking Act 1979 that all institutions providing the same services and competing in the same market places should, so far as is possible, be subject to the same prudential controls.

It should be added that the 'First Banking Co-ordination Directive' adopted in Brussels in 1977 exempted the building societies from the requirement that they should obtain authorisation before commencing their activities for only a limited period of time. Accordingly, a Statutory Instrument in 1981 required the Registrar of Friendly Societies to give positive authorisation for each new society and effectively confirmed existing authorisations. In deciding whether to authorise a society, the two main criteria are that the society's capital must be at least £50 000 and that the business is 'effectively directed by two individuals of sufficiently good repute and sufficient experience to perform their duties'.

As we have seen, Article 1 of the Banking Act requires that, apart from the Bank of England and the institutions specifically listed as exempt in Schedule 1 of the Act, all institutions which accept deposits must be either 'recognised banks' or 'licensed deposit-taking institutions'. And Schedule 2 of the Act lays down the minimum criteria to be observed by the Bank in granting to an institution either *recognition* as a bank or a *licence* to take deposits.

The minimum requirements for a *recognised bank* are that

1. The institution, or in the case of a new institution its shareholder, 'enjoys, and has for a reasonable period of time enjoyed, a high reputation and standing in the financial community' (Schedule 2, para. 1)
2. The institution provides or will provide in the United Kingdom 'either a wide range of banking services or a highly specialised banking service'. A 'wide range of banking services' means all of the following:
   (a) current or deposit account facilities in sterling or foreign currency for members of the public or for bodies corporate or the acceptance of funds in sterling or foreign currency in the wholesale money markets;
   (b) finance in the form of overdraft or loan facilities in sterling or foreign currency for members of the public or for bodies corporate or the lending of

funds in sterling or foreign currency in the wholesale money markets;

(c) foreign exchange services for domestic and foreign customers;

(d) finance through the medium of bills of exchange and promissory notes together with finance for foreign trade and documentation in connection with foreign trade; and

(e) financial advice for members of the public or for bodies corporate on investment management services and facilities for arranging the purchase and sale of securities in sterling or foreign currency. (para. 2)

The Bank of England is given discretion under the Act, when determining whether to give an institution the status of a recognised bank, to disregard the fact that it does not or will not provide one or two of the services specified in (c) to (e) above: that is, the Bank may choose to recognise an institution provided it takes deposits, makes loans and provides just one of the three remaining services specified. The Act is curiously silent on the definition of a 'highly specialised banking service'; and at the time of writing the discount houses are believed to be the only institutions to be recognised as banks on this basis.

3. the business of the institution is carried on 'with integrity and prudence and with those professional skills which are consistent with the range and scale of the institution's activities'. (para. 3)
4. 'At least two individuals effectively direct the business of the institution'. (para. 4)
5. The institution has net assets (defined as paid-up capital and reserves) of not less than £5m in the case of an institution providing a wide range of banking services and £250 000 in the case of an institution providing a highly specialised banking service. (para. 5)
6. The institution maintains net assets which, 'together with other financial resources available to the institution of such a nature and amount as are considered appropriate by the Bank, are of an amount which is commensurate with the scale of the institution's operations'. (para. 6)

The minimum requirements for *licensed institutions* are that

1. 'Every person who is a director, controller or manager of the institution is a fit and proper person to hold that position'. (para. 7)
2. 'At least two individuals effectively direct the business of the institution'. (para. 8)
3. The institution has net assets of at least £250 000 (para. 9)
4. The institution conducts its business in a prudent manner and, in particular,
   (a) maintains 'net assets of such an amount as, together with other financial resources available to it of such a nature and amount as are considered appropriate by the Bank, is sufficient to safeguard the interest of depositors' having regard to 'the scale and nature of the liabilities of the institution and the sources and amounts of deposits accepted by it'; and 'the nature of the assets and the degree of risk attached to them'.
   (b) maintains 'adequate liquidity having regard to the relationship between its liquid assets and its liabilities and also to the times at which its liabilities fall due and its assets mature'; and
   (c) makes 'adequate provision for bad and doubtful debts and obligations of a contingent nature'. (para. 10)

This two-tier system of authorisation caused some misunderstanding and unhappiness when the recognitions and licenses were first granted following the passing of the Act, in that many regarded the label of licensed deposit-taker as in some sense inferior to that of recognised bank. In a speech delivered in May 1980, the Governor of the Bank went out of his way to correct the misunderstanding and dispel the unhappiness:

> Under the Act, all institutions which seek to take deposits must be authorised. Clearly not every such institution is a bank. A judgement, a discrimination, about which is and which is not is therefore inevitable. Hence the so-called two-tier structure and the relative tests in the Act.

The Governor went on, later in the same speech:

> Perhaps the most important structural feature laid down by the Act is the two-tier system. This structure has as its objective to distinguish that kind of business which is recognisably a fully-fledged banking operation on the one hand from that which is something different on the other. The distinction in practice is more one of function than of status.

In admitting that 'the Bank has been presented with some difficult decisions at the margin', he added:

> let me say a little more about how we see the borderline. It is not intended, and was never intended, to be a great divide. We are concerned, as we have always been, to permit and encourage progression for those institutions which may wish to move from the licensed deposit-taker category to that of recognised bank. Clearly not all will wish to make this move. For the Act provides that the distinctive attributes of a fully-fledged bank are not only, on the one hand, the high reputation and standing that it will have built up over time in the financial community, but also, on the other, the provision in reasonable depth of a wide range of banking services in this country – a criterion which many institutions will have no interest in meeting.
>
> Therefore classification as a licensed deposit-taker is not to be seen of itself as impugning the status of an institution – and certainly not the integrity and competence of its management or the good name of the institution generally. This point is worth repetition. As further lists are published, it will be very clear that a wide variety of institutions is covered in the category of licensed deposit-taker. For example, it will include a number who, for very good reasons, have not sought, or do not want, to provide the range of services which go to make up the business of a fully-fledged bank. In addition it will embrace a number of institutions of overseas provenance, including branches of major foreign banks which are of undoubted standing and reputation but which have not been in business long

> enough in the United Kingdom to have built up their range of service here to the level required of a recognised bank.[3]

The unhappiness the Governor was trying to dispel by emphasising that the distinction between the two tiers is in practice one of function rather than status, was that felt by those who felt slighted by being licensed rather than recognised. No doubt some of this unhappiness in some cases was a reflection of wounded pride; but a more tangible worry was that a licensed deposit-taker would not be able to obtain deposits in the interbank market – or anywhere else – at as fine rates of interest or in the same amounts as if it had been a recognised bank: that is, there was a very real fear that the distinction between recognised banks and licensed institutions would become one of the criteria utilised by banks and other depositors in assessing the credit risk of the institution in question. The Governor went straight to this point and emphasised that the Bank

> would not expect the market to make crude judgements of credit-worthiness based merely on the distinction between recognised banks and licensed deposit-takers. Indeed, I should regard the market as failing in professional expertise if it were to base its assessment on this distinction alone. There can be no justification for charging a particular institution, which in every other respect remains unchanged, more for its money following publication of its name in the list of licensed deposit-taking institutions. The division between licensed deposit-takers and recognised banks has . . . a marked functional character and some licensed deposit-takers will undoubtedly be stronger and of greater repute than some recognised banks.[4]

The supervision of banks

As we have seen, recognised banks and licensed institutions are both required to meet criteria covering legal form, prudence and management. Recognised banks must in addition meet exacting requirements relating to their range of services and their reputation and standing. In both cases the requirements are continuing ones, so that the Bank of England, as the supervising authority specifically appointed by the Act, must satisfy itself not only that they are met before an institution is recognised or licensed but also that they continue to be met so long as that recognition or licence is in force. And this requires a system of continuing and regular supervision of all recognised banks and licensed institutions by the Bank. (For simplicity, the term 'bank' will be used in this section to cover both recognised banks and licensed institutions.)

The requirements as to legal form and minimum net assets are straightforward enough to monitor, as in the question of whether an institution is providing a sufficiently wide range of banking services to qualify as a recognised bank. The questions as to the reputation and standing of an institution in the financial community, as to whether its business is carried on with 'integrity and prudence and with those professional skills which are consistent with the range and scale of the institution's activities', as to whether its net assets and other financial resources available are 'of an amount which is commensurate with the scale of the institution's operations' or, in the case of licensed institutions, are 'sufficient to safeguard the interest of depositors', as to whether the institution maintains adequate liquidity and makes adequate provision for bad and doubtful debts and obligations of a contingent nature: all these questions are not susceptible to a simple ticking-off on a check-list by the Bank of England as supervisor, but are complex questions involving subjective decisions by the Bank.

The role of the Bank of England as the supervisory authority, appointed by the Banking Act, has been both fashioned and made easier by its long-standing relationship with the British banking community. And the fact that this relationship is probably unique in any major financial centre is reflected in the fact that the Bank's style of supervision is probably unique as well – and the envy of many commercial bankers in many other centres. The Bank itself described this relationship to the Wilson Committee in the following terms:

> The Bank's role in the City has been determined as it has grown up among the institutions and markets which constitute the City, and it continues to evolve with them. The Bank's central banking functions – notably as adviser to the Government and executor of domestic monetary and exchange rate policy – give them traditional and unquestioned responsibility and authority over banks and money markets, while at the same time inevitably involving close working relations with City institutions in general. To a considerable degree, therefore, Bank Governors have been able to play the rôle of confidant or arbiter of the City and guardian of its standards. The Bank's rôle was accepted the more easily because players could feel that, as referee, they were both independent of faction and understood the game, while being at the same time able to keep in view the wide issues.[5]

Most, if not all, British bankers would warmly endorse this concept of the Bank as referee with a full player's knowledge of the game. But they would probably go further. To many bankers, part of the unique charm of the Bank's role as referee is that it carries on an endless dialogue with the players as to how the rules should be modified to accord with changing conditions: the rules which all are obliged to obey are thus hammered out in a debate in which all are allowed to participate. This aspect of the Bank's approach to supervision survived, and was even enhanced by, the passing of the Banking Act in 1979. As we saw in Chapter 4, the Bank initiated, following the passing of the Act, detailed debates with and within the British banking community on the key questions as to how to measure the capital adequacy, liquidity and foreign currency exposure of institutions; and the papers which it published following these debates represented very much a consensus of the views of the supervisors and the supervised.

Speaking at a time when this debate on the three papers was in full swing, the Governor of the Bank underlined this principle of participation by the banking community in formulating the general principles of supervision:

By and large . . . a successful supervisory regime will want the banking system to breathe comfortably and will seek to ensure that its basic tenets are essentially consistent with the institutions' own perception of commercial prudence. It must certainly be the Bank of England's endeavour to carry the weight of banking opinion with it on the general supervisory principles to be applied, for it is the spirit in which they are followed which matters: prudent banking can never be ensured by the mechanical application of a particular set of rules. It is for these reasons that the Bank continues, within the new statutory framework, to attach great importance, as it always has done, to consulting extensively with the banking community as it develops its supervisory guidelines.[6]

The point was reiterated in November 1982, when the initial debates on the supervisory guidelines had been concluded, by Mr Peter Cooke, an associate director of the Bank of England and Head of Banking Supervision, when he drew attention to the 'process of dialogue which is at the heart of the system'. He emphasised that these three papers were 'initially issued as discussion documents for we believe that, certainly in the long term, but more often than not also in the short term, the interests of bank managements and of those concerned with the prudential soundness of banks is the same'.[7] The debates from which the three papers emerged were but a preliminary stage of the permanent and continuing dialogue which the Bank conducts on the basis of regular bilateral meetings with the management of recognised banks and licensed institutions – as well as of those institutions hoping to achieve the one or the other status. As Mr Cooke put it:

it is judgements about management which are at the heart of our supervisory process – not only from the evidence of the balance sheet and the profit performance but from face to face discussions with senior management of all supervised institutions. The Bank's system is designed to enable the supervisor to sit alongside management, sharing in his thinking. Although we have no wish to be directly involved in management we certainly regard it as of crucial importance to have a good understanding of the thrust of management in a business.

If the process of dialogue lies at the heart of the British system of banking supervision, a second characteristic – almost as important and probably as unique – is the flexibility shown by the Bank in fulfilling its supervisory responsibilities. Again, the point was highlighted by Mr Peter Cooke in the address quoted above when he emphasised that although the Bank's supervisory role

> is now statutorily underpinned, the day-to-day fulfilment of that role is still handled without recourse to detailed legal provisions. The framework of the regime and the general principles of supervision to which the Bank must have regard are set out in the statute, but the application of those general principles are left to be handled in a way which can be responsive to the particular features of individual institutions and developments in the market-place.

From these two basic principles of dialogue and flexibility has emerged the British mechanism of banking supervision: regular meetings several times a year, between an individual bank's management and the supervisors, to discuss the bank's philosophy, business, balance sheet and profit and loss, backed up by regular statistical returns. The business of banking is a business of calculated risks, and much of these discussions between a bank's management and the supervisors will centre on the type and scale of the risks being run. When it comes to the risks involved in liquidity, foreign currency exposure and gearing or capital adequacy, the discussions take place within the framework of the three papers described in Chapter 4; but it is worth re-emphasising that these papers deal only with the methods of assessing the risks being run, the actual level of risk of each type appropriate to the individual bank in question remains the subject of bilateral agreement between its management and the supervisors. In Mr Cooke's description of the three papers, 'we have concentrated on outlining our approach to the measurement of certain aspects of a bank's business rather than specifying the absolute levels to be maintained in applying the system of measurement'.

As we saw in Chapter 4, the actual level of risk to which a bank can reasonably expose itself in these three areas is entirely a matter of judgement by that bank's management, endorsed by the supervisor. The supervisor can probe into the reasoning behind any particular level; but under the British system there is no simple scale to which the bank or its supervisors can refer. If a common set of absolute levels emerges, it will be by the consensus of individual decisions rather than the imposition of a central decision on all banks. It is true that the Bank deliberately compares the level of risk being undertaken by institutions in the same area of business and of similar size: in Mr Cooke's words, 'it is the Bank's practice to engage in peer group analysis – checking particular judgements of adequacy of balance sheet and profit performance against similar institutions'. And most bankers welcome this opportunity to compare, behind a veil of anonymity, their own decisions with those of their competitors and fellow bankers. But, as Mr Cooke went on, 'at the same time there is no wish on the Bank's part to stamp all our variegated institutions with a standard range of supermarket categorisations, each group clearly distinguished from each other, with identical labels for capital, liquidity, overall size or area of activity'.

But within the velvet glove of British supervisory arrangements, there always ultimately remains the iron hand of the Bank of England as ultimate arbiter. The point has been made fairly but firmly by Mr Cooke:

> I should make it clear . . . that notwithstanding this emphasis, and in my view very proper emphasis, which we put on flexibility and letting managements manage, there will always be a point at which the supervisor must be the final arbiter. Hopefully this only arises infrequently and when there is no alternative. It is also important that the arbiter's ruling should be readily accepted. That is why the Bank as an institution has always set out to be closely involved in the market. The professionals must be prepared to accept the referee's decision. There will always be some aspects of

> supervision where there can be no absolute or objective basis for applying judgement. Capital adequacy is perhaps the most obvious example. In this area particularly there will be occasions when the supervisor has to say you may go no further. It has been interesting recently to note several cases where banks who have previously chafed at a regime required by the Bank have subsequently come to settle without complaint within the guideline applied as circumstances have changed.

Here, then, is the firm but gentle way in which the Bank of England monitors the risks to which banks expose themselves in matters of capital adequacy, liquidity and foreign currency exposure – and nudges the management of a bank whose exposure has got much out of line with the consensus opinion of prudence. But what about the other risks discussed in Chapter 4, to which banks inevitably expose themselves – the credit risks? It is probably in this area that the British supervisory arrangements differ most markedly from those in other leading financial centres. Again, the British arrangements have been clearly described by Mr Cooke:

> It is generally, although far from exclusively, the case that most of the losses incurred by banks arise from their lending. And it is in this area that the system of supervision in this country gives rise to the most questioning. How, one is asked, can the Bank supervise effectively without a system of inspection or examination of the books of the banks and in particular the credit files. Our response to this is that we rely on proven management quality, historic loan loss experience and the monitoring of management's own view of evolving profitability and major problem loans through the year, together with regular returns of the sectoral and country breakdown of lending and the largest exposures. This we believe gives us at least as good an overview of the quality of the assets of a bank as sending in a team of inspectors to look at the loan documentation. We of course have to rely on management baring their soul to us several times a year, but find in practice that it gives us at least as good a picture as a sampling of lending which is the

common feature of most inspection systems. We also learn rather quickly whose soul baring we can depend upon. Now I would not claim that this aspect of supervision is not capable of improvement, but in general we believe it serves us rather well.

A crucial prerequisite for this relatively informal British system is mutual trust between the banks and the supervisors. As Mr Cooke remarked:

> Of course, this system can be abused, but happily setting out to hoodwink the supervisor is not a popular bankers' pastime in this country; if it were so the system would have to be modified. In particular cases, however, we can always mount special investigations of all and every aspect of a bank's business if we feel this is necessary.

Another prerequisite of the British system is a competent accountancy profession, providing an auditing service for banks on which the supervisory authorities in the Bank as well as the shareholders can rely. In Mr Cooke's words, 'I think it may be said that one of the main reasons why in this country we have managed to maintain a system of supervision which does not involve an examination procedure is because of the reliance we can place upon the auditor's work'. Conversely, many British bankers take great comfort from the fact that they are not subjected to the apparently duplicated enquiries of both auditors and bank examiners which are suffered by many of their fellow bankers in other financial centres.

Though the work of a bank's auditor complements the role of the supervisor, there is an important distinction to be made between their two roles. This was described by Mr Cooke in a passage which is worth quoting in full:

> For the supervisor the primary responsibility is to a bank's depositors; for the auditor it is to the shareholders. Both share a duty to form an opinion on the condition of a bank. The auditor's task is to report on the information presented by directors in the company's accounts (perhaps with a formal disclaimer if it appears unsatisfactory) so that the

shareholders can make an assessment on which they may themselves act as they deem fit. The depositor on the other hand merits a more active protection, and the supervisor has thus not only to form his own judgement of a bank's condition but also to undertake whatever action appears necessary to protect depositors' interests. The auditor, one may say, is concerned primarily with establishing the truth of facts presented to him by management and the appropriateness of the judgements made in relation to those facts, while the supervisor's concern extends to the implication of those facts and judgements for the future viability of the business. This reflects the different character of shareholders and depositors. The shareholder knowingly undertakes a risk activity which may involve loss; the depositor reasonably expects to get his money back, an expectation now partially reinforced by statute.

Mr Cooke summarised the relationship between his staff of supervisors and the auditors of banks in the following terms:

> Links between auditors and supervisory authorities are not as close in the United Kingdom as in most other countries because the Bank does not insist that prudential returns should be audited. However, considerable reliance is placed on auditors by the Bank because of the absence of regular inspection as part of the supervisory process. To a considerable extent, the Bank depends on the bank's auditors to verify valuations of assets, liabilities and reserves, and relies, to a degree at least, on their judgement of the adequacy of internal control systems.

One particular matter which involves bankers, their auditors and the supervisors and which is the subject of much public comment in the early 1980s is the question of provisions against bad and doubtful debts. At the end of each accounting period, every bank discusses with its auditors what provision out of that period's profits it should make for bad and doubtful debts on the books at the end of the period. These provisions fall into two groups: specific and general. Specific provisions are made against specific debts and are in principle allowed by the tax authorities as deductions from taxable profits. General provisions are intended to cover the debts in the books of the bank at the end of the accounting period which while already going bad have not yet been identified as such. General provisions, which are not tax-allowable, are usually calculated fairly crudely as a proportion of the total loans of a bank, or as a proportion of total loans within different categories, industrial or geographical; and clearly the proportion is struck against the economic background in which the bank is operating. Most British banks, for example, would make higher general provisions in respect of their domestic lending in the very early 1980s than they would have done in, say, the very early 1970s. (A fine but relevant distinction is drawn between debts which are *already* bad or doubtful, but unidentified as such at the balance sheet date, and debts which, while good at the balance sheet date may go bad thereafter: the former are covered by the general provisions for bad and doubtful debts and the latter, as we saw in Chapter 4, by the capital and reserves – the 'net assets' – of the bank.)

The decisions as to the size of specific or general provisions for bad and doubtful debts are made by a bank in consultation with its auditors. They are bound to be highly subjective. We saw in Chapter 4 some of the factors to be taken into account in assessing a borrower's ability to repay a loan in the future: it is a very fine judgement to decide that these factors have changed sufficiently since the loan was made to make its repayment sufficiently doubtful to justify a provision; it is an even finer judgement to decide whether such a provision should represent, say, 10 per cent or 20 per cent of the outstanding loan. In these circumstances, it is not surprising that two different banks and their respective auditors may well conclude that provisions of different sizes are appropriate for identical loans to identical borrowers.

This lack of uniformity in making provisions was highlighted in the early 1980s by the 'doubtfulness' of loans to sovereign borrowers to such countries as Mexico, Brazil and Argentina. The doubtfulness of these debts is even less easy to quantify than the doubtfulness of loans to commercial and industrial corporations; and their treatment for provisions is correspondingly more varied. As Mr Cooke observed in the address quoted above:

> bankers, auditors and supervisors are all having to wrestle with the difficult issue of deciding what if any provisions should be made against banks' international portfolios, particularly in relation to indebtedness in cases where problems have arisen or are imminent in meeting capital and/or interest payments on outstanding lending. At one extreme, some may say that this is not a problem – countries don't go bust, they say. Ultimately it will all come good, so provisions for capital at least are not required. Others may say that for countries X and Y there appears to be no prospect of repayment of their borrowing over what to bankers would appear to be a reasonable time horizon, so we should write it all off. The reality and the practice, as so often, no doubt lies somewhere between these two extremes and I have no magic formula to offer today.

Mr Cooke went on to spell out the apparent inconsistency in the approach to provisions against loans to sovereign borrowers by different banks:

> First, there can be no doubt, and I have found no bankers to contest it, that over the last two or three years the quality of assets in many major banks' portfolios have undergone some deterioration. Second, it cannot be denied that different loans to the same sovereign borrower have the same quality, albeit perhaps different maturities, no matter in which bank's balance sheet they appear. In an ideal world it would seem reasonable to treat such assets in the same way. Third, managements of banks do in practice view such identical or almost identical assets differently and there is considerable diversity of treatment. At the same time, there is a marked reluctance among most supervisory authorities to take action which deprives management of their responsibility as the prime judges of the quality of the assets in their book.

This diversity of treatment has infuriated many commentators, particularly those responsible for assessing the published profitability of banks in the context of the price of their shares on stock exchanges. Thus, for example, Mr John Plender commenting in the *Financial Times* on the varying levels of profitability published by British, US and European banks in the accounts for 1982 and on the underlying diversity of treatment for provisions, criticised all three parties concerned: the banks, the supervisors and the auditors. On the latter two he wrote that 'the different views of bank profitability reflect, among other things, a lack of co-ordination between regulating authorities around the world; also the failure of the accountancy profession to develop, in conjunction with the regulators, a coherent approach to banking provisions'.[8]

The view of the British bank supervisors was clearly expressed by Mr Cooke:

> As far as decisions about provisioning policy are concerned, I recognise that auditors (not to mention tax authorities) as well as bank managements have difficult judgements to make. There will need to be wide discussion – among bankers, between bankers and auditors, between bankers and supervisors and between different supervisory authorities. Out of these, hopefully, some reasonable and sensible consensus will emerge. In this process the supervisor, while allowing bankers and auditors to make their judgements may have to be prepared to make his judgements on their judgements in the light of the overall picture as it emerges and to react as necessary in the supervisory assessment of the individual institution.

This comment by Mr Cooke typifies in a very practical way the underlying approach of the Bank of England to the supervision of banks and at the same time explains, at least in part, the considerable respect it has earned in the British banking community. The basic principle is that the bankers should be allowed to manage their banks and make their own judgements as to risks, valuations and provisions. The supervisor is not a fundamentalist high priest with divinely-given rules as to how these judgements should be made, to impose on the bankers from on high. His function rather, is to assist and educate the banker in taking his own decisions, feeding into him, if appropriate, his knowledge – 'washed' into a suitably anonymous form – of what judgements other banks are making in similar circumstances. It is only when a bank strays significantly outside the current conventional wisdom in making its judgements that the supervisor feels obliged to exercise his authority and say, in Mr Cooke's words, 'you may go no further'.

The Deposit Protection Scheme

The establishment of a Deposit Protection Scheme was the third main purpose of the Banking Act 1979. The scheme, which is set out in Part II of the Act, provides that relatively small depositors with an institution which becomes insolvent will receive payments representing 75 per cent of their protected deposits from a Deposit Protection Fund. The Fund itself is financed by contributions from recognised banks and licensed institutions and is administered by a Deposit Protection Board, whose members are drawn from the Bank of England and the contributing institutions.

The scheme effectively insures 75 per cent of the deposits made by any one depositor, up to a maximum of £10 000 with the UK offices of any one institution; it is limited to sterling deposits and does not include deposits in other currencies whether or not they are made with British banks. Secured deposits and deposits with an original term of more than five years are excluded. The relatively low maximum of £10 000 satisfies the political requirement of 'consumer protection' for the relatively small personal depositor; it provides little protection to larger depositors, such as other banks lending through the interbank market. The reasoning for this is quite simply that the larger depositors should be expected to make their own credit judgements and look after themselves. The limitation of cover to 75 per cent of any deposit involves even the small depositor in *some* responsibility in assessing the credit risk; and this seems eminently fair to discourage such depositors from shopping round to obtain the highest rate of interest, regardless of the credit-worthiness of the institution accepting the deposit.

Initial contributions to the Fund, which were made in July 1982, were required by the Act to produce in aggregate a total of not less than £5m and not more than £6m; the Board can call for much larger contributions should the need arise. As has been pointed out elsewhere, this is a decision taken at a fairly early stage in the drafting of the legislation that

> the scheme should involve a relatively small paid-up element and rely on something akin to a guarantee arrangement for generating additional amounts if necessary. It was felt that the credibility of the scheme would be enhanced if there were a physical fund, but that there was no need to generate a fund large enough to cater for any eventuality. Thus the scheme stands somewhere between the approach adopted in Germany, which has no paid-up component and relies entirely on guarantees, and the system operated by the Federal Deposit Insurance Corporation in the United States, which involves a very substantial physical fund.[9]

With the exception of one specific group of institutions, all recognised banks and licensed institutions are obliged to contribute to the Fund: this, of course, excludes those institutions exempt from the whole Act, which were discussed earlier in this chapter. The one exempt group comprises those overseas institutions whose sterling deposits with their UK offices are as well protected by some similar scheme in their home country as they would be under the British deposit protection scheme. In such cases, the institution will pay no contributions and their depositors will enjoy no protection under the scheme. In fact, as Mr Morison and his colleagues have pointed out, 'it seems likely that few foreign deposit protection schemes or arrangements currently in force provide the necessary protection for sterling deposits with U.K. offices: generally they apply only to deposits in that country's own currency'.[10]

The initial contributions were calculated as a fixed proportion of each contributor's 'deposit base', with the important imposition of a minimum contribution of £2500 and a maximum contribution of £300 000. The 'deposit base' of an institution is defined as the average for the three months March, April and May 1982, of sterling deposits with the UK offices of that institution, other than

(a) secured deposits;
(b) deposits which had an original term to maturity of more than five years; and
(c) deposits in respect of which the institution has in the United Kingdom issued a sterling certificate of deposit. (Section 23(b))

If necessary, further contributions can be called for up to almost unlimited amounts: the only limitation is that no contributing institution shall be required to pay a further contribution if (or to the extent that) the amount of that contribution raises its cumulative contributions to 0.3 per cent of its deposit base.

This allocation of contributions to be called from the differing contributing institutions was the most controversial aspect of the scheme, in the debate which accompanied the drafting of the legislation. The clearing banks, in particular, made the not unreasonable point that to base the allocation on the size of deposit base would be to call for the largest contributions from the largest banks, particularly themselves, which, almost by definition, were the least likely to go bust; and this point was mitigated only to a small extent by the maximum and minimum contributions finally laid down by the Act. Apart from the logical impossibility of devising a realistic method of allocation which would extract the largest contributions from those institutions most likely to go bust, the rationale which prevailed in the final formula was that the deposit protection scheme was intended to enhance the stability of the sterling deposit-taking banking community as a whole, and was thus in the interests of that community: in these circumstances, it seemed reasonable to call for contributions based on the size of an institution's participation in that community.

But, quite aside from their complaint about the financial cost of the scheme to themselves, the clearing banks had another reason for being distinctly unenthusiastic about the proposal for a deposit protection scheme: the bruising experience they had recently endured as members of the Bank of England's Lifeboat to recycle deposits in the secondary banking crisis, described in Chapter 1. The Lifeboat, it will be recalled, was set up in December 1973 as a Control Committee of the Bank of England and the English and Scottish clearing banks, under the chairmanship of the Deputy Governor. Its purpose had nothing to do with deposit protection. It was rather to recycle back to the deposit-taking institutions in trouble those deposits which had been withdrawn from them (and which had almost invariably ended up directly or indirectly with the clearing banks) as a result of the general collapse of confidence in the financial markets. In recording the criteria by which the committee decided whether a company should be assisted, the Bank listed first 'that the company seeking support was currently trading solvently and, on the basis of best estimates possible at that time, was likely to remain solvent provided it received liquidity support by way of re-cycled deposits'. Again, recalling the situation at the time the Lifeboat was launched, the Bank remarked that 'while it was at this stage expected that the majority of the situations would be solved by re-cycling the lost deposits until confidence was re-established, it was common ground that, if the initial investigation showed an already unviable position, no support would be given'.[11]

In the event, of course, several of those institutions which were assisted turned out to be suffering from more chronic diseases than the simple illiquidity brought on by an external collapse of confidence in the markets; and as a result of these diseases the banks contributing to the Lifeboat had to make very substantial provisions. In the light of this experience, it is not surprising that the English and Scottish clearing banks were very chary about giving any further support of this nature. Having contributed massively, and initially unknowingly, to a deposit protection scheme of a sort – under a genuine misapprehension that they were simply contributing to a mechanism for recycling – they were reasonably cautious, even hostile, in responding to the Banking Bill's proposals for further contributions to such a scheme in which the clearing banks again were called upon to shoulder the heaviest burden.

In the event, the relatively low maximum level of insured deposits in the scheme as finally enacted leaves the clearing banks and other contributors less exposed to the risk of financial loss through the insolvency of other institutions than the clearing banks found themselves as members of the Lifeboat. And it is much to be hoped that the arrangements for authorisation and licensing and for the supervision of deposit-taking institutions laid down by the Act and described in this chapter will greatly reduce the recurrence of illiquidity and insolvency amongst such institutions on the scale experienced in 1973–4. But it is worth remarking that, in the event of another flight of confidence and of consequent problems of liquidity for some deposit-taking institutions, neither the deposit protection scheme nor anything else in the Banking Act would provide any help by way of a Lifeboat or in any other form.

The Deposit Protection Scheme was brought into being by Statutory Instrument in February 1982. The initial contributions were levied later that year, assessed by reference to the average of each institution's sterling deposit base in the three months March, April and May. The first call on the Fund was made in respect of payments totalling £1.2m to depositors with Merbro Finance (NI), a licensed deposit-taker in Northern Ireland which became insolvent and went into liquidation in May 1982.

THE INTERNATIONAL CO-ORDINATION OF SUPERVISION

The Basle committee of banking supervisory authorities

One of the most significant developments in banking throughout the world in the late 1960s and the 1970s has been the international spreading of their activities by individual banking institutions. The British banking community has experienced this in two ways. First, as 'parent' banks,

British banks – particularly the clearing banks – have built up considerable networks of subsidiaries, branches and representative offices in other financial centres in the United States, the rest of Europe, Japan, Hong Kong and Singapore as well as in other countries where they have participated in local banking; secondly, as 'host' to the ever-growing list of subsidiary and associated corporations, branches and representative offices which have been set up in London by banks with head offices outside Britain. But it is a development which has also embraced the banking communities of many other countries: bankers in other European centres, the United States, Japan and Hong Kong, for example, have all experienced this same internationalisation both in setting up their own subsidiaries and branches in other financial centres and in playing host to the subsidiaries and branches of banks from other countries in their own financial centres.

As Mr Cooke has pointed out:

> the expansion of a bank beyond national frontiers poses immediate supervisory problems. A different legal system and supervisory regime will impinge on those activities. The supervisors of the bank proposing to expand, the parent bank, will want to be assured that its operations abroad can be properly conducted. As they are not physically on the spot to supervise those activities themselves, they need to assure themselves of the adequacy of supervision of foreign establishments by the relevant authorities receiving branches or subsidiaries of foreign banks within their own territories. These host countries will have similar concerns. Failure of a foreign bank operating in their country could cause losses to local depositors and might damage confidence in the local banking system. They will wish, therefore, to investigate the quality of the home country supervision of a bank seeking to expand into their market.[12]

Mr Cooke went on:

> The first major problems, then, which arise for the supervisory authorities whose banks are involved in inter-

> national banking business, are the allocation of supervisory responsibilities and the closely related need for supervisors to have access to information on an international level. It is, I think, generally recognised that at the beginning of the 1970s supervisory authorities had not addressed themselves sufficiently to these questions, and that techniques of supervision had lagged behind developments in international banking business and the growth of euro-markets.

Since Mr Cooke was himself, as Chairman of the Committee of Banking Supervisory Authorities described below, a principal architect of the arrangements to fill this gap, as well as a major participant in them, it is worth quoting his description of them in full:

> The events of 1973-74 after the first oil shock and the spectacular failure of two international banks highlighted this lacuna in a dramatic way. They led to the establishment by the governors of the central banks of the Group of Ten major industrialised countries and Luxembourg and Switzerland of a standing committee of banking supervisory authorities. The first task of the Committee was to address itself to the division of supervisory responsibilities among its members for international banking business. The understandings which resulted from these discussions led to the document which has come to be known as the Concordat and which sets out the respective responsibilities of the parent bank's supervisory authority and the supervisory authority of the country in which a branch or subsidiary of that parent bank operates. The basic objectives were to ensure that no foreign establishment of a bank operating internationally escaped effective supervision and, to that end, that there was a clear understanding between the different authorities – parent and host – about the nature of the supervisory responsibilities borne by each in respect of international banking activities undertaken in their territories.

The division of responsibilities set out in the Concordat was as follows:

Supervision was deemed to be the joint responsibility of parent and host authorities, with both having a duty to ensure that surveillance of banks' foreign establishments was adequate. The supervision of liquidity was seen as the responsibility of host authorities in the first instance (on the grounds that foreign establishments generally have to conform to local rules on liquidity management). The solvency of branches, which are an integral part of the parent bank, was seen as primarily a matter for parent authorities, whilst that of subsidiaries fell rather to the host; though it was recognised that parent supervisors, in their supervision of the parent bank, needed to take account of its foreign subsidiaries and joint ventures in view of its moral commitment in their regard.

A later recommendation of the Committee, which developed out of the Concordat, was that supervision of banks' international business should be carried out on the basis of consolidated data, in order to provide a global picture of a bank's activities. This tended to reinforce the perception of an overall supervisory duty of the parent authority to monitor the totality of a bank's international operations, including both branches and subsidiaries. The principles of the Concordat and the techniques of consolidation, as applied in major countries, now forms the framework within which the supervision of banks' international business is undertaken.

The Concordat was drawn up in 1975 by the authorities of the Group of Ten countries, Luxembourg and Switzerland who comprise the members of the supervisors' committee in Basle. As Mr Cooke has pointed out in another address, the banks supervised by members of the Supervisors Committee

> conduct very much the greater part of the volume of international banking business . . . in addition, since 1975 an increasing number of countries outside the Group of Ten have given their support to achieving this fundamental objective as more and more countries have been drawn into the network of international supervisory co-operation, particularly as a consequence of international conferences

of eighty or more countries' supervisory authorities held in London in 1979 and in Washington in 1981.

Indeed by December 1982 the proper supervision of banks had been effectively extended throughout the non-Communist world, and Mr Cooke could reasonably declare his belief that

> the essential structure is in place within which international banking can operate soundly and confidently. It is misleading to imply that there are large areas of the international banking system which escape supervision. There are no rogue herds of unregulated bankers tramping through international markets. It is true that there are a few, but now only a very few, territories around the world where banking companies are licensed and allowed to operate without any serious efforts to accompany a licence with effective supervision. But such institutions are miniscule in relation to the market as a whole, widely known and recognised for what they are, generally regarded as unacceptable counterparties by the banking community at large, and in no position to undermine the strength of the system as a whole.[13]

Later in the same address, Mr Cooke emphasised that the supervisory net now extends to cover the offshore centres which, some years previously, had been

> felt to be a major Achilles' heel in the system. Improved supervisory procedures in most of those centres and the increased resort to consolidated supervision by parent banks and parent banks' supervisors have significantly modified those earlier views. Indeed, the Basle Committee has developed close and valuable links with all the significant offshore centres who constituted themselves into a formal group two years ago.

The Concordat received considerable publicity at the time of the spectacular collapse of the Banco Ambrosiano in Italy in June 1982; and, indeed, the whole Ambrosiano affair highlighted the need, stressed by Mr Cooke, for the techniques of supervision to keep up with the developments in international banking business. The Banco Ambrosiano, a commercial bank based in Milan whose shares were quoted on the Milan Stock Exchange, had built up a complicated network of subsidiaries and associated companies overseas, notably in Luxembourg, Nassau, Nicaragua and Peru. The Luxembourg subsidiary, Banco Ambrosiano Holdings (BAH), which was owned as to 69 per cent by Banco Ambrosiano in Milan, took very considerable deposits from many international banks through the interbank market in eurocurrency deposits; and it seems that most of these deposits were on-lent to other non-Italian companies in the Ambrosiano group. In excess of 400 million US dollars of these deposits were outstanding when the parent bank collapsed in June 1982.

The collapse of Banco Ambrosiano was triggered by a crisis of confidence amongst its depositors following the macabre death of its chairman, Sig. Roberto Calvi, whose body was found hanging from scaffolding under Blackfriars Bridge in London on 18 June 1982, ten days after he had mysteriously disappeared from Milan. The immediate reaction of the Bank of Italy was to organise a Lifeboat operation, not dissimilar from that organised by the Bank of England to stem the withdrawal of deposits from British secondary banks in 1973–5, whereby seven leading Italian banks provided 457 billion lira (around US $325m) in emergency liquidity to fill the hole left by the flight of deposits. In fact, the problem quickly turned out to be one of insolvency rather than illiquidity and Banco Ambrosiano was declared insolvent by a Milan bankruptcy Court on 26 August 1982, a new Bank Nuovo Banco Ambrosiano (NBA) being immediately created to take over its entire Italian operations. The precise causes of the insolvency, which almost certainly involved fraud on a massive scale, have not become clear at the time of writing. At the time of the parent company's collapse, the Luxembourg subsidiary, BAH, suffered a similar withdrawal of deposits, but the Bank of Italy did not feel the same obligation to mount a Lifeboat operation to fill the hole left by this withdrawal, and BAH was left to default on its loans and deposits.

Three points are worth making about the Ambrosiano affair in the context of this chapter. First, it must not be taken as British banking smugness to suggest that had the Bank of Italy been able to supervise Banco Ambrosiano's affairs on a consolidated basis in the manner described in this chapter as British practice, it is inconceivable that the bank's affairs could have got into the tangled mess that they did, including fraud on a scale sufficient to make the bank insolvent. But the Bank of Italy's position was quite different from that of the Bank of England in relation to the banks it supervised. For one thing, the Bank of Italy simply did not at the time possess the statutory powers to supervise Italian banks – and, if necessary, force changes in their senior management, by wielding the threat of withdrawal of authorisation – which the Bank of England now enjoys under the Banking Act 1979; though it is expected that the Italian Parliament will pass legislation at least reducing this gap, in the wake of the Ambrosiano affair. And for another thing, it is clear from all the reports that the Bank of Italy did not enjoy that relationship of trust and respect with Sig. Calvi which, as we have seen, lies at the heart of the British arrangements for supervision. Indeed, it seems very possible that Sig. Calvi's flight from Italy in June was precipitated by a letter addressed to him by the surveillance department of the Bank of Italy, asking for urgent explanations of Banco Ambrosiano's heavy exposure overseas, particularly in Latin America, asking for this exposure to be reduced and requiring that the contents of the letter be made known to his fellow directors.

The second point worth making about the Ambrosiano affair relates to the refusal of the Bank of Italy to mount a rescue operation for the depositors with the Luxembourg subsidiary, BAH, as well as those of the parent company in Italy. In the words of one informed report, the Bank of Italy has

> consistently argued that since B.A.H. was only 69 per cent owned by Banco Ambrosiano in Milan the Italian shareholder was not responsible for its debts and neither therefore was the Bank of Italy. Furthermore, it has pointed out, neither it nor the Luxembourg authorities

could be expected to take responsibility for loans made from one off-shore centre (Luxembourg) to another (Panama) via a third category of off-shore centre (Latin America).[14]

Some critics of the Bank of Italy suggested that the Concordat described in this section obliged the Bank of Italy to mount such a rescue operation. This assertion has been firmly denied by Mr Cooke:

> I must stress yet again [he said in his description of the principles of the Concordat and the technique of consolidation] that these arrangements, worked out between the major industrialised countries and increasingly accepted and applied by other supervisory authorities round the world, relate to *supervisory* responsibilities not *lender of last resort* responsibilities. It is thus wrong to say that the recent events surrounding the demise of the Banco Ambrosiano demonstrate the ineffectiveness of the Concordat understandings. In any event, as a number of others commenting on that situation have indicated, there can be no guarantee that any authority will automatically undertake to stand behind any banking institution in all circumstances, especially where it appears that fraud is involved.

The third point worth making about the Ambrosiano affair relates to the position of the Luxembourg authorities. We have seen that the Concordat put primary responsibility for the liquidity and solvency of a subsidiary in the hands of the host country's supervisors but that the principle of consolidated supervision placed the overall supervisory duty with the parent bank's supervisory authority 'to monitor the totality of a bank's international operations, including both branches and subsidiaries'. Recognising the principle of consolidated supervision and to 'comply with the philosophy' of the Basle Concordat, the Luxembourg banking Commission amended its rules in April 1981 to lift banking secrecy and enable all relevant items on the assets side of a bank's balance sheet to be freely passed through the parent bank on to the parent authority, though banking secrecy remains for deposits with

Luxembourg banks of non-banking customers. More pertinently, in the wake of the Ambrosiano affair, the Luxembourg authorities obtained guarantees from the six Italian banks with branches in Luxembourg that they would cover any eventual debt by their affiliates.

A revised version of the Concordat was published by the Supervisors' Committee in May 1983. In a covering letter, Mr Cooke explained that 'the primary motivation for the revision was the need to incorporate understandings, agreed since 1975, on applying the principle of consolidated supervision to banks' international business'. These included guidelines for the division of responsibilities between parent and host authorities in supervising foreign establishments. The paper makes clear that there is a role for both the host and the parent supervisory authority in the supervision of the liquidity of banks' foreign establishments; the supervision of solvency is primarily the responsibility of the parent authority as regards branches, whilst in the case of subsidiaries it is the joint responsibility of both host and parent authorities:

> In addition to incorporating the principle of consolidated supervision [Mr Cooke went on] the paper contains several other modifications to the 1975 Concordat. First, in reiterating the objective of the original document that no international banking operation should escape effective supervision, it examines further ways in which any supervisory gaps can be prevented, in particular those gaps which arise from inadequate supervisory standards in certain countries or from the existence of holding companies and non-banking companies within banking groups. It stresses the importance of close co-operation between host and parent authorities in dealing with all such cases and puts more emphasis than in the original document on the generally overlapping nature of responsibilities rather than a strict allocation of responsibilities in particular circumstances. [And] finally, the new paper makes explicit what was implicit in the earlier paper – that it addresses supervisory responsibilities and not responsibilities for lender of last resort support. The Committee is a committee of supervisors and in many countries this function is

undertaken by authorities which are not central banks. The Committee is thus not the most appropriate forum to deal with questions of lender of last resort.

The first major problems which were identified by Mr Cooke in his 1982 address as arising for the supervisory authorities whose banks were involved in international banking business were the allocation of supervisory responsibilities and the need for supervisors to have access to information on an international level. It remains to record Mr Cooke's report of progress on the second of these problems as well as the first. 'In the course of building up the apparatus of supervisory co-operation in recent years, a great deal of importance has been attached to the improved flows of information both within banking groups and between banking authorities. These flows have of course to be subject to the requirements of banking secrecy provisions in different countries, but these are not nearly as constraining as might be supposed. In my view there are very few cases where effective consolidated supervision is frustrated by an inability to supply information on grounds of banking secrecy. Secrecy regulations operate stringently most particularly in respect of the details of individual depositors' business. They do not normally impede aggregated liability data, and information on the assets side of the balance sheet important for judgements of risk. It has been a notable development in recent years that legislative provisions have been introduced in a number of countries, including in our own Banking Act, to temper banking secrecy constraints on information flows. In particular cases, such provisions authorise supervisory authorities to disclose information to other supervisory authorities where it is judged such disclosure would be of assistance to those authorities in the exercise of their responsibilities.

One final point made by Mr Cooke is worth quoting as it is highly relevant both to the philosophy underlying the supervisory techniques described in this chapter and also to the next section on the EEC. Concluding his remarks on the international aspects of supervision, Mr Cooke observed:

so over recent years there has grown up an international

framework of supervision and the means to give effect to it through co-operative endeavour and exchanges of information. But there has also been a by-product in this process – a general improvement in supervisory techniques as a common perception of best practice emerges. This has been one of the significant benefits of discussions in Basle and in other groups like the E.E.C. Contact Group of European Community supervisors, the offshore supervisors group, as well as in the two major international conferences of supervisory authorities in London in 1979 and in Washington in 1981. We have all learnt a great deal about each other's systems and I can think of a number of cases where in this country we have improved our techniques by borrowing some of our colleagues' better ideas. Others too I believe have learnt something from us.

Just as it is desirable within the British banking community and between that community and the Bank of England to have some common framework of concepts in which to discuss the techniques of managing the risk-taking by banks, in all its aspects, and its supervision by the prudential authorities, so it is as desirable within the international banking community, for the benefit of its members and their national supervisors, that the techniques of risk analysis and supervision should be similar in all financial centres. We have seen how a common basis of risk analysis, management and supervision has emerged in Britain from a continuing debate within the banking community and between it and the supervisory authorities; and this basis can be expected to be the subject of continuing modifications, resultant from this debate, to adjust to changing circumstances in the future. The framework is now in place for a similar continuing debate between the supervisory authorities of different countries, from which will emerge, it is to be hoped, a gradual synchronisation of techniques for the management and regulation of banks on an international level and a common reaction to new problems and developments as they appear.

The role of the European Commission

One of the long-term ambitions of the Commission of the European Economic Community (EEC) in Brussels is to create a 'common market' in banking throughout the EEC. This aim is founded solidly on the Treaty of Rome which established the EEC in 1957. Article 57 of the Treaty required the EEC to issue directives 'for the co-ordination of the provisions laid down by law, regulation or administrative action in Member States concerning the taking up and pursuit of activities as self-employed persons'; and the term 'self-employed persons' in this context was used to cover companies and firms as well as self-employed persons in the normal sense. These directives are to be issued by the Council of the EEC, on which each member state is represented, acting on a proposal from the Commission; and Article 57 specifically requires that the Council's decision should be unanimous on 'measures concerned with the protection of savings, in particular the granting of credit and the exercise of the banking profession'.

A directive[15] was adopted in 1973 which formally prohibited discrimination on grounds of nationality against banks from one member state seeking to establish themselves or provide banking services in another member state; banks and other financial institutions were also required to abolish administrative practices which discriminated in favour of national institutions. Although this directive was seen by its authors as a first step in the development of a common market in banking, its practical effects were limited because of the wide divergencies in national supervisory practices.

The goal of a common market in banking was therefore seen to require a further directive harmonising the banking regulations in each member state into one common code of regulations. When Britain joined the EEC in 1973 a proposal for a draft directive[16] to achieve this end had already been drawn up. This draft represented a thoroughgoing harmonisation of the banking legislation of the six original member states: it seemed to embody the most *dirigiste* provisions and characteristics of the systems then in operation in those six member states and would have been quite incompatible with the British system of supervision and regulation. This latter, while less formalised than the system described in this chapter, bore all the same hallmarks of flexibility and 'dialogue' between the supervisors and the supervised. Largely through the influence of the British authorities, strongly supported by the British banking community through the British Bankers' Association, this first draft was abandoned and a more gradualist approach was adopted. This gradualist approach was enshrined in the First Council Directive on the 'co-ordination of laws, regulations and administrative provisions relating to the taking up and pursuit of the business of credit institutions' (hereinafter referred to as the First Banking Co-ordination Directive). This directive was finally adopted by the Council of the European Community in December 1977 and, as we have seen, was one of the factors which prompted the passing of the British Banking Act in 1979.

A principal characteristic of this First Banking Co-ordination Directive is that it leaves ultimate responsibility for banking supervision and regulation firmly in the hands of the national authorities (in Britain's case, the Bank of England); and it seeks to achieve the object of harmonisation by encouraging these national authorities to harmonise their existing regulations rather than by imposing a new set of 'Community' regulations from Brussels. The directive requires member states to have a system of prior authorisation for credit institutions before they commence business and lays down certain minimum criteria for such authorisation; and it covers in general terms principles for continuing supervision, conditions for withdrawal of authorisation, provisions rationalising the controls applicable in one member state to the branch or subsidiary of a bank from another member state and for the uniform treatment throughout the EEC of banks from outside it. It also established an Advisory Committee, consisting of senior officials engaged in the field of banking legislation and supervision in the member states, to be involved in implementing the requirements of the directive and, as important, in preparing new proposals for the co-ordination of regulations and supervision.

Although the immediate requirements of the First Banking

Co-ordination Directive appear to be much more modest than those of the earlier draft of July 1972, the ultimate aim of a true common market in banking was the same; and the First Banking Co-ordination Directive was seen as but the first step towards this aim. The point is well made in the following passage in the preamble to the directive:

> In order to make it easier to take up and pursue the business of credit institutions, it is necessary to eliminate the most obstructive differences between the laws of the Member States as regards the rules to which these institutions are subject . . . However, given the extent of these differences, the conditions required for a common market for credit institutions cannot be created by means of a single Directive . . . it is therefore necessary to proceed by successive stages.

As in the earlier draft 'the purpose of co-ordination is to achieve a system whereby credit institutions having their head office in one Member State are exempt from any national authorisation requirement when setting up branches in other Member States'; but whereas the first draft sought to achieve this purpose by the immediate imposition of a common set of regulations, the First Banking Co-ordination Directive seeks to achieve it by the gradual harmonisation of existing national regulations.

As we have seen, the directive requires all member states to have a system of prior authorisation of credit institutions, such as that established in Britain by the Banking Act 1979. It laid down five minimum conditions for such prior authorisation, all of which are included in less specific and demanding form than the criteria for recognition or licensing set out in the Banking Act. These conditions are that

(i) the credit institution must possess separate 'own funds' or net assets;
(ii) it must possess adequate minimum own funds;
(iii) there shall be at least two persons who effectively direct the institution's business;
(iv) those persons must be of 'sufficiently good repute' and have 'sufficient experience' to perform their duties; and

(v) applications for authorisation must be accompanied by a 'programme of operations' setting out, *inter alia*, the types of business envisaged and the structural organisation of the institution. (Article 3)

In listing these requirements it is worth noting the passage in the preamble which states that 'the eventual aim is to introduce uniform authorisation requirements throughout the Community for comparable types of credit institution . . . at the initial stage it is necessary, however, to specify only certain minimum requirements to be imposed by all Member States'.

Although the Directive does not lay down specifically the principles and concepts to be used in the supervision of credit institutions, Article 6 does require that

1. Pending subsequent co-ordination, the competent authorities shall, for the purposes of observation and, if necessary, in addition to such coefficients as may be applied by them, establish ratios between the various assets and/or liabilities of credit institutions with a view to monitoring their solvency and liquidity and the other measures which may serve to ensure that savings are protected.

   To this end, the Advisory Committee shall decide on the content of the various factors of the observation ratios referred to in this first subparagraph and lay down the method to be applied in calculating them.

   Where appropriate, the Advisory Committee shall be guided by technical consultations between the supervisory authorities of the categories of institutions concerned.
2. The observation ratios established in pursuance of paragraph 1 shall be calculated at least every six months.
3. The Advisory Committee shall examine the results of analyses carried out by the supervisory authorities referred to in the third subparagraph of paragraph 1 on the basis of the calculations referred to in paragraph 2.
4. The Advisory Committee may make suggestions to the

Commission with a view to co-ordinating the coefficients applicable in the Member States.

Article 7 of the directive requires that the national supervisory authorities should collaborate closely in the supervision of banks in one member state with branches or subsidiaries in one or more other member states and should swap sufficient information to facilitate such supervision:

1. The competent authorities of the Member States concerned shall collaborate closely in order to supervise the activities of credit institutions operating, in particular by having established branches there, in one or more Member States other than that in which their head offices are situated. They shall supply one another with all information concerning the management and ownership of such credit institutions that is likely to facilitate their supervision and the examination of the conditions for their authorisation and all information likely to facilitate the monitoring of their liquidity and solvency.
2. The competent authorities may also, for the purposes and within the meaning of Article 6, lay down ratios applicable to the branches referred to in this Article by reference to the factors laid down in Article 6.
3. The Advisory Committee shall take account of the adjustments necessitated by the specific situation of the branches in relation to national regulations.

Article 9 of the directive lays down a uniform treatment throughout the EEC of banks from outside it:

1. Member States shall not apply to branches of credit institutions having their head office outside the Community, when commencing or carrying on their business, provisions which result in more favourable treatment than that accorded to branches of credit institutions having their head office in the Community.
2. The competent authorities shall notify the Commission and Advisory Committee of all authorisations for branches granted to credit institutions having their head office outside the Community.

3. Without prejudice to paragraph 1, the Community may, through agreements concluded in accordance with the Treaty with one or more third countries, agree to apply provisions which on the basis of reciprocity, accord to branches of a credit institution having its head office outside the Community identical treatment throughout the territory of the Community.

Article 11 of the directive provides that 'an "Advisory Committee of the Competent Authorities of the Member States of the European Economic Community" shall be set up alongside the Commission'. It further provides that

> the tasks of the Advisory Committee shall be to assist the Commission in ensuring the proper implementation of both this Directive and Council Directive 73/183/EEC of 28th June, 1973 on the abolition of restrictions on freedom of establishment and freedom to provide services in respect of self employed activities of banks and other financial institutions in so far as it relates to credit institutions. Further it shall carry out the other tasks prescribed by this Directive and shall assist the Commission in the preparation of new proposals to the Council concerning further co-ordination in the sphere of credit institutions.

Article 11 also provides that the Advisory Committee 'shall not concern itself with concrete problems relating to individual credit institutions', thus implying that it should concern itself only with matters of policy. And it provides that the Advisory Committee should be composed of not more than three representatives from each Member State and from the Commission; there is no provision for representation from the commercial banks. Britain is represented on the Committee by HM Treasury, the Bank of England and the Registry of Friendly Societies. The Committee held its inaugural meeting in June 1979 and meetings have been held half-yearly since then. Whilst the Committee may invite qualified persons and experts to participate in its meetings, the discussions and outcome are confidential unless otherwise decided. The Committee works in close collaboration with the 'Contact

Committee', an informal group of representatives from the banking supervisory authorities of each Member State, on which a representative of the Commission sits as an observer.

The Advisory Committee is clearly seen as the main vehicle through which a common code of co-ordinated banking regulations can be brought about, both by harmonising existing national regulations and by guiding the Commission in its drafting of new directives to achieve this end. As we have seen, the First Banking Co-ordination Directive gave the Advisory Committee a perceptible nudge into harmonising techniques for measuring solvency and liquidity by requiring national regulatory authorities to establish, initially for observation purposes, 'ratios between the various assets and/or liabilities of credit institutions with a view to monitoring their solvency and liquidity and other measures which may serve to ensure that savings are protected' and providing that the Advisory Committee 'decide on the content of the various factors of the observation ratios . . . and lay down the method to be applied in calculating them'. These observation ratios have, indeed, been one of the major initial preoccupations of the Committee. They have been calculated, on a sample basis, for two ratios for assessing bank solvency (a risk–assets ratio and a gearing ratio), a ratio for assessing the profitability of banks and a ratio for assessing their liquidity.

The risk–asset ratio and the gearing ratio calculated by the Advisory Committee are similar in concept to the risk–asset ratio and gearing ratio now used as a central tool for the management and supervision of British banks and described in Chapter 4. The gearing ratio relates 'own funds' or capital and reserves to total liabilities (which under the EEC definition include acceptances). The risk–asset ratio relates own funds to risk assets, which are divided into four groups carrying weightings of zero, 20 per cent, 50 per cent and 100 per cent. To determine which weighting applies, each asset is categorised by two scales. One scale divides risk assets into three groups, according to the nature of the borrower: governments (central and local), credit institutions and private sector excluding credit institutions. The other scale is not directly recognised in the British weightings and is rather more controversial: it divides all assets by reference to the country of origin of borrower into two zones, one comprising all member countries of the EEC plus the other main industrialised countries of the non-Communist world, and the other comprising the rest of the world. Trial calculations of both the gearing and the risk–asset ratios were first made in 1981, based on figures for up to 20 of the largest banks in each member state; and the exercise was repeated in 1982 and 1983, the definitions in each calculation being slightly revised in the light of experience gained in the previous calculation and comments from the national supervisory authorities, through the Advisory Committee, the European Commission and the commercial banks themselves. (It is worth noting that the bankers themselves are given the opportunity to comment on any proposals for the harmonisation of banking regulations which emerge either from the Commission or the Advisory Committee, through the 'Banking Federation of the European Community' (hereinafter referred to as the Banking Federation), an umbrella trade association whose membership consists of the national banking trade associations of each member state, the British Bankers' Association being the British member.) When the calculation of solvency ratios was first proposed by the Advisory Committee in October 1980, two further ratios were included: a fixed assets ratio and a large exposures ratio. The fixed assets ratio has been discontinued and the large exposures ratio postponed, pending a more detailed examination of the problems of definition and comparability.

The profitability ratio proposed by the Advisory Committee related gross profits to total assets; a second ratio was added in December 1982 relating *net* profits to total assets. Gross profits are taken after the deduction of general expenses but before the deduction of depreciation, provisions, taxation, appropriations to reserves and dividend payments; net profits comprise gross profit less general provisions and taxation but before appropriation to reserves and the payment of dividends. Total assets represent the total assets on the balance sheet (sometimes described as 'total footings') less contingent liabilities. The results of the first trial calculation were issued in January 1982 and were based on figures taken from the published annual accounts for the year 1980 of up to twenty of the largest banks in each Member State. The exercise was repeated in the first quarter of 1982 and 1983. It is difficult to see what use can be made of this ratio from the point of view of the national bank supervisors, since the ratio of any particular bank will clearly depend to a large extent on the type of business which it undertakes, the quality of the assets it holds and the consequent return on those assets. The Banking Federation takes comfort from the fact that the calculation of this ratio requires no additional reporting information from individual banks.

The liquidity ratio proposed by the Advisory Committee relates liquid assets to short-term liabilities. Liquid assets are defined to include notes and coins, balances and deposits with other banks with maturities up to three months, money market instruments and debt securities quoted on a recognised stock exchange; short-term liabilities are defined as all liabilities, with maturities up to three months, to other banks and to customers. The first calculation of this ratio was made using figures as at 30 September 1981, on a sample of up to twenty of the largest banks in each Member State; a second calculation was made on the same sample of banks, using figures as at 30 September 1982. As at present calculated, the ratio is probably of limited value: in particular, by concentrating on the comparison between short-term liabilities and liquid assets, it reflects more of the traditional approach to liquidity and ignores the more modern approach, described in Chapter 4, which takes into account the forward mismatch of commitments and the consequent expected flow of funds. From the point of view of British banks, the calculation of this ratio involves no additional reporting information from individual banks, since the Bank of England makes the calculation using statistics already available to it from existing returns.

So far, these ratios have been calculated purely for 'observation' purposes; and even as observation ratios, they have been seen very much as trial runs. In their comments on the Advisory Committee's proposals for the calculation of the ratios, the Banking Federation has consistently warned of the dangers of making the ratios 'normative' or compulsory, rather than for observation purposes: it has warned, for example, of the dangers inherent in comparing the ratios of different sorts of banks, of different sizes, operating in different markets and environments and also of the dangers of comparing the ratios of banks in different Member States until more common accounting definitions and conventions have been established throughout the EEC. As we have seen already, a common system of banking supervision and a common conceptual framework on which such a system can be based, is likely to emerge only as the result of a synthesis of the national mechanisms and conceptual frameworks which obtain in individual countries, rather than of the imposition of a new common mechanism and framework by some supra-national authority. This synthesis is likely to emerge from a continuing debate between the national supervisory authorities, within and between the different national banking communities and between the supervisory authorities and the banking communities on a national and international level. In a European context, the EC Commission has a role to play in this debate, acting as a sort of catalyst for the process of synthesis or harmonisation; and the observation ratios proposed in the First Banking Co-ordination Directive and calculated by the Advisory Committee should be seen, not as having an immediate supervisory use in themselves, but rather as focal points for the debate out of which harmonised ratios and concepts will ultimately emerge.

Apart from observation ratios, it is understood that the Advisory Committee has concerned itself with three other main topics: the supervision of credit institutions on a consolidated basis, the winding up of credit institutions and plans by the EC Commission for a Second Council Directive on Credit Institutions.

The proposal that banks within the EEC should be supervised on a consolidated basis was put forward in a draft directive prepared jointly by the EC Commission and the Advisory Committee, published in September 1981. Its aim is 'to provide for overall supervision of a credit institution operating in several Member States by the competent authorities in the Member State where it has its head office, in consultation as appropriate with the competent authorities of the other Member States concerned'.[17] A revised draft was published in February 1983, incorporating amendments, among others, recommended by the European Parliament. The proposal will, when adopted, put into effect one of the principles set out in the First Banking Co-ordination Directive; it is also entirely consistent with the Basle Concordat on the allocation of supervisory responsibilities issued by the Cooke Committee of banking supervisory authorities, described above. The draft directive proposes the consolidation for supervisory purposes of all subsidiaries and 'participations', which are defined as the ownership of 25 per cent or more of one credit institution by another. Some flexibility and discretion is allowed to the national supervisory authorities. For example, they may decide whether consolidation should be on a full or a pro rata basis where a credit institution holds a participation of 50 per cent or more in another institution; they also have discretion to decide whether and how consolidation is to be affected in situations where effective control does not exist, notwithstanding the size of the shareholding. The draft directive proposes that supervision on a consolidated basis should be carried out at least once a year by the supervisory authority of the country in which the credit institution has its head office. The proposal for this directive was approved by the European Parliament at the end of December 1982; and was formally adopted by the Council of Ministers in June 1983.

The draft directive on the Re-organisation and the Winding-up of Credit Institutions was first introduced in April 1981, following a recommendation by the Advisory Committee that the implications of the winding-up of credit institutions needed to be considered from the standpoint of the protection of savers and the financial system as a whole; it has since been the subject of considerable revision. The current proposal (dated July 1982) lays down the broad principles to be adopted by supervisory authorities in dealing with credit institutions in financial difficulties which have branches in other Member States. It allows consultation between supervisory authorities in different Member States before any measures are taken. Although the principle of 'home country' control is largely adopted, the authorities of the 'host country' are permitted to introduce certain limited 'reorganisation' measures where the financial difficulties of the credit institution are not great. The proposal also seeks to establish certain principles in respect of deposit protection arrangements: for example, that host country authorities should ensure that, where branches of banks whose head office is in another Member State have had to comply with the host country's authorisation procedure, as laid down in the First Banking Co-ordination Directive, those branches shall be party to arrangements for the protection of depositors in the host country, unless their deposits are at least as well protected by arrangements in the home country. Where no pre-authorisation procedure has been adopted, the home country's deposit protection arrangements will apply. At the time of writing (March 1983) this proposal still has some way to go before it is formally adopted and in force as a directive.

The final topic with which the Advisory Committee has concerned itself is the plans by the EC Commission for a second Council Directive on Credit Institutions (or Second Banking Directive). These plans were issued by the Commission as a consultative document in December 1981. Their aim was threefold: to develop the original framework established by the First Banking Co-ordination Directive; to resolve difficulties encountered by national supervisory authorities concerning cross-border activities of credit institutions including those which have their head offices outside the EEC; and to eliminate discriminatory practices preventing the cross-border establishment of branches and subsidiaries within the EEC. It is too early to tell what practical measures will finally emerge from this new initiative by the Commission; in any event, it is likely to be some years before such measures are actually put into effect. But it is worth noting that the EC Commission, in the pursuit of its role as laid down by the Treaty of Rome, to create a common market in banking, is clearly not content simply to stage-manage the debate between national supervisory authorities and the national banking communities on how best to co-ordinate and harmonise national prudential regulations within the EEC, but is determined to contribute its own initiatives to achieve that end.

NOTES

1. *First Council Directive* (77/780/EEC), article 3, para. (1).
2. Morison, Tillett and Welch, *Banking Act 1979* (Butterworth, 1979) p. 23, para. 66.
3. Speech given by the Governor at the *Financial Times* luncheon for representatives of the foreign banking community in London on 20 March 1980. Reprinted in *Bank of England Quarterly Bulletin* (June 1980) p. 206.
4. Ibid., pp. 206–7.
5. 'Regulation in the City and the Bank of England's role', reprinted in *Bank of England Quarterly Bulletin* (September 1978) p. 380, para. 9.
6. Speech of 20 May 1980, *Bank of England Quarterly Bulletin* (June 1980) p. 207.
7. 'The role of the banking supervisor', reprinted in *Bank of England Quarterly Bulletin* (December 1982) p. 548. All quotations of Mr Cooke's views given in this section are taken from this address.
8. John Plender, 'Of Profits and Imprudence', *Financial Times*, 18 February 1983.
9. Morison, Tillett and Welch, *Banking Act 1979*, p. 74.
10. Ibid., p. 82.
11. 'Secondary Banking Crisis and the Bank of England's Support Operations', *Bank of England Quarterly Bulletin* (June 1978) p. 233, paras 28, 29.
12. All the quotations in this section, unless otherwise attributed, are from Mr Cooke's address, 'The Role of the Banking Supervisor', reprinted in *Bank of England Quarterly Bulletin* (December 1982). The letter quoted on pp. 279–80 was dated 8 June 1983 and was addressed to all British banks by Mr Cooke in his capacity as Head of Banking Supervision, Bank of England. The revised version of the Concordat was entitled 'Principles for the Supervision of Banks' Foreign Establishments' and dated May 1983; it was distributed to national supervisory authorities worldwide from whom it is available to banks.
13. W. P. Cooke, 'Speech to the Financial Times World Banking Conference in London, 9 December 1982', reprinted in *Bank of England Quarterly Bulletin* (March 1983) p. 63.

14. James Buxton, article on the Bank of Italy's handling of the Ambrosiano affair, *Financial Times* supplement on Italian Banking, 17 November 1982.
15. 'Directive on Freedom of Establishment and Freedom to Supply Services for Banks and other Financial Institutions' (73/183).
16. This proposal, which bore the reference number XIV/508/72 and was issued in July 1972, was never formally published.
17. The draft directive bears the Commission's reference: 'COM(81) final 9.9.81'. The revised draft published in February 1983 bears the reference 'OJ 1983 C40/6–11.2.83'. The Directive was finally adopted on 13 June 1983.

6 The Banking System and National Policy

THE BANKING SYSTEM AND MONETARY POLICY

The importance of the money supply

We saw in Chapter 1 that the 1970s and early 1980s witnessed the build-up of considerable pressures which led successive British governments – and governments elsewhere in the industrialised world – to become much more preoccupied with the banking system than they had been previously. One group of such pressures was the gradual acceptance by the British authorities, and to some extent at least by the public at large, of the importance of control over the money supply as a crucial weapon in the control of inflation and economic policy generally. But to identify and recognise this importance of control of the money supply is one thing; to identify an accurate and durable definition of 'money supply' and then methods of controlling it which do not conflict too painfully with other objectives of policy is quite another. From the early 1970s right through to the time of writing in 1983, a great debate has developed amongst academic economists, economic journalists, Treasury and Bank of England officials and practising bankers as to how some sort of control can be imposed on the supply of money. Participants in the debate include on the one hand those who believe, in an almost theological sense, that strict control of the money supply, if only the authorities had the guts to enforce it, would turn out to be a panacea, if not solving all problems at least providing a basis for achieving simultaneously the five objectives of policy listed by the Radcliffe Committee and quoted in Chapter 1. On the other hand, it includes those who see no such panacea in a policy of controlling the money supply but simply believe that some such control is a necessary, though certainly not a sufficient, condition for controlling inflation.

One of the purposes of this book is to explain to the participants in this debate some of the practical consequences of some of their theoretical proposals on the financial markets and institutions of the real world: to map out some of the complex real terrain over which their intellectual battles are fought. Listening to the debate, and observing the gradual establishment of control of the money supply as a key element of economic policy, practising bankers may be forgiven for feeling that they are involved in an elaborate laboratory experiment, possibly involving some pretty major vivisection, in which they are the guinea-pigs and the experimenters have varying respect and regard for their interests, comfort or even survival. If this book can help to explain to some of the experimenters how practising banking guinea-pigs respond to certain policy stimuli without knives being wielded, blood shed and lives lost, then at least a part of its purpose will have been achieved.

Whilst it is not a purpose of this book to contribute to the wider political debate as to the precise emphasis to be given to monetary control, in comparison with the other aims of national policy, it is nevertheless taken for granted that *some* such control is an essential part of economic government. One of the enduring tasks of practising bankers is to encourage their borrowing customers to limit their plans and ambitions to what they can reasonably afford; to limit their borrowing to what they can reasonably expect to repay with interest within a reasonable period of time; in short, to cut their coats according to their cloth. Whilst many businesses and individuals express great gratitude to their bankers for the provision of finance to help them realise their ambitions, practising bankers soon come to accept that an occupational hazard of their trade is to incur the frustrated displeasure of some of their customers resultant from pointing out to them the financial impropriety, or sometimes arithmetical nonsense, implicit in some of their ambitions and dreams. This frustration of the over-ambitious – and, even more so, of the spendthrift – individual to whom a banker has been obliged to explain the facts of financial life is a familiar part of their day-to-day routine to most practising bankers, dealing with individuals and finance directors or boards of companies; it therefore comes as no surprise to find the same frustrations voiced at a national level, when the more forceful plans and ambitions of politicians and others run up against financial reality. To this extent a day-to-day 'micro' experience of practising bankers is directly applicable to the 'macro' context of national economic policy. Seen through the spectacles of a practising banker, the frustrated anguish of politicians and others whose ambitions on a national scale for, say, dramatic increases in the social services – or, for that matter, in the provision of national defence – far outrun their willingness to take measures to provide the necessary financial resources are effectively no different from the frustrated anguish of the visionary entrepreneur whose cash flow forecasts simply cannot be made to demonstrate that a borrowing made from his banker has any chance of being repaid with interest within a reasonable period of time – or, indeed, from the equally frustrated anguish of the spendthrift individual whose unfortunate banker is obliged to shoulder the task of forcing him to live within his means.

Some bankers sometimes will, of course, err on the side of caution when agreeing or not to lend to their customers: the factors which they should and do take into account when taking such decisions were discussed in Chapter 4. But it may be worth noticing in passing that even the most perfect banker will *inevitably* find himself turning down requests for borrowing which the customer regards as reasonable and that his role will thus *inevitably* be seen by some as the frustrator of their proper ambitions. The same point applies on a macro, national scale, except that the distinctive roles of banker and borrower are blurred. A government whose spending ambitions run ahead of its willingness or ability to raise money by taxes, or by saving on other expenses, is in a sense its own banker: it can, in the end, arrange for the gap to be filled by increasing the money supply – with an almost mathematical inflationary consequence. At the simplest level, the case for control of the money supply is, in part, the case for closing, or at the very least limiting, this opportunity for governments to arrange for the country to live beyond its means. No banker would claim that absolute precision is possible in fixing a target for the money supply, even assuming that the means were to hand to make the target attainable, any more than he would claim that it is a matter of precise mathematics rather than practical judgement to know when to give the visionary entrepreneur the benefit of the doubt and increase his loan or when to call a firm halt to the spendthrift's borrowing. But equally, no practising banker would have any doubt that *some* control over the money supply is essential. It is for this reason that the Barber boom of 1973–4, described in Chapter 1, was contemptuously regarded as irresponsible by many bankers at the time – and by many more in retrospect. It is for this reason, too, that most bankers applauded the appeal of the Labour Government in 1976 for a loan from the IMF, with all its disciplinary strings attached, notwithstanding the ambitions for social expenditure of many members of the Government, which ran far ahead of the financial resources available. In short, it is a premise of this whole book that some sort of control over the money supply is as essential a part of responsible economic government as some sort of control over borrowings is of responsible financial management by corporations or individuals.

Measuring the money supply

The first problem confronted in any attempt to control the money supply lies in defining and measuring the concept one is trying to control. To revert to the analogy of an individual or corporation, the concept of the 'money supply' available to that individual or corporation is simple enough: it is the aggregate amount of cash and credit available. As we have seen, the cash and credit available to individuals and corporations is a major factor in the planning of their activities and is sometimes a major constraint on some of their ambitions. On the 'micro' level of the individual or corporation, the amount of this cash and credit available is relatively easy to calculate; but since the credit element is likely to include commitments made to the individual or corporation by their bankers – which are as yet undrawn, subject to continual amendment and of necessity unrecorded in any central way – it is by definition impossible to add up the cash and credit position of each economic unit in the economy and so arrive at a 'money supply' figure for the economy as a whole.

Indeed, like so many analogies which are taken too far, an attempt to move from the 'micro' concept of a 'money supply' for individuals and corporations, which is generally recognisable and comprehensible to both such entities and their bankers, to a more 'macro' concept of the money supply of the economy as a whole is fraught with definitional problems and conceptual pitfalls. In particular, the 'money supply' available to an individual or corporation, the size of which is crucial to decisions about future expenditure and plans for expansion or contraction, includes credit lines available, whereas the 'money supply' in the economy as a whole specifically *excludes* such credit lines unless they are drawn. And even when credit lines are drawn, they should not in themselves be included in the definition of money supply without causing total conceptual confusion. As Mr Roger Brown has explained very clearly in a recent textbook, 'an increase in bank lending usually leads to an increase in the stock of bank deposits and the money supply. *But bank deposits should not be confused with bank credit or lending – the two things are quite different*. When a bank lends it has a claim on the borrower. Bank deposits, on the other hand, are claims by the public on the banks.'[1] And it is the public's claims on the banks, *not* the banks' claims on their borrowers, which are included in any statistical measure of the money supply in the economy as a whole.

And there is another reason why the aggregation of all cash positions and credit available to individuals and corporations would not make a realistic and meaningful measure of the money supply: that is, that one of the biggest operators in the economy, and much the largest user of credit has *no* effective limit placed on the credit available to it – the British Government. It is for this reason that any serious attempt to control the money supply as a whole must involve a serious and successful attempt to control the Government's borrowings. It is a function of the bankers to put a limit on the credit available to individuals and corporations, and thus controls, instructions or even exhortations to the banking community can have some effect on the money supply, to the extent that it represents the sum of the cash and credit available to these individuals and corporations; but such controls, instructions and exhortations will be absolutely useless in controlling the money supply unless they are accompanied by self-restraint (in the absence of restraining bankers) exercised by the Government on its own borrowings.

A measure of the money supply must therefore be found by another route. In Britain, the measure to which most significance is attached is '£M_3': this is calculated as the sum of notes and coin in circulation with the public and all sterling deposits held by UK residents with UK banks – including both sight and time deposits, interest bearing and non-interest bearing, and those held by both the private and public sectors. Expanding on this definition, the British authorities have remarked that

> apart from notes and coin, the £M_3 money stock consists of liabilities of the banking system. In considering how [policy] instruments affect monetary conditions, it is sometimes helpful to examine how a particular control will affect items on the asset side of the banking system balance sheet – the credit counterparts of the money stock. Indeed, by accounting identity, the change in £M_3 equals the P.S.B.R. [Public Sector Borrowing Requirement] *less* sales of public sector debt outside the banking system *plus* the increase in bank lending to the private and overseas sectors *plus* the net external inflow to the private sector *less* the increase in banks' non-deposit liabilities. Useful though this widely known identity is, it must be emphasized that the counterparts are not independent. Policy action on one of them will typically induce changes in the others so that a change in any one rarely has an exactly equal effect on the money supply.[2]

As we saw in Chapter 1, the Chancellor of the Exchequer was at pains in his 1982 Budget to ease the spotlight from this single measure of money supply: he announced that in future the authorities would instead take into account a range of other measures of the money supply, and less specific indicators of its movements as well. These further measures of money supply, known as M_1, PSL_2, as well as £M_3, were described in Chapter 1 and need not detain us again.

If measuring the money supply on a macroeconomic, or national, level is not as simple and straightforward as measuring the 'money supply' of an individual or corporation, its control is even more complex. The action and reaction of the authorities and the financial institutions and markets in any attempt to control the money supply is an infinitely more complicated pattern of relationships.

A close inspection of how money is actually created should make this point clear. Much the largest element in any definition of the money supply consists of deposits with banks and other financial institutions. These deposits can be increased by a bank, almost literally by a stroke of the pen. For example, if a customer wishes to borrow £100 from his bank, and his bank manager agrees to lend it to him, then the bank will open a new advance account in the name of the customer, debit that account with £100 and credit that £100 to the customer's current account in its books. At this point, the bank in question will have increased its total assets by £100 (represented by the new advance account in the name of the customer); more importantly, in the present context, it will have increased its total liabilities by £100 as well (represented by the increase in the customer's credit balance on his current account), and this, by definition, will show up as an increase of £100 in the money supply. What the customer does with the £100 addition to his current credit balance does not alter the fact that by the simple act of opening an advance account, debiting it with £100 and crediting that £100 the customer's current account, the bank has increased the money supply by £100.

It is worth following this example through one further stage. The customer will probably have wanted the extra £100 to enable him to make some payment. If he pays the full amount away to, say, a shopkeeper's account with another bank, then the original increase in the money supply of £100 remains intact: the customer's credit balance is reduced by £100, thereby reducing his bank's liabilities by £100, but the shopkeeper's credit balance is increased by £100, thereby increasing *his* bank's liabilities by £100. If, on the other hand, the shopkeeper uses his £100 to reduce a borrowing from his bank, then he will reduce his credit balance with his bank by £100 (thereby reducing his bank's liabilities) and at the same time reduce the debit balance on his advance account by £100 (thereby reducing his bank's assets by the same amount). At this point, the total money supply will revert to its size before the original customer borrowed the £100.

Several points should be made about this simple example. First, it is clearly within the power of bank managers up and down the country, within the limits laid down by directives from their head offices, to increase the money supply at the stroke of a pen: to the extent that they have the authority to lend money to customers, they effectively have the same authority to increase the money supply. Second, neither the local bank manager, nor any other banker, has the ability to increase his lendings, and thus the money supply, entirely on his own initiative: an increase in bank lendings requires not only a willing lender but as importantly a customer who wishes to increase his borrowings. In short, there are two necessary conditions for an increase in the money supply: a demand from the public, or the government, for an increase in credit and a banking system willing and able to meet that demand.

A third point to be made about our simple example relates to the second stage: that is, whether the shopkeeper uses the £100 to increase his credit balance or to reduce a borrowing. As we have seen, if he uses it to reduce a borrowing the immediate result will be a reduction in the money supply. In most cases, the decision to reduce the borrowing is entirely in the hands of the shopkeeper: his bank is unlikely to refuse to allow him to repay. Thus, in effect, reductions in the money supply can take place without any initiatives by the banking system at all: the banking system is simply reacting in a passive way to a change in the demand for credit from the public.

To summarise the lessons to be drawn from our simple example, it may be said that the increases in the money supply result from an increase in the satisfied demand for credit within the economy. To the extent that this demand for credit comes from the government it is satisfied automatically by increases in the government's borrowing through the financial markets, in the manner described in Chapter 3; the banking system has neither the authority nor the opportunity to influence this process. To the extent that the demand for credit comes from the private sector, it is satisfied by the banking system granting credit facilities to its individual and corporate customers. To the surprise of many commentators, there is no mechanism available for the precise control of the extent of this credit creation and thus of potential increases in the money supply. As we saw in Chapter 4, the cash ratio and, subsequently, the liquidity ratio, appeared in the past to provide some brake on the willingness of individual banks to grant credit and thus to increase the size of their balance sheets and, effectively, of the money supply; and the gearing ratio and risk assets ratio provide a comparable brake today. But these brakes are, by their very nature, imprecise and, in any case, can be blunted in their application as a brake by increases in a bank's capital. It is in recognition of this lack of precise control over the creation of credit, that attention has been turned in recent years to the concept of controlling the creation of credit by the banking system by controlling the monetary base of that system. To this concept we now turn.

Monetary base control

A major complication in controlling the money supply on a macroeconomic or national basis is that no mechanism exists by which the supply of money can simply be turned off. In the analogy of the individual or corporation, the 'money supply' is ultimately controllable by the individual's or corporation's bankers, who have it in their power to say 'not a penny more' and require the borrower to take the consequences. As became clear in the description in Chapter 3 of the Discount

Market and the market in sterling interbank deposits, such a neat switch simply does not, and in the nature of the case cannot, exist to limit the money supply on a national scale. As we saw in that chapter, one of the principal functions of the Bank of England in the money markets is the maintenance of orderly markets, not least in smoothing out the effects of the Bank's own activities as banker to the biggest and lumpiest borrower of all, the Government itself. And this responsibility for the maintenance of orderly markets and, derivatively, for 'accommodating' financial institutions totally excludes the possibility of the Bank of England as the ultimate source of credit in the banking system, saying 'not a penny more' in a national context. As Tim Congdon puts it in a passage quoted in Chapter 3, 'there may be a trade off between the exactitude of money supply control and the microeconomic efficiency of the financial system'.[3]

The only meaningful way in which the Bank *could* control the money supply by saying 'not a penny more' would be to do so, not as the ultimate source of credit to the banking system, but in its capacity as banker to the Government. If the Government's own availability of credit was subject to the same disciplines of its bankers as is the credit available to every other borrower, it is probable that the failure to control the money supply in the 1970s, and the inflationary consequences of that failure, would not have reached the disastrous proportions that it did. But any remnant of the traditional relationship between a banker and a borrowing customer which may still have existed was effectively extinguished by the Bank of England Act 1946, which (in Section 4(1)) gave a general statutory power to the Treasury to issue to the Bank such directions 'as, after consultation with the Governor of the Bank they think necessary in the public interest'. As the Radcliffe Committee commented, this section of the Act carries the clear implication 'that the will of the Government, formally expressed in the form of a direction, is paramount'.[4]

In the late 1970s several proposals were put forward for a fairly automatic or mechanistic method of controlling the money supply by controlling the money base of the banking system. In the words of a joint consultative paper prepared on the subject of 'monetary control' by the Treasury and the

Bank of England and published by the Government in March 1980:

> In concept a monetary base scheme is very simple. The banks keep at least a known proportion of their deposits (which, currency in the hands of the public apart, constitute the money supply) in base money, however specified, either because there is a mandatory requirement on them to do so or because they can be relied on to do so over a period for prudential reasons. [The term 'base money' includes 'bankers deposits at the Central Bank and may also include notes and coin held by either or both the banks and the public'.] The authorities then either:
> (a) control the amount of base money in existence and so the total growth of the money supply, since the banks' balance sheets cannot exceed a specified multiple of the base;
> or
> (b) use divergencies of the base money figure from the desired trend as a trigger for a change in interest rates intended to correct the divergence.
>
> In the former case if there is a tendency for the money supply to grow too fast, banks compete in an attempt to secure the base assets which they require to match the growth in deposits. This increases interest rates. This approach therefore is intended to provide a means for the markets to generate the interest rates necessary to bring the rate of growth of the money supply back towards the desired path. The latter case is intended to provide for more rapid and automatic adjustments in interest rates than the present discretionary changes since the timing of changes is determined by movements in the base. But the amount of the change would either be discretionary or determined by a scale set in advance by the authorities, rather than by a market process balancing the supply and demand for such a base asset.[5]

The consultation paper goes on to comment that

> the translation of this apparently simple concept into

> practice raises a number of inter-related problems: as to how the scheme should be specified, as to how the authorities would control the base if the variant was of the first type, and as to how the banks and other financial institutions would behave in the changed environment. There are therefore a large number of potential schemes within the monetary base approach.

The paper divided these schemes into two groups: those where the bankers' need for base assets stems from their own requirements for operating their business, rather than from a mandatory requirement imposed by the authorities ('schemes without a mandatory requirement') and those where there is a mandatory relationship between the base assets held by a bank and its deposits – as, for example, in the United States ('schemes with a mandatory requirement').

Since this book is concerned with the British banking system as it is, rather than as it might be, this is not the place to describe in detail any of the many variations of the proposal for 'monetary base control' or their implications for the institutions and markets of the existing system.[6] In this context it is necessary to make only three comments. First, it is the considered conclusion of the consultation paper quoted above that a move to a system of monetary base control would not necessarily be an improvement on the present arrangements. On schemes *without* a mandatory requirement, it concludes that 'given the known costs and uncertain benefits, the case for a scheme on this basis has not been made out' (para. 4.9). After discussing the theoretical and practical operational difficulties involved in a monetary base control system *with* a mandatory requirement to hold base assets, the paper concluded by recording the authors' doubt as whether such a system 'would produce the desired results. None of the schemes so far suggested appear to give a reasonable prospect of doing so. Moreover, there would be severe practical difficulties in operating such schemes with any precision' (para. 4.16).

The second comment to be made about monetary base control is that in its most rigid form, at least, it would almost certainly destroy the elaborate market mechanisms described in Chapter 3. In the words of a paper written by economists in the Bank of England's Economic Intelligence Department:

> the conclusion . . . is that strict control of the base (which would, of course, imply an end to all the present lender of last resort facilities) would continually threaten frequent and potentially massive movements in interest rates, if not complete instability. Changes in the base would inevitably carry implications for interest rates, and the greater the emphasis on control of the base the less the possibility that the central bank could intervene to ameliorate any interest-rate fluctuations. In the strictest form of control (the day-to-day regulation. . .), the problem would, of course, be at its most acute as no adjustment time (e.g. for the banks to curtail their loans to the non-bank public) would be available. Indeed it is highly dubious whether such a system could possibly work, mainly because of the time it would take for markets to adjust to the interest-rate changes induced by the banks in their attempts to meet their reserve requirements. But even for control over longer periods of time, strict control of the base would throw onto financial markets the whole burden of adjustment at present 'shared' by the Bank of England's lender of last resort facilities, its open-market operations, its foreign exchange intervention, and the permitted short-term variability in the level of balances held by the clearing banks at the Bank of England.[7]

One of the roles of the institutions and financial markets which make up the British banking system which has probably not been emphasised enough in this book so far is highlighted by the same authors later in their paper in the following terms. Concluding that an attempt to use monetary base control rigorously over short periods would be neither desirable nor feasible, they comment, 'indeed, because it is the rôle of the banking system to absorb and to meet shocks occurring in the demand or supply of money and credit within the economy, the search for tight short-term control of the money stock, for example, on a week to week basis, would seem to be misguided'. In fairness, it should also be quoted that their next sentence reads: 'this is *not*, however, to deny the possibility of improving control techniques for influencing monetary developments over a longer horizon measured, say, in terms of four to six months'.[8]

Indeed, the debate on monetary base control in Britain is by no means closed. Writing of the new arrangements for monetary control which were successively introduced from August 1981, the Bank of England commented in March 1982 that

> the money market arrangements now in place provide a framework within which it might be possible to operate some form of monetary base control, although it is not currently being so used. Control of the monetary base implies giving priority to the amount of official money market intervention rather than to the rate at which it is transacted. In its extreme form, where the control is sought over a very short period, the authorities would be obliged to forgo all control over interest rates. As was made clear following the discussions which led to the introduction of the present monetary arrangements, the repercussions of changing to such a system in the United Kingdom would be uncertain. Nevertheless, the new arrangements may facilitate study of the relationship between monetary base and other economic developments, in particular by allowing the banks freedom to determine, given the prevailing monetary situation, how much of the stock of monetary base they hold, i.e. their holdings of notes and coin plus their operational balances at the Bank of England.[9]

The third comment to be made about the concept of monetary base control is that although the proposed control is often presented as an almost mechanical device, it does, in fact, rely heavily on changes in interest rates as the force which transmits changes in the monetary base to the real economy of borrowers and lenders; and it is the institutions and markets of the banking system which provide the mechanism for this transmission. If the purposes of monetary base control can be achieved by influencing the level of interest rates without the traumatic effects on the existing mechanism which a move to full-blooded monetary base control seems to imply, then the case for the latter becomes pretty redundant. The question of interest rates and how they can be influenced is discussed later in this chapter.

Instruments for controlling the money supply

If a simple on/off switch is not available to the authorities for controlling the money supply, what instruments *are* available? In its introduction to the Green Paper on monetary control prepared by the Treasury and the Bank of England and published in 1980, the British Government was quite clear that

> the main instruments must continue to be fiscal policy and interest rates. The Government is satisfied that these provide the means to achieve its medium term objectives. In particular it intends to bring down over time the Public Sector Borrowing Requirement (PSBR) as a proportion of national output. But there may be room for improvement in monetary control over shorter periods.[10]

The paper on monetary control itself opens with the statement that 'there are a number of policy instruments available to the authorities in influencing monetary conditions. Of these the main ones are fiscal policy, debt management, administered changes in short term interest rates, direct controls on the financial system and operations in the foreign exchange markets.[11]

Of these policy instruments, fiscal policy has a major influence on movements in the money supply. As the paper on monetary control points out, 'tax and expenditure policies are the main means by which the Government affects the P.S.B.R., although these policies also affect the other counterparts of the money stock' (para. 1.3). As we have seen, the PSBR is itself an important ingredient of £M_3, the most used measure of the money supply, by simple accounting identity: perhaps more interestingly, this accounting identity simply reflects the point made earlier in this chapter that, everything else being equal, an increase in the Government's borrowing is bound to result in an increase in the money supply. The consultation paper remarks that

> it is impossible to forecast the P.S.B.R. with precision and therefore very difficult to control it closely. Its size in any period depends on the level of economic activity and the inflation rate as well as the fiscal stance. And over short periods – a year or less – it can fluctuate markedly, even after adjusting for seasonal factors, due to minor variations in the pattern from month to month of Government expenditure and receipts. (para. 1.3)

To a banker, all this, while perfectly valid, sounds very much like the response he gets from his corporate customers, when he asks them for a cash flow forecast to back up their request for an increase in their borrowings; and we saw in Chapter 4 the importance such forecasts play in a banker's decision as to the credit-worthiness of his customer. Two lessons should be drawn in the present context. First, it is difficult to forecast the PSBR with any precision on a week-to-week or month-to-month basis, just as it is difficult to forecast cash flows in a large and complex corporation over the same time-span: it is therefore as futile to attempt a precise control over the money supply over that same time-span as it is to control the precise level of a corporation's borrowings. But secondly, some control over the Government's borrowings over the medium term are as essential for the health of the economy as a similar control over the borrowings of a corporation: the difference is that failure to exert such control in the case of the corporation will quite simply cause it to go bust, while failure in the case of the Government will have one of two consequences, each detrimental to the health of the economy. Either it will cause an increase in the money supply and thus in rampant inflation; or alternatively if the failure to control the public sector's borrowing is combined with a successful policy to contain the rate of increase in the money supply, then this will cause an exaggerated squeeze on the 'money supply' or credit available to the private sector. Whilst it is difficult to be too precise in analysing cause and effect in very recent economic history, it does seem that the severity of the monetary squeeze on the private sector of the British economy, and particularly on private industry, in the first year or so of the Thatcher Government from 1979, as reflected in unusually high real rates of interest and an unusually high exchange rate for the pound against the currencies of Britain's main trading partners, might have been less destructive without necessarily being less effective, if that government had been quicker in taking control over public sector spending and the PSBR. How such control should be executed over the PSBR lies outside the scope of this book.

A second policy instrument for influencing monetary conditions is the management of the National Debt. This management, which is undertaken by the Bank of England on behalf of the Government falls into two main parts: the management of the issues of, and market in, Treasury bills and the management of the issues of, and markets in Government bonds or 'gilt-edged' securities. The Bank's role in relation to Treasury bills was discussed in some detail in Chapter 3. The only point worth repeating is to note the stimulating effect on the market for eligible bills of the Bank's 'over-funding' in the bond markets in 1980 to 1983 and its use of the surplus funds thus made available to buy commercial bills in the market. This manoeuvre effectively took long-term funds out of the non-bank private sector (the pension funds and other investment institutions, for example) and put them back, via the bill market, into short-term loans to commerce and industry. The Bank's role in relation to government bonds, whilst indirectly relevant to the banking system, is a highly technical subject in its own right which probably lies outside the scope of this book.[12]

A third policy instrument for influencing monetary conditions is, of course, the short-term rate of interest; and this is discussed in the next section. As the authors of *Monetary Control* pointed out:

> using the basic weapons of fiscal policy, gilt-edged funding and short-term interest rates, the monetary authorities can achieve the first requisite of control of the money supply – control, say, over a year or more. However, there have been substantial swings in the rate of monetary growth, not

> only from month to month, but also from quarter to quarter. Given both the volatility and short-term unpredictability of all the counterparts, it is almost certainly unrealistic to think in terms of a smooth path from month to month. This could only be achieved, if at all, by massive swings in interest rates, and then would probably involve significant switches back and forth between closely substitutable forms of liquidity just inside and just outside the definition of the target. Such month to month control is not necessary to achieve the desired restraining impact of monetary growth on the growth of prices and nominal incomes, since that is essentially a medium term relationship. But there would be advantage in shortening the period within which it is possible to exercise control if it were practical to find a way of doing this. If there were smoother growth of the money supply from quarter to quarter, there would be more complete confidence in the Government's policies, and so expectations could be affected favourably to a greater extent – both in the financial markets and elsewhere in the economy.[13]

The solution adopted in Britain in recent years to the problem of smoothing the growth in the money supply from month to month or quarter to quarter is the imposition of quantitative controls on the banking system. The most recent example was the Supplementary Special Deposits (SSD) scheme, or 'corset', which was first introduced in 1973 and finally abandoned in June 1980. The problems and limitations of such controls have been well described in *Monetary Control*; and the quotation which follows perhaps makes the problems more vivid when read against the background of the descriptions of institutions and markets set out in Chapters 3 and 4:

> Various forms of quantitative controls have been used, or suggested, to supplement the main instruments of monetary policy. Such controls can be applied either to the assets side of the financial institutions concerned – as with the ceilings on bank lending in the 1960s – or to their liabilities, as in the Supplementary Special Deposit (S.S.D.) scheme. The general pros and cons are, however, the same in either

case. A more useful distinction can be drawn between permanent and temporary controls, a point returned to below.

The main purpose of introducing such controls in this country has been to reduce the need to raise interest rates, at least in the short term, by causing banks to ration their lending. It has generally been recognised that, in time, lending rates will still tend to rise. But controls have more recently been seen as a way of bridging the time-lag before other policies have their effect. They have also, on occasion, provided reassurance to financial markets that the Government is concerned to hold its monetary policy, thereby helping to end a hiatus in gilt sales. A particular reason behind the form of the S.S.D. scheme was the desire to affect relative interest rates – especially those on bank deposits vis-à-vis other short term assets – to a greater extent than could be achieved through the more general instruments of Minimum Lending Rate (M.L.R.) and open market operations.

If such control is effective, it will almost certainly reduce competition within the controlled sector and between that sector and uncontrolled institutions doing similar business. It will involve some resource cost and loss of efficiency. There may also be prudential risks for – almost by definition – uncontrolled forms of business are less likely to be within the ambit of regulation by the monetary authorities.

If the control becomes permanent, the resource costs and prudential risks may in time be considerable. There is also the danger that funds are disintermediated, that is, business increasingly moves out of the controlled sector. The aggregate most directly affected by the control (£M_3 in the case of the S.S.D. scheme) becomes an increasingly distorted measure of the monetary position. This distortion soon becomes apparent, and causes both the statistic and the policy to decline in value.

If the control is occasional and temporary, resource costs and prudential risks would be much less significant. Distortion of the target aggregate may still occur as exemplified by the build-up of the so-called bill leak in 1978, when the

> S.S.D. scheme was reintroduced. A different problem arises, however, because the controlled institutions may anticipate the reintroduction of the control and, at the worst, actually precipitate the action they have been expecting. Something of this sort occurred in the first few months of 1978. There is no obvious solution to the problem. A final difficulty with temporary controls is that, if conditions do not improve as quickly as was hoped when the controls were adopted, it becomes difficult to take them off, because of the likelihood of reintermediation and risk of appearing to ease the stance of policy.
>
> The distortion of monetary indicators by a quantitative control is less misleading if it can be measured. For example, with the S.S.D. scheme, it has at least been possible to monitor the main form of disintermediation hitherto: the bill leak. However, other forms are less easily measurable especially now that United Kingdom residents are free to transact business abroad in sterling or in foreign currency.[14]

There is little to add to this statement of the pros and, particularly, the cons of quantitative controls, and the 'corset' in particular, on the banking system, from the point of view of the authorities – or indeed of the banks themselves. The banks would probably emphasise even more strongly their distaste for the effects the 'corset' had in driving business outside the banking system which would normally have flowed through it. The point was made in more detail later in *Monetary Control*, where it was noted that the 'corset'

> succeeded, after it was first introduced in December 1973, in its immediate objective of causing the change in relative interest rates necessary to remove the incentive for round tripping. ['Round-tripping' was defined as involving borrowing funds from a bank which, because relative interest rates make it profitable, are then redeposited with the same or another bank.] It appears also to have had the effect of inhibiting the development by the banks of new types of business. But a major effect has been to divert flows into uncontrolled channels. On occasions, the banks have

> reduced their holdings of short-term public sector debt which has been taken up by others outside the banking system. This will have reduced £M_3, but with little effect on the underlying liquidity of the economy since there is virtually no difference for that liquidity between, say, an industrial company holding a Treasury Bill itself, or the company holding a bank's Certificate of Deposit and that bank holding a Treasury Bill. More recently, the most obvious form of avoidance has been the growth in holdings outside the banking system of bank-accepted commercial bills.[15] To the holder such bills are no less liquid than a certificate of deposit of comparable term, and to the borrower they are a very close substitute for direct bank credit. These are but two of many possible forms of such disintermediation. Any attempt to stop them by redefining the scheme would only lead to disintermediation into other forms, which would be more likely to carry the problems referred to in the previous Chapter [and quoted above]. They are difficult to measure so their extent would be unknown. There could be prudential risk, either for those involved or for the financial system as a whole.[16]

Before leaving this discussion on the banking system and methods of controlling the money supply, one further comment should be made. And that is to emphasise how new the whole experiment of such control really is. While the underlying theological and purely practical arguments may be pretty clear-cut in justification for *some* sort of control over the money supply, the identification of a reliable and durable measure of the money supply is still at a very early and experimental stage. And the identification of a method of controlling the money supply without chaotic side-effects in the financial system and the real economy as a whole is at an equally preliminary stage. Whatever the theoretical arguments, the efficacy of the various measures of the money supply and the methods of its control can only be tested by practical experience in the real world; and it is a tribute to the British authorities, and particularly, the Bank of England, that the experiments have so far been conducted in a manner which has furthered the debate without causing lasting damage to the financial system or the economy at large. The jeers of the most fundamentalist theologians of 'monetarism' at the supposed 'pussy-footing' of the authorities in the early years of the Thatcher Government from 1979 and the equally shrill conclusions of some commentators that the 1982 Budget Speech marked the effective end of the monetarist experiment were both equally wide of the mark.

The proper and main conclusions to be drawn on the experiment so far are that some sort of control of the money supply is likely, and ought, to remain a key weapon in the armoury of economic policy; that the use of tight monetary targets for a single monetary aggregate is wrong on two counts, in that the targets must be flexible and should encompass several separate measures of the money supply; and that any attempt to restrict the money supply without exercising a comparable restriction on public borrowing will have a distorting effect on the financial system (including a sharp rise in the rate of interest) and on the economy as a whole (including an exaggerated cash squeeze on the private sector). A further conclusion is that, in the absence of effective exchange controls, it is impossible to achieve a reasonable and separate control on both the domestic rates of interest and the rate of exchange for sterling. To these two policy instruments, their relationship to the banking system and their effect on each other, we now turn.

Interest rates, the exchange rate and the banks

The level of interest rates and, more particularly, changes in that level have for long been regarded as a principal instrument of monetary policy. Surveying the British monetary system and its recent history in 1959, the Radcliffe Committee concluded that

> monetary policy must take its influence upon the structure of interest rates as its proper method of affecting financial conditions and eventually, through them, the level of demand. There is no doubt that it has, and can, exert this influence through the management of the National Debt which, if burdensome to the financial authorities in other

> respects, affords in this respect an instrument of singular potency. In our view debt management has become the fundamental domestic task of the central bank. It is not open to the monetary authorities to be neutral in their handling of this task. They must have and consciously exercise a positive policy about interest rates, long as well as short, and about the relationship between them.[17]

As we have seen, conventional views of the conduct of economic policy in general and monetary policy in particular have changed considerably since 1959; but the rate of interest, and particularly the short-term rate of interest has retained a central position in any discussions of such policy. Thus, for example, the rate of interest was listed in the paper on monetary control quoted in the last section as being one of the main policy instruments available to the authorities in influencing monetary conditions.

This is not the place to discuss in any detail the precise ways in which interest rates effect the real economy through their impact on the decisions of borrowers and lenders. It is sufficient to note, by quoting again from *Monetary Control*, that the effects on the money supply which, in a sense, mirror these decisions, are complex and take some time to work their way through the system:

> Short-term interest rates have a complex effect on the money supply; they affect all the counterparts but in differing directions, in differing degrees and with varying time profiles. A rise in rates will increase the P.S.B.R. through the cost of Government borrowing and affect the timing and amount of tax receipts. It will also affect both the amount and composition of external flows and so the exchange rate. A rise will tend to increase gilt sales both by raising yields and also by affecting expectations about future trends in interest rates. In the short run, however, the effect may be perverse if the rise is viewed as a harbinger of yet higher long-term rates. It will also decrease the level of bank lending to the private sector but this is likely to take some months to occur.
>
> Bank lending to the private sector is determined by a

number of factors including the financial position of the company sector, consumer confidence and inflationary expectations, as well as interest rates. Moreover the growth in lending exhibits sharp month to month fluctuations in response to normal commercial demand from industrial and other customers. Because of this and the delay before interest rates have their full effects, it is not feasible for the authorities to exercise an exact control over bank lending through interest rates in the short run.[18]

In spite of these cautions, interest-rate manipulation remains a prime instrument of monetary policy. And it is difficult to see why this should not continue to be the case. As we saw in a previous section, increases in the money supply originating in the private sector are a direct consequence of increases in the credit made available to the private sector by the banking system; and these increases in credit availability are the result not only of banks granting credit but equally of individuals and corporations demanding more credit. And there is no doubt that, in the medium term at least, the demand for credit in the private sector is heavily influenced by the price of that credit, the rate of interest. (Enough has probably been said about increases in the money supply originating in the public sector where, of course, the demand for credit is almost totally unaffected by its price and must therefore be curbed by other means.)

If interest-rate manipulation remains a prime instrument of monetary policy, how can this be achieved? The authors of the paper, *Monetary Control*, were quite clear that

> the level of short-term interest rates at any time is determined by the interaction between the markets and the authorities. The short-term interest rates generated by the markets are not necessarily those needed to achieve the monetary target. Markets respond to the current supply and demand for particular types of funds and their expectations about future movements in interest rates. Market operators will take a view about future trends in the domestic and world economies – notably the domestic inflation rate, and interest rates elsewhere – but also about

any actions which they believe the authorities need to take to achieve the monetary targets.[19]

As we saw in Chapter 3, the principal contact between the Bank of England and the sterling money markets is made in the Discount Market. At the risk of repetition, it is worth emphasising that the Bank's operations in the Discount Market have two separate but related functions: to smooth out the inevitable humps in the movements of funds between the Bank, as the Government's bankers, and the rest of the banking system – and thus 'accommodate' the market to this end – but at the same time to influence the overall level of interest rates in accordance with its perception of the requirements of monetary policy.

The Bank's participation in the discount market is conducted primarily through the purchase and sale of bills – either Treasury bills or eligible commercial bills. The Bank has described how it uses these transactions to influence the level of interest rates in the following way:

> Pre-determined dealing rates having been abandoned, the discount houses compete to sell paper to the Bank, or buy from it when in surplus, through their choice of the rates at which they offer to do business. The Bank can influence interest rates by its reactions to these offers. If the Bank is content with the pattern of rates implied by the offers, it is generally prepared to accept sufficient to balance the market. But if the rates which are offered conflict with the Bank's interest rate objective, all or part of the offers may be rejected; in this case, if the houses are short of funds, they may have a chance to submit further offers (e.g. if the rejection came at the morning session . . .), and the Bank again decides which offers to accept. In addition to, or separately from, any bill operations, the Bank may let the houses know that it is willing to lend, at an interest rate of its own choosing. Such occasions are exceptional, and are in contrast with the earlier arrangements under which the houses could at times borrow continuously.[20]

Two examples of occasions when the Bank may decide to lend in this latter way were quoted in Chapter 3.

Although the Bank confines its operations to the Discount Market, its influence on the rates of interest in that market is quickly spread to the interbank market in sterling deposits through the many banks who operate in both markets and would quickly arbitrage out any interest rate differentials which appeared between the two. And the interbank rates are quickly reflected in the rates which individual banks charge and pay for loans and deposits. This is because many banks calculate the rate of interest they charge their borrowers as being an agreed margin above the cost of funds for the appropriate maturity; and, equally, they pay interest on their deposits at a rate either equal to, or related to, the rate paid in the interbank market (small deposits commanding a rate lower than the market rate, the differential depending mainly on size).

Interbank rates are also reflected, if not very precisely, in the Base Rates published by the clearing banks and to which their overdraft lending and deposit rates are directly related. The relationship between interbank rates and clearing bank base rates has been clearly described by Mr John Quinton, senior General Manager of Barclays Bank. 'The reason why wholesale (inter-bank) rates are crucial to the clearers in pitching base rate is that they represent the bank's marginal cost of funds.' This has come about because 'the clearing banks' traditional deposit base – savings and cheque accounts – has diminished as a proportion of total deposits in recent years. Competition, particularly from the building societies but also from National Savings, has increased the clearers' dependence upon the wholesale markets. Rather more than one-third of Barclays' deposits is now raised at market related rates'.

But this causal chain from the Bank of England's 'intervention rate' – the rate at which it will buy or sell bills – via the interbank deposit market to the level at which a clearing bank will fix its base rate is not altogether precise. Mr Quinton gives two reasons why this is so. First,

> banks do not alter base rate from week to week, so any base rate decision will be influenced by a view of how long current market conditions – the level of money rates – will

prevail and the likely direction of the next change. Because of this, the banks will take into account what they perceive to be the underlying trend of both financial and general economic conditions – including the authorities' attitude to exchange rate and money supply pressures. Although base rate decisions cannot depart far from commercial criteria – the cost of the banks' funds and the pressure of competition in financial markets – wider considerations may also come into play, including the condition of industry.

Mr Quinton set out his second reason as follows:

There is a generally held misconception that intervention rates are fundamental to any judgement by a clearing bank on the appropriate level of its base rate. They are not – unless intervention rates themselves move market rates, especially the three-month rate. Intervention rates certainly provide the pivot to the entire interest rate spectrum, but those who relate base rate prospects to the Bank of England's intervention rates overlook the point that the clearers cannot raise deposits at those rates. It is the rate at which the banks can raise deposits that determines both what they can pay to investors and charge to customers. Because very short-term rates are dominated by the Bank of England's intervention rate, the three-month rate will be influenced by the market's expectations about possible future movements in the Bank's dealing rates for seven-day bills. As a result, the notion that market forces have a completely independent life of their own is largely fallacious although underlying pressures will of course influence the Bank's policy.

Commenting on which interbank rates are taken into account by the clearing banks in setting their base rates, Mr Quinton pointed out that

the three month rate is particularly significant; it is fairly stable and corresponds to standard money market maturities. However, shorter-term rates, from overnight to seven-day, are also relevant, for if they are too high in relation to base rate large corporate customers may borrow on overdraft and lend back through the wholesale market at the higher rate. The banks have sought, not wholly successfully, to eliminate such misuse of overdraft facilities.[21]

But in spite of the Bank of England's ability to control very precisely the very short-term interest rates obtaining in the Discount Market and in spite of the clear link between the Discount Market and the interbank market, there can be circumstances in which the Bank is unable to control rates in the interbank market and is even obliged to follow that market rather than lead it. The reason for this is the arbitrage into and out of the domestic markets for sterling deposits out of and into the eurocurrency markets, made possible by the swap market in foreign exchange described in Chapter 3. In the absence of exchange control, any increase in domestic UK sterling interest rates can cause an inflow of almost infinite proportions into the domestic market if the rate of interest available in that market for, say, three-month deposits exceeds the cost of three-month eurodollar deposits plus (or minus) the discount (or premium) between the spot rate and the three-month forward rate for sterling against dollars. Such a movement of funds is, of course, even less controllable if the spot exchange rate for sterling against US dollars is fixed within fairly narrow bands (as it was prior to 1972) and if the markets believe that that exchange rate will be maintained. In these circumstances, the difference between the spot and forward rates of exchange for sterling against dollars – the 'swap cost' – is likely to remain stable, no matter how great the movement of funds from dollars into sterling, and this movement of funds is thus likely to continue until either the interest rate for domestic sterling deposits eases downwards or the interest rate on eurodollar deposit eases upwards. If the spot and forward rates for sterling are allowed to float freely, the market itself may put an end to this movement of funds, in that the spot purchases of sterling might drive the spot rate up so high that the foreign exchange markets might reckon that in three months' time it was more likely to be lower than higher: this combined with the selling pressure on sterling three months forward generated by swaps would, in theory at least, widen out the discount between spot and forward sterling and thus increase the cost of manufacturing eurosterling through the swap. But this self-correcting mechanism only works if the Bank of England really does allow the spot exchange rate for sterling to float freely against dollars – or against any other major currency, for we saw in Chapter 3 how closely connected by arbitrage are the markets for sterling against dollars, D-Marks, Swiss francs, Japanese yen and other major currencies.

The conclusion must be that it is impossible, in conditions freed from any exchange control and in the context of the huge markets in eurocurrency deposits and foreign exchange described in Chapter 3, to control both domestic interest rates and the rate of exchange for sterling. Indeed, experience is too short since the abolition of exchange control in 1979 to demonstrate how wild the fluctuations in the exchange rate must be to limit the effect of external interest rates on internal interest rates or, for that matter, how wild the fluctuations in domestic interest rates must be to limit the effect of external interest rates on the exchange rate for sterling. Experience *has* shown, and for other countries as well as Britain, that a wide disparity between interest rates in, say, the eurodollar market and the domestic deposit market can cause pressures on domestic interest rates and the exchange rate which are unwelcome to domestic policy makers. Examples of this experience are the very high domestic rates of interest which were forced on the British authorities by external factors in the autumn of 1981 and, again, the pressures from external factors which forced British interest rates to higher levels than the Government would clearly have liked for reasons of domestic economic policy in January 1983.

The same point was made in the context of monetary control, in the consultation paper already quoted:

> External flows can exert a powerful influence on domestic monetary conditions, both directly through their impact on monetary growth and indirectly through changes in the exchange rate. Provided that intervention is small or self-balancing so that the exchange rate mainly reflects

market forces, the direct effects of external flows on the money supply are likely to be small. However, there is no way in which the domestic money supply can be completely isolated from external flows because even if in total there is no net inflow or outflow, changes in the composition of flows between the various sectors of the economy and abroad will still affect the money supply.[22]

What conclusions can be drawn from this rather gloomy discussion? The first and perhaps the most important one is that, whatever the theoretical attractions of a tight and rigid control of the domestic money supply, such control is simply not attainable with any great precision – at least for a country in Britain's present position. As the Governor of the Bank put it in a speech in March 1982:

we are a relatively small country with a relatively very large financial centre exposed to international monetary forces acting in a turbulent world. At the same time, our domestic monetary policy remains crucial to success in the steady, unremitting fight against inflation. Recent experience serves, I believe, to confirm the judgement that arrangements that allow maximum flexibility of response, that leave as much room as possible for the free play of market forces, and that enable us to operate with a somewhat lower profile than before, are best suited to our times and enable us to pursue as steady a course as is practicable.

This very flexibility has become associated with the now well-known fact that policy has regard to a number of indicators, including the exchange rate, rather than to any single monetary aggregate. This might give an impression that policy lacks coherence. But I would suggest that the consistency and steadiness of our behaviour in pursuit of the ultimate objectives of policy is more important than the apparent intellectual coherence and presentational simplicity of concentration on a single monetary aggregate. Of course it would be best if we could successfully combine both; but hard experience has taught us that that is not our world.[23]

The second lesson concerns the banking system. The Governor preceded the comments quoted above by remarking that

> last week saw a further modest but welcome reduction on interest rates from the exceptionally high level reached last autumn. Market opinion, responding to the coalminers' ballot, to a relatively robust performance of sterling in the exchange markets, and to a less gloomy view of domestic monetary trends, became more favourable. The Bank, in its daily operations in the money market, was able to take a similar attitude and acted to encourage a modest fall. This episode marks a further brief chapter in the story of the new monetary arrangements introduced last August; and I think provides further evidence of their virtues.

What the Governor was admitting, however gracefully, was that there are moments when the Bank has to follow 'the market', or at least keep in step with it, rather than lead it, when it comes to interest rates. It is important to emphasise that this 'market' to which so much influence is apparently conceded consists *not* of the banking system itself, but rather of the myriad of borrowers and lenders, buyers and sellers of currency throughout the world, who are the customers of that system.

OFFICIAL INTERVENTION IN CREDIT DECISIONS

The banks as executors of monetary policy

As we have seen, a principal function of the banking system is the collection of deposits from those with surplus funds and their on-lending to organisations and individuals in need of credit. A by-product of this function is to give the banking system a key role in the working of a free-enterprise economy: the allocation of limited resources of credit between those who need them. In normal circumstances, the main criterion observed by bankers in this allocation is their assessment of the ability of the borrower to repay the principal amount borrowed plus interest over a reasonable period of time, that is, their assessment of the 'credit risk' of the borrower.

In the absence of any particular preferred pattern of allocation laid down by the head offices of banks, the Bank of England or anybody else, the exact allocation of credit between types of borrowers, property developers and manufacturing industry, for example, emerges as a by-product of hundreds of decisions taken every day by individual bankers. Some exponents of the free-enterprise system describe approvingly this allocation of credit as being effected by the 'hidden hand' of the market place, implying by their approval both that the allocation resulting from many thousands of credit decisions taken by individual bankers on purely commercial grounds is *prima facie* more likely to be beneficial to the economy at large than any other allocation. Also that those who complain about the resultant allocation should take note that no individual, let alone government official, is responsible for that allocation, that there are therefore no ears for such complaints to fall on and that the complainants had better therefore accept the existing allocation as a simple fact of economic life. It is worth remarking that whilst most practising bankers would probably approve of both these implications, they would nevertheless point out that in practical terms they, the bankers, are effectively the agents of the 'hidden hand' in allocating credit and, rightly or wrongly, find themselves the recipients of many of the complaints about that allocation.

It is a general principle of bankers that they should tailor their lendings so that they roughly equal a reasonably stable proportion of their incoming deposits: precisely what this proportion should be was discussed in Chapter 4. They are clearly unable to let lendings run ahead of their capital and deposits since, quite simply, they cannot lend what they do not have: and to take on deposits and effectively incur an actual or notional rate of interest thereby without actually on-lending them at a profit would be a very expensive exercise indeed. When credit throughout the economy is tight, it is probable that individual lending bankers up and down the country will have many more applications for loans than they have funds to lend and their job as allocators of credit thus takes on the additional and emotionally-charged characteristic of 'rationer' of funds as well and, in the absence of any specific directives from above, they will apply their existing criteria for credit assessment with even greater stringency. When credit in the economy as a whole is easy, lending bankers will take a more relaxed view in applying their criteria for credit assessment, and under the continual pressure to lend out the funds available to them, will probably give some pretty marginal applicants for loans the benefit of the doubt.

In many ways, a time of easy money is a deceptive and dangerous situation for lending bankers, for the pressures on them to lend out the funds available will almost certainly cause them to lower their standards of lending; and the pressures of competition from other bankers, equally anxious to lend out their surplus funds available, will probably encourage them to lend at even narrower margins of gross profit. The explosion of lending, much of it on much-lowered standards of credit risk assessment, which followed the 'Barber boom' in the money supply in 1972 and 1973, is a practical case in point; and the secondary banking crisis which followed it is a clear example of the inherent dangers in such a lending boom and consequent lowering of standards.

But it is worth noting that the penalties for increasing lending at the expense of lowering standards in credit assessment will not always be incurred entirely by the lending bankers. If money supply is increased dramatically, as in the 'Barber boom', and the bankers are given more money to lend, the result, as we have seen, is an almost inevitable increase in the rate of price inflation. And a steady rate of inflation has the insidious effect, among others, of reducing or sometimes eliminating the consequences of financial imprudence. Thus, for example, a company whose cash flow forecasts would not justify additional borrowing on the basis of constant prices might well find that the sums work out quite differently and advantageously if they are adjusted to take account of a reasonably high rate of inflation. Or again, and more simply, a property speculator who borrows money to invest in property which would probably bankrupt him if prices remained stable or fell, would probably be rewarded by substantial profits if prices continued to rise with inflation. Equally, the bankers who lent to both these borrowers might well have bad debts on their hands if prices remained stable; whilst an inflation of prices would permit both borrowers to repay their loans comfortably on time, together with the interest due.

But the converse of this is also true. An easy money supply may well give rise to a boom in lending and a lowering of lending standards; it will also give rise to an inflation of prices which may, but not always, 'bail out' both the borrower and the lender of the 'low standard' loans and shield them from the consequences of their imprudence. A tight money policy is unlikely, by definition, so to increase the lendable funds in the hands of bankers as to cause them to lower their standards in fresh credit assessments; but it may well, if accompanied as anticipated by a fall in price inflation, make *existing* loans look very risky indeed. These loans would have been made on assessments which looked reasonable at the time they were made and which wrote in some expectation of future price inflation. In other words, a tight money policy accompanied and followed by a reduction in price inflation, as was experienced in Britain in 1981 and 1982, may well result in individual and corporate borrowers from the banking system looking a great deal less credit-worthy than they did before the tight money policy was imposed, to the consequent discomfort of themselves and their bankers. This last point provides one explanation of why 1981 and 1982 saw so many British examples of companies whose credit rating, in the eyes of their bankers, had suddenly deteriorated fast and whose bankers, often with substantial existing loans outstanding to the borrowers concerned, were tempted suddenly to cry 'not a penny more' and to refuse to increase their lendings further.

We have seen that in the British economy the allocation of credit between potential borrowers in the private sector is, generally speaking, effected by the decision of a great many lending bankers up and down the country applying their commercial lending criteria to the cases of the applicant borrowers and that the consequent allocation has no preconceived pattern or logic. There have, of course, always been those who regard this *laissez-faire* approach to credit allocation as being totally contrary to the national interest and a system in which the basic decisions on credit allocation are taken by individual lending bankers rather than by some official guardian of the national interest as a gross abdication of the proper responsibilities of government to run the national economy. A practical example of this view is to be seen in the socialist Mitterrand government which took office in France in 1981 and which clearly and explicitly expects bankers to pay attention to the views and plans of government officials in Paris when making their decisions on the allocation of credit.

This is not the place for any significant participation in this highly political debate. It is a premise of this book that the main decisions as to the allocation of credit in Britain are, and should remain, in the hands of lending bankers; and our purpose is to discuss how those decisions are taken and how, if at all, they should be influenced by the central government. This premise is based on two simple factors. First, as a practical matter of fact, decisions as to the allocation of credit *are* in the hands of lending bankers though many arguments have been put forward for allowing other factors to influence their decisions. The second factor is a firm belief that the allocation of credit *ought* to be in the hands of practical bankers; and this belief in its turn has two separate facets: first that it is important for the health of the economy that decisions of credit allocation should be taken predominantly for commercial reasons and secondly that to leave the decisions to be taken in a decentralised way by hundreds and thousands of individual bankers is a better guarantee that commercial criteria will prevail than any other system of decision – taking which has been proposed. This is not to say that non-commercial criteria should never intrude – as, for example, the level of unemployment in any particular geographical area: it is rather to say that the basic decision for credit allocation should rest on a commercial analysis of the credit risk involved and that any distortion of decisions taken in this way should be clearly seen to be such a distortion and should require clear and public justification.

Some recent criticisms of banks' domestic lending decisions

The system of credit allocation based on the commercial decisions of many individual bankers has been both highlighted and subjected to increasing criticism in the 1970s and early 1980s and the pressures for government intervention to distort these decisions have become correspondingly greater. These pressures can be traced to two main causes: an increasing dissatisfaction with the growth performance of the British economy since the 1960s and the harshness of the consequences of an allocation of credit on an undistorted commercial basis which has been demonstrated by the economic policy of the Thatcher Government since 1979 based, as we have seen, on a greater attention to controlling the money supply than was shown by its predecessors.

One of the commonest, and most valid, criticisms of British economic policy in the 1960s and 1970s has been the low rate of growth in the economy, both in absolute terms and in comparison with other developed economies in Europe and the United States. The figures demonstrating this disappointing record, as measured by practically any indicator one chooses to take, have been so well documented as to require no further repetition here.

We have seen how the underlying strategy of economic policy to achieve the five ends listed by the Radcliffe Committee was based, from 1945 into the early 1970s, on the manipulation of 'demand' and how this gradually gave way in the middle 1970s to control of the money supply as an equal or more important basis of policy. One of the gnawing frustrations of the period of demand management was the inability of the policy-makers to engender a steady and reasonable rate of economic growth. In the context of a 'demand management' strategy, the classic method of achieving growth was to engineer easy credit, low interest rates and an easy fiscal policy, implying low taxation and a budget deficit. One attempt to break out of 'stop–go' into a steady and virtuous spiral of growth was the period of expansion in 1963–4 engineered by Mr Reginald Maudling, the then Chancellor of the Exchequer: whilst this experiment was cut short, as it were, in midstream by the election of October

1964 and the consequent change of government, it was already clear that the price to be paid for such expansion in terms of balance-of-payments deficits and inflationary pressures would almost certainly have caused it to be brought to an end in any case.

A more recent attempt to break out of 'stop–go' policies and launch a strategy of economic expansion was made by the Conservative Government of Mr Edward Heath which came to power in June 1970. Again, this strategy was based firmly in the context of demand management: it involved substantial budget deficits and an expansionary monetary policy, the 'Barber boom', which saw the money supply growing by over 25 per cent in both 1972 and 1973. This was accompanied by the introduction in September 1971 of Competition and Credit Control – a major liberating new deal for the banking world which swept away many of the restrictions on bank lending which had existed up till then. To oversimplify, the strategy was based on the assumption that the encouragement to the banks to lend would act in two beneficial ways: as a stimulus to personal demands for goods and services – through personal loans, hire purchase, and the like – and as a consequent stimulus to industrial investment to provide the productive capacity to meet these consumer demands – through the provision of loans to industry to finance this industrial investment, and also to satisfy the accompanying need for increased working capital: for example to finance an increase in stocks. This experiment, too, was cut short in midstream by the General Election of February 1974 which brought the Labour Government to power under Sir Harold Wilson. But by February 1974, it was already clear that the strategy of economic expansion was not working out as planned. First the massive expansion of credit under the 'Barber boom' led to, and fuelled, a frightening increase in price inflation. Secondly, and as importantly in this context, the practical bankers took advantage of the massive new amount of credit put at their disposal together with their reinforced freedom from controls, to lend not to industry for manufacturing investment but rather to property speculators and financial speculators: far from sowing the seeds of a virtuous economic expansion, the expansionist monetary policy thus sowed the seeds of both the property crash and secondary banking crisis of 1973–5.

Noting the explosion in money supply in 1971–3, Margaret Reid has traced through the statistics to show the uses to which this newly available credit was put:

> In the two-and-a-quarter years between September 1971, when Competition and Credit Control was launched, and December 1973, when the secondary banking crisis broke out, the supply of money, according to the most widely accepted measure, sterling M_3, which includes bank deposit accounts, rose by 73 per cent to £33 200m.[24] More striking and ominous was the much stronger upsurge in bank lending. By December 1973, total sterling bank advances to U.K. resident borrowers had risen to two-and-a-half times their October 1971 level, a climb of 148 per cent to £20,057m. The clearing banks were no slouches, since they raised their lending by 112 per cent to £11,379m, while foreign banks in Britain, also liberated from lending ceilings, sharply increased their advances too. But 'other U.K. banks', broadly the secondary sector of listed banks, as distinct from the 'junior' section 123 concerns, boosted their lending many times over, from £395m to £3366m.[25] Even adjusting for the fact that five sizeable finance houses or secondary banks were included in the statistics after being re-designated as part of the banking system on receiving section 127 status in January 1972, the level of lending by 'other banks' probably more than trebled.[26] [It should perhaps be added that these 'other banks' included, besides the secondary banks, the merchant bank subsidiaries of the clearing banks.]
>
> The pattern of the lending was striking. In the two years November 1973 active and aggressive borrowers in the property and financial sector more than quadrupled their bank loans to £6,347m. It is a remarkable fact that by then these categories owed more to the banks than the whole of manufacturing industry, whose advances had risen to £6,337m,[25] over the same period, an increase of 73 per cent. Individuals almost trebled their borrowing to £4,076m., spurred on by the tax concession on interest [in the Budget

of March 1972, making interest above £35 a year offsettable against tax] and the boom to a stock market peak in 1972 (when the *Financial Times* 30 share index reached a record 543.6 on May 19). Another factor stimulating bank borrowing by individuals was the opportunity for rich pickings through stagging – seeking short-term profits on – new share issues.

Miss Reid has some colourful comments to make on the practical bankers:

> Long established restrictive attitudes within the High Street clearing banks were abandoned in the tussle for new lending business. Sedate bank managers from the big High Street clearers shed their didactic 'no-man' image and became like salesmen, actively marketing that commodity then in plentiful supply, money. New personal loan schemes, packages for small firms and longer-term loans for industry abounded, while managers became more open-handed with overdrafts to individuals, who borrowed heavily to play the stock market boom which was well under way.[27]

The result of this was, as we have seen, a long way from the purpose of Mr Heath and his Government; and it is, perhaps, understandable that in surveying the wreckage of the property collapse and the secondary banking crisis – and the continuing stagnation in industrial investment – some members of that government should feel some bitterness towards the practical bankers. We gave bankers the expansion of credit at low rates of interest, they might have argued, to enable them to finance the real investment which British industry was thought to need as a necessary condition for sustained economic growth, and all they did was to squander these resources on loans to speculators in the property and financial markets. Small wonder, in a way, that even senior members of the Conservative party were heard muttering about the 'irresponsibility' of the bankers.

If the last attempts at 'demand management' as the central core of economic policy focused attention in this way on the role of practical bankers as the main allocators of credit, the same thing happened in the first attempts to place control of the money supply as that central core. One of the main purposes of controlling the money supply is to limit, or even eliminate, the progress of price inflation. But a secondary effect of this policy, and every bit as important, is to allow the normal financial disciplines to apply to individuals and corporations in the management of their affairs. We have seen already how inflation can blunt these disciplines and permit individuals and corporations to borrow more than they prudently should and postpone or even duck completely the awkward decisions of management – to close down unprofitable plant, to turn a blind eye to excess manning, to fail to adopt new techniques of production through inertia or fear of labour reprisals, for example. We have seen, too, how a sudden pull on the rein by imposing some control over the supply of money, with an attendant fall in the rate of price inflation can and does have a devastating effect on the disciplinary pressures on corporations and individuals (and, consequentially, since the pressures bear across the whole economy, on the total level of unemployment).

It is a matter of practical fact that many companies, and many bits of other companies, have gone to the wall basically as a result of the control of the money supply effected, however imperfectly, by the Thatcher Government since 1979; it is a matter of practical fact that a great many of those companies and operations would have modified their policies or gone out of business in a more humane way at some earlier time over the last twenty years or so, if they had not been shielded from harsh economic reality by price inflation. But it is also a matter of fact that the conditions which have caused this purge – particularly high nominal rates of interest, high and possibly rising real rates of interest and, for individuals, static or falling real after-tax incomes – have aborted many a bright and potentially profitable idea and have stifled the enthusiasm of many a budding entrepreneur. Finally, it is a practical matter of fact that the apparent agent for the 'hidden hand' of monetary policy in forcing these disciplines is always the practical banker – whether it is calling a halt on the borrowing of companies such as Laker Airways or Stone-

Platt Industries and forcing them into bankruptcy, or forcing companies to close a redundant plant or sack a redundant workforce, or failing to support a young entrepreneur with a bright idea because of doubts of his ability to pay the high real rates of interest prevailing, or simply forcing a spendthrift individual to realise that the feather-bedding provided by inflation is over and he must henceforth learn to live within his means. Put in these terms, it is easy to see why the monetary policy of the Thatcher Government and the disciplines it imposed should have caused a groundswell of criticism of practical bankers and their decisions on the allocation of credit, and calls for Government intervention to influence those decisions in the future.

To all these criticisms, the bankers have a very proper riposte: that in 1971–3 and again in 1979–83, all they were doing was to pursue their own trade of lending out the funds available to them, to those borrowers which represented the most sensible commercial risks. If the resultant pattern of lending over the whole economy was not entirely to the satisfaction of the Government, this was not necessarily, or even probably, the fault of the bankers. If the collective decisions of individual bankers cause a higher proportion of lending to go to, say, property speculation than the Government thinks appropriate or a lower proportion to go to, say, heavy industrial investment, this could be the result of three separate reasons. First, that the bankers have done their credit assessments and simply got them wrong – in which case, provided the Government does not interfere, it can rest assured that the banks will in due time reap the rewards of their own folly. Secondly, that the environment in which the bankers took their individual commercial decisions contained blemishes which could distort those decisions, such as the prevalence of a higher rate of price inflation and the consequent attraction of real estate and other 'real' assets as security for bank lending – in which case, the government must take responsibility for setting this environment and for the distortions it contains. Thirdly, that the commercial criteria followed by the bankers in their allocation of credit to, say, an expanding service industry and away from, say, heavy engineering were a great deal more conducive to the health and growth of the economy than an allocation based on less commercial criteria and favoured by the Government – in which case the country, if not the Government itself, should be thankful that the credit allocation based on the collective commercial decisions of the banking system represents some bulwark for the protection of the economy from a government's doctrinal prejudices and follies.

This is not to say that the allocation of credit on purely commercial criteria will necessarily lead to the best of all possible worlds. There may, for example, be acceptable political reasons for distorting the geographical allocation of credit in order to assist particularly depressed areas; or the industrial allocation of credit in order to encourage entrepreneurs to start up small businesses on their own or to encourage the growth of some industry thought to have a strategic importance; or the personal allocation of credit in order to encourage, say, the individual ownership of residential property. But practising bankers would plead two points already made in this book about such distortions. First, that the Government should effect these distortions itself by, for example, the granting of tax advantages and subsidies, and should resist the temptation to abdicate responsibility for effecting them to the lending bankers by giving them 'directives' as to how to allocate credit, overriding the bankers' own commercial decisions. Secondly, the bankers plead that these distortions should be specific and overt and should be effected by attaching the tax advantages and subsidies to the favoured takers of credit and not to any group of lenders, thus reducing the possibility of fostering unfair competition between groups of lending institutions.

Lifeboats for domestic industrial borrowers

One of the features of the British economic scene in the early 1980s has been the large and growing number of industrial and commercial corporations whose creditworthiness has, in the eyes of their bankers, suddenly deteriorated fast and tempted these bankers to decide to throw no more good money after bad and to state firmly, 'not a penny more'. In simplest terms, this deterioration reflects an ever-growing level of indebtedness to banks by these corporations, accompanied by an ever-prolonged absence of recovery in their trading profits.

This deterioration, and the reaction of bankers to it, was highlighted by Mr C. W. McMahon, the Deputy Governor of the Bank of England in a lecture given in November 1982:

> There is no single unambiguous indicator of a Company's financial position. But one frequently used is that of income gearing – the proportion of profits absorbed by interest charges. On this basis, the position of companies, both in the United Kingdom and overseas, has deteriorated sharply in recent years: partly because of declining profitability and partly because inflation has led to higher nominal interest rates. The Bank of England has studied a sample of 1,200 U.K.-listed industrial and commercial companies: for these, the average cover for interest has, over the past decade, been halved – from 9 times to 4½ times. In respect of the smaller listed companies within the sample the decline in cover has been even greater, although from a higher level at the start of the period.[28]

Mr McMahon analysed the factors behind this deterioration in the following terms:

> Lower profitability has reduced the capacity of firms to generate their own cash flow to provide for working capital, modernisation and expansion. Companies' fixed and working capital requirements have been met to a greater degree than was previously customary by recourse to borrowing. Moreover, from the early 1970s, the corporate debenture market, which had traditionally provided a ready source of fixed-interest long-term funding, ceased to be used; and dependence by companies on short and medium-term borrowing at variable interest rates increased markedly. This brought a dramatic increase in companies' dependence on banks. Between 1967 and 1973 the percentage of bank borrowings in companies' total new outside finance rose from 30% to 70%; between 1973 and 1982 it rose further, from 70% to 80%.

> Within the total figures for corporate indebtedness, the Bank of England's work on the balance sheets of listed industrial and commercial companies suggests that there have been some significant developments in the maturity structure of corporate bank debt. There has been an increase in the proportion of bank debt raised by term lending rather than overdraft. Since overdraft facilities are – at least notionally – repayable on demand, this development should have improved companies' liquidity positions. However, this development has not prevented a significant shortening in the average maturity of company debt as a whole in that, since 1973, there has been a marked increase from about 30% to 37% in the proportion of companies' total debt repayable within a year.

He summarised later in the lecture:

> Thus we have seen the indebtedness of the corporate sector increase considerably over the last few years; banks have become the dominant – indeed virtually the exclusive – source of new outside finance. The average maturity of overall debt has become shorter, probably reflecting decisions by borrowers rather than lenders. There has been an increased reluctance by companies to enter into long-term commitments at times of uncertainty associated with high inflation. This appears to have more than offset the fact that the banks have acted to move the maturity structure in the other direction, for instance by increased term lending in place of overdraft facilities.

From the immediate point of view of the lending bankers this deterioration in the financial condition of many of their corporate borrowers was worrying enough. As time went on, without any appreciable alleviation in the conditions of high interest rates and weak demand for their products, more and more of these corporate borrowers seemed to be reaching a condition where there appeared to be no realistic hope that they would ever repay their loans together with interest accrued in the forseeable future. But from the point of view of the national authorities there was a deeper and even more worrying implication: that when the recession finally eased and a recovery in demand actually occurred, great sections of British industry and commerce would be too debilitated financially to respond. The worry was clearly expressed by Mr McMahon:

> The combination of past high inflation and low growth has left financial problems that will persist, whatever the future may hold. And despite these problems, companies will have to continue to attract outside funds. Indeed, as the economy recovers, the financing requirement may be substantial. Many companies will be starting from a position where profits are low; and where stocks, working capital and activity have been sharply cut back. Moreover companies will also need much new investment to face the intense competition which is bound to confront them. Investment now must compensate for the relative dearth of investment in manufacturing over the past few years of low demand and excess capacity. Economic upturn is likely therefore to give rise to financial difficulties, which in somes cases may be severe. It is important that arrangements should be in place so that finance will not be an unnecessary impediment to recovery.
>
> We start, unfortunately, from a position where, as a result of the length and severity of the recession, a number of companies are currently in difficulties and in need of active assistance from their banks. In these situations the Bank of England is occasionally able to play a role.

When the Bank first intervened to alleviate this problem in 1981, many commentators saw it as an unjustified pursuit of the precedent established by the formation of the Lifeboat to contain the secondary banking crisis in 1973–5; and considerable criticism developed from two independent sources. First, there were the purist 'monetarists' who saw the financial debility of much of British commerce and industry as a consequence and reflection of supposedly flabby management which the monetary disciplines of tight money, high interest rates and a high exchange rate were intended to cure. In the eyes of these critics, any attempt by the Bank of

England to protect such commercial and industrial corporations from the disciplines of monetary policy would simply render those disciplines less effective and prolong the agonising period before the purge of the flabbiness had gone sufficiently far to allow the Government to alleviate the disciplines. These critics appeared to have something in common with those who ridiculed the Bank of England's actions to 'accommodate' the money markets at a time when the whole stance of Government policy was intended to tighten monetary conditions, except that they saw no justification for 'accommodating' apparently incompetent corporate managements, whatever the arguments for 'accommodating' the money markets. The second group of critics was to be found amongst the bankers themselves. This group saw the precedent of the Lifeboat for secondary banks as being totally irrelevant: it was always accepted that the earlier Lifeboat was to ameliorate conditions of *illiquidity*, not *insolvency*, whereas in organising Lifeboats for British industry the Bank seemed bent on persuading lending bankers to continue support for individual corporations beyond the point where their own best analysis demonstrated that the borrower's solvency was in serious doubt, or at least at serious risk.

To assess the validity of these criticisms, it is as well to inspect what the Bank of England's policy of creating Lifeboats for domestic industrial borrowers really amounts to. Again, the policy was clearly stated by Mr McMahon:

> Our Industrial Finance Division at the Bank attempts to monitor the progress of many individual companies, keeping in close touch with both the companies themselves and their bankers. The aim is jointly to identify major problems as early as possible. If a difficulty arises it may sometimes help to bring together all the banks involved with the company, and encourage them to agree a mutually beneficial solution. In this way it may be possible to avoid the situation where one bank takes unilateral action at the expense of the other banks, without full knowledge of the overall situation, and in the fear that other banks may be contemplating similar action. If, on the other hand, the

banks concerned can agree on a uniform approach, they – and the company – may well be able to devise an alternative outcome that could benefit them all more. We have, I believe, had considerable success, both in helping to bring about agreement in individual cases, and more generally, in making banks and companies aware of the need for frankness and completeness in exchanging information. Early resolution of problems in this way can often prevent them becoming more intractable later on.

The Bank of England's role can only be marginal; and it is satisfying to see how the banking system as a whole has also been responding in a flexible and innovative way to the developing situation.

One such response noted approvingly by Mr McMahon, to which we shall return, was that 'most banks have improved and tightened their own monitoring of their corporate customers'; another, much more controversial one is that 'there have in some cases been debt conversions and modest investments in equity by leading bankers'. This latter, he remarked,

> has been materially helpful in mitigating the short-term cash constraints of some of their customers and restoring, to some extent, their balance sheet position, thereby permitting them a somewhat longer time horizon in which restructuring decisions can be put into effect. There are, nevertheless, severe limits, above all prudential, on how far banks can go in the direction of becoming shareholders: the stability of British banks – such a striking feature in the context of the world as a whole – would be much less evident now, if they had become shareholders on a large scale in the past. But judicious exercise of this option may, in suitable cases, both preserve a viable enterprise, and protect the bank's own investment in it.

Be that as it may, it would be wrong to see the encouragement of banks to make equity investments in their borrowing customers as a major or even significant part of the Bank's role in forming industrial Lifeboats; indeed, in searching for methods of filling this need for debt conversions into longer maturities and investments in equity, the Bank has been much more active in soliciting the interest of the investment institutions and other large holders of investible funds, both through the medium of the Stock Exchange and by direct private placement.

In simplest terms, the purpose of the formation of industrial Lifeboats by the Bank of England is twofold. First, it encourages lending bankers to stay their hand in saying 'not a penny more' and putting a corporation into liquidation until it is satisfied that all alternative courses of action, aimed to save the corporation in question, have either been tried or clearly demonstrated to be of no avail. This is not to say that the lending banks have been brow-beaten or simply encouraged to distort their commercial judgements by applying weaker criteria for credit-worthiness than would otherwise be the case. It *is* to say that lending bankers have become much more involved in monitoring the present financial condition and future plans of their corporate customers. To take a simple example, it may be that a borrowing customer has diversified too fast into new areas of activity in such a way that the continued viability of the total operations of the customer requires the injection of further borrowing which neither its balance sheet nor its profit projections justify. A solution to the problem, possibly the only realistic one, is for certain of the activities of the borrower to be hived off and sold to another corporation: this has the dual effect of putting cash in the hands of the selling corporation, with which to reduce its borrowings, and thus its gearing, and at the same time giving the activities which have been sold off access to further borrowings, assuming that the buyer's financial condition is healthier than the seller's. One way of relieving this would be to put the borrowing corporation into liquidation, thus forcing the break-up and distribution of the productive assets which is really needed. Another would be for the borrower to sit down with its bankers and agree what surgery is required in the form of selling off assets to achieve or regain financial viability; and this is precisely the purpose of most of the industrial Lifeboats. By effecting the surgery before rather than after a liquidation, the lending banks are not necessarily distorting their commercial judgement and will almost certainly be at less of a risk of loss than if a liquidation had proceeded; and although the borrower may have been obliged to drop some of its ambitions in diversification, it will at least have avoided the traumatic experience of liquidation, with its inevitable discomfort to workers, shareholders, lending bankers and other creditors.

Two points are worth making about this first purpose of industrial Lifeboats. First, it simply concentrates the minds of lending bankers on the monitoring of the financial condition and prospects of their borrowing customers. This function is, in any case, an important part of the continuing risk analysis which, as we saw in Chapter 4, is a major part of the job of the lending banker. This aspect of the Lifeboats can scarcely be said to distort the commercial judgement of the bankers: rather, it should refine that judgement and, by introducing the panoply and formality of Bank of England intervention, it should make the practical consequences of that judgement more acceptable to the borrowing customer. Secondly, this process of monitoring the financial condition and prospects of the borrower often involves the commissioning by the lending banker – but at the expense of the borrowing customer – of a detailcd accountant's report on that condition and those prospects: although often seen as irksome and sometimes even offensive, to the borrowing customer, these reports provide an essential background against which banker and borrower can discuss, for example, cash flow forecasts and future projections of profits.

The second, and as important, purpose of the formation of industrial Lifeboats is to prevent a jockeying of position between several lending bankers, to the detriment of the borrower. A main preoccupation of a lending banker is to get his loan repaid plus interest, when due. If a corporation is borrowing from only one bank, then that bank can be repaid only out of the cash flow generated by the borrower. If, on the other hand, a corporation is borrowing from several banks, then one of them can probably be repaid out of other borrowings from other banks. It is worth remarking that one of the results of the intense competition between banks in recent years for domestic lending business to British borrowers as well as to international borrowers has been that most industrial and commercial corporations of any size have at least two lending bankers and some of the larger ones have as many as thirty or forty. Indeed, it is fair to say that this trend towards multi-banking, with industrial and commercial borrowers taking loans from a wide group of banks, has probably gone too far to be healthy and is creating problems of its own. Most bankers would agree that a prudent corporate treasurer is well advised to seek more than a single source of bank finance; but excessive multi-banking is in the best interest of neither the borrower nor its long-term bankers. Many borrowers have come to learn that some of the most competitive banks which have seduced them into taking loans in recent years are the first to bail out when the going gets rough – a sort of banker's application of the accounting convention for stock valuation of 'last in, first out' or LIFO; and the tasks of credit appraisal and continuing monitoring are inevitably rendered more difficult by an excess of multi-banking. If the pressures of recession and monetary stringency which threw up the need for industrial Lifeboats in the early 1980s have the additional effect of reducing some of the 'over-competition' which developed in British banking in the 1970s, they may well remove at source one of the underlying factors giving rise to that need.

If a lending bank becomes apprehensive, as a result of its credit assessment, about the future viability of a borrower and if it knows that there are other lending bankers who have given commitments to lend, as yet undrawn, which last further ahead in time than its own commitment, then prudence suggests that it should call its loan for repayment out of increased borrowings from the other banks while the going is good. Equally, if the lending bank is lending unsecured, it may well feel that its apprehension would be sufficiently allayed, if it continued its loan but took adequate security against it such that, by any reasonable estimate, the proceeds of the sale of the security, in the event of a liquidation, would be more than sufficient to repay the loan. In this case, too, the first bank to ask for security – just like the first bank to call for repayment – would be doing so at the direct expense of the other banks lending to the borrower concerned. It is easy to see that either of these situations could well result in a sort of musical chairs stampede: all banks lending to the borrower would try to avoid being the last lender to call its loan, or to take adequate security. The consequent withdrawal of loans from the borrower might well precipitate its financial demise; and the penalty for being the last bank to call its loan would thus be not only to find itself the only remaining lender to the borrower but the only remaining lender to a borrower that had been mortally afflicted by a haemorrhage of cash caused by the withdrawal of loans by other banks.

It is to lessen the risk of such a musical chairs stampede which is a main purpose of the formation of industrial Lifeboats. To some extent, therefore, these industrial Lifeboats have something in common with those created during the secondary banking crisis in 1973–5. Where a credit analysis or an accountant's report suggests that an industrial borrower is perfectly solvent and likely to remain so, *provided* that all banks continue their existing lines, then the Bank of England, in persuading all the lending banks to do just that could be said to be solving a crisis of illiquidity for the borrower, rather than of insolvency – an interpretation which makes its action pretty non-controversial. It must be remembered that a 'Lifeboat' situation will only have arisen because one or more lending bank is apprehensive about its loans being repaid; and for this reason, it is probably important – if rather undignified, in the eyes of some bankers – for the Bank of England to lend its authority to the request to *all* banks lending to the borrower in question to refrain from calling their loans.

But the situation of most industrial and commercial borrowers for whom Lifeboats have been formed is seldom as simple as to allow a neat and obviously acceptable distinction to be drawn between illiquidity and insolvency. As we have seen in Chapter 4, credit analysis and cash flow forecasting is by no means an exact science and leaves plenty of room for disagreement, even with the benefit of elaborate accountants' reports. It may well be, for example, that one lending bank believes that a borrower is beyond salvation and that any delay in appointing a liquidator is simply prolonging the agony and increasing the ultimate loss to all lending banks, whereas other lending banks are disposed to give the borrower one more chance to put its house in order. Any such difference in view between lending bankers comes into much sharper focus if continuing support of the borrower involves *increasing* the loans from the bankers rather than just holding them at their existing levels.

The 'Lifeboat' activities of the Bank of England have no ultimate remedies for this sort of fundamental difference of view. They rely heavily, and in most cases successfully, on the good old British premise that reasonable men confronted with a common problem can probably be relied on to come up with a commonly acceptable solution. The Bank of England's most important function is probably to get all the lending bankers round the same table, persuade them to disclose to each other the exact amounts and terms of their loans to the common borrower, including the security actually taken by each lending bank, and encourage them to discuss together each one's assessment of the financial condition of the borrower, preferably and if necessary against the background of a detailed accountants' report. If this process of consultation and mutual disclosure does not end in unanimity among the banks, then ultimately the Bank of England has no final powers of coercion, though the respect with which it is traditionally held in the City means that a single bank must feel very sure of its grounds for non-co-operation before refusing to participate in an industrial Lifeboat.

For the sake of completeness, it should be recorded that where a Lifeboat has been put together for an industrial or commercial company, the lending banks participating in the Lifeboat will usually take collectively all the security available (that is, all the security not already given away to holders of prior charges, such as debenture-holders), and will devise a priority agreement setting out the pecking order by which each of them may dip into this common pot of security, in the event of a liquidation. This pecking order will reflect as best it can the priorities enjoyed by each lending bank when the Lifeboat was formed. And it is worth noting that an individual bank's view of its own priority can be much shaken by sitting round a table with other lending banks and hearing their views of *their* priorities. Sometimes these surprises are the result of straight dishonesty by the borrower – as, for example, in the case of the borrower who has devised a method to give a first charge over the same asset to two or more lenders. More often, they are the result of more innocent imperfections in the channels of communication between borrowers and their lending banks.

The formation of industrial Lifeboats was prompted in large part by the increasingly heavy reliance on bank finance by British industrial corporations in the late 1970s and early 1980s and also by the stringent disciplines engendered by a policy of monetary control designed to squeeze inflation out of the British economy. It is to be hoped that both these factors will reduce throughout the 1980s, thus reducing the need for the Lifeboats. As Mr McMahon remarked in his summary of the lecture quoted above:

> banks have played a major role in providing external finance to companies in recent years as the result of past inflation and recession and the consequent demise of alternative forms of company financing. For the future, companies will need new outside finance, quite probably on a substantial scale, and it seems that perhaps the banks may not play so dominant a role in this as they have played over the past few years. I believe that the financial health of the corporate sector is best assisted by the diversification of forms of corporate finance, including the generation of new sources of equity capital, and by a reversal of the trend of recent years towards shortening the maturity of company borrowing. The recent revival of the corporate bond market is perhaps an indicator of future developments, and it is – I believe – an indicator that we should all welcome.

Most British practising bankers would join Mr McMahon in welcoming any reduction in the reliance of British industrial corporations on bank finance and would hope too that the need for forming industrial Lifeboats will reduce as the 1980s proceed. But there are several lessons from the experience of these Lifeboats which will probably stick. First, the value of continued monitoring of a borrower's financial condition is probably more widely appreciated than it was before the Lifeboats were put together: lending banks have become, and will remain, much more willing to discuss its financial condition with the borrower's management and to participate in discussions as to its financial planning. And secondly, the banks have learnt the very real value of comparing notes on each other's loans to any one borrower and the security which they believed they enjoyed for those loans: it would be surprising if some more formal arrangements for exchanging this information did not survive the eventual and hoped-for redundancy of the Lifeboats themselves.

It may be worth remarking that in several European countries, a mechanism exists for the exchange between banks of credit information about their borrowing customers. Such 'credit information exchanges' exist in Belgium, France, Germany and Italy; and a similar system is being developed in Luxembourg. The systems vary; but their purpose is that each subscribing bank should feed information relating to its borrowers into a central, computerised data bank and should have the right to call from that data bank for all the information available on any one of its borrowers. A proposal has been put forward by the European Commission in Brussels that an EEC credit information exchange should be established into which all banks resident within the European Community would feed information on all their loans, down to a specified minimum, to borrowers resident both inside and outside the European Community. This proposal, which was first introduced in a discussion document in July 1979, was designed to further the aim of the European Commission noted in Chapter 5 of creating a 'common market' in banking. Although there are clear advantages to be gained by individual banks from exchanging information about their respective lendings to mutual customers, there is considerable doubt as to whether the proposal of the European Commission is the most effective way of doing so. In particular, a main criticism of the original proposal was that the benefits which would accrue would not justify the costs involved.

Some recent criticisms of banks' international lending decisions

If British bankers have been criticised by their governments of all political persuasions, and others, for some of the credit decisions they have taken in relation to their lending to domestic borrowers, they have also, together with many of their banking colleagues in other financial centres, come in for some sharp criticism for their decisions in relation to their lending to overseas, particularly sovereign, borrowers. We saw in Chapter 1 the dimensions of the recycling problem set for the world financial system by the massive hikes in the price of oil in 1973 and again in 1979 and 1980, and the resultant transfer of massive cash resources from the oil-consuming countries to the oil-producers. We saw, too, how this problem was effectively solved, almost single-handed, by the commercial banking system taking in deposits from the oil producers and lending them on to those in need, the oil consumers. By the end of 1982, it was clear that the original problem of simply recycling a vast and continuing flow of funds, which had poured into the coffers of the oil-producers was already much less formidable and might even disappear completely, for two main reasons. First, several of the oil-exporting countries had now got under way considerable development plans, based on forecasts of substantial oil revenues, which were absorbing ever-increasing imports from the developed oil-consumers at ever increasing costs in foreign exchange: examples include Bahrain and Oman in the Middle East, together with Nigeria and Indonesia. In addition, the war between two other potential oil producers, Iraq and Iran, had had the effect of increasing their imports from the West and at the same time reducing the flow of oil exports to pay for them. Secondly, and even more importantly, the world surplus of oil brought about by the price increases of the 1970s, and by the world-wide recession for which those price increases were in part responsible, had had the effect of reducing the oil exports of many OPEC members and at the same time weakening the price of oil in early 1982 and again more dramatically in 1983. These factors have in turn drastically reduced the income of many oil-producers –

Mexico, Venezuela and Nigeria being three obvious examples.

For these reasons, the simple problem of recycling may well turn out to have passed its peak and to that extent to be more manageable. Certainly, fears that the collective balance sheets of the commercial banks operating in the international arena had little more room to go on recycling at the rate experienced in the 1970s and up to 1981 can now be seen to be redundant. But if the basic recycling problem may have eased, the consequences of the way the commercial banking system stepped into the breach and handled it in the early years seem likely to cause a whole set of new problems which will be with us for several years to come.

By definition, lending operations in the international arena – and particularly those involved in the recycling of oil money – involve banks in lending funds across national frontiers to borrowers in foreign countries. Sometimes these borrowers are commercial organisations independent of the government of their country of residence; more often they are either the governments themselves, entities wholly-owned by the governments (such as nationalised industries) or companies carrying the guarantee of the governments in one form or another. A further important group of such borrowers are banks with head offices in the borrowing country in question which have deliberately and substantially tapped the eurocurrency interbank markets for deposits, either directly or through branches or subsidiaries established in London, and then channelled these funds back into their country of residence in the form of loans to public or private sector borrowers. In any event, a loan even to a private corporation in a particular foreign country carries with it certain risks attaching to its country of residence; and the ultimate such risk is that residents of that country will be forbidden to repay their overseas debts – for political, balance-of-payments or any other reason.

In their efforts to find borrowers of the massive funds being deposited with them by the oil-producers, the international commercial banks were driven by the logic of the situation to lend these funds to those who needed them – those countries for whom the rise in the price of their imported oil had created an immediate balance-of-payments problem. Some of these oil-importing countries had developed economies, such as those of Western Europe, for whom the readjustment involved in righting the balance-of-payments imbalance caused by the price rise was possible, if inconvenient and sometimes painful, over a relatively short period of time: for these countries the bankers had little difficulty in agreeing to make what was essentially a short- to medium-term loan. But many other oil-importing countries were less well placed, being less developed, or ruled by governments lacking either the will or the ability to make the necessary adjustments; many of these were themselves very dependent on the export earnings from their production of commodities.

In retrospect, and to some cautious bankers at the time, the ease with which some of the major Western commercial banks poured loans into these oil-importing countries – and others in trouble with their balance-of-payments – from the first oil price rise in 1973 right up to the early months of 1982 was breathtaking. But gradually problems caught up with them. First, many countries borrowed so much that their annual bill for interest, even when the loans were first taken out, took a significant proportion of their export earnings. Secondly, since most of the borrowings were at rates of interest which moved with the rates in the eurocurrency markets, being adjusted every three or six months, the rocketing rates of interest in the eurodollar markets in 1981 and 1982, pushed up by rates in the domestic money markets in the United States, increased their annual bill for interest to levels far in excess of those they had originally budgeted and, in many cases, far in excess of their ability to pay. Thirdly, the slump in prices for many raw materials, caused by the world recession and reflecting a decline in world price inflation, meant that many borrowers received an income from their exports far lower than they had budgeted for, thus reducing still further their ability to pay the interest on their loans, let alone to start repaying the loans themselves. Fourthly, and reflecting the second and third problems, the combination of sky-high rates of interest and slowing inflation caused the *real* rate of interest they were paying to be almost crippling by any standards of economic management (comparable to the pressures on corporate managements in the domestic economy, mentioned above, from a tight monetary policy allied to a slowing in the rate of inflation).

With all these factors reaching a crescendo in 1981 and 1982, it is not surprising that those two years saw one country after another announcing that it was unable to repay its debts to the international commercial banking system, when due. Such announcements came from Eastern Europe, particularly Poland and Romania, with whom negotiations for rescheduling their debts to Western commercial banks dragged on from 1981 into 1982 and beyond; from less developed oil-importing countries like Brazil, Argentina and many smaller states such as Zaire, North Korea, Turkey and Chile; and, possibly most dramatically of all, from some oil-exporting countries themselves, whose oil revenues have fallen short of their appetite for imports, such as Nigeria and Mexico.

If a corporate or personal borrower advised its lending bank that it is unable to repay its debts on time, then the usual procedure would be for the borrower and its banker together to make a detailed study of its future prospects and cash flow forecasts, in the hope of agreeing some adjustments to its policies which showed prospects of improving the cash flow and thus of the repayment of the debts. If no such adjustments could realistically be expected to achieve this end, then the banker would, in the last resort, put the borrower into liquidation. The situation is complicated if there are several lending banks involved and, as we saw in the last section, there is a case for a central authority to intervene in such situations to get the lending bankers round a table for a free and frank exchange of views and information in an attempt to discourage the more nervous bankers from recalling their loans too precipitately and thus forcing a liquidation which might have been avoided.

If a sovereign borrower advises it lending banks that it is unable to repay its debts on time, the situation is rather different for six main reasons. First, in Britain and most other countries, a corporation is prohibited by law from trading while insolvent; there is thus a point beyond which a borrowing corporation and its bankers cannot go on rescheduling debts or devising other methods of preventing the corporation's financial collapse, no matter how willing and keen both parties are to do so. On the other hand, there is no such cut-off point for sovereign borrowers, who from a legal point of view can go on borrowing and rescheduling as much as they like, provided they can find willing lenders.

The second difference btween the threat of default by a commercial borrower and a sovereign borrower is that, in the case of sovereign borrowers, there are almost always a great many more lending banks involved than in the case of a corporate domestic borrower. In the case of the latter, it would be unusual to find more than thirty or forty banks involved, and for smaller borrowers the number would be very much less; in the case of Mexico, when it threatened to default at the end of 1982, there were no less than 1400 individual banks around the world who were providing that country with loans totalling over $80 000 million. Not only did these large numbers of lending banks greatly complicate the practical arrangements for negotiation between the borrower and the lending banks; they also complicated the very assessment of the actual exposure of the lenders to the borrower. As Mr Peter Leslie, Senior General Manager of Barclays Bank International, has remarked on the problems of rescheduling sovereign risks: 'resolving the discrepancies between what the debtor thinks he has borrowed and what the commercial banks think they have lent, together with aspects of commitments, standbys, and in advised lines, has proved a much bigger task than expected'.[29]

The third difference between the threat of default by a commercial borrower and a sovereign borrower is that the distinction between a crisis of *illiquidity* and a crisis of *insolvency*, discussed earlier in this chapter is much less easily, if at all, applicable to sovereign borrowers. There are, sadly, many occasions when a banker, with the best will in the world, cannot agree that there is any course of action available to a corporate borrower which is likely to enable the borrower to repay his outstanding debts, plus interest, within a realistic time-span; and in these circumstances, the banker has no alternative but to put the company into liquidation. But it is a bold banker who accepts categorically that a sovereign state is unable to repay its debts within a reasonable time-span, provided it adopts internal economic policies to achieve the required surplus in its current balance of payments; indeed, the experience of the post-war years suggests that countries which have been required by the International Monetary Fund (IMF), as a condition of loans from that institution, to undertake the economic adjustment necessary to restore their credit-worthiness, have proved their political and economic capability to do just that. In other words, there is a very strong case for assuming that, given the political will, a sovereign borrower need never 'go bust' in the sense that its bankers must give up hope of getting their money back.

The fourth difference between the threat of default by a commercial borrower and a sovereign borrower is that the default of the sovereign borrower could be much more painful to the lending banker. If a commercial borrower defaults and its bankers decide it is not worth putting further good money after bad, the borrower is put into liquidation: unless the bankers have allowed the situation to drag on longer and deteriorate further than prudence would dictate, they should expect to salvage a proportion of their outstanding loans in a liquidation. If a sovereign borrower simply walks away from its debts, the odds must be that, short of military action, the lending banks will have little chance of salvaging any of their outstanding loans at all.

The fifth difference between the threat of default by a commercial borrower and a sovereign borrower is quite simply the size of the exposure which individual banks have allowed themselves to undertake to individual sovereign borrowers. We saw in Chapter 4 how most banks will set a limit on their maximum lendings to any one borrower, as a matter of common prudence. Based, no doubt, on the premise, discussed in that chapter, that sovereign states 'do not go bust', most lending banks appear to have undertaken far greater exposures to sovereign risks than would be deemed appropriate by any standards for normal commercial risks, in relationship to the lending banks' capital resources. It has been estimated, for example, that the nine largest US banks had by December 1982 (and before the increases which were part of the rescue package discussed in the next section) lent the equivalent of 50 per cent of their capital and reserves to Mexico alone.[30] Another estimate made early in 1983 put the figures into a more global perspective: 'the loan portfolio to countries on the "problem list" now approaches $200 billion, which compares with the published equity capital of the top 100 banks of $150 billion'.[31] In the context of these figures, it is easy to see why individual banks are much more reluctant to contemplate a total default by a sovereign borrower than they would be a total default by a commercial borrower.

The sixth difference between the threat of default by a commercial borrower and a sovereign borrower is that a default by the latter would almost certainly excite the interest of national monetary, prudential and political authorities to a much greater extent than a default by a commercial borrower, however large. The official interest, and the calls for official intervention, in the protracted negotiations for rescheduling the Polish debt in 1981 and 1982 were one example; the official interest by national authorities in Britain, the United States and elsewhere on the negotiations for the rescheduling of the Mexican debt in 1982 and 1983 was another. This interest derives partly from the sheer scale of the debts of some of the borrowing countries, noted above, which suggests that a default by any one of the larger borrowers would play havoc with the balance sheets of money-lending banks and certainly force them to reduce their lendings, at least temporarily, both domestically and internationally; partly from the detrimental effect that this would have on financial institutions and markets, both domestically and internationally, and their ability to provide finance for both trade and investment; and partly from the probable effect it would generate on the diplomatic relationship between the government of the defaulting country and those of the countries of residence of the lending banks.

For all these reasons, the situation reached by the world's commercial banks in early 1983 in respect of their loans to sovereign borrowers had excited much more comment and criticism from official and unofficial commentators than they had probably ever experienced in relation to their loans to commercial borrowers. The first and obvious criticism was the scale of their exposure to borrowers who turned out to be apparently unsound. The criticisms have been aimed at two targets: the major banks who took the deliberate view that sovereign borrowers 'do not go bust' and continued to lend to them ever-increasing amounts without putting in place the sort of financial disciplines which they would certainly have demanded as a condition for the continued support of commercial borrowers; and the many thousands of smaller banks, in London, throughout the United States and elsewhere who made little pretence at any serious credit assessment of the sovereign risks they were undertaking on the simple premise that sovereign risks 'do not go bust' and, in any case, what was good enough for their bigger fellow bankers was good enough for them. In a sense the full validity of these criticisms will never be known, particularly as far as the bigger banks are concerned: if by, say, the end of the 1980s no sovereign borrower of any size *has* gone bust and the current huge loans are being repaid in an orderly way, it will be difficult to sustain too serious a criticism of the basic premise on which those loans were made. The criticism of the smaller banks may turn out to be equally hollow; but, as we shall see in the next section, they may forfeit their immunity from the criticism if they refuse to play *their* role in achieving an end to the story where no sovereign risk has gone bust.

At this stage it is worth noting that the commercial banks did step in and play a vital role in cushioning the real economies of the world from the oil price shocks of 1973 and 1979–80 and that, at the time, the problems of the sovereign borrowers appeared nothing like as acute as they appeared in the early 1980s. As the Governor of the Bank of England has recorded very fairly:

> Following the first oil shock, there was general approval of the helpful role the banks played in the recycling of oil exporters' surplus funds to the importers of oil. The only qualification was that it was desirable for a larger proportion of financing to come from conditional financing through official sources, with its stress on policies to redress imbalances. In the event, the bulk of the financing was provided by the banks. This cushioned the shock, and

> borrowers were given the chance to respond more gradually to the sudden and dramatic change in their circumstances. Looking back after the second oil shock of 1979/80 and its consequences, we may now be able to conclude that the respective contributions of financing and of adjustment – especially given the stock of debt which had built up in the meantime – were not after all so appropriate. But it is right to remember that many of the assumptions shared by borrowers and lenders have been invalidated by the recent performance of the world economy in a way that few could or did fully anticipate. Non-one expected real rates of interest to remain so high for so long. Most underestimated both the length and the depth of the recession.[32]

Not only were the commercial banks criticised for their supposed imprudence reflected in the extent of their exposure to sovereign borrowers who turned out to be unable to repay their debts on the due dates; those banks which showed a reluctance to continue these loans, sometimes in increased amounts, when they fell due in 1982 and 1983 came in for criticism every bit as sharp. In other words, there were an increasing number of cases where banks were officially cajoled into extending loans beyond a point where their prudent judgement required them to say 'not a penny more'. The need for this stretching of bankers' prudence in their international lending was put succinctly by Dr Arthur Burns, a former Chairman of the Federal Reserve System: 'banks have been very foolish', he said to a meeting of bankers early in 1982, 'We must now pray that they will go on being foolish'.[33]

The same point was spelled out at greater length by Mr Christopher McMahon, the Deputy Governor of the Bank of England, at a speech in London on 26 May 1982:

> At a time when banks have been made rather more sharply aware of the risks involved in their exposure to particular countries in difficulties there could be a problem if they began more generally to withdraw from, or at least to run down their involvement in, individual countries or groups of countries, without a fully-balanced assessment of those

countries' positions. We have seen similar behaviour in respect of involvement in lending to companies, both domestically and internationally. Excessive prudence can be as dangerous in some circumstances as excessive exuberance in others.[34]

Mr McMahon described very precisely the dilemma facing international bankers when a borrowing country begins to experience debt difficulties, noting again its similarity with the dilemma faced by domestic bankers in their dealings with companies:

> Prudent banking practice may suggest that exposure should be reduced, by the refusal of requests for new credit and the termination of existing lines or deposits as they mature; on the other hand, action of this sort, if precipitate or taken simultaneously by a number of the country's creditors, may well hasten and exacerbate the very difficulties from which the banks are trying to escape. Action by a single bank taken in its own narrow interests can easily prove detrimental not only to its own longer-term interest, but also to the interests of the wider banking community. In such circumstances there can be no guiding rule, but each case must be judged on its individual merits.

From the central banker's point of view, the problem would be compounded if individual banks began to withdraw loans not only from an individual sovereign borrower which seemed to be heading for trouble, but from whole groups of sovereign borrowers whose position appeared to be much more sound. For the Bank of England, the precedent of the secondary banking crisis of 1973–5 was still very much in mind, in which the collapse of one unsound secondary bank caused a withdrawal of deposits from a whole sector of institutions and in which, in the Bank's own words, 'the problem was to avoid a widening circle of collapse through the contagion of fear'.[35] As Mr McMahon continued:

> a more widespread difficulty might arise if problems deriving from a particular rescheduling caused banks to

react defensively towards other indebted countries, precipitating difficulties for them. Banks must consider carefully whether the difficulties faced by a country are transient or whether they reflect fundamental malajustment or mismanagement.

The central banks, and the Bank of England in particular, have taken two types of action to alleviate the threat of an international liquidity crisis resulting from a widening withdrawal of confidence and thus of lendings from sovereign borrowers. First, as Mr McMahon, pointed out:

> as long ago as September 1974 the Governors of the Group of Ten central banks stated publicly in the wake of the Herstatt affair that they were satisfied that means were available for the provision of temporary liquidity to the euro-markets and would be used if and when necessary. That statement still stands. As was also said in 1974, however, it would not be practicable or advisable to lay down in advance detailed rules and procedures for the provision of such liquidity. In particular, if such provision were to be in any sense automatic or if the factors or criteria which determined it were precisely specificd, there would be a danger that the disciplines of the market would be overridden – if the arrangcments looked too restrictive – or undermined, if they looked too lax.

The second type of action taken by the central banks, again with the Bank of England playing a leading role, has been to create international Lifeboats of banks to support sovereign borrowers comparable to those formed to support domestic borrowers and described earlier in this chapter. These Lifeboats are the subject of the next section.

A third criticism endured by commercial banks in this whole drama of sovereign lending has been the treatment they have given to sovereign debts in default in their annual published accounts. The criticisms have been aimed at the size of the provisions made, for example, by the major US banks and British clearing banks in their published accounts for the year ended 31 December 1982, against loans to sovereign borrowers; they have also been aimed at the wide diversity of treatment of identical loans to sovereign borrowers in the accounts of different banks. Both these criticisms have been levelled at the supervisors and auditors of banks as well as their managements: they were discussed in some detail in Chapter 4 in the context of supervision. In the present context, one further comment on this topic by the Governor of the Bank of England should be noted, since it bears directly on the Bank's philosophy behind its role in putting together Lifeboats for sovereign borrowers – the subject of the next section:

> An important concern of supervisors, [he said in February 1983] is to ensure that banks make proper provision in the form of sums set aside for the possible future inability of borrowers to repay debt when due. One aspect of this is the adequacy of provisioning in banks' accounts for rescheduled sovereign debt. This has naturally been a matter for discussion between central banks. It soon became clear that no across-the-board rules could be applied: accounting practices and conventions vary too much from country to country, as do the circumstances of individual banks. It has, however, been recognised that where a country has adopted a programme of economic adjustment under I.M.F. auspices, it is not inconsistent for banks to grant new lending to it while at the same time making provision in their accounts against part of their outstanding claims on that country, to recognise that the quality of those assets has deteriorated. In the right circumstances additional lending can be a justifiable and prudent way of seeking to improve their quality in the longer term.[36]

International Lifeboats for sovereign borrowers

As we have seen, 1981 and 1982 saw one sovereign borrower after another advising its commercial banking lenders that it was unable to repay its debts when due, the biggest shock probably being Mexico's announcement to that effect in August 1982. Such a situation was fraught with dangers: that banks individually would try to withdraw all their loans and deposits from the hard-pressed borrower, as and when they become due; that sovereign borrowers would thus be deprived of any chance of rescheduling their debts in an orderly way; that faced with this prospect, these borrowers would thus have no alternative but to default on their existing debts as they came up for repayment – and probably on interest payments as well. It was feared that this in turn would make frightening inroads into the profits and balance sheets of many of the lending banks; this in *its* turn would cause a flight of confidence from those banks, not only in the international eurodeposit markets but in their national domestic money markets as well; and that as a consequence of all that, there would be a complete collapse of the international financial system and the domestic financial systems of the major economies, to the detriment of the whole of the non-Communist world. The situation was, if you like, comparable in a world-wide context to that which faced the Bank of England in the secondary banking crisis in Britain in 1973.

As in the secondary banking crisis in Britain, the first clear need was for some central authority to grip the situation and prevent the free play of the immediate individual self-interest of the participating banks, which would certainly have resulted in the disastrous scenario depicted above: that is, in short, to set up Lifeboats for sovereign borrowers. It is difficult at this early stage after the initial formation of the international Lifeboats for sovereign borrowers, and from the point of view of an outside observer, to identify those responsible for taking this initiative. The Governor of the Bank of England clearly played a leading role, as did Mr Paul Volcker (the Chairman of the Board of Governors of the Federal Reserve System in Washington), Mr Jacques de Larosière (the Managing Director of the IMF) and Dr Fritz Leutwiler (the President of the Bank for International Settlements (BIS) in Basle). In these circumstances, it was fitting that one of the last major speeches made by Lord Richardson before he retired from the Governorship of the Bank of England in June 1983 dealt specifically with the establishment of this mechanism for international Lifeboats.

The actual procedure adopted in setting up Lifeboats for

sovereign borrowers has been picturesquely described by Margaret Reid in the following terms:

> The formula cobbled together in last August's Mexican panic has been repeatedly copied. Hard-pressed borrower state agrees, after borrowing upsurge, that the party's over and the time has come to retrench with 'adjustment' policies. Once this is agreed, the International Monetary Fund (I.M.F.) lends a judicious sum ($3.8 billion to Mexico and probably $6 billion to Brazil). Reassured that the world's bank manager (the I.M.F.) has been heeded, the far larger commercial bank creditors reschedule (extend) their present lending – and add some more (but smaller rations than lately). Pending the wrapping up of these deals, the leading nations' central banks – via the Bank for International Settlements (B.I.S.) – put up bridging finance, often covered by Government guarantees. Also, sometimes, a Government (as with the U.S. for Mexico and Yugoslavia) rushes in with more emergency help.[37]

Looking back on the first six months of such Lifeboat formation, which followed the Mexican failure in August 1982, Lord Richardson commented as follows:

> I regard the most important and heartening aspect of the response to the debt problems of recent months to have been the way in which borrowers, the International Monetary Fund, governments, central banks and commercial banks have quickly and informally concerted arrangements for mobilising assistance. It is true that the response has been pragmatic and ad hoc – it had to be; but it is noteworthy that the interdependence between these participants was so quickly recognised. Our achievement so far in containing the situation has hinged vitally on the willingness of each to perform its particular role. I want to say a few words about each in turn.
>
> I start with the borrowers. The essential is that they should be willing to undertake the economic adjustment necessary to restore their creditworthiness. In most cases this means working out an economic programme with the International Monetary Fund. This is an indispensable first

step, and the earlier it is taken the better. The World Bank and other international lending agencies may also have a part to play.[38]

Of the five participants in the arrangements listed by the Governor, it is difficult to identify the one whose willingness to perform its particular role was most crucial to the initial success of the Lifeboats – or whose continued willingness is most crucial to the continuing of that success. But the borrowers themselves have a strong claim to that position. It should not be underestimated how much political courage was required by the governments of at least some of the borrowing countries to submit to the disciplines of an IMF-designed programme to adjust their internal economy in such a way as to reduce the need for external borrowing and improve the external balance of payments. Such programmes must almost inevitably cause some sacrifice of cherished ambitions for public expenditure and economic growth and almost inevitably result in a greater degree of austerity for the population at large. It is a measure of the importance of this courage and commitment on the part of the governments of borrowing countries that the main doubts voiced by the sceptics on the ultimate success of the Lifeboats centre entirely on the political will and ability of these borrowing governments to effect the programmes proposed by the IMF. In other words, the whole success of the Lifeboats depends ultimately on the proposition that sovereign states 'do not go bust'; and whether or not this proposition turns out to be valid depends crucially on the political nerve and control of the governments of those borrowing sovereign states.

The second participant in the Lifeboats is the IMF. The IMF was set up at the famous international monetary conference held in Bretton Woods, New Hampshire in July 1944, which attempted to lay down the ground rules and establish the institutional framework necessary for the development of the international financial system after the Second World War. The purposes of the IMF were set out clearly in Article 1 of its Articles of Agreement, in the following terms:

1. To promote international monetary co-operation through a permanent institution which provides the machinery for

consultation and collaboration on international monetary problems.
2. To facilitate the expansion and balanced growth of international trade, and to contribute thereby to the promotion and maintenance of high levels of employment and real income and to the development of the productive resources of all members as primary objectives of economic policy.
3. To promote exchange stability, to maintain orderly exchange arrangements among members, and to avoid competitive exchange depreciation.
4. To assist in the establishment of a multilateral system of payments in respect of current transactions between members and in the elimination of foreign exchange restrictions which hamper the growth of world trade.
5. To give confidence to members by making the Fund's resources available to them under adequate safeguards, thus providing them with opportunity to correct maladjustments in their balance of payments without resorting to measures destructive of national and international prosperity.
6. In accordance with the above, to shorten the duration and lessen the degree of disequilibrium in the international balances of payments of members.

In the context of these purposes, particularly numbers 1, 5 and 6, the sovereign debt problems of the early 1980s provided a classic opportunity for the IMF to play a role; indeed, it might reasonably be argued that had it failed to play a role it would have failed to undertake its proper responsibilities. This point has been well made by Mr Peter Leslie of Barclays Bank International, who joined it with an interesting criticism of the IMF's inactivity in the 1970s. Writing of the arrangements for the rescheduling of sovereign debts, he remarked that

> the re-emergence of the International Monetary Fund as a key ingredient in this role is the event which more than any other has enabled a degree of confidence in the international system to be restored. The ability – or capability – of

the IMF to negotiate effective conditionality and to give its official seal of approval to internal economic and financial reconstruction is something which commercial banks cannot really achieve. I use the word 're-emergence' advisedly, since the part that the IMF played in the 1970s, compared with the days of Bretton Woods, was a relatively silent one. Indeed, later historians may well ask: where were the IMF, the Bank for International Settlements, central banks and official monetary corporations generally in the 1970s? And it is, of course, easy for us to see now that the abdication of their essential role of leadership of world financial order and the filling of this vacuum by the commercial banks, highly praised at the time, has been one of the elements that has brought the world to its present state of disorder.[39]

In playing the role it has, the IMF came up against three formidable difficulties – one political, one intellectual and one financial. The political difficulty arose from the fact that at the end of 1982 the IMF had 146 member countries, including nearly every important country in the non-Communist world with the exception of Switzerland. The Fund is run by a conference comprising a Governor from each of its members, a more restricted executive body responsible for most of the operation decisions, and international staff. In addition, an Interim Committee was established in 1974 consisting of 22 Governors, which meets twice a year. This Committee advises the full Board of Governors, particularly in dealing with sudden disturbances which might threaten the international monetary system. With this widely spread group of members – all of whom have a right to ask for assistance from the IMF to tide them over temporary balance-of-payments crises and all of whom carry the ultimate responsibility of bearing their share of the costs of any bad loans which the IMF itself makes – the Fund has to tread very warily before committing too substantial a proportion of its resources to one or two major sovereign borrowers, such as Mexico, Brazil or Argentina. Some of the smaller members might well have feared that major loans to such countries might pre-empt resources which would otherwise be available for them, if the need arose; larger members, such as the

United States, might well have questioned the use of *their* resources to 'bail out' either 'spendthrift' sovereign borrowers or 'imprudent' lending bankers, or both.

The intellectual difficulty for the IMF was simply the enormous increase in its workload of devising, and subsequently monitoring, individual national economic programmes for the borrowing countries to achieve the required adjustments. With thirty-five odd years of experience behind it, the staff of the IMF is, of course, better equipped to devise such programmes than it would have been in earlier years; but it should be remembered that in the sovereign debt crises, even more than in other requests for borrowing, the IMF has been under tremendous pressure to devise adjustment techniques to minimise the resultant austerity – and not only because of the effects such austerity would have on the national economy concerned, but also because of the effects it might have on the level of world trade and the attempts of the Western world to pull itself out of recession.

The financial difficulty for the IMF was simply to avoid running out of its resources available to lend, not only to the crisis-ridden sovereign borrowers but also to other member countries who might be forced by the same basic factors of low commodity prices, low world demand for exports and high real rates of interest to ask for balance-of-payments loans in the future. The IMF obtains its lendable resources from three main sources: the contributions of its members; additional contributions by the 'Group of Ten' (ten of the largest industrial country members of the Fund) under the 'General Arrangements to Borrow' (GAB), first established in 1962; and specially negotiated loans, principally from Saudi Arabia. Intensive activity over the last months of 1982 and the beginning of 1983 secured substantially increased contributions from all three sources: in February 1983 agreement was announced for a 47.5 per cent increase in quota subscriptions – the basic subscription of each member country to the Fund – from 61 billion Special Drawing Rights (SDRs) (equivalent to US $67bn) to 90 billion SDRs (US $98.5bn); agreement was also announced to increase the contributions made by the Group of Ten under the GAB from 6.4 billion SDRs (US $7bn) to 17 billion SDRs (US $18.7bn); and the agreement of Saudi Arabia was announced to provide a further loan to the IMF of between $3bn and $4bn with an additional $1.5bn to $2bn in a parallel arrangement with the GAB.[40] These increases should provide the IMF with sufficient resources to play its role in Lifeboats for sovereign borrowers at least until the end of 1983, and hopefully beyond.

The third group of participants in the Lifeboats for sovereign borrowers, as listed by Lord Richardson, was national governments. Their role, principally as subscribers to the IMF, lay behind the political difficulty of the IMF mentioned above; it was highlighted by the Governor in the following terms:

> In turning to the role of governments, you will perhaps permit me to remind you – and this is sometimes forgotten by commercial bankers naturally concerned that burdens should be equitably shared – that the resources of the I.M.F. and other international financial institutions derive from public funds. The new resources likely to be available as a result of an increase in Fund quotas and the G.A.B. will constitute a substantial new commitment of funds by governments.

The fourth group of participants in the Lifeboats for sovereign borrowers was the central banks, including the 'central bankers' central bank', the Bank for International Settlements. The Governor depicted their role as twofold: as providers of short-term crisis funds to bridge the gap before more permanent arrangements have been made and as the supervisors of the commercial banks. As to the first role, he commented that

> it is a feature of the liquidity crises that beset countries that they break very suddenly. A loss of confidence for whatever reason can stem the expected inflow of funds to a borrower and a haemorrhage of existing finance can seriously exacerbate the problem. There is almost inevitably a gap of weeks or months before confidence can be restored, normally through agreement on a carefully

> structured Fund programme, and funds begin to flow again. There may often therefore be a need for bridging finance, which can be supplied either by banks themselves or by official bodies, or partly by one and partly by the other. Over the past few months there have been occasions when it has seemed appropriate for the Bank for International Settlements to organise temporary support, generally with the backing of a number of central banks. This seems to me to have had a positive effect on confidence. There are, however, important limitations on the scope of B.I.S. action which need to be understood and respected if it is to play such a role. The resources of the B.I.S. are to a large extent the national reserves of central banks. This means that the B.I.S. must maintain a high degree of liquidity. Its lending can thus only be of a short-term bridging nature, and there must be unambiguous terra firma at the other end of the bridge. Hence the importance of the availability of adequate and unencumbered collateral, or the clear promise of Fund or other resources from which the bridging loan can be repaid.

As to the second role of central banks, as supervisors of the commercial banks, the Governor remarked that

> international co-operation in this field has been greatly developed over the past decade, and important progress has been made in ensuring that banks throughout the world are adequately supervised and that supervisors apply so far as practicable a consistent and co-ordinated set of principles.

Referring to the international co-ordination of supervision described in Chapter 5, he commented that

> under the auspices of the Basle Supervisors Committee and other supervisory groups worldwide, patient and largely unpublicised work continues to improve both the coverage and content of supervision. I believe that the fruits of that co-operation are making their contribution in the present difficult conjuncture.

Co-ordination of the views of national bank supervisors on the question of provisions for sovereign debts, for example, was mentioned in the previous section.

The fifth and final group of participants in the Lifeboats for sovereign borrowers were the commercial banks themselves. The Governor remarked:

> On bank lending as a whole, there would, I think, be general assent to two propositions. . . . First, that, given the state of the world economy the rate of increase of international bank lending reached by 1981 had become unsustainable. And, second, that given borrowers' reliance on capital inflows, too precipitate a reduction in the international lending of banks would generate an insupportable burden of adjustment. Figures for international lending in 1982 endorse the first proposition. The commercial banking system's constructive response in the last six months in the problem country cases bears witness to the acceptance of the second.
>
> This response has not come without effort. In the first place there was the sheer problem of communication given the numbers of banks involved. The establishment of advisory or liaison groups of banks to deal with each separate case has obviously been a great organisational help. The commitment of time and management and other resources in the wider interest by the relatively small group of banks most heavily engaged has been commendable. I welcome too the decision to create the Institute of International Finance.[41] This should be helpful as a focus for the gathering, analysis and dissemination of information which should benefit borrowing countries and lenders alike.
>
> As well as the organisational challenge, there has been a need to change attitudes of mind. What has been required is a shared recognition that the participation of commercial banks in international lending involves responsibilities which the banking community as a whole cannot avoid. The leading central banks quickly realised that rescue packages could succeed only if implemented as a whole and if the burden was seen to be widely spread. Given the importance of London as a major financial

> centre it has fallen naturally to the Bank of England to play a prominent role in the process of co-ordination and encouragement. This we have willingly done.

The Governor went on in a key passage in our present context:

> I will illustrate the nature of the problems, and our involvement by reference to the inter-bank market. The foreign branches of banks from some countries in difficulty had taken very short-term deposits from other banks and largely lent them back at longer term to their home countries. These short-term deposits were so large that any significant withdrawal of them would have jeopardised the whole package of support facilities. Moreover, if some banks succeeded in reducing their exposure, others would be strongly tempted to follow suit. In order to help the banks obtain a better appreciation of the situation as a whole we felt it right to let the market know that we regarded maintenance of exposure to these branches as very desirable given the needs of the moment. Parallel action was taken by our American counterparts in New York. The final decision on how to respond to the situation has been one for the bankers themselves, our part having been to ensure that they were aware of the broader considerations. Their response has been positive.

Some commercial bankers would smile wryly at this attribution by the Governor of the final decision as to whether to maintain their exposure to these branches to the bankers themselves. As one of the fifty-five London banks lending to Mexico, who were urged by the Bank of England to maintain their exposure, as part of the Lifeboat package put together for that country in December 1982, Mr Stanislas Yassukovich, the managing director of the European Banking Company (a London-based consortium bank) declared angrily that

> for the first time in our history as independent bankers we have been robbed of our freedom of action in taking a decision on whether to make a loan or not. We have been

told that if we don't make a loan, our standing in the market could be prejudiced. It seems to me to be a fundamental interference with the independence of a bank . . . We were pretty well told by the deputy governor [of the Bank of England] that if we did not step into line we would be on the carpet. What can you do under those circumstances? Here for the first time is a situation where 55 banks have been told: 'you have a bad loan, yet we are insisting you put more money into that situation in order to save the system'. If people think through the implications of that they will be horrified. It is going to accelerate the process of people dropping out of the market.[42]

In response to this criticism, the Bank of England might well respond that if people thought through the implications of a withdrawal by all commercial banks of their loans to problem sovereign borrowers they would be equally horrified. Indeed, just such a response came, not so much from the Bank of England, but from some of the larger banks involved in the Lifeboats. Writing in April 1983, Mr Peter Leslie of Barclays Bank International, for example, has remarked rather sharply that

> we, the commercial bankers, have to realise that we are all in this together. We may have been shortsighted when we went into cross-border lending but we must be awake enough on that point now. Yet there are still banks – particularly the smaller banks – who came in on the 'me too' basis and who are now trying to reduce their exposure and cut their lines in an attempt to transfer their troubles to the big brigade. Until the need for co-operation is fully realised, I fear that it may be necessary to recognise what is on all other grounds deeply antipathetic: that the unilateral declaration by a borrower of a short-term moratorium is a necessary ingredient to successful re-scheduling.[43]

Here is a classic example of the conflict which sometimes occurs between the immediate self-interest of participants in a market and the health or even survival of the market itself. In such situations some compromise has to be reached between the commercial banks – as the guardians of their own self-interest – and the central banks – as the guardians of the interests of the markets as a whole. If such a conflict of interest were to arise in a nursery of children playing a game in which all sides had got themselves into a position where nobody was willing to make the next move for fear of losing points, a supra-nursery nanny would simply solve the problem by closing down the game, cancelling the scores and announcing tea-time. Regrettably, the real world of banking is simply not like that. There *is* no supra-world authority able to cancel or at least take over in unlimited amounts the loans which banks have granted in the past and now wish to have repaid. The only possible solution to the problem is through a series of compromises between the parties concerned: the borrowers, the IMF, governments, central banks and commercial banks.

It would be as foolhardly to forecast as it would be impertinent to recommend exactly what compromises will be reached and how the problem of sovereign borrowers in difficulties will ultimately be solved. But three points may reasonably be made. First, the compromises will not be reached easily; and the extent of, and limitations on, the supposed responsibilities of all five parties will be loudly and publicly proclaimed. There will be other voices besides those of Mr Yassukovitch pointing out the consequences of too great a coercion of the commercial banks by the central banks, to go beyond what they, the commercial banks, regard as the limits of prudence; and such voices will not be confined to the commercial banks themselves. Dr Fritz Leutwiler, for example, the President of the BIS and President of the Swiss National Bank has warned of the dangers of too great pressures from the central banks on the commercial banks to restore and maintain credit limits for interbank deposits with banks with head offices in major debtor countries, such as Mexico or Brazil, on the very practical grounds that such pressures might create problems for the central banks as to their precise responsibilities in the interbank markets should the commercial interbank lines prove difficult to recover.[44]

The interests of national governments in the debate have been forcibly expressed by both Senators and members of the

House of Representatives in Washington. Taking advantage of the opportunity provided by the need for Congressional approval for the increase in the US subscription to the IMF in early 1983, they demanded much more stringent control over the foreign lending of overseas banks. Senator Jake Garn of the Senate Banking Committee is reported to have told the US bank supervisors that 'the price of an $8.4 million increase in the IMF authorisation in Congress is going to be legislation so that lawmakers can go home and say we did not bail out the banks'.[45] Again in the US Congress, Mr Fernand St Germain, the Chairman of the House Banking Committee, is reported to have laid at least part of the blame for the sovereign debt crisis at the door of the Basle Committee of Banking Supervisors on the grounds that their supervision was inadequate and that they 'watched while international lending expanded out of control at record-breaking rates'.[46]

In Britain, the Treasury and Civil Service Committee of the House of Commons produced a Report on *International Monetary Arrangements: International Lending By Banks* in March 1983. Whilst generally applauding the action taken by the parties concerned to put together international Lifeboats for sovereign borrowers such as Mexico, the Committee enunciated the same principle as that spelled out in the US Congress that the government should not bail out the banks. Remarking that they saw 'no need to attempt to apportion praise or blame for the origin of present difficulties', the Committee went on to comment that 'some banks undoubtedly contributed to their problems by relaxing their traditional standard of prudence'.[47] And again, in admitting that debt crises 'may also create a need for the authorities of the industrial countries to provide lender-of-last-resort facilities to banks if there is a serious interruption of debt-service payments', and recognising that the distinction between illiquidity and insolvency crises of banks may not always be clear cut, the Committee echoed the views of their fellow legislators in Washington in the following words:

> Depositors should be protected even if a bank does make loans that turn out to be imprudent. But the authorities have no comparable obligation to protect the interests of

management and shareholders. Imprudent lending should be penalised by demanding a change in management, where it has been at fault, before a rescue operation is mounted and by ensuring that losses reduce the value of shareholders' equity before there is any call on the public purse.[48]

The second point to be made about the outcome of the present problems is that it is perfectly possible in early 1983 to envisage a scenario in which the financial pressures on the stricken sovereign borrowers are much eased: a scenario, for example, in which real and nominal interest rates are significantly lower than they were in 1982 and early 1983, in which real oil prices are significantly lower than they were in 1982, and in which world economic recovery is reflected in a resumption of growth in industrial countries and a revival of demand for the exports of the less developed countries. If this scenario comes to pass, then the debts of the stricken borrowers will become more manageable and the compromises between the parties concerned will become less tense. If it does not, then the compromises will become more tense and more difficult to achieve; but nothing will alter the fact that they provide the *only* way through the problem.

The third point to be made is that uncoordinated lending to sovereign borrowers by many different commercial banks carries with it risks which are now plain for all to see and to which no responsible banker should allow himself to be exposed again. When the dust has settled, there are three developments which will probably emerge from the present crisis and which, indeed, are already in train. First, any reallocation of liquid financial resources between sovereign nations on the scale achieved in the recycling of the oil money in the 1970s and early 1980s will almost certainly involve a larger participation in its early stages by the IMF, in pursuit of its purposes listed above, with a correspondingly smaller participation being undertaken by the commercial banking system. Secondly, in making their credit assessments of sovereign risks, commercial banks will almost certainly compare notes with fellow lenders, both official and unofficial, in much more detail than they ever have in the past; the establishment of the Institute of International Finance has already laid the foundation for such an exchange of information and views. And thirdly, whilst it is to be hoped that the simple faith of many credit analysts that sovereign states 'do not go bust' will not be proved wrong, it is now clear that it will continue to be right only if the sovereign borrowers observe some discipline in their internal economic policies designed to achieve that end. It may well be the case that much greater liaison will develop between the commercial banks and the IMF and that the principle, forged in the present crisis, will become firmly established that the banks will extend loans to sovereign borrowers beyond a certain point only on the basis that the borrower has agreed a programme of economic retrenchment with the IMF. In the Governor's words,

> the closer contact which has recently come about between the banks and the I.M.F. has a lasting value. From the point of view of the Fund, it must be right and natural that, in devising programmes for countries in balance-of-payments deficit, it should have some sense of the amount of private finance likely to be available. And from the point of view of the banks, their lending plainly needs to pay more regard to how far such countries are committed to economic programmes likely to restore reasonable economic performance.

One final point should be made. There is a clear frustration implicit in much of the comment on the Lifeboats for sovereign borrowers, deriving from the fact that the arrangements are very *ad hoc* and represent immediate reactions to immediate problems rather than a clearly thought-out strategy. The Governor himself, in taking comfort in February 1983 from what had been achieved over the past six months, added 'but it has been emergency management aimed at fighting fires'.

This book has been about the principles observed by banking managements in managing the business of their banks, and the principles by which those managements are supervised by the appropriate authorities. One of the points which has emerged is that the principles of both bankers and supervisors have been hammered out on the anvil of practical experience rather than produced as intellectually elegant blueprints drawn up in ivory towers. The practical experience of the 1970s has wrought unprecedented developments and refinements in the approach of both bankers and supervisors in many different ways; the practical experience of the sovereign debtors and their Lifeboats in the early 1980s seem likely to have a similar effect. But the changes will be developments and refinements of existing arrangements and principles; there is no reason to suppose that they will involve a wholesale redrawing of the map of banking institutions and their markets or a major reassessment of the principles for their management and supervision.

NOTES

1. Roger Brown, *A Guide to Monetary Policy* (Banking Information Service, 1982) p. 4, para. 1.14. The italics are Mr Brown's.
2. *Monetary Control*, Cmnd 7858 (HMSO, March 1980) p. 1, para. 1.2.
3. Tim Congdon, *Monetary Control in Britain* (Macmillan, 1982) p. x.
4. *Report of the Committee on the Working of the Monetary System*, Cmnd 827 (HMSO, 1959) pp. 271–2, para. 761.
5. *Monetary Control*, Cmnd 7858 (HMSO, March 1980) p. 8, paras 4.1, 4.2, 4.3, 4.5.
6. The proposal is discussed in some detail in Chapter 4 of the paper on monetary control already quoted and in annex B to that paper which examines more fully the 'issues which might arise when considering how a monetary base control system might operate, and the concomitant problems'. The question of 'whether monetary base control should be the means by which the authorities control the monetary aggregates' is discussed with great clarity by M. D. K. W. Foot, C. A. E. Goodhart and A. C. Hotson of the Economic Intelligence Department of the Bank of England in a paper entitled 'Monetary Base Control', *Bank of England Quarterly Bulletin* (June 1979) p. 149. The paper includes an appendix describing the monetary reserve requirements imposed on the banking system by the central

banks of the United States, Canada, West Germany, Switzerland, Spain and Italy.

7. Foot, Goodhart and Hotson, 'Monetary Base Control' (see note 6 above), p. 153, para. 29.
8. Ibid., para. 48.
9. 'Role of the Bank of England in the Money Market', *Bank of England Quarterly Bulletin* (March 1982) p. 94.
10. *Monetary Control*, p. iii, para. 5.
11. Ibid., p. 1, para. 1.1.
12. A description of the objectives and techniques of the Bank's management of the gilt-edged market and a discussion of a number of proposals for changes may be found in an article entitled 'The Gilt-edged Market', *Bank of England Quarterly Bulletin* (June 1979) pp. 137–48.
13. *Monetary Control*, pp. 2–3, paras 1.9–1.11.
14. Ibid., pp. 3, 4, paras 1.12–1.17.
15. For a description of these bank-accepted commercial bills and their use in the British banking system, see Chapter 3, pp. 111ff.
16. Ibid., p. 5, paras 2.2, 2.3.
17. *Report of the Committee on the Working of the Monetary System*, Cmnd 827 (HMSO, 1959) p. 337, para. 982.
18. *Monetary Control*, p. 2, paras 1.6, 1.7.
19. Ibid., p. 6, para. 3.1.
20. 'The Role of the Bank of England in the Money Market', *Bank of England Quarterly Bulletin* (March 1982) p. 90.
21. John Quinton, 'Bank base rates', *Barclays Briefing*, No. 58 (February 1983). (A quarterly information service published by Barclays Bank.)
22. *Monetary Control*, p. 2, para. 1.8.
23. Governor of the Bank of England, Address to the Finance Houses Association on 28 January 1982, reprinted in *Bank of England Quarterly Bulletin* (March 1982) p. 102.
24. *Bank of England Quarterly Bulletin* (March 1974) table 12/1, col. 2.
25. *Bank of England Quarterly Bulletin* (March 1972 and March 1974) table 8.
26. Margaret Reid, *The Secondary Banking Crisis 1973–75* (Macmillan, 1982) p. 60.
27. Ibid., p. 59.

28. *Banks and Industry* (Lecture by the Deputy Governor to the Institute of Bankers in Bristol, 23 November 1982) reprinted in *Bank of England Quarterly Bulletin* (December 1982) pp. 506–10. The unattributed quotations in this section are all taken from this lecture.
29. Peter Leslie, 'Techniques of re-scheduling: the latest lessons', *The Banker*, April 1983, p. 28.
30. *The Economist*, 11 December 1982, p. 11.
31. 'The Lex Column', *Financial Times*, 24 January 1983.
32. Governor of the Bank of England, Speech at the Annual Banquet of the Overseas Bankers Club, 8 February 1983, reprinted in *Bank of England Quarterly Bulletin* (March 1983) p. 39.
33. Quoted in leading article, *Financial Times*, 29 May 1982.
34. Speech to the *Financial Times* annual lunch for the foreign banking community in London, 26 May 1982, reprinted in *Bank of England Quarterly Bulletin* (June 1982) pp. 270–1.
35. *Bank of England Quarterly Bulletin* (June 1978) p. 233, para. 25.
36. Speech by the Governor of the Bank of England to the Overseas Bankers Club, 8 February 1983 reprinted in *Bank of England Quarterly Bulletin* (March 1983) pp. 40–1.
37. Margaret Reid's weekly column 'Financial World', *Investors' Chronicle*, 18 February 1983.
38. Speech by the Governor of the Bank of England to the Overseas Bankers Club, 8 February 1983, reprinted in *Bank of England Quarterly Bulletin* (March 1983) p. 39. Unattributed quotations in the rest of this section are taken from this speech.
39. Leslie, 'Techniques of re-scheduling: the latest lessons', p. 23.
40. Figures reported in *Financial Times*, 12 February 1983.
41. See Chapter 4, pp. 185–6.
42. Quoted in William Hall, 'The small banks get nervous', *Financial Times*, 21 December 1982.
43. Leslie, 'Techniques of re-scheduling: the latest lessons', p. 24.
44. Dr Fritz Leutwiler at a private meeting of bankers in London in April 1983, as reported in the *Financial Times*, 22 April 1983.
45. Reported in the *Financial Times*, 18 April 1983.
46. Reported in the *Financial Times*, 21 April 1983.
47. Fourth Report from the Treasury and Civil Service Committee of the House of Commons, *International Monetary Arrange-*

ments: International Lending By Banks, vol. I Report (HMSO, March 1983) para. 4.5.

48. Ibid., para. 5.22. The Committee adds a footnote to this paragraph that 'this point was made to us on several occasions in the course of our visit to Washington'. The point is covered in some detail in the oral evidence taken by the Committee in Washington in January 1983 from Professors William Bronson, Stanley Black, Richard Cooper and Ronald McKinnon and Dr Fred Bergsten, published in the Minutes of Evidence forming volume II of the Report, Questions 1182–202.

Bibliography

1 OFFICIAL PREOCCUPATION WITH THE BANKING SYSTEM

Bank of England, 'The secondary banking crisis and the Bank of England's support operations', *Bank of England Quarterly Bulletin* (June 1978).
Congdon, Tim, *Monetary Control in Britain* (Macmillan, 1982).
Crockett, Andrew, *International Money: Issues and Analysis* (Nelson, 1977).
Fforde, J. S., 'Setting monetary objectives', *Bank of England Quarterly Bulletin* (June 1983).
Monetary Control, Cmnd 7858 (HMSO, 1980).
Radcliffe Committee (Committee on the Working of the Monetary System), *Report*, Cmnd 827 (HMSO, 1959).
Reid, Margaret, *The Secondary Banking Crisis 1973–5* (Macmillan, 1982).
Williamson, John, *The Failure of World Monetary Reform* (Nelson, 1977).

2 THE INSTITUTIONS OF BRITISH BANKING

Committee of London Clearing Banks, *The London Clearing Banks* (Evidence by the CLCB to the Wilson Committee) (CLCB, 1978).
Perry, F. E., *The Elements of Banking*, 3rd edn (Methuen and Institute of Bankers, 1981).
Revell, Jack, *The British Financial System* (Macmillan, 1973).
Wilson Committee, (Committee to Review the Functioning of Financial Institutions): *Report* and *Appendices*, Cmnd 7937 (HMSO, 1980); *Evidence on the Financing of Industry and Trade, vol. 5* (HMSO, 1978); *Second Stage Evidence*, vol. 4 (HMSO, 1979).

3 THE FINANCIAL MARKETS OF LONDON

Accepting Houses Committee, *Written Evidence to the Wilson Committee*, Written Evidence on the Financing of Industry and Trade, vol. 5 (HMSO, 1978).

Bank of England, 'The Exchange Equalisation Account: its origins and development', *Bank of England Quarterly Bulletin* (December 1968).
Bank of England, 'The foreign exchange market in London', *Bank of England Quarterly Bulletin* (December 1980).
Bank of England, 'The role of the Bank of England in the money market', *Bank of England Quarterly Bulletin* (March 1982).
Coleby, A. L., 'Bills of exchange: current issues in historical perspective', *Bank of England Quarterly Bulletin* (December 1982).
Coleby, A. L., 'The Bank's operational procedures for setting monetary objectives', *Bank of England Quarterly Bulletin* (June 1983).
Gerrard & National Discount Company, *The London Bill Market*, 3rd edn (Gerrard & National, 1981).
Gillett Brothers Discount Co., Ltd, *The Bill on London*, 4th edn (Methuen, 1976).
Shaw, E. R., *The London Money Market*, 3rd edn (Heinemann, 1981).

4 THE RISKS OF BANKING

Bank of England, 'The capital and liquidity adequacy of banks', *Bank of England Quarterly Bulletin* (September 1975).
Bank of England, 'Foreign currency exposure', *Bank of England Quarterly Bulletin* (June 1981).
Bank of England, 'The measurement of capital', *Bank of England Quarterly Bulletin* (September 1980).
Bank of England, 'The measurement of liquidity', *Bank of England Quarterly Bulletin* (September 1982).
Bank of England, 'Prudential arrangements for the discount market', *Bank of England Quarterly Bulletin* (June 1982).
Burton, F. M. and Inoue, Hisashi, 'Country risk evaluation methods: a survey of systems in use', *The Banker* (January 1983).
Committee of London Clearing Bankers, *The London Clearing Banks* (CLCB, 1978).
Krayenbuchi, T. E., 'How country risk should be monitored', *The Banker* (May. 1983).
Lascelles, David, 'US bank regulation after the debt "crisis" ', *The Banker* (January 1983).
Lomax, Dr David, 'Sovereign risk analysis now', *The Banker* (January 1983).
Manning Dacey, W., *The British Banking Mechanism*, 2nd edn (Hutchinson, 1958).
Perry, F. E., *The Elements of Banking*, 3rd edn (Methuen and Institute of Bankers, 1981).
Sayers, R. S., *Modern Banking*, 7th edn (Oxford University Press, 1967).
Wilson Committee, *Evidence* on the Financing of Industry and Trade, vol. 5: Written Evidence by the Accepting Houses Committee (HMSO, 1978).

5 THE PRUDENTIAL SUPERVISION OF BANKS

Banking Act 1979 (HMSO, 1979).

Bank of England, 'Regulation in the City and the Bank of England's role', *Bank of England Quarterly Bulletin* (June 1980).

Commission of the European Economic Community, *First Banking Co-ordination Directive* (published by the Commission as document 77/780/EEC 1977).

Cooke, W. P., 'The role of the Banking Supervisor', *Bank of England Quarterly Bulletin* (December 1982).

Cooke, W. P., 'The international banking scene: a supervisory perspective', *Bank of England Quarterly Bulletin* (March 1983).

Morison, Ian, Tillett, Paul and Welch, June, *The Banking Act 1979* (Butterworth, 1979).

6 THE BANKING SYSTEM AND NATIONAL POLICY

Bank of England, 'The role of the Bank of England in the money market', *Bank of England Quarterly Bulletin* (March 1982).

Brown, Roger, *A Guide to Monetary Policy* (Banking Information Service, 1982).

Carter, H. and Partington, I., *Applied Economics in Banking and Finance* (Oxford University Press, 1981).

Coleby, A. L., 'The Bank's operational procedures for meeting monetary objectives', *Bank of England Quarterly Bulletin* (June 1983).

Congdon, Tim, *Monetary Control in Britain* (Macmillan, 1982).

Crockett, A., *Money: Theory, Policy and Institutions* (Nelson, 1973).

Fforde, J. S., 'Setting monetary objectives', *Bank of England Quarterly Bulletin* (June 1983).

Foot, M. D. K. W., Goodhart, C. A. E. and Hotson, A. C., 'Monetary base control', *Bank of England Quarterly Bulletin* (June 1979).

Group of Thirty, *Risks in International Bank Lending* (First Report of the International Banking Study Group of the Group of Thirty, New York, 1982).

Group of Thirty, *Commercial Banks and the Restructuring of Cross-border Debt* (Group of Thirty, New York, 1983).

Guth, Dr Wilfred, 'International debt crisis: the next phase', *The Banker* (July 1983).

House of Commons (Treasury and Civil Service Committee), *International Monetary Arrangements: International Lending by Banks, vol. 1* (HMSO, March 1983).

Leslie, Peter, 'Techniques of re-scheduling: the latest lessons', *The Banker* (April 1983).

McMahon, C. W., 'Banks and industry', *Bank of England Quarterly Bulletin* (December 1982).

Mendelsohn, M. S., 'International debt crisis: the practical lessons of restructuring', *The Banker* (July 1983).
Monetary Control, Cmnd 7858 (HMSO, 1980).

Index

NOTES:

1. The Notes referred to in brackets relate to the page references immediately preceding them.
2. The word 'Bank' in sub-headings refers to Bank of England.